BORGES AND JOYCE
AN INFINITE CONVERSATION

# LEGENDA

LEGENDA, founded in 1995 by the European Humanities Research Centre of the University of Oxford, is now a joint imprint of the Modern Humanities Research Association and Routledge. Titles range from medieval texts to contemporary cinema and form a widely comparative view of the modern humanities, including works on Arabic, Catalan, English, French, German, Greek, Italian, Portuguese, Russian, Spanish, and Yiddish literature. An Editorial Board of distinguished academic specialists works in collaboration with leading scholarly bodies such as the Society for French Studies and the British Comparative Literature Association.

# MHRA

The Modern Humanities Research Association (MHRA) encourages and promotes advanced study and research in the field of the modern humanities, especially modern European languages and literature, including English, and also cinema. It also aims to break down the barriers between scholars working in different disciplines and to maintain the unity of humanistic scholarship in the face of increasing specialization. The Association fulfils this purpose primarily through the publication of journals, bibliographies, monographs and other aids to research.

Routledge is a global publisher of academic books, journals and online resources in the humanities and social sciences. Founded in 1836, it has published many of the greatest thinkers and scholars of the last hundred years, including Adorno, Einstein, Russell, Popper, Wittgenstein, Jung, Bohm, Hayek, McLuhan, Marcuse and Sartre. Today Routledge is one of the world's leading academic publishers in the Humanities and Social Sciences. It publishes thousands of books and journals each year, serving scholars, instructors, and professional communities worldwide.

www.routledge.com

# EDITORIAL BOARD

*Chairman*
Professor Colin Davis, Royal Holloway, University of London

Professor Malcolm Cook, University of Exeter (French)
Professor Robin Fiddian, Wadham College, Oxford (Spanish)
Professor Paul Garner, University of Leeds (Spanish)
Professor Marian Hobson Jeanneret,
Queen Mary University of London (French)
Professor Catriona Kelly, New College, Oxford (Russian)
Professor Martin McLaughlin, Magdalen College, Oxford (Italian)
Professor Martin Maiden, Trinity College, Oxford (Linguistics)
Professor Peter Matthews, St John's College, Cambridge (Linguistics)
Dr Stephen Parkinson, Linacre College, Oxford (Portuguese)
Professor Ritchie Robertson, The Queen's College, Oxford (German)
Professor Lesley Sharpe, University of Exeter (German)
Professor David Shepherd, University of Sheffield (Russian)
Professor Michael Sheringham, All Soul's College, Oxford (French)
Professor Alison Sinclair, Clare College, Cambridge (Spanish)
Professor David Treece, King's College London (Portuguese)

*Managing Editor*
Dr Graham Nelson
41 Wellington Square, Oxford OX1 2JF, UK

legenda@mhra.org.uk
www.legenda.mhra.org.uk

STUDIES IN COMPARATIVE LITERATURE

*Editorial Committee*
Professor Stephen Bann, University of Bristol (Chairman)
Professor Duncan Large, University of Swansea
Dr Elinor Shaffer, School of Advanced Study, London

*Studies in Comparative Literature* are produced in close collaboration with the British Comparative Literature Association, and range widely across comparative and theoretical topics in literary and translation studies, accommodating research at the interface between different artistic media and between the humanities and the sciences.

PUBLISHED IN THIS SERIES

1. *Breeches and Metaphysics: Thackeray's German Discourse*, by S. S. Prawer
2. *Hölderlin and the Dynamics of Translation*, by Charlie Louth
3. *Aeneas Takes the Metro: The Presence of Virgil in Twentieth-Century French Literature*, by Fiona Cox
4. *Metaphor and Materiality: German Literature and the World-View of Science 1780–1955*, by Peter D. Smith
5. *Marguerite Yourcenar: Reading the Visual*, by Nigel Saint
6. *Treny: The Laments of Kochanowski*, translated by Adam Czerniawski and with an introduction by Donald Davie
7. *Neither a Borrower: Forging Traditions in French, Chinese and Arabic Poetry*, by Richard Serrano
8. *The Anatomy of Laughter*, edited by Toby Garfitt, Edith McMorran and Jane Taylor
9. *Dilettantism and its Values: From Weimar Classicism to the fin de siècle*, by Richard Hibbitt
10. *The Fantastic in France and Russia in the Nineteenth Century: In Pursuit of Hesitation*, by Claire Whitehead
11. *Singing Poets: Literature and Popular Music in France and Greece*, by Dimitris Papanikolaou
12. *Wanderers Across Language: Exile in Irish and Polish Literature of the Twentieth Century*, by Kinga Olszewska
13. *Moving Scenes: The Aesthetics of German Travel Writing on England 1783–1830*, by Alison E. Martin
14. *Henry James and the Second Empire*, by Angus Wrenn
15. *Platonic Coleridge*, by James Vigus
16. *Imagining Jewish Art*, by Aaron Rosen
17. *Alienation and Theatricality: Diderot after Brecht*, by Phoebe von Held
18. *Turning into Sterne: Viktor Shklovskii and Literary Reception*, by Emily Finer
19. *Yeats and Pessoa: Parallel Poetic Styles*, by Patricia Silva McNeill
20. *Aestheticism and the Philosophy of Death: Walter Pater and Post-Hegelianism*, by Giles Whiteley
21. *Blake, Lavater and Physiognomy*, by Sibylle Erle
22. *Rethinking the Concept of the Grotesque: Crashaw, Baudelaire, Magritte*, by Shun-Liang Chao
23. *The Art of Comparison: How Novels and Critics Compare*, by Catherine Brown
24. *Borges and Joyce: An Infinite Conversation*, by Patricia Novillo-Corvalán

# Borges and Joyce

*An Infinite Conversation*

❖

Patricia Novillo-Corvalán

LONDON AND NEW YORK

2011

First published 2011 by Modern Humanities Research Association and Routledge

2 Park Square, Milton Park, Abingdon, Oxfordshire OX14 4RN
52 Vanderbilt Avenue, New York, NY 10017

*Routledge is an imprint of the Taylor & Francis Group, an informa business*

First issued in paperback 2020

Copyright © Modern Humanities Research Association and Taylor & Francis 2011

All rights reserved. No part of this book may be reprinted or reproduced or utilised in any form or by any electronic, mechanical, or other means, now known or hereafter invented, including photocopying and recording, or in any information storage or retrieval system, without permission in writing from the publishers.

Notice:
Product or corporate names may be trademarks or registered trademarks, and are used only for identification and explanation without intent to infringe.

ISBN 978-1-907625-05-3 (hbk)
ISBN 978-0-367-60231-4 (pbk)

# CONTENTS

| | | |
|---|---|---:|
| | *Acknowledgments* | ix |
| | *Abbreviations* | x |
| | Introduction: Towards Comparative Literature | 1 |
| 1 | *Ulysses* in Transit, from Paris to Buenos Aires: The Cross-Cultural Transactions of Larbaud, Borges, and Güiraldes | 12 |
| 2 | Borges's Reception of Joyce in the Argentine Press | 40 |
| 3 | James Joyce, Author of 'Funes the Memorious' | 68 |
| 4 | In Praise of Darkness: Homer, Joyce, Borges | 93 |
| 5 | Architects of Labyrinths: Dante, Joyce, Borges | 117 |
| 6 | Joyce's and Borges's Afterlives of Shakespeare | 151 |
| | Conclusion: The Afterlives of James Joyce in Argentina | 172 |
| | *Bibliography* | 175 |
| | *Index* | 191 |

# ACKNOWLEDGEMENTS

A book devoted to the study of two giants of Western literature requires, in turn, a colossal dedication and an even larger degree of help and personal and intellectual support. As a result, I owe a great deal of gratitude to my two doctoral supervisors, Joe Brooker and William Rowe, who enthusiastically accompanied me throughout this journey and patiently read several drafts of this study. I am also hugely indebted to the Arts and Humanities Research Council for awarding me a doctoral scholarship and overseas research funding. My warm thanks also go to my two thesis examiners, Jason Wilson and Richard Brown, whose eye for detail and pertinent suggestions greatly improved this book. *Muchas gracias también* to Robin Fiddian, reader for Legenda, whose patient and exhaustive reading of the manuscript pruned from it numerous imperfections and added insightful remarks. I am grateful to Graham Nelson, editor of Legenda, for his unfaltering advice and support. My warm thanks also go the School of English & Humanities at Birkbeck College, which provided me with a friendly and intellectually stimulating learning environment, especially to Tom Healy, Sandra Clark, Aoife Monks, and the late, and much missed, Sally Ledger. I also gained enormously from the lively discussions with fellow Joyceans at the University of London 'Charles Peake *Ulysses* Seminar', superbly led by Andrew Gibson, where we would spend two hours on a Friday evening perusing just a few lines from Joyce's modernist masterpiece (and later, in true Irish style, extend those discussions in the pub).

    I am also grateful to Alejandro Vaccaro, who generously put at my disposal his vast Borges collection, and introduced me to the 'Asociación Borgesiana' in Buenos Aires. Cecilia Smyth, the director of the 'Museo Güiraldes' in San Antonio de Areco, Buenos Aires, kindly opened the doors of the museum to me and allowed me access to their rare first edition of the 1929 French translation of *Ulysses*. My parents, Sofanor Novillo-Corvalán and Patricia Doherty de Novillo-Corvalán, have been a continuous source of inspiration, and helped me find books and articles of extreme importance for this project. My final and largest thanks go to my husband, Adam Elston, for his encouragement, love, and dedication, and for helping me throughout all stages of my academic career. This book is dedicated to him.

Earlier versions of chapters in this study have been previously published in the following journals: sections of Chapter 1 in *James Joyce Broadsheet*, 79 (2008), 1; a shorter version of Chapter 3 appeared in *Variaciones Borges*, 26 (2008), 59–82; an earlier version of Chapter 6 in *Comparative Literature*, 60.3 (2008), 207–27. I am most grateful to the editors of these journals for their advice in the writing of these articles.

# ABBREVIATIONS

OC     Jorge Luis Borges, *Obras completas*, 3 vols (Buenos Aires: Emecé, 1990); vol. 4 (Barcelona: Emecé: 1996)
OCC    Jorge Luis Borges, *Obras completas en colaboración* (Buenos Aires: Emecé, 1991)
IA      Jorge Luis Borges, *El idioma de los argentinos* (Buenos Aires: Seix Barral, 1994)
TE     Jorge Luis Borges, *El tamaño de mi esperanza* (Buenos Aires: Seix Barral, 1993)
Inq.     Jorge Luis Borges, *Inquisiciones* (Buenos Aires: Seix Barral, 1995)
TR     Jorge Luis Borges, *Textos recobrados*, 3 vols (vol. 1, Barcelona: Emecé, 1997), (vol. 2, Bogotá: Emecé, 2001), (vol. 3, Buenos Aires: Emecé, 2003)
CF     Jorge Luis Borges, *Collected Fictions*, trans. by Andrew Hurley (New York: Penguin, 1999)
SNF    Jorge Luis Borges, *Selected Non-Fictions*, ed. by Eliot Weinberger, trans. by Esther Allen, Suzanne Jill Levine, and Eliot Weinberger (Viking: New York, 1999)
SP     Jorge Luis Borges, *Selected Poems*, ed. by Alexander Coleman, trans. by Willis Barnstone, Alexander Coleman, Robert Fitzgerald, Stephen Kessler, Kenneth Krabbenhoft, Eric McHenry, W. S. Merwin, Alastair Reid, Hoyt Rogers, Mark Strand, Charles Tomlinson, Alan S. Trueblood, John Updike (London: Penguin, 1999)
L      Jorge Luis Borges, *Labyrinths: Selected Stories and Other Writings*, ed. by Donald A. Yates & James E. Irby, preface by André Maurois, 2nd edn (London: Penguin, 2000)
A      Jorge Luis Borges, 'An Autobiographical Essay', in *Critical Essays on Jorge Luis Borges*, ed. by Jaime Alazraki (Boston, MA: G. K. Hall & Co, 1987), pp. 21–55.
U      James Joyce, *Ulysses*, ed. by Hans Walter Gabler, with Wolfhard Steppe and Claus Melchior, afterword by Michael Groden, 4th edn (London: Bodley Head, 2002)
E      James Joyce, *Exiles*, intro. by Conor McPherson (London: Nick Hern Books: 2006)
P      James Joyce, *A Portrait of the Artist as a Young Man*, ed. by Jeri Johnson (London and New York: Oxford University Press, 2000)
FW    James Joyce, *Finnegans Wake*, with an intro. by Seamus Deane, 2nd edn (London: Penguin, 2000)
D      James Joyce, *Dubliners*, with an intro. and notes by Terence Brown, 2nd edn (London: Penguin, 2000)
JJI     Richard Ellmann, *James Joyce* (New York: Oxford University Press, 1959)
JJII    Richard Ellmann, *James Joyce: New and Revised Edition* (New York: Oxford University Press, 1983)
Letters   James Joyce, *Letters of James Joyce*, vol. 1 ed. by Stuart Gilbert (New York: Viking Press, 1957, reissued with corrections 1966); vols 2 and 3 ed. by Richard Ellmann (New York: Viking Press, 1966)
SL     James Joyce, *Selected Letters*, ed. by Richard Ellmann, 2nd edn (London: Faber & Faber, 1992)

Note: English translations of Borges's works belonging to the editions quoted above are cited parenthetically within the body of the book. All other, unreferenced, translations of Borges's works are my own.

# INTRODUCTION

## Towards Comparative Literature

In 1993 Susan Bassnett concluded her book-length study *Comparative Literature* with the provocative assertion: 'Comparative literature as a discipline has had its day. Crosscultural work in women's studies, in post-colonial theory, in cultural studies has changed the face of literary studies generally. We should look upon translation studies as the principal discipline from now on, with comparative literature as a valued but subsidiary subject area.'[1] On the one hand, Bassnett was trying to shake the deeply laid foundations of the nineteenth-century edifice which has long been associated with a type of comparative practice renowned for its restrictiveness and inescapable Eurocentric impulses. On the other, she was eager to offer her support to the emerging discipline of translation studies which she carefully presented as a substitutional discourse, a surrogate discipline born to replace a declining, almost extinct, comparative literature. But as Bassnett herself has been able to corroborate, in the last two decades comparative literature was not only able to survive her fatalistic scholarly oracles, but also managed to stay alive and well, despite the numerous challenges it had to face at the turn of the twentieth century. This challenging period has been characterized by a revaluation of its priorities, principles, methodologies and linguistic, cultural, and literary practices, particularly in the light of a much-needed shift from a localized European perspective to a broad-spectrum globalist approach. Moreover, the value, function, and future of comparative literature became the subject of the American Comparative Literature Association (ACLA) collection of essays *Comparative Literature in the Age of Multiculturalism* (1995),[2] which gathered a fascinating range of responses from distinguished comparatists such as Jonathan Culler, Anthony Appiah, and Mary Louise Pratt. This momentous debate highlighted, above all, the important fact that comparative literature needed to become multicultural in its focus and interdisciplinary in its method, forging complex intersections with, for example, the critical discourses of gender studies, postcolonialism, cultural studies, translation studies, and a broad range of cross-cultural issues. Ten years down the line, the ACLA report extended — in a rather predictable move — its multiculturalist concerns onto the wider phenomenon of globalization, thus resulting in the much-awaited sequel, *Comparative Literature in an Age of Globalisation*, ed. by Haun Saussy (2006).[3] At the beginning of the twenty-first century, Saussy victoriously proclaims: 'Comparative literature has, in a sense, won its battles [...] The controversy is over. Comparative literature is not only legitimate: now, as often as not, ours is the first violin that sets the tone for the whole orchestra'.[4] The discipline has become a major paradigm in an increasingly globalized world, even if, admittedly, it usually fails to gain the recognition it deserves. The ubiquitousness of comparative literature ideas, Saussy argues, is evident in the way in which 'what comparatists elaborated, argued, and propagated in the laboratories of their small, self-selecting profession has gone out into the world and won over people who have no particular loyalty to institutional bodies of comparative literature'.[5] Indeed, Saussy teasingly suggests that comparative literature ought to levy a tax to English and History departments 'every time they cited Auerbach, de Man, Said, Derrida, or Spivak'.[6]

But going back to the eschatological predictions of the demise of a discipline, we are now able to see, with hindsight, that rather than becoming a subsidiary or appendix to, say, translation studies — as Bassnett had announced — comparativism in general welcomed these decisive critical perspectives and used them as a resource to foster a wider, globally orientated twenty-first-century practice. In a recent essay published in the journal of the British Comparative Literature Association (BCLA), Bassnett inevitably reconsidered her unjust death penalty and vindicated a renewed model of the old discipline: 'Today, looking at that proposition, it appears fundamentally flawed: translation studies has not developed very far at all over three decades and comparison remains at the heart of much translation studies scholarship.'[7] As Bassnett also justifiably argues regarding her 1993 claim: 'The basis of my case was that debates about a so-called crisis in comparative literature stemmed from a legacy of nineteenth-century positivism and a failure to consider the political implications of intercultural transfer processes.'[8] In this context, Bassnett aspired to reposition comparative literature as a pluralized, global forum which had to break free from the shackles of its Eurocentric heritage.

This urgency for the rebirth of a truly international discipline has recently become the subject of Gayatri Spivak's reflections in *Death of a Discipline* (2003). Yet this is another apocalyptic warning by a leading figure in comparative literature, translation studies, and postcolonialism, as Spivak unambiguously warns us that her book will be read as the 'last gasp of a dying discipline'.[9] If the rebirth of the discipline must be at the cost of ditching the corpse of a nineteenth-century inheritance, then the new face of comparative literature, stresses Spivak, has to prioritize the 'national literatures of the global South but also of the countless indigenous languages in the world [...] The literatures in English produced by the former British colonies in Africa and Asia [...] And who can deny the Spanish and Portuguese literature of Latin America?'[10] But Spivak's claim that the dying discipline could only survive through the exclusion of the 'Western European "nations"'[11] ought to be questioned, particularly since the convenient label of homogeneity can no longer serve as the defining characteristic of a European cultural identity. Indeed, as Lucia Boldrini has pointed out: 'Many European countries have no imperial history if not a passive one, having themselves been "colonised", subjugated or controlled by other political powers. A "decolonising" of the European mind needs to take place'.[12] This is, above all, the case of postcolonial Ireland, and our understanding of Joyce lies precisely in recognizing Ireland as both an inward and outward force within Europe, in the sense that Joyce, as Emer Nolan notes, '[in his] writings about Ireland may not provide a coherent critique of either colonised or colonialist; but their ambiguities and hesitations testify to the uncertain divided consciousness of the colonial subject'.[13]

Therefore I propose the comparative study of the literary relationship between Borges and Joyce as a suitable model for the type of comparatist practice which illustrates the cultural, literary, linguistic, and geographical concerns that the discipline is aspiring to address at this crucial junction. And in this vital comparative process of reading, studying, teaching, and translating literary texts, the relations of Borges and Joyce with the canonical tradition of Homer, Dante, and Shakespeare remain at the forefront of the book. In this sense, a study of Borges and Joyce cannot ignore their complex interplay with the canon as is shown in their respective reinvention of a foundational body of writings from a marginal standpoint, as they infiltrate a vast European archive with their autochthonous Irish and Argentine viewpoints, deftly combining reverence and irreverence. Ultimately, Borges's and Joyce's idiosyncratic readings of Homer, Dante, and Shakespeare stand as yet another metaphor for the fecund forces at stake in the act of translation, recreation, and transcreation, particularly if viewed through the light of the Brazilian translation movement known as 'Cannibalism', following the *antropófago* poetics proposed by Haroldo de Campos, who proclaimed that Western discourses are devoured by colonial writers through a transformative practice that absorbs their canonical nutrients and enriches them with elements from their own cultures.[14] The Brazilian anthropophagi movement brings to mind Walter Benjamin's groundbreaking essay 'The Task of the Translator' (1923). Both translation processes involve the biological metaphors of death (original) and rebirth (translation). They endorse an inverted *modus operandi* in which the translation gives life to the original by extending and enhancing its lifespan, rather than vice-versa, as had been commonly held in traditional translation approaches. An apt view of Borges's overall attitude towards the Western archive is skilfully conveyed by Suzanne Jill Levine: 'As cannibalistic reader and fanatically original (re)writer *par excellence*, Borges made European writers such as the "excessive" Joyce his own. Like Joyce, Borges was drawn to the vast canonical works they both inherited as readers, particularly Homer's epics and Dante's encompassing allegories.'[15]

As things stand, the lesson we can learn from comparative literature today is that the strength of the discipline lies in its utopian aspiration to embrace the concerns of a global, or planetary — as Spivak puts it — literary, linguistic, and cultural spectrum. This thirst for change and renewal, explains Robert Weninger, is why 'Comparative Literature as a discipline is at yet another crossroads — except that the crossroads would not seem to be the same in every part of the world'.[16] And these crossroads, these important global intersections, are also a characteristic of the international turn of Joyce studies, which is testimony to the proliferation of translations and creative responses worldwide. And these comparative (and Joycean) crossroads can be found along the several roads that lead to a number of worldwide destinations across both sides of the Atlantic.

## Towards Borges and Joyce

This book examines the interface between two of the most revolutionary writers of the twentieth century, James Joyce and Jorge Luis Borges. The relationship consists of a fascinating series of parallels: both are renowned for their polyglot abilities, prodigious memories, cyclical conception of time and labyrinthine creations, for their condition as European émigrés and blind bards of Dublin and Buenos Aires, and, of course, for not being awarded the Nobel Prize for Literature. Yet at the same time, Borges and Joyce largely differ in relation to the central aesthetic of their creative projects: the epic scale of the Irishman contrasts with the compressed *ficción* of the Argentine. Throughout this study I will argue that Joyce's aesthetic of expansion and Borges's aesthetic of compression, for all their self-evident disparity, may be bridged in order to create a *tertium comparationis* in which their textual conversation takes place.

James Joyce's work loomed large throughout all stages of Borges's oeuvre. A chronological survey of the numerous writings Borges exclusively dedicated to Joyce reveals a most impressive and heterogeneous catalogue. As early as 1925 a youthful Borges published a pioneering review of *Ulysses* and a fragmentary translation of 'Penelope' in the Buenos Aires avant-garde review *Proa* [*Prow*]. In the late 1930s a more mature Borges, on his way to becoming the modern master of the compressed, metaphysical *ficción*, continued and developed his dissemination of Joyce's works with ensuing reviews of *Work in Progress* and *Finnegans Wake*, as well as a fascinating miscellany of papers on Joyce's life and works which appeared in the cultural and artistic journal *Sur* [*South*] and the mass-marketed, à la mode women's magazine *El Hogar* [*Home*]. In the 1940s he incorporated two excerpts of *Ulysses* into his *Anthology of Fantastic Literature* and declared in his 1941 obituary of Joyce that *Ulysses* stood as the precursor of Ireneo Funes, his Uruguayan gaucho endowed with an infinite memory. In the decades that followed, until his death on 14 June 1986 (two days before Bloomsday), he repeatedly returned to Joyce's work in his poems, fictions, and in numerous interviews, whereby the lingering shadow of his blind predecessor grew larger and larger. The towering presence of a writer of the stature of Borges in the reception of Joyce's works in the Hispanic world is, ultimately, indisputable, as is the important fact that in 1946 he penned a unique review of the first complete translation of *Ulysses* into Spanish by fellow Argentine writer J. Salas Subirat. It soon becomes clear that Borges invented himself as the unofficial Hispanic promoter of Joyce, holding behind him the torch that would illuminate the path onto Joyce's works for successive generations of readers.

If a writer of the stature of Jorge Luis Borges took part in the act of reading and disseminating Joyce, then the distinctive, compressed aesthetic of his *ficciones* strove to create an image of Joyce as the artificer of intricately woven labyrinths whose sheer size, encyclopaedic scope, and infinite nature, both fascinated and horrified him. Thus, I will argue that Borges sought to forge a version of Joyce refracted through his own condensatory impulses, hence offering a fragmentary translation of Molly Bloom's unpunctuated soliloquy; the ideal insomniac reader of *Ulysses* and *Finnegans Wake* in his celebrated short story 'Funes the Memorious'; a gothic reading of *Ulysses* as a fantastic short story in his *Anthology of Fantastic Literature*; an irreverent résumé of *Ulysses* in several of his fictions; and the final affirmation that his arduous journey through Joyce's geography involved not a one-way trip but numerous excursions (or short cuts) through an inexhaustible and ever-shifting landscape. As in 'Pierre Menard, Author of the *Quixote*', the undeniable richness of an exercise in translation and rewriting is that we are now able to access a Borgesian version of Joyce, as much as Joyce's distinctive cadences and metaphors resonate throughout Borges's oeuvre. Alas, Borges and Joyce never met in life.

In this way, this book argues that Borges created himself as a 'precursor' of Joyce (in the Borgesian sense of the word). This raises momentous issues. What kind of Joyce emerges, then, from Borges's idiosyncratic reading? What kind of Joyce emerges from the perspective of a writer located, as Sarlo claims, in a 'culturally marginal nation'[17] and yet who indiscriminately drenched himself with world literature? The Joyce(s) that are refracted through Borges's complex prism allow the creation of an infinite conversation between the literatures of Ireland and Argentina, between the point of view of two writers who considered themselves European outsiders, but at the same time embraced a whole Western tradition. Above all, the Borgesian formula shifts Joyce's epic proportions into the compressed and intricately woven microcosm of the *ficción*, thus allowing the reader to experience the novelistic scope of Joyce's *Ulysses* within the confines of a nutshell. A Borgesian exercise of tremendous audacity, irony, and creativity, which fittingly describes his relationship with Joyce, was to reduce 'la vida entera de un hombre a dos o tres escenas' (*OC1* 289) ['a person's entire life to two or three scenes'] (*CF* 3),[18] and, even more remarkably, to claim that it is a 'desvarío laborioso y empobrecedor el de componer vastos libros; el de explayar en quinientas páginas una idea cuya exposición oral cabe en pocos minutos' (*OC1* 429) ['It is a laborious madness and an impoverishing one, the madness of composing vast books — setting out in five hundred pages an idea that can be perfectly related orally in five minutes'] (*CF* 67). Further, Borges set himself the task of offering summaries and commentaries of real and imaginary works, an undertaking he carried out, again and again, with Joyce's oeuvre. A compulsive creator of literary genealogies, heterogeneous catalogues, and the study of a writer's precursors, Borges exposed the endless possibilities of literary combinations which allowed him to freely compare, contrast, parody, and venerate an unlimited number of texts. This eccentric practice brings to mind the conclusion reached by the French critic Gérard Genette in his study *Palimpsests*, whereby he wrote that Borges created 'the utopia of a Literature in a perpetual state of transfusion, a transtextual perfusion, constantly present to itself in its totality and as a Totality all of whose authors are but one and all its books one vast, one infinite Book'.[19]

## Borges's Infinite Conversation with Joyce

For all the pioneering and creative impetus of Borges's early reception, the reader may be surprised to learn that the journalistic papers he exclusively dedicated to Joyce remained dormant for nearly half a century in the dusty shelves of long-forgotten Argentine archives and have only been exhumed in the last two decades.

Why, then, was Borges's critical reception of Joyce plunged into the dark abyss of oblivion? First of all, this phenomenon ought to be explained by the crucial fact that the majority of Borges's papers on Joyce (including his fragmentary translation of 'Penelope') were originally produced for a series of Buenos Aires periodicals. The difficulties begin when we consider that a large proportion of Borges's journalistic production was excluded from the authorized edition of the *Obras completas* [*Collected Works*]. Despite the claim of their title, the *Obras completas* only gathered the writings of Borges that had been previously published in book form, hence excluding a vast journalistic production, as well as a large proportion of assorted writings from his formative years. Moreover, Borges's 1925 review of *Ulysses* — in which he proudly described himself as the 'primer aventurero hispánico' (*Inq* 23) [first Hispanic adventurer] of Joyce's epic geography — was subsequently included in his essay collection *Inquisiciones* (1925) [*Inquisitions*]. Yet this book was subject to a similar fate, since later in his life Borges mercilessly excluded it from the *Obras completas*, along with *El tamaño de mi esperanza* (1926) [*The Extent of my Hope*] and *El idioma de los argentinos* (1928) [*The Language of the Argentines*] considering them baroque aberrations of his early years. Consequently, Borges's journalistic papers on Joyce remained, until their recent re-emergence in the last two decades, a peripheral group of writings either unauthorized from the approved corpus of his *Obras completas* (as in *Inquisiciones*) or scattered in the various editions of the magazines in which they had been originally published. For example, Borges's biographer Emir Rodríguez Monegal has argued that, far from presenting a totality, the incongruous partiality of the *Obras completas* aims to bring together not the total Borges, but rather the canonical Borges: 'They are far from complete, and, in a sense, they are closer to being the official or canonical edition; that is, the edition by which Borges wants to be judged.'[20] James Woodall, in his biography *The Man in the Mirror of the Book*, has humorously claimed that Borges, like Joyce, entrusted the disordered editions to the patient work of future scholars:

> The problems really begin with Borges himself. His habit of changing texts from edition to edition, of suppressing, or excising, sometimes re-introducing in modified form, words, phrases, lines — mainly in the poetry — has landed any potential bibliographer with a lifetime's toil. A Borgesian joke of the highest order, it might be thought, recalling James Joyce's comment that he wrote in the way he did in order to keep the professors busy for centuries.[21]

The real implications of Borges's editorial toil, suggest Helft and Pauls, became particularly noticeable after his death, which was followed by the gradual unearthing of a large collection of journalistic and miscellaneous writings which had been gathering dust in the archives of Argentine libraries for several decades.[22] The most important compilation of Borges's journalistic production was published in 1986 with the aptly titled collection *Textos cautivos* [*Captive Texts*][23] that gathers Borges's numerous writings for the illustrated magazine *El Hogar*. The determining factor here is that in this collection was reprinted Borges's 1937 biographical sketch of Joyce, as well as one of his 1939 reviews of the *Wake*. As expected, this edition was followed by a book-length volume of Borges's contributions for the magazine of the newspaper *Crítica*,[24] and then by a collection of his writings for *Sur*, thus adding the missing sequels to Borges's most copious journalistic production. The *Sur* publication brought back to life Borges's largely forgotten 1941 obituary of Joyce — in which he argues that *Ulysses* stands as a precursor to his short story 'Funes the Memorious' — as well as resurrecting his other 1939 review of the *Wake*. But far from being conclusive, these publications only heralded the beginning of what started to be seen as a series of proliferating *addenda* to an ever-increasingly deficient *Obras completas*. Only with the recent publication of an entirely new collection, appropriately titled *Textos recobrados* [*Recovered Texts*], which follows a similar principle of regaining, rescuing, and freeing a large body of Borges's work that was already implicit in *Captive Texts*, have we begun to get a closer approximation of the extent of Borges's oeuvre in general and of his lifelong obsession with Joyce in particular.[25] Indeed, *Recovered Texts* was decisive in resuscitating one of Borges's most fascinating early responses to Joyce: his 1925 fragmentary translation of Molly's Bloom's long unpunctuated soliloquy. The idea of picturing the youthful, avant-gardist Borges undertaking a translation of the last two pages of 'Penelope' cannot but stand at odds with the larger image of the blind Argentine bard later renowned, as much for his erudite fictions, as for his spartan, library-bound, mythical existence. Thus, it seems an irony that Jorge Luis Borges gifted the Hispanic world with a translation of Molly Bloom's sexually charged reverie, particularly an excerpt that is included in Paul Vanderham's list of passages 'deemed obscene or otherwise objectionable by various governmental and editorial authorities between 1918 and 1934'.[26] Looking back on Borges's writing career we become particularly aware of the large gulf that stands between his wholehearted embrace of Molly's sexuality as an avant-gardist and passionate young man, and the ensuing metaphysical and asexual tone that the mature writer would develop in his *ficciones*. Further, the promissory aspect of Borges's early journalistic reception of Joyce in the cultural Argentine scene may well explain why in the 1930s the owner of the Buenos Aires daily *Crítica* commissioned Borges with the difficult task of undertaking a complete translation of *Ulysses* into Spanish. According to an account by one of Borges's colleagues of *Crítica*,[27] Borges gave an unequivocal 'Yes' and the newspaper promptly telegraphed London, only to find out that the Joyce estate had already awarded the translation rights to Salas Subirat, whose complete translation of *Ulysses* finally appeared in 1945. Borges's 1946 review of this translation, once again, has been reissued in *Recovered Texts*.

The majority of Borges's papers on Joyce, thus, formed part of a large corpus of writings which were produced during an industrious journalistic activity spanning several decades. On the one hand it is undeniable that the journalistic context in which the majority of these writings were produced provided a decisive medium for the diffusion of Joyce's work in the Hispanic world — just think of the readers of the mass-marketed magazine *Home* reading a review of the *Wake* sandwiched in between publicity spaces for luxury chocolates and ladies' lingerie. On the other hand this circumstance had the adverse effect of restricting their posterior status as peripheral writings, thus masking a significant aspect of Borges's activity as a writer, critic, and translator. In this light, one of the most important lessons we can learn from this shift in Borges's publication history is that the extent of his literary relationship with Joyce has finally come into full view. This raises important questions. What knowledge ought we to have of Borges's lifelong fixation with his Irish predecessor and, at the same time, his inseparable thoughts on how to distance himself from Joyce's aesthetic of expansion in his attempt to forge his super-condensed *ficciones*? In the same vein, did the young, avant-gardist Borges contemplate in the mirror of Joyce's art a reflection of the creative tendencies he sought to emulate in the 1920s as he aspired to elevate the city of Buenos Aires to worldwide recognition, as Joyce had done with Dublin? And how did the mature Borges dramatize his complex relationship with Joyce in his public declarations and, most importantly, in the compressed *ficciones* that would eventually place him alongside Joyce, as one of the most revolutionary writers of twentieth-century literature? Any attempt to listen to the resounding echoes of the infinite conversation held between Borges and Joyce may only disclose the intriguing yet timeless quality of such exchange. To overhear Borges's meditations on Joyce throughout his life, or what the young Argentine poet said of his Irish *maestro* — with whom he shared the Homeric affliction of an impending blindness — in his 1925 review of *Ulysses* and translation of 'Penelope', or, equally, by shifting chronologies and assessing what Joyce would have made of Borges, is to participate in a pluralistic forum that inscribes our blind bards within the larger canvas of world literature.[28]

**Epic Proportions versus Compressed *Ficciones***

Whilst in this study I take as a point of departure Borges's renowned anti-novelistic stance, I will show that the dynamic that characterizes his literary relationship with Joyce simultaneously orchestrated sympathy and antipathy, praise and scorn, and affiliation and disaffiliation. In this sense, we could not speak of Borges's relationship with Joyce without alluding to the ambiguity, unpredictability, and contradictoriness of his responses to the Irish writer. Even what has so far been considered Borges's most celebratory writing, his 1925 *Proa* review of *Ulysses*, indisputably betrayed an early uneasiness with the epic scope and inherent difficulties of *Ulysses*, which led him to compare Joyce with the baroque experiments of the seventeenth-century Spanish writer Luis de Góngora. This becomes particularly apparent in Borges's oxymoronic remark in a 1982 interview with Seamus Heaney and Richard Kearney: 'I did recognize from the beginning that I had before me a marvellously tortuous book.'[29] Behind the ambiguousness of Borges's approach, I will demonstrate, lies a deeper realization that Joyce's work served him as a looking-glass wherein he was able to find a reflection of the metaphysical, literary, and linguistic issues that occupied him during his career as a writer, critic, and translator. For one thing, Borges continuously gazed, both compelled and horrified, at the sheer scale of Joyce's novelistic experiments in a conscious endeavour to reposition his aesthetic of brevity as the antithetical response to Joyce's epic legacy. Moreover, Borges's constant peeping through the multilayered texture of Joyce's vast novelistic tableau served him as an excuse to foster a literary debate which enabled him to discuss a wide range of concerns including: the act of reading and interpretation; infinity and total recollection; translation as an act of recreation;

translation as an impossibility; the category of literary genres; the heterogeneous catalogue; the literary tradition of the blind bard; and a self-examination of his role as the Hispanic publicist of Joyce. Finally, Borges had to confront the broader, more difficult issues concerning two marginal writers from Ireland and Argentina respectively, in relation to what he deemed as their unquestionable 'right' to a Western tradition — as he boldly stressed in his celebrated lecture 'The Argentine Writer and Tradition' (1953) — thus urging fellow Argentine writers to follow the example of the Irish who had taken all European subjects 'sin supersticiones, con una irreverencia que puede tener, y ya tiene, consecuencias afortunadas' (*OC1* 273) ['without superstition and with an irreverence that can have, and already has had, fortunate consequences'] (*SNF* 426). At the heart of Borges's irreverential call for action is the assumption that the inheritance of several crowded centuries of Western discourses implies a radical rethinking of a tradition which must be affected, modified, and reinvigorated by the twentieth-century writer, Irish or Argentine. At various times in his life, Borges leaned to the mirror of Joyce's art to recognize the shifting, composite silhouettes of Homer, Dante, and Shakespeare in an attempt to see how their canonical significance has been redeployed across history, culture, and language. The enormous scope of these enquiries and the encyclopaedic nature of Joyce's enterprise kept Borges occupied during a time span of nearly sixty years; from the youthful, avant-garde gesture of his 1925 review and translation of *Ulysses*, to the moving testimony of a blind and elderly man who in 1982 joined the Bloomsday celebrations to commemorate the centenary of Joyce's birth in Dublin. In the extraordinary trajectory of this journey is encapsulated the full arch of Borges's relationship with Joyce, and the fascinating, yet intriguing literary conversation between two icons of twentieth-century literature.

Chapters 1 and 2 examine, analyse, and document the complex relationship between Borges and Joyce from a literary, historical, and cultural perspective by offering a comprehensive study of Borges's reception of Joyce from 1925 to 1946 in the Buenos Aires reviews *Proa*, *El Hogar*, *Sur*, and *Los Anales de Buenos Aires*. The focus of Chapter 3 is on Borges's 1941 obituary of Joyce in which he proclaimed *Ulysses* to be one of the precursors of his then work-in-progress, 'Funes the Memorious'. With his usual irreverence and customary cheek, he proposed that the story's paralysed hero from Fray Bentos — who had been gifted with an infallible memory — represented the ideal 'monstrous' reader of *Ulysses* and *Finnegans Wake*. The final three chapters discuss the way in which Borges and Joyce conjured up the ghosts of Homer, Dante, and Shakespeare. The central interrelatedness at stake in these chapters also lays emphasis on the crucial fact that Dante was a reader of Homer, as much as Shakespeare was a reader of a deeply mediated Homeric and Dantean tradition. Moreover, each of these triangular studies shows that the lingering spirits of Homer, Dante, and Shakespeare haunted Borges and Joyce throughout their career as writers: their restless phantasms crept up, time and again, in the fabric of their works, eager to be reborn in a new language, culture, and history. The idea of resurrecting the dead appealed to Borges and Joyce, eager to devour their Western legacy and to transubstantiate it into the very essence of their arts.

## Notes to the Introduction

1. Susan Bassnett, *Comparative Literature: A Critical Introduction* (Oxford: Blackwell 1993), p. 161.
2. *Comparative Literature in the Age of Multiculturalism*, ed. by Charles Bernheimer (Baltimore, MD, and London: Johns Hopkins University Press, 1995).
3. *Comparative Literature in an Age of Globalization*, ed. by Haun Saussy (Baltimore, MD: Johns Hopkins University Press, 2006).
4. Saussy, p. 3.
5. Saussy, p. 4.
6. Saussy, p. 4.
7. Susan Bassnett, 'Comparative Literature in the Twenty-First Century', *Comparative Critical Studies*, 3.1–2 (2006), 3–11 (p. 6).
8. Bassnett, 'Comparative Literature in the Twenty-First Century', p. 6.
9. Gayatri Spivak, *Death of a Discipline* (New York: Columbia University Press, 2003), p. xii.
10. Spivak, p. 15.
11. Spivak, p. 8.
12. Lucia Boldrini, 'Comparative Literature in the Twenty-First Century', in *Comparative Critical Studies*, 3.1–2 (2006), 13–23 (p. 15).
13. Emer Nolan, *James Joyce and Nationalism* (London: Routledge, 1995), p. 130.
14. See Else Ribeiro Pires Vieira, 'Liberating Calibans: Readings of Antropofagia and Haroldo de Campos' Poetics of Transcreation', in *Post-colonial Translation: Theory and Practice*, ed. by Susan Bassnett and Harish Trivedi (London and New York: Routledge, 1999), pp. 95–113.
15. Suzanne Jill Levine, 'Notes to Borges's Notes on Joyce: Infinite Affinities', *Comparative Literature*, 49.4 (1997), 344–58 (pp. 345–46).
16. Robert Weninger, 'Comparative Literature at a Crossroads?: An Introduction', *Comparative Critical Studies*, 3.1–2 (2006), xi–xix (xiv).
17. Beatriz Sarlo, *A Writer on the Edge*, ed. by John King (London and New York: Verso, 1993), p. 47.
18. All English translations of Borges's works belong to the editions listed in the bibliography and will be cited parenthetically within the body of the book. All other unreferenced translations are mine.
19. Gérard Genette, *Palimpsests: Literature in the Second Degree*, trans. by Channa Newman and Claude Doubinsky (Lincoln and London: University of Nebraska Press, 1997), p. 400.
20. Emir Rodríguez Monegal, *Jorge Luis Borges: A Literary Biography* (New York: Dutton, 1978), pp. 268–69.
21. James Woodall, *The Man in the Mirror of the Book: A Life of Jorge Luis Borges* (London: Sceptre, 1996), p. 278.
22. Nicolás Helft and Alan Pauls, *El factor Borges: nueve ensayos ilustrados* (Buenos Aires: Fondo de Cultura Económica, 2000), pp. 128–39. They also suggest that this posthumous phase of Borges's publication history has merited the designation of 'invisible work', in an appropriate analogy with the similarly neglected period in the oeuvre of the French symbolist writer, Pierre Menard. See Helft and Pauls, p. 129.
23. Jorge Luis Borges, *Textos cautivos: ensayos y reseñas en 'El Hogar' (1936–1939)*, edición de Sacerio-Garí y Emir Rodríguez Monegal (Buenos Aires: Tusquets Editores, 1986).
24. Jorge Luis Borges, *Borges en revista multicolor: obras, reseñas y traducciones inéditas*, investigación y recopilación de Irma Zangara (Buenos Aires: Editorial Atlántida, 1995).
25. Interestingly, the ambitious 1999 English edition of Borges's non-fictional work incorporated a variety of writings from the *Obras completas*, magazines, and other previously unpublished texts in an attempt to distance itself from the obvious difficulties of the Spanish editions. See Jorge Luis Borges, *Selected Non-Fictions*, ed. by Eliot Weinberger (New York: Viking, 1999).
26. Paul Vanderham, *James Joyce and Censorship: The Trials of Ulysses* (London: Macmillan, 1998), pp. 169 and 210.
27. See Ulises Petit de Murat, '¿Quién sos vos para no discutirme?' *La Maga*, año 1, 22 (10 June 1992), p. 17. Petit de Murat also agreed to collaborate with Borges in the translation of *Ulysses*.

28. In the last three decades, the relationship between Borges and Joyce has attracted the attention of several critics who have produced a variety of critical essays which explore certain aspects of their literary relationship. For example, Schwartz, 'Borges y la primera hoja de *Ulysses*', *Revista Norteamericana*, 100–01 (1977), 721–26; Sánchez Robayna, 'Borges y Joyce', *Insula*, 437 (1983), 1, 12; Levine, 'Notes to Borges's Notes on Joyce: Infinite Affinities', *Comparative Literature*, 49 (1997), 344–59; Chitarroni, 'Borges y Joyce', in *Joyce o la travesía del lenguaje: psicoanálisis y literatura*, Lasic y Szumiraj (compiladoras) (Buenos Aires: Fondo de Cultura Económica, 1993), pp. 17–24; Salgado, 'Barroco Joyce: Jorge Luis Borges's and José Lezama Lima's Antagonistic Readings', in *Transcultural Joyce*, ed. by Karen Lawrence (Cambridge: Cambridge University Press, 1998), pp. 63–97; Vegh, 'A Meeting in the Western Canon: Borges's Conversation with Joyce', in *English Joyce Studies: Joyce's Audiences*, ed. by John Nash (Amsterdam: Rodopi, 2000), pp. 86–97; Rice, 'Subtle Reflections of/upon Joyce in/by Borges', *Journal of Modern Literature*, 24 (2000), 47–62; Waisman, 'Borges Reads Joyce: The Role of Translation in the Creation of Texts', *Variaciones Borges*, 9 (2000), 59–73 and *Borges and Translation: The Irreverence of the Periphery* (Lewisburg: Bucknell University Press, 2005); Willson, 'Borges, traductor de Joyce', in *La Constelación del Sur: traductores y traducciones en la literatura argentina del siglo XX* (Buenos Aires: Siglo veintiuno, 2004). It is also important to mention Murillo's *The Cyclical Night: Irony in James Joyce and Jorge Luis Borges* (Cambridge, MA: Harvard University Press, 1968). Yet, despite its promising title, this is not a comparative study but rather a separate, yet insightful investigation of their works. In the introduction, however, Murillo highlights important parallels between Borges and Joyce but declares that 'some basic differences between them restrict the possibilities of a comparative study', p. x. To some extent, my own study originated as a response to Murillo's thwarted comparativism, in an attempt to show that a global, open model of comparative literature welcomes not only neat resemblances but also divergences and contradictions.
29. Richard Kearney, *Transitions: Narratives in Modern Irish Culture* (Manchester: Manchester University Press, 1988), pp. 47–57 (48).

CHAPTER 1

# *Ulysses* in Transit, from Paris to Buenos Aires: The Cross-Cultural Transactions of Larbaud, Borges, and Güiraldes

In an interview with Seamus Heaney and Richard Kearney that took place during the centennial celebrations of Joyce's birth in Dublin, 16 June 1982, a blind and elderly Borges — who attended the symposium as a guest of honour[1] — spoke about his first encounter with Joyce: 'Let us go back to the early nineteen twenties. A friend of mine gave me a first edition of *Ulysses* which had just been published by Sylvia Beach in Paris'.[2] The friend who bestowed upon the young, avant-gardist Borges an *editio princeps* of *Ulysses* was Ricardo Güiraldes (1886–1927), the celebrated Argentine writer whose gaucho masterpiece *Don Segundo Sombra* (1926)[3] became an instant best-seller during his lifetime and rapidly achieved the status of national treasure. Güiraldes had, in turn, secured his copy of *Ulysses* through his close friendship with the French critic, writer and translator, Valery Larbaud. According to the accounts wherein Sylvia Beach methodically recorded the subscribers to the first publication of *Ulysses*, Güiraldes purchased copy no. 47 of the 100 copies of the deluxe Dutch handmade paper edition sold at 350 Francs each.[4] In a letter of 22 February 1922, Larbaud asked Beach to reserve him three copies of *Ulysses*, one for Güiraldes, the second for his wife, Adelina del Carril, and the third for Victoria Ocampo, the Argentine writer, critic, and founder of the influential Buenos Aires review *Sur* [*South*].[5] The Larbaud–Güiraldes financial and cultural exchange signified the immediate migration of the newly released *Ulysses* to the remote and distant geography of Buenos Aires.

In his seminal essay 'The Task of the Translator' Walter Benjamin defies traditional approaches to translation and proposes that the original owes its surviving life to the translation and not vice-versa. Thus the original is endowed with an 'afterlife', a utopian survival by means of which it depends upon the translation for its ever-recurring existence.[6] Drawing on this suggestive metaphor, Karen Lawrence asserts in *Transcultural Joyce* that: '[Joyce's texts] are carried metempsychotically across cultural, linguistic, national, and gender divides to undergo a "change of manners".'[7] On its auspicious transatlantic journey to Argentina, Güiraldes's copy of *Ulysses* embarked on the nomadic, transnational trajectory of the translated text.

The voyage of the book culminated, nearly two years later, in Borges's 1925 review of *Ulysses* and fragmentary translation of 'Penelope' which appeared in the Buenos Aires avant-garde review *Proa* [*Prow*]. Following his avant-gardist impulses, Borges equated the innovative *Ulysses* with the futuristic title of the review, and infused his translation of 'Penelope' with his current nationalistic agenda by rendering Molly Bloom's unpunctuated soliloquy into a distinctive type of Spanish saturated with Argentine diction. If Joyce's Eveline failed to elope to the distant promise of Buenos Aires, then Borges's Molly Bloom embodies the unfulfilled fate of her literary sister and proudly incarnates her new Argentine identity. What is, then, the itinerary followed by *Ulysses* in its migration to the Southern Hemisphere? And, upon arrival, how did 'Penelope' undergo its transformative process as an Argentine résumé of *Ulysses*? In order to answer these questions and to understand the crucial role that Borges played in the early reception of *Ulysses* in the Hispanic world, it is essential to provide a preliminary survey of the complex interactions that contributed to the dissemination of Joyce in Spain and Latin America. This chapter seeks to uncover a literary map that charts the early reception of Joyce in Argentina by focusing on Borges's 1925 review of *Ulysses* and fragmentary translation of 'Penelope'. It starts with a historical exploration of the cultural negotiations between Larbaud and Güiraldes which resulted in the safe arrival of *Ulysses* in Buenos Aires. It then discusses Borges's review and translation, particularly through the rich symbolic meaning conveyed by the nautical image of *Proa*. It demonstrates that the voyage of *Ulysses* to South America signified not only the exportation of a notoriously expensive and controversial commodity, but also the shifting of history, literature, and language across geographical boundaries, and the complex ways in which these cultural forces were received in Argentina.

### Valery Larbaud, Promoter of Joyce (and Latin America)

Not insignificantly, Richard Ellmann begins the second chapter of the 'Paris' period of his biography, *James Joyce*, with an unreserved tribute to Larbaud:

> Valery Larbaud, among the principal French writers of the 1920s, had the distinction of being the most receptive to the achievements of others. The excellence of his own work in poetry and the novel lent authority to his generous recognition of fellow talents. Besides his creative understanding of the literature in his own language, he was well versed in Italian and English literature. He was to make available to a French audience such writers as Coleridge and Landor. Most recently he had translated Samuel Butler. Though a man of subtlety and refinement, he had a most winning simplicity and directness. (*JJII* 499)

Ellmann summarizes the creative, critical, and philological skills that earned Larbaud a prominent place in French literary circles and which, most of all, contributed to his successful diffusion of *Ulysses*. Notwithstanding Ellmann's endeavour to pay full justice to the wide-ranging literary pursuits and polyglot abilities of Joyce's devoted campaigner, he fails to mention that, as well as English and Italian, Larbaud was equally proficient in Spanish, and had been deeply involved in the promotion of works from Spain and Latin America.[8] What are the consequences of this omission?

Or more precisely, how can Larbaud's simultaneous interest in the Hispanic world be recovered and reintegrated into the main critical narrative of his role as the publicist of Joyce? To begin with, John L. Brown draws attention to Larbaud's deep involvement with Spanish and Latin American literature during the early 1920s, a crucial period that may be read in conjunction with Larbaud's timely meeting with Joyce and his subsequent promotion of *Ulysses*: 'On his return from Alicante in 1919, Larbaud increasingly devoted himself to Spanish literature and somewhat later, because of his friendship with the Argentinian, Ricardo Güiraldes, and the Mexican, Alfonso Reyes, to Latin American writing'.[9] Further, Brown claims that Larbaud's encounter with Güiraldes 'contributed to Larbaud's interest in Latin American literature, which was to be one of his major areas of critical activity during the 1920s', as well as asserting that 'through Güiraldes, Larbaud came to know two other Argentine writers, Jorge Luis Borges and the novelist Manuel Gálvez'.[10] More recently, the decisive influence of Valery Larbaud within the wider European spectrum has become the recurrent narrative thread interweaving many of the outstanding essays of *The Reception of James Joyce in Europe*.[11] What this wide-ranging collection makes evident is the crucial fact that for many European writers and critics unacquainted with *Ulysses*, Larbaud's early reviews and fragmentary translations proved essential in the early dissemination of Joyce in their respective countries. For example, in a review of *The Reception of James Joyce in Europe*, Fritz Senn points out that 'the most referred-to author [of the compilation] is Valery Larbaud. I count some thirty entries in the index; T. S. Eliot gets twenty-four. His lecture at Adrienne Monnier's *La Maison des Amis des Livres*, on 7 December 1921, was often reprinted and quoted and may well have been the point of departure for reviewers who did not always rely on first-hand impressions'.[12]

Ricardo Güiraldes belonged to one of the most illustrious and prosperous land-owning families of Argentina at the turn of the twentieth century, his privileged social status and unlimited wealth enabling him to lead an untroubled lifestyle of literature and travels. These journeys involved frequent expeditions to Paris, which in those days was the undisputed Mecca for many well-off Latin Americans. In this respect, we can recognize in Güiraldes a mirror image of Larbaud, who also belonged to an affluent French family, enjoying the benefits of an existence free from financial troubles, and who devoted himself to a successful literary career and frequent expeditions across several European countries. Güiraldes's first encounter with Larbaud took place in 71 rue du Cardinal Lemoine — Larbaud's Paris residence — in the autumn of 1919. By the time Larbaud formally met Joyce in December 1920 and was 'raving mad over *Ulysses*' (*JJII* 499), his relationship with Güiraldes had become fully consolidated. Larbaud's ensuing promotion of *Ulysses* coincided with his endorsement of Güiraldes's work in the *Nouvelle Revue Française*,[13] one of the most prestigious literary reviews in Paris. But the relationship between the two men went much further. Indeed, there was a fundamental Latin American connection between Larbaud and Güiraldes, which would have largely contributed to the rapid development of their personal and literary relationship. Larbaud's celebrated fictional persona, Archibald Olson Barnabooth, was a young South American multi-millionaire who journeyed across Europe in a quest for self-knowledge.

Moreover, Larbaud's novella *Fermina Márquez* was based on his adolescent days at the illustrious Sainte-Barbe-des-Champs school, whose renowned educational excellence made it very popular with affluent Latin American families.[14] Sylvia Beach pertinently recalled: 'He [Larbaud] was sent to a school attended by a great many Argentinians, and it was there that he learned to speak Spanish like a native.'[15] Güiraldes manifested his gratitude to Valery Larbaud by symbolically naming a character of his gaucho elegy *Don Segundo Sombra* with a Hispanic variation of his first name, Valerio Lares.

Meanwhile, in March 1922 the restless Güiraldes embarked on yet another voyage across the Atlantic, arriving in Paris at the precise moment the recently published *Ulysses* was receiving considerable attention there, as well as raising an intense climate of speculation in the rest of Europe and the United States. In spite of Güiraldes's brief sojourn in the French capital, that saw him returning to Buenos Aires at the end of the same year, he nonetheless managed to purchase a copy of *Ulysses* via the intercession of Larbaud and Beach. Yet it remains an irony that the Francophile Güiraldes, although possessing no knowledge of the English language, nevertheless paved the way for the diffusion of a book in a language he ignored. This eccentric impulse, however, can be explained by his desire to present to Argentine intellectual circles the latest episode in French literary affairs and, equally, as a gesture of gratitude and renewed support for Valery Larbaud. In the end, thus, the journey of *Ulysses* from Paris to Buenos Aires involved a complex process of migration that not only enabled its physical appearance on Argentine soil, but also presupposed the existence of a readership that would guarantee its eventual consumption in the receiving culture. All literary works strive to find their readers; in 1924 *Ulysses* found its match in the avant-garde, nationalistic expression of Jorge Luis Borges, who was at the time one of the most promising men of letters of the young generation. Borges's fluency in English, Spanish, French, German, and a solid Latin education, his unique erudition and close association with the introduction of avant-gardism in Argentina made him, for the time being, the ideal reader of Joyce. Borges had brought back from his European excursions the Spanish movement *Ultraísmo*, of which he had been a dedicated theorist and practitioner, with regular contributions in the Spanish periodicals *Grecia*, *Ultra*, and *Tableros*.[16] The purposeful Güiraldes, then, entrusted the book to the accomplished twenty-five-year-old poet. Yet the gift of the book came at a price; Güiraldes asked Borges to undertake the translation of *Ulysses*, albeit fragmentary, for the review *Proa*. In a letter of 26 October 1924 to Guillermo de Torre, Borges alludes to Güiraldes's request and enthusiastically announced his forthcoming translation of the last two pages of 'Penelope'.[17] (We should also bear in mind that Larbaud's correspondence with Güiraldes included several references to Joyce's life and works, ranging from his frequent eye operations to all kind of editorial matters related to *Ulysses*, which would have provided relevant additional information for Borges.)[18] At the same time, Borges's fragmentary translation of 'Penelope' into Spanish coincided with two significant events in the reception of Joyce that were taking place in France and Spain. In 1924 the Spanish poet, critic, and translator Dámaso Alonso, who is known mainly as one of the members of the influential 'generación del 27', agreed to undertake the first translation of *A Portrait of the Artist as a Young Man* into Spanish. Signed under the pseudonym of Alonso Donado, *El artista adolescente (retrato)* was published in Madrid in 1926 and had the added advantage of claiming a certain degree of collaboration with the author, as Alonso held an epistolary correspondence with Joyce (see *Letters III* 128–30). Undoubtedly, any attempt to translate Joyce in the mid-twenties ought to have been inspired by the influential translation of *A Portrait* (1924) into French by Ludmila Savitsky and, above all, by the beginning of the difficult venture headed by Monnier and Beach to publish a French translation of *Ulysses*. Whilst Larbaud was the favoured recipient for such a vast enterprise, he nevertheless opted to limit his services to supervisor of the edition, with the gargantuan task to be eventually undertaken by Auguste Morel.

If during his lifetime Güiraldes served as the central, yet unacknowledged link in the promotion of Joyce in Latin America, after his untimely death from cancer in Paris in 1927 a series of circumstances strengthened his posthumous association with the Irish writer. Just as in 1922 he purchased copy n47 of the first edition of *Ulysses*, so the first numbered copy of the 1929 translation of *Ulysses* into French was specially printed for Güiraldes's widow, Adelina del Carril de Güiraldes. This unique N.1 copy, part of a limited edition of twenty-five copies on Hollande van Gelder paper, displays the following typescripted dedicatory: 'Exemplaire imprimé pour Madame Adeline del Carril de Güiraldes'.[19] By dedicating the first number of this edition to Güiraldes's widow, Monnier and Larbaud paid their respects to Güiraldes and presented it as homage to the surviving wife of their deceased friend.[20] Last, but not least, Güiraldes died in Paris in 1927 in an apartment located in 7 rue Edmond Valentin. Coincidentally, Joyce resided there in the years 1934–39, which amounts to a record number of five years, without a doubt, an unusually long period for his customarily nomadic lifestyle. The flat belonged to Güiraldes's friend, the Argentine Alfredo González Garaño.[21]

### 'Fallen on his feet in Buenos Ayres' (*D 32*): *Ulysses* in Argentina

In the effervescent climate of Argentina in the 1920s, an avant-garde manifesto did not come exempt from the customary challenge to social, linguistic, and cultural conventions. Therefore, in 1924 the founders of *Proa*, Güiraldes, Borges, Brandán Caraffa, and Pablo Rojas Paz proclaimed thus: 'Trabajamos en el sitio más libre y más duro del barco, mientras en los camarotes duermen los burgueses de la literatura. Por la posición que hemos elegido, ellos forzosamente han de pasar detrás nuestro en el honor del camino'[22] [While we work in the forefront and most difficult place of the ship, the bourgeois men of letters are sleeping in their cabins. Due to our chosen position, they shall be forced to go behind us in this honourable journey]. The underlying sense of defiance at stake here has been magnificently captured by the Buenos Aires avant-garde painter, writer, mystic, and inventor of languages, Xul Solar, who, according to Borges was 'our [Argentine] William Blake' (*A* 41). In 1923 Solar produced an imposing watercolour painting depicting three figures with disproportionately long necks and elongated arms with daggers (most surely representing three of the founders) aboard the ship *Proa*. In the tempestuous sea of the picture are three monstrous oceanic creatures emerging from the water and engaging in a fierce battle with the three sailors, who boldly encounter their hideous opponents with unbending courage and resolution.[23] In this way, Borges, Güiraldes et al. carefully branded the futuristic *Proa* as an innovative, rebellious periodical for a new literary generation. In the joint preface that launched the second phase of the journal, its members declared that, among other things: '*Proa* aspira a revelar en sus páginas la inquietud integral de los espíritus fecundos que viven esta hora' (*TR1* 190) [[*Proa*] aspires to disclose in its pages the fundamental concerns of the creative spirits of this time]. In his autobiographical essay, Borges reflected that their contributions to *Proa* were aimed at 'renewing both prose and poetry' (*A* 41), particularly through their attempt to create new metaphors and striking poetical images. As editors of an avant-garde journal, the young founders of *Proa* aimed to introduce Argentine audiences to the latest literary and artistic innovations from both home and abroad. Thus, the January 1925 issue of *Proa* perfectly illustrated the overall aims of the review, bringing together an exceptional issue that contained, amongst other things, Borges's pioneering review of *Ulysses* and fragmentary translation of 'Penelope'; a full-page portrait of Joyce; articles on Neo-dadaism and Surrealism by the Spanish poet and critic Guillermo de Torre; two illustrations by Borges's sister, Norah; a first-hand account of Parisian literary life by Güiraldes; and two poems by Leopoldo Marechal, who, twenty-four years later, would publish the experimental city novel *Adán Buenosayres*, which Robin William Fiddian has aptly defined as 'the first "Argentinian *Ulysses*"'.[24]

What were the cultural repercussions, then, of publishing a review and a translation of *Ulysses* in the Buenos Aires of the early twenties? If we consider that *Ulysses* had become outlawed in the United States, a legal procedure thereafter replicated in England, Ireland, and most English-speaking countries, this was, without a doubt, an act of great editorial audacity. Furthermore, the United States ban had come into place as the direct result of the serialization of several episodes in the avant-garde Chicago monthly, *The Little Review*, edited by Margaret Anderson and Jane Heap. As previously stated in the Introduction, Borges translated one of the so-called 'obscene' fragments from Molly's eroticized soliloquy. *Proa*'s editorial decision acquires further significance if viewed in relation to a pertinent parallel drawn by Valery Larbaud. In 1925 he perceptively identified an analogy between *Proa* and *The Little Review*, both periodicals of the Americas, North and South, and representative of the latest European avant-garde sects and, hence, eager to endorse the dissemination of the most noteworthy events in the literary world. Larbaud unveiled this parallel in a tribute to *Proa* on its untimely closure: 'Nous apprenons avec chagrin la disparition de la revue d'avant-garde *Proa*' [We have learned with great sadness of the disappearance of the avant-garde magazine *Proa*], emphasizing that, 'C'est là qu'ont paru la plupart des études et des notes réunies par J. L. Borges en "Inquisiciones"' [in this magazine appeared most of the studies and notes compiled by Jorge Luis Borges in *Inquisiciones*].[25] His note concluded with a positive parallel between *Proa* and *The Little Review*: 'Cependant *Proa* n'aura pas été inutile; elle aura donné à l'Amérique du Sud une revue littéraire comparable à celles des États-Unis: *The Dial* et surtout *The Little Review*' [*Proa*, however, has not been in vain, it has conferred on South America a literary magazine which may be compared to others in the United States: *The Dial* and, above all, the *Little Review*].[26] For Larbaud, *Proa*'s editorial decision to translate fragments from 'Penelope' and to introduce the work of James Joyce mirrored *The Little Review*'s previous serialization of *Ulysses*, particularly their controversial publication of 'Nausicaa'. However, unlike *The Little Review*, the fragmentary translation of *Ulysses* published in *Proa* did not fall prey to overzealous censorship, and heralded instead the beginning of Latin America's enduring love affair with Joyce.

More generally, the decisive point in Borges's participation in the *Proa* cultural project and his relationship with the avant-garde is clearly expressed in his 1969 poem-tribute 'Invocation to Joyce'. Here a blind and elderly Borges looks back to his *ultraista* forays from the wider perspective of the numerous avant-garde trends that flourished during this innovative period in the first few decades of the twentieth-century. Due to its importance, the poem is included below:

> Dispersos en dispersas capitales,
> solitarios y muchos,
> jugábamos a ser el primer Adán
> que dio nombre a las cosas.
> Por los vastos declives de la noche
> Que lindan con la aurora,
> Buscamos (lo recuerdo aún) las palabras
> de la luna, de la muerte, de la mañana
> y de los otros hábitos del hombre.
> Fuimos el imagismo, el cubismo,
> los conventículos y las sectas
> que las crédulas universidades veneran.
> Inventamos la falta de puntuación,
> la omisión de mayúsculas,
> las estrofas en forma de paloma
> de los bibliotecarios de Alejandría.
> Ceniza, la labor de nuestras manos
> y un fuego ardiente nuestra fe.
> Tú, mientras tanto, forjabas
> en las ciudades del destierro,
> en aquel destierro que fue
> tu aborrecido y elegido instrumento,
> el arma de tu arte,
> erigías tus arduos laberintos,
> infinitesimales e infinitos,
> admirablemente mezquinos,
> más populosos que la historia.
> Habremos muerto sin haber divisado
> la biforme fiera o la rosa
> que son el centro de tu dédalo,
> pero la memoria tiene sus talismanes,
> sus ecos de Virgilio,
> y así en las calles de la noche perduran
> tus infiernos espléndidos,
> tantas cadencias y metáforas tuyas,

los oros de tu sombra.
Qué importa nuestra cobardía si hay en la tierra
un solo hombre valiente
qué importa la tristeza si hubo en el tiempo
alguien que se dijo feliz,
qué importa mi perdida generación,
ese vago espejo,
si tus libros la justifican.
Yo soy los otros. Yo soy todos aquellos
que ha rescatado tu obstinado rigor.
Soy los que no conoces y los que salvas. (*OC2* 382–83)

[Scattered over scattered cities
alone and many
we played at being that Adam
who gave names to all living things.
Down the long slopes of night
that border on the dawn
we sought (I still remember) words
for the moon, for death, for the morning,
and for man's other habits.
We were imagism, cubism,
the conventicles and sects
respected now by credulous universities.
We invented the omission of punctuation
and capital letters,
stanzas in the shape of a dove
from the librarians of Alexandria.
Ashes, the labor of our hands,
and a burning fire our faith.
You, all the while,
in cities of exile,
in that exile that was
your detested and chosen instrument,
the weapon of your craft,
erected your pathless labyrinths,
infinitesimal and infinite,
wondrously paltry,
more populous than history.
We shall die without sighting
the twofold beast or the rose
that are the center of your maze,
but memory holds its talismans,
its echoes of Virgil,
and so in the streets of night
your splendid hells survive,
so many of your cadences and metaphors,
the treasures of your darkness.
What does our cowardice matter if on this earth
there is one brave man,
what does sadness matter if in time past
somebody thought himself happy,

> what does my lost generation matter,
> that dim mirror,
> if your books justify us?
> I am the others. I am all those
> who have been rescued by your pains and care.
> I am those unknown to you and saved by you.][27]

In a larger way, the mature Borges is invoking here James Joyce's Modernist legacy, particularly the distinctive 'cadencias' of Joyce's unique music which stood in opposition to the cacophonous discords of other vanguard movements. Thus Borges argues that the glowing fire of his lost avant-garde generation has turned to ash, and that their fervent, cutting-edge poetics have only survived in the curricula of 'crédulas universidades'. But this ephemeral existence, however, is justified by the long-lasting work of James Joyce, who, unlike the short-lived vanguard trends, has endured the test of time, and therefore enfolds them with the luminosity of his later glory. This becomes particularly apparent in the last three lines of the poem, in which Borges shifts the plural pronoun 'we' — used as a choral device that brings in the myriad avant-garde voices — into the singular first person pronoun 'I' of Borges the poet, who speaks to Joyce in the present tense and pays homage to his pervasive literary influence. In this final mystical vision, a humble and reverential Borges elevates his blind predecessor as the redeemer and saviour of the literary vagaries of his yesteryears, and as the continuing inspiration of his art. Once the blind and elderly Borges has summoned the ghost of Joyce as his guide and *maestro*, he is following in the footsteps of Virgil, who also sought the guidance of another blind bard, Homer. He is also following in the footsteps of Dante, who looked upon Virgil as the legendary figure to lead him through the shadowy confines of the Otherworld. In staging an imaginary conversation with Joyce's phantasm, Borges is also inaugurating a poetic tradition that will be followed by two Poets Laureate from the Caribbean and Ireland respectively, Derek Walcott and Seamus Heaney. In Book V of *Omeros* Walcott's poet-narrator elevates Joyce as 'our age's Omeros, undimmed Master/and true tenor of the place', and has a vision of the ghost of Joyce as it appears at nightfall to walk the streets of his beloved Dublin:

> I leant on the mossed embankment just as if he
> bloomed there every dusk with eye-patch and tilted hat,
> rakish cane on one shoulder.[28]

Just as Borges and Walcott paid tribute to their Irish predecessor, so Heaney similarly conjured up an encounter with the spectre of Joyce in *Station Island*. Amongst the numerous ghosts which Heaney stumbles upon during this physical and spiritual voyage of self-discovery is the looming phantom of Joyce:

> Like a convalescent, I took the hand
> stretched down from the jetty, sensed again
> an alien comfort as I stepped on ground
> to find the helping hand still gripping mine,
> fish-cold and bony, but whether to guide
> or to be guided I could not be certain
> for the tall man in step at my side

> seemed blind; though he walked straight as a rush
> upon his ashplant, his eyes fixed straight ahead.[29]

Like Borges and Walcott, Heaney is able to capture Joyce's distinctive silhouette by means of a brief descriptive passage that condenses his archetypal image. The dream vision that follows stages Heaney's dialogue with the spectre, who advises him on his career and role as a poet: 'Your obligation / is not discharged by any common rite. / What you do you must do on your own. / The main thing is to write for the joy of it'.[30] Ultimately, what Borges, Walcott, and Heaney are saying here is that the haunting phantom of Joyce has become their guide and inspiration in their journeys through literature. The three poets are paying homage to the vast literary tradition encompassed in Joyce's work, as the elongated shadow of Joyce has also enwrapped the kindred spirits that preceded him: Homer, Virgil, and Dante.[31]

## Sailing Through Turbulent Waters: *Ulysses* and the Review *Proa*

Borges opened his 1925 review of *Ulysses* with a boastful declaration: 'Soy EL PRIMER AVENTURERO[32] hispánico que ha arribado al libro de Joyce: país enmarañado y montaraz que Valery Larbaud ha recorrido y cuya contextura ha trazado con impecable precisión cartográfica (*N. R. F., XVIII*)' (*Inq.* 23) ['I am the first traveller from the Hispanic world to set foot upon the shores of *Ulysses*, a lush wilderness already traversed by Valery Larbaud, who traced its dense texture with the impeccable precision of a mapmaker'] (*SNF* 12). What is implicit in Borges's emphatic assertion is not only his belief that he is the first Hispanic explorer of the epic *Ulysses*, but also the awareness that he was touring Joyce's geography for the later enlightenment of the Spanish-speaking world. And yet Borges's proud claim to be Joyce's first Hispanic critic and translator had been undermined by the Spanish writer Antonio Marichalar who, just two months previously, had published an article on Joyce and fragmentary translations of 'Ithaca' and 'Penelope' in the November 1924 issue of the Spanish review *Revista de Occidente* [*The Western Review*].[33] Indeed, the youthful, impetuous Borges was unaware of the fact that Marichalar was also competing for the honour to render the first pages of *Ulysses* into Spanish. But as far as Borges had been able to see, his only predecessor in charting a path through Joyce's *terra incognita* was Larbaud, to whom he refers to as a rigorous mapmaker. Undoubtedly, he is also alluding to the schemata of Homeric and symbolic correspondences that Joyce had lent to Larbaud in order to help him with the preparation of his public lecture. It is well known that the diagram of correspondences proposes a system of parallels between the eighteen episodes of *Ulysses*, by assigning a specific hour, scene, organ, art, colour, symbol and technique to each Homeric title. Joyce had lent the schemata to several critics and writers, including Larbaud, Carlo Linati, and Stuart Gilbert, amongst others. Regarding the Homeric parallels Borges duly stated: 'Joyce pinta una jornada contemporánea y agolpa en su decurso una variedad de episodios que son la equivalencia espiritual de los que informan la *Odisea* (*Inq.* 27) ['Joyce portrays a day in modern life and accumulates a variety of episodes in its course which equal in spirit those events that inform the *Odyssey*'] (*SNF* 14). Borges also sketched a biographical profile of Joyce with material collated from Larbaud's 1921 Paris lecture (although the emphasis on Joyce's faultless Latin is definitely Borges's):

> [Joyce] nació el ochenta y dos en Dublín, hijo de una familia prócer y piadosamente católica. Lo han educado los jesuitas; sabemos que posee una cultura clásica, que no comete erróneas cantidades en la dicción de frases latinas, que ha frecuentado el escolasticismo, que ha repartido sus andanzas por diversas tierras de Europa y que sus hijos han nacido en Italia (*Inq.* 24–25).
>
> [He [Joyce] was born in Dublin in 1882, into an eminent and piously Catholic family. He was educated by the Jesuits. We know that he possesses a classical culture, that he is not unfamiliar with scholasticism, that there are no errors of diction in his Latin phrases, that he has wandered the various countries of Europe, and that his children were born in Italy (*SNF* 13).]

But for all of Borges's initial arrogance and the grandiosity of his claim to be the first Hispanic reader of *Ulysses*, he soon laid bare his aesthetics of compression that stood in opposition to the grand epic scale of Joyce's *Ulysses*, and described his reading as '[lo] inestudioso y transitorio de mi estadía en sus confines' (*Inq.* 23) ['[my] visit within its borders has been inattentive and transient'] (*SNF* 12). In a broad sense — and looking ahead to Borges's subsequent development as a writer — what Joyce rendered on the vast and open canvas of the novelistic genre, Borges later contracted within the tight confines of the short story. Hence, a tongue-in-cheek Borges openly and unreservedly confessed to not having read *Ulysses* in its entirety: 'Confieso no haber desbrozado las setecientas páginas que lo integran, confieso haberlo practicado solamente a retazos' (*Inq.* 23) ['I confess that I have not cleared a path through all seven hundred pages, I confess to having examined only bits and pieces'] (*SNF* 12). Borges justified this claim, however, by arguing that notwithstanding his incomplete reading, he still professed to know the book with 'esa aventurera y legítima certidumbre que hay en nosotros, al afirmar nuestro conocimiento de la ciudad, sin adjudicarnos por ello la intimidad de cuantas calles incluye' (*Inq.* 23) ['with that bold and legitimate certainty with which we assert our knowledge of a city, without ever laying claim to the intimacy of all the many streets it includes'] (*SNF* 12). Apart from conveying Borges's fragmentary reading of *Ulysses*, this statement reveals an even more significant aspect of his understanding of Joyce, as Borges uses the image of the city for his own purposes. In a larger way, what Joyce had done for Dublin, the young Borges aimed to do for his native Buenos Aires. 'Joyce, in his exile in Trieste,' writes Jason Wilson, 'in his myopic dedication to writing, had turned his beloved Dublin into the site of a new myth. Borges had hoped to do the same with Buenos Aires.'[34] The youthful Borges may have wandered around the labyrinthine streets of *Ulysses* much in the way that has been described by Colin MacCabe: '*Ulysses* is a voyage through meaning: a voyage through all the discourses available in English in 1904. As Bloom and Stephen move through Dublin so the writing moves through the city of words that is English.'[35] The Joycean aesthetic that Borges consciously pursued in the 1920s is clearly discernible in his aspiration to chart a literary mythology of Buenos Aires. It is also surely relevant to note that their first books of fiction and poetry respectively are entitled with the names of their native cities: *Dubliners* (1914) and *Fervour of Buenos*

*Aires* (1923). In these collections of stories and poems the writers undertake the task of elevating Dublin and Buenos Aires respectively to worldwide recognition by mapping a spatial and cultural landscape of their metropolis. This intersection is furthered from a biographical standpoint, since Borges and Joyce are writing from the perspective of young, aspiring writers, inasmuch as Joyce completed *Dubliners* at the age of twenty-five and Borges was about to turn the same age when *Fervour of Buenos Aires* was released. Borges alluded in the review to Joyce's biographical trajectory, including his birth in Dublin, in 1882, and his voluntary exile in Europe, as well as the important fact that Joyce 'ha compuesto canciones, cuentos breves y una novela de catedralicio grandor' (*Inq.* 24–25) ['He has composed lyrics, short stories, and a novel of cathedral-like grandeur'] (*SNF* 13).

Yet Borges's voyage — or shortcut — through the labyrinth of *Ulysses* suggested an additional, larger metaphor, which amalgamated his pioneering reception of Joyce with his role as editor and founder of *Proa*. This dual impulse is conveyed in the self-conscious statement: 'Joyce es audaz como una proa y universal como la rosa de los vientos' (*TR1* 28) ['Joyce is as bold as the prow of a ship, and as universal as a mariner's compass'] (*SNF* 14). Therefore in 1925 Borges applied to the newly discovered *Ulysses* the symbolism of the futuristic journal caption taken from navigational terminology. The result of this insightful fusion is the suggestion that *Ulysses* shared with *Proa* the same bold and perilous enterprise of pointing towards new directions. 'The image of the prow', argues Beatriz Vegh, 'represented for the editors a visual reality symbolizing what the journal valued and wished to enhance in the literary and artistic horizons and productions of their country: audacity, analytical approach, directional newness, fervour, dissatisfaction with conventional norms and intellectual unrest.'[36] The ideological foundations of *Proa* — especially as they had been laid out in the 1924 anti-bourgeois manifesto of the review — are also reflected in Borges's profound conviction of the power of *Ulysses* as a revolutionary book, its ultimate all-inclusiveness, as well as the relevance of its ontological enquiries:

> En las páginas del *Ulises* bulle con alborotos de picadero la realidad total. No la mediocre realidad de quienes solo advierten en el mundo las abstraídas operaciones del alma y su miedo ambicioso de no sobreponerse a la muerte, ni esa otra realidad que entra por los sentidos y en que conviven nuestra carne y la acera, la luna y el aljibe. La dualidad de la existencia está en él: esa inquietación ontológica que no se asombra meramente de ser, sino de ser en este mundo preciso, donde hay zaguanes y palabras y naipes y escrituras eléctricas en la limpidez de las noches (*Inq.* 26).

> [A total reality teems vociferously in the pages of *Ulysses*, and not the mediocre reality of those who notice in the world only the abstract operations of the mind and its ambitious fear of not being able to overcome death, nor that other reality that enters only our senses, juxtaposing our flesh and the streets, the moon and the well. The duality of existence dwells within this book, an ontological anxiety that is amazed not merely at being, but at being in this particular world where there are entranceways and words and playing cards and electric writing upon the translucence of the night (*SNF* 13–14).]

For Borges, then, the metaphor of the prow served various purposes simultaneously.

It transmitted the cutting-edge principles of the review (they were, so to speak, navigating on the tempestuous currents of literature, language, and culture), it described Joyce's audacious mapping of previously uncharted territories, and it illustrated, additionally, Homer's myth of the seafaring Ulysses. Such a suggestive tableau of nautical imagery recalls, to a further extent, Joyce's comment to Arthur Power that 'the modern writer must be an adventurer above all, willing to take every risk, and be prepared to founder in his effort if need be. In other words we must write dangerously.'[37] Borges also extended the marine imagery of 'prow' with the cartographical symbol of the 'rose of winds'. Like the *rosa ventorum* that showed the directions of the eight winds and served as a central diagram to maps and charts, Joyce's *Ulysses* became a universal literary compass with which to navigate the vast sea of literature. This analogy acquires added relevance in relation to the manifesto that opened the magazine, in which Borges et al. referred to the audacity of the prow symbol and declared: 'Creemos que por lo menos podemos ostentar la brújula del viajero' (*TR1* 189) [We believe we can at least display a traveller's compass]. Such an array of prows, compasses, and seafaring devices equally addresses the naturalistic impulses that characterized Joyce's writing of *Ulysses*. In this vein, Frank Budgen described Joyce's making of *Ulysses* to that of 'an engineer at work with compass and slide-rule, a surveyor with theodolite and measuring chain or, more Ulyssean perhaps, a ship's officer taking the sun, reading the log and calculating current drift and leeway.'[38]

Nevertheless, for all his energetic exploration of Joyce's epic geography, the *ultraist* adventurer ended his journey through the currents of *Ulysses* emphasizing, once more, his reluctance to read the book in its entirety, along with the impossibility of him carrying the hefty volume to Neuquén, a province located in the West of Argentina, 'en la imposibilidad de llevarme el *Ulises* al Neuquén y de estudiarlo en su pausada quietud' (*Inq.* 28) ['I have not the ambition to take *Ulysses* to Neuquen and study it in quiet repose'] (*SNF* 14). But in a final, unexpected twist, he added as a closing quotation the not entirely innocent remark made by the Spanish Golden Age playwright, Lope de Vega, in his attempt at deciphering the baroque experiments of Góngora: 'Quiero hacer mías las decentes palabras que confesó Lope de Vega acerca de Góngora: *Sea lo que fuere, yo he de estimar y amar el divino genio deste Cavallero, tomando del lo que entendiere con humildad y admirando con veneración lo que no alcanzare a entender*' (*Inq.* 28) ['I wish to make mine Lope de Vega's respectful words regarding Góngora: Be what it may, I will always esteem and adore the divine genius of this Gentleman, taking from him what I understand with humility and admiring with veneration what I am unable to understand'] (*SNF* 15).[39] The anticlimactic closure of the review with a comparative reading of Joyce and Góngora ambivalently refracted through the perception of Lope de Vega's hesitant stance, takes us to the heart of Borges's conflictual relationship with Joyce. As the passionate, avant-gardist Borges gave way to the emergence of the mature, self-composed author of the utterly compact and metaphysical *ficción*, so the gulf between Joyce's aesthetics of expansion and Borges's aesthetics of compression became even greater. Furthermore, this statement also invalidates critical claims that highlighted the 'unconditional, celebratory reverence' of Borges's review,[40] but instead reveals a more complex, hybrid texture that marks the beginning of Borges's admiration but also serious reservations towards Joyce.

## Jorge Luis Borges, Translator of *Ulysses*

If Valery Larbaud has been unanimously recognized as the European promoter of *Ulysses*, then Jorge Luis Borges fulfils a similar role in the Hispanic world.[41] Just as Sylvia Beach and Adrienne Monnier considered Larbaud the most suitable candidate for the French translation of *Ulysses*, the Uruguayan Natalio Botana (the owner of the Argentine newspaper *Crítica*) similarly commissioned Borges to undertake the difficult task of translating *Ulysses* into Spanish. As stated in the introduction, Borges gave an unequivocal 'Yes' and Botana promptly telegraphed London, only to find out that the Joyce estate had already awarded the translation rights to fellow Argentine J. Salas Subirat, whose complete translation of *Ulysses* finally appeared in 1945.[42] How much different would the reception of James Joyce have been in the Hispanic world had we had a complete translation of *Ulysses* by a writer of the stature of Jorge Luis Borges? Whilst it is tempting to be allured by the attractiveness of envisaging a fusion between two of the most revolutionary writers of the twentieth century, we should not be fooled here by Borges's impetuous agreement to undertake a project of such magnitude. Undoubtedly, it remains highly questionable whether Borges, for all his repeated adherence to an aesthetic of brevity, his encapsulation of infinity in a small iridescent sphere known as the Aleph, and his tongue-in-cheek habit of providing commentaries and summaries of real and imaginary books, would have been able to tackle the epic proportions of Joyce's modernist novel. Indeed, Borges's aesthetics of brevity can only produce an abridged rendering of *Ulysses*, a miniaturized version of Joyce's epic proportions filtered through his own economical impulses. One plausible conclusion we may extract from this is that Borges is only capable of providing us with an abridged translation of *Ulysses*. Like 'Pierre Menard, Author of the *Quixote*' who opted for rewriting selected paragraphs from Cervantes's *Don Quixote*, Borges confined himself to a fragmentary translation of Joyce. But we should recognize that if Cervantes was the subject of Borges's humorous exercise, it was Joyce who was very much in the background of Borges's reflections on reading and translation. Borges's celebrated technique of 'anacronismo deliberado y de las atribuciones erróneas' (*OC1*: 450) [deliberate anachronism and erroneous attributions], prides itself in eschewing literary chronologies and challenging stable notions of authorship. This might validate the claim that Joyce's *Ulysses* precedes Homer's *Odyssey*, inasmuch as the Hispanic reader is now prompted to read 'Penelope' refracted through the idiosyncratic prism of Borges. Consequently, since Borges neither translated a complete version of *Ulysses*, nor acted as supervisor (like Larbaud in France) of the unabridged rendering into Spanish, his role as translator of Joyce will be examined mainly through his fragmentary version of 'Penelope', as well as in relation to his reception of Salas Subirat's translation in the Buenos Aires press.[43]

### Molly Bloom's Obscene Passages

As I have argued in the introduction, the idea of picturing the youthful, avant-gardist Borges undertaking a translation of the last two pages of Molly's erotic, unpunctuated soliloquy cannot but stand at odds with the received image of the blind Argentine bard, later renowned as much for his erudite *ficciones* as for his spartan, library-bound mythical existence. Of equal relevance is the crucial fact that during the early reception of *Ulysses*, the absence of punctuation and uninterrupted use of the innovatory technique of interior monologue in 'Penelope' turned the episode into a stylistic curiosity to most critics and commentators. Besides this revolutionary literary novelty, the episode had also earned a reputation for its unabashed obscenity, with its prolific allusions to male and female genitals, sexual practices, and scatology. Significantly, in a letter to Frank Budgen, Joyce himself boldly referred to 'Penelope' as 'probably more obscene than any preceding episode' (*JJII* 501), and explained, without inhibitions, how the metaphor of the female body is employed throughout the episode: 'It turns like the huge earth ball slowly surely and evenly round and round spinning, its four cardinal points being the female breasts, arse, womb and cunt [...]' (*JJII* 501). Regarding the fascinating critical history of 'Penelope' Richard Brown would claim that: 'Critics have been reading the episode now for more than eighty years and the transition even between the kinds of reading practised during the past twenty or so years is striking, especially as regards the treatment of the body.'[44] Again, Kathleen McCormick has skilfully summarized the numerous readings to which the body of Molly Bloom has been subjected: 'Seen as obscene by many reviewers in the twenties, an earth goddess in the thirties and forties, a whore in the fifties and sixties, a realistic product of her historical formation in the seventies, and most recently a symbol of "écriture feminine," Molly Bloom has been the subject of intense critical debate throughout the history of the reception of *Ulysses*'.[45] Borges's fragmentary translation of 'Penelope', as we shall soon discover, provides just one more fascinating reading in the larger narrative of Molly's critical reception. Borges had the foresight to gift Latin America with the first translation of Molly Bloom's sexually charged reverie. If Borges's fragmentary translation is partly explained by his reluctance to perform a complete reading of the book, the fact that the fragments in question belong to 'Penelope' poses a different question altogether: why 'Penelope'?[46] To begin with Edwin Williamson has suggested that Borges's entanglement in the sensuous web of 'Penelope' coincided with his infatuation with the Argentine poet, Norah Lange, the muse of Borges's literary generation, a red-haired beauty of Norwegian extraction. 'Running broadly in parallel to Borges's reflections on Joyce', argues Williamson, 'we find a growing fascination with Norah Lange. On October 26 he told Guillermo de Torre that he was thinking of translating a passage from *Ulysses*, and in the same letter referred no fewer than three times to Norah, asking his Spanish friend what he thought of her poems'.[47] Williamson's conjecture about Borges's infatuation with the teenage Norah has certainly produced a stir in the seemingly uneventful life of the ivory-towerish Borges. Further, previous biographers of Borges had presented this relationship as pure literary camaraderie, particularly since Lange had been closely involved with Borges in introducing the *ultraist* movement in Buenos Aires.[48] Williamson's hypothesis implies, moreover, a further onomastic parallel between Borges and Joyce, in a nominal analogy that links both 'Nora(h)s' as inspirational muses. In addition, Suzanne Jill Levine views Borges's decision to translate Molly Bloom's sexually charged reverie, as the confluence of 'hedonistic' and 'esthetic' impulses: 'Homer's seafaring adventure on the one hand and Joyce's sexual adventure on the other appealed, respectively, to Borges the boy and Borges the man'.[49]

Beyond Borges's biographical context, the complex motives behind his translation of 'Penelope' ought to be considered in relation to the Francophone reception of Joyce. In this sense, it must be stressed that the trend to offer fragmentary translations of 'Penelope' was not a Borgesian peculiarity but had rather been initiated by Valery Larbaud during his *Ulysses* campaign in Paris. In his famous 1921 lecture, Larbaud himself had commissioned the translation of several excerpts of *Ulysses*, including the six final pages from 'Penelope'. Furthermore, in the Parisian literary review *Commerce*, founded in 1924 by Paul Valery, Fargue and Larbaud himself,[50] the last four pages of 'Penelope' appeared in a translation jointly signed by 'MM. Valery Larbaud et Auguste Morel'.[51] Since Larbaud had promptly sent a copy of this first issue to Güiraldes at the time he had been actively collaborating with Borges in *Proa*, it is valid to conclude that Borges had full access to these French translations. Just as Borges had closely followed Larbaud's 1921 lecture on Joyce published in the *Nouvelle Revue Française*, so he had similar access to the translations published in *Commerce*, which offered French audiences a preview of *Ulysses* that ironically disclosed its ending, rather than beginning. Thus, Borges continued the translation history of *Ulysses* heralded by Larbaud in France, and similarly privileged a fragmentary rendering of the closing pages of 'Penelope'. In this manner, a translation is no longer envisaged as an isolated exercise, but as part of an interactive sequence in which the translator engages in conversation not only with the 'original' but also with its existing afterlives.

The oxymoronic device of introducing a book by its ending rather than beginning, certainly appealed to Borges, who opted for presenting Hispanic readers with a sexually charged preamble — and finale — of the last two pages. Jorge Schwartz, for instance, celebrates Borges's translation strategy: 'The fact that "The Last Page of *Ulysses*" became the first page of *Ulysses* published in the Spanish language, is an oxymoron whose symmetry would have pleased Borges'.[52] Similarly Waisman argues that: 'The last page of *Ulysses* in English thus becomes the first page of *Ulysses* into Spanish; the last page of Joyce's great work becomes the first page of what would be a long and interesting textual dialogue that Borges holds with Joyce throughout his life'.[53] Moreover, this translation tactic in which the ending becomes *mutatis mutandis* the beginning of *Ulysses*, converges with Joyce's conception of 'Penelope' as an infinite episode with 'no beginning, middle or end' (*Letters I* 172) since Molly's incessant flow of memories not only bring back her own past, but also circularly remember the whole book.

## The Task of the Translator

It is noteworthy that Borges defied traditional approaches to translation that conceived the original as a sacrosanct, definitive text, and instead argued that the so-called original is nothing but a *borrador* [draft] of an incomplete and unstable text. In a 1946 review of Salas Subirat's complete translation of *Ulysses* into Spanish, Borges reiterated this unconventional stance and privileged a translation of *Ulysses* that championed a re-creative, manipulative strategy. He concluded the review with a verdict that served as a warning to prospective translators of Joyce: 'Joyce dilata y reforma el idioma inglés: su traductor tiene el deber de ensayar libertades congéneres' (*TR2* 235) [Joyce expands and renovates the English language: the task of his translator is to exercise a similar freedom]. These radical precepts are conspicuously perceptible in his translation of 'Penelope', particularly since he aimed to present an autonomous version of Molly Bloom, namely, a résumé of 'Penelope' specifically written for the readership of *Proa* in 1925 and which is notorious for the several liberties taken with the original. Therefore, Borges's immediate reaction back in 1925 was to approach language in an essentially Joycean way, that is, as a protean, flexible, and unfinished material. Appropriately, in his 1926 essay 'The Infinite Language' — which was published one year after his translation of 'Penelope' — he proposed a type of linguistic usage that promotes inventiveness and expansion, as part of a linguistic manifesto in which he encouraged writers to experiment with the Spanish language. Such call for action is exemplified with the coinage 'amillonar' [millioning] that, much like a Joycean virtuoso performance, turns the numeral *millón* [million] into a verb: 'Lo grandioso es amillonar el idioma' (*TE* 39) [the grandiosity of millioning language]. This also meant that in his 1925 review of *Ulysses* Borges employed the noun *millonario* [millionaire] to refer to the stylistic *tour de force* of Joyce's revolutionary book: '[Joyce] es millonario de vocablos y estilos' (*Inq.* 27) ['He is a millionaire of words and styles'] (*SNF* 14). Consequently, Borges concluded 'The Infinite Language' with an exhortation to fellow Argentine writers to regard the Spanish language not as a fixed idiom but as an unfinished sketch (*TE* 43). Borges's 'politics of language', writes Beatriz Sarlo, 'is based on the conviction that this language is a historic and modifiable instrument which can therefore both resist the system and offer a canvas on which to place the imprints of a sensibility and of a nation'.[54] Yet it must be mentioned that the mature Borges later repudiated the passionate nationalistic outbursts and linguistic experiments of his young self. Following this trend, in 1946 Borges acknowledged the various difficulties entailed in any rendering of Joyce's 'verbal mastery' into the Romance languages:

> El inglés (como el alemán) es un idioma casi monosilábico, apto para la formación de voces compuestas. Joyce fue notoriamente feliz en tales conjunciones. El español (como el italiano, como el francés) consta de inmanejables polisílabos que es difícil unir (*TR2* 234).
>
> [English (like German) is an almost monosyllabic language, suitable for the formation of compound words. Joyce was notoriously successful with those conjunctions. Spanish (like Italian, like French) contains unmanageable polysyllables that are very difficult to bring together.]

The polyglot Borges exemplified this claim with an excerpt from the French translation of *Ulysses*, by Morel, Larbaud et al. He compared and contrasted Joyce's inventive compound phrases with the not-so-convincing French rendering that unsuccessfully turned their prior compactness into a string of single word units: 'Joyce, que había escrito en el *Ulises*: *bridebed, childbed, bed of death, ghastcondled* (sic), tuvo que resignarse a esta nulidad en la versión francesa: *lit nuptial, lit de parturition, lit de mort aux spectrales bougies*' (*TR2* 234) [Joyce who had written in *Ulysses*: *bridebed, childbed, bed of death, ghastcondled* (sic), had to resign himself to this nullity in the French version: *lit nuptial, lit de parturition, lit de mort aux spectrales bougies*]. Significantly, in the 'The Infinite Language' Borges had already advocated a more flexible use of prepositions in the Spanish language, proposing a more liberal usage of prefixes, infixes, and suffixes based on the model of the Germanic languages: 'Esta licencia de añadirle prefijos a cualquier nombre sustantivo, verbo o epíteto, ya existe en alemán, idioma siempre enriquecible y sin límites que atesora muchas preposiciones de difícil igualación castellana' (*TE* 41) [The practice of adding prefixes to any noun, verb, or epithet already exists in German, an ever expanding and limitless language that contains prepositions of difficult equivalence in Spanish]. Whereas this observation evinces Borges's scepticism regarding the verbal elasticity of the Spanish language, on the other hand, he is calling for a linguistic reform that aims to transcend traditional views that resisted regional variations or innovative permutations. Borges's youthful faith in the possibility of moving towards a more manageable Spanish language re-appeared in his praise of Salas Subirat's occasional virtuoso performances in his translation of *Ulysses*:

> Muy superiores son aquellos pasajes en que el texto español es no menos neológico que el original. Verbigracia, éste, de la página 743: *que no era un árbolcielo, no un antrocielo, no un bestiacielo, no un hombrecielo,* que recta e inventivamente traduce: *that it was not a heaventree, not a heavengrot, not a heavenbeast, not a heavenman* (*TR2* 234).
>
> [Far more superior are those passages in which the Spanish text is no less neological than the original. For example, this one, from page 743: *que no era un árbolcielo, no un antrocielo, no un bestiacielo, no un hombrecielo,* that directly and inventively translates: *that it was not a heaventree, not a heavengrot, not a heavenbeast, not a heavenman.*]

This compelling example from Salas's translation demonstrates that rather than obeying strict linguistic limitations in the morphological structure of the Romance languages, the creativity and resourcefulness of the translator plays a significant role in the translation. And yet the linguistic difficulty in providing a match for all of Joyce's verbal experiments obliged Borges to conclude his review with the statement: '*A priori*, una versión cabal del *Ulises* me parece imposible' (*TR2* 234) [*A priori*, an exact version of *Ulysses* seems to me impossible]. Similarly, in 1982 Borges declared to Kearney and Heaney: 'Joyce's obsession with language makes him very difficult if not impossible to translate. Especially into Spanish — as I first discovered when I first translated a passage from Molly's soliloquy in 1925.'[55] But for Borges, it must be stressed, *Ulysses* is untranslatable only if the translator aims to produce a literal version of the text. Contrariwise, the ideal non-English version of *Ulysses* should strive to re-create Joyce's linguistic polyvalence, rather than to merely provide a strict semantic equivalence. Thus, according to Borges, prospective translators of *Ulysses* must engage in an analogous linguistic playfulness and hence, share as much authorship as Joyce himself. In *Borges and Translation* Efraín Kristal summarizes Borges's complex stance regarding the translatability of Joyce's *Ulysses*:

> At times Borges referred to *Ulysses* as an impossible challenge to a translator, by which he meant it would be impossible to render all of Joyce's verbal experiments into any other language. On other occasions he denied that the novel was untranslatable, recommending that it be used as a pretext for the creation of another work. For Borges some works of literature are more translatable than others, but no work of literature is untranslatable in principle, because a translator can always take the necessary liberties to achieve what any creative writer should strive for: a convincing work of literature.[56]

The various difficulties inherent in the translation of Joyce's last two texts are noteworthy, and even Joyce himself momentarily expressed certain doubts on the vast enterprise of rendering *Ulysses* into other languages: 'At first he had thought, as he told Daniel Hummel, that the book could not be translated into another language' (*JJII* 561). The difficulty of translating Joyce's *Ulysses* and *Finnegans Wake*, argues John Paul Riquelme, is because 'Joyce's texts already contain so many dislocations, which are themselves translations. These elements have already undergone a process of substitution and transformation that we may recognize and reenact when we encounter them'.[57] Borges's belief in re-creating a text, or using it as a 'pre-text' for the creation of another, was a radical practice shared by Joyce. It is well known that Joyce played an active role in the French and Italian translations of his own work, particularly in the Italian re-creation of 'Anna Livia Plurabelle' in which the English version is recontextualized into a primarily Italian setting. In this respect, Rosa Maria Bollettieri Bosinelli notes that: 'The ideal reader of this text is undoubtedly an Italian reader, who is offered the chance of hearing Anna Livia's "silly and extravagant chatter" in the framework of a familiar, Italianized context'.[58] Likewise, Borges applied this translation method to his own works, and actively engaged in collaborative enterprises that bestowed unprecedented freedom upon his translators.[59] In this light, Borges conceived translation as a collective project, just as he declared in 1937 that 'más que la obra de un solo hombre, el *Ulises* parece la labor de muchas generaciones' (*OC4* 251) [rather than the work of a single man, *Ulysses* seems the work of many generations]. Borges and Joyce adhered, ultimately, to a re-creative translation practice that negated both traditional beliefs in faithful renditions or the more literal word-for-word equivalence.[60]

### 'I haven't forgotten it all' (*U* 18.1472): Un-Translating Molly into Spanish

It has now become clear that Borges aimed to present an autonomous version of 'Penelope' specifically written for the readership of the review *Proa*. Faced with this challenging task, the young Borges may have asked himself: how can I translate a passage of a book renowned for its difficulty and controversy in a manner both comprehensible and introductory to an Argentine audience unfamiliar with *Ulysses*, without hindering the linguistic, stylistic, and cultural complexity of the original? Borges's immediate answer to this question was to come up with his own *in medias res* of 'Penelope': 'shall I wear a white rose' (*U* 18.1553–54) ['usaré una rosa blanca'] (*TR1* 201). What better way than to begin Molly's monologue with her recurrent intonation of the popular song by H. S. Clarke and E. B. Farmer?[61] Borges also decided to celebrate in his translation the stylistic trademark of 'Penelope', lack of punctuation, which gives the illusion of uninterruptedness of Molly's thoughts. Another remarkable feature of Borges's fragmentary rendering of Molly Bloom's unpunctuated soliloquy is its distinctive colloquial tone rich in Argentine diction, which not only provided the appropriate idioms to convey the eroticism of the episode, but also added a distinctive linguistic significance to Molly's notorious polyvalence. Inevitably, a vital consideration that Borges confronted in translating *Ulysses* into Spanish is whether Joyce's text should be rendered in the peninsular or Argentine inflection of the language. Borges, who was aware of an analogous colonial situation between Spain/Argentina and England/Ireland, followed Joyce's example in privileging his own vernacular dialect and proudly bestowed a distinctive Argentine idiosyncrasy upon Molly Bloom. In his review of *Ulysses* that preceded the translation he appropriately remarked: 'James Joyce es irlandés. Siempre los irlandeses fueron agitadores famosos de la literatura de Inglaterra' (*Inq.* 24) ['James Joyce is Irish. The Irish have always been famous for being the iconoclasts of the British Isles'] (*SNF* 12). In effect, Borges's decision to present readers of *Proa* with an Argentine-speaking version of Molly Bloom corresponded to the literary credo he professed in the mid-twenties, in which he advocated a colloquial use of River Plate Spanish. This search for an Argentine 'essence' is conveyed in his 1928 essay 'The Language of the Argentines' whereby he proclaimed that, 'el no escrito idioma argentino sigue *diciéndonos*' (*IA* 145) [the unwritten Argentine language still *speaks us*]. As a corroboration of his linguistic conviction to give literacy to a primarily oral vernacular, Borges innovatively rendered Molly Bloom with the Argentine second person pronoun 'vos'. In other words, Borges challenged conventional practices that still employed the standard Spanish 'tú' as the customary norm for written texts, and instead utilized the River Plate spoken vernacular form: 'para vos brilla el sol' (*TR1* 201) [the sun shines for you'] (Joyce *U* 18.1571–72).[62] 'We must recall that in the 20s', writes Beatriz Vegh, 'Borges wanted to capture in his writing the essence of a certain Argentine tone of voice, a form of national identity that had been ignored by those who wanted the country to be just progressive and modern.'[63]

Amongst the other lexical choices and inflections from River Plate Spanish that Borges deliberately included in his colloquial, yet ideologically charged translation of 'Penelope', is the reiterated use of the adjective 'lindo/a', hence rendering Molly's 'a nice plant' (*U* 18.1556) to 'una linda planta' (*TR1* 201) and 'beautiful country' (*U* 18.1559) to the superlative form of 'campo lindísimo' (*TR1* 201).[64] This lexical choice becomes more apparent if examined in conjunction with 'The Language of the Argentines' in which Borges raises the issue of the differences between peninsular Spanish and the Argentine variation of the imperial language: 'No hemos variado [los argentinos] el sentido intrínseco de las palabras, pero sí su connotación [...] La palabra *súbdito* [...] es decente en España y denigrativa en América [...] Nuestro *lindo* es palabra que se juega entera para elogiar; el de los españoles no es aprobativo con tantas ganas' (*IA* 147) [[Argentines] have not changed the intrinsic meaning of a word, but rather its connotation [...] The word *subject* [...] is respectful in Spain but pejorative in Latin America. Our *lindo* is a word that bursts with compliments; the one of the Spaniards does not praise with the same emphasis]. What Borges aspired to do with his usage of a specific type of Argentine Spanish was, ultimately, to demonstrate that it is possible to turn an allegedly colloquial dialect into a valid literary form. Moreover, the informality of the vernacular also appealed to Borges as an adequate solution to convey the linguistic illusion of uninterruptedness of Molly's unpunctuated interior monologue. Several critics and translators have praised this element, for instance, Conde Parrilla states that: 'Borges's one page of "Penelope" has the noteworthy feature of its genuinely colloquial style';[65] Schwartz similarly says: '[Borges] twists and turns the language to suit Molly's interior monologue';[66] while Waisman claims: 'Borges finds ways to translate the orality of Molly's monologue'.[67] Finally, Levine has remarked that: 'Many Hispanic readers have agreed that the Latin American translators of North American and English literature (among them writers such as Borges and the Cuban Lino Novas Calvo), because of the very nature of their Argentine or Cuban brand of Spanish, produced more vivid and colloquial translations than their Spanish cousins'.[68]

But in order to turn his fragmentary excerpt into an independent piece, Borges also legitimized a translation practice that promoted the deliberate omission of certain details from the text. In relation to Borges's aesthetic of omission Kristal offers a useful synopsis:

> (1) Borges's most common practice as a translator was to remove what he once called the 'padding' of a work: words and passages that seem redundant, superfluous, or inconsequential. (2) He removed textual distractions. This stratagem involves cutting part of the content of a literary work that might distract attention from another aspect Borges would prefer to highlight. (3) Borges often added a major or minor nuance not in the original: changing a title, for instance. (4) Borges sometimes rewrote a work in the light of another, as when he inscribes a post-Nietzschean sensibility to his translation of Angelus Silesius.[69]

As has been noted by Willson,[70] Joyce's Irish setting on 'Howth head', among the rhododendrons, is strategically deleted and the two lovers are placed instead in a more universal pastoral setting 'tirados en el pasto' [lying on the grass] (*TR1* 201). If Borges deleted the crucial setting of Howth he retained, on the other hand, Molly's allusion to the popular Lipton's store in central Dublin, '[the] tea, wine, spirit, and provisions merchants [located] in 59–61 Dame Street'[71] and noticeably conveyed Molly's indulgence for sumptuous patisserie as: 'esas masas divinas de lo de Lipton' (*TR1* 201), 'those fairy cakes in Liptons' (*U* 18.1554). Borges also excluded several nominal references, principally the names of Molly's lovers that his *Proa* readers would have ignored or found confusing, and replaced them with the anonymous versions of 'fulano y zutano' [Mr so and so] (*TR1* 201). This translation preference highlighted, most of all, the interchangeability of all her male suitors, which goes hand-in-hand with Molly's subsequent reflection at the decisive moment she accepts Blooms amorous proposal: 'and I thought well as well him as another' (*U*

18. 1604–05). Other significant appellative changes are his rendering of 'Hester' into the Hispanic version of 'Ester' and 'old captain Groves' into the more generic version of 'capitán'. To crown the protean onomastics of his translation, Borges follows Molly's final orgasmic 'Yes' with the Hispanic version of Joyce's first name, whose authorial signature is distinctively turned into Jaime Joyce. Borges, however, erased Joyce's final signature: 'Trieste-Zurich-Paris 1914–1921'.

## Infinitely Translatable: Molly Bloom

Apart from restoring to Molly her alleged Spanish fluency — albeit in the River Plate variant: 'I wonder could I get my tongue round any of the Spanish como esta usted muy bien gracias y usted see I haven't forgotten it all' (*U* 18.1471–72) — Borges also offers an audacious recreation of her controversial 'obscene' passages. According to Suzanne Jill Levine '[Borges gets] closer to the breathless ecstatic language of the original than any of the subsequent versions'.[72] The prior versions to which Levine is referring here are, of course, the complete translations by Salas Subirat and Valverde, both of which diminished the erotic significance of the episode.[73] Levine's emphasis on the inadequacy of these two versions, cannot but emphasize the fact that Borges's pioneering 1925 translation, produced at a time when the Joyce critical industry was almost non-existent and the obscenity of *Ulysses* remained a subject of controversial debate, did not fail to recreate the erotic impulses of Joyce's text. Borges's translation not only preserved Molly's sexual references, but also enhanced Joyce's version by introducing a further sexual duplicity. He rendered Molly's idiom: 'I wouldn't give a snap of my two fingers' (*U* 18.1564) with the brief vernacular expression 'me importa un pito' (*TR1* 201) which not only functions as a valid equivalent to the English, but also carries sexual undertones due to the polysemy of the word 'pito' in Spanish, which means 'whistle' but is also a vulgar word for penis. Another noteworthy aspect of Borges's translation of 'Penelope' is his rendering of Leopold Bloom's romantic appellation to Molly as 'mountain flower' (a phrase that is repeatedly evoked in Molly's erotic ruminations) into the idiosyncratic expression 'flor serrana', that contrasts with the four-worded, 'flor de la montaña' employed by Salas Subirat, Valverde, and more recently, by García Tortosa.[74] Not only has Borges convincingly rendered the iterative phrase into a suitable two-worded epithet, but in doing so, he is then able to provide a fitting translation to Joyce's deliberate variation of the expression as 'Flower of the mountain', which signals a typographical (capital letter) and grammatical (added preposition and article) alteration. Joyce introduced this variant of the phrase in order to specifically refer to Molly's upbringing in Gibraltar, a place of both nature and nurture that contributed to her Spanish distinctiveness:

> and the glorious sunsets and the figtrees in the Alameda gardens yes and all the queer little streets and the pink and blue and yellow houses and the rosegardens and the jessamine and geraniums and cactuses and Gibraltar as a girl where I was a Flower of the mountain yes when I put the rose in my hair like the Andalusian girls (*U* 18.1599–1603).

For comparative purposes Borges's translation of this excerpt goes thus:

> y los ocasos brillantes y las higueras en la Alameda sí y las callecitas rarísimas y
> las casas rosadas y amarillas y azules, y los rosales y jazmines y geranios y tunas
> y Gibraltar de jovencita cuando yo era una Flor de la Montaña sí cuando me
> até la rosa en el pelo como las chicas andaluzas (*TR1* 202).

Andrew Gibson has persuasively argued that Joyce may have borrowed Molly Bloom's distinctive designation Flower of the mountain from 'the literature of Gibraltar [which] refers to a botanical specimen, the *flora calpensis* ("flower of Calpe", the ancient name for Gibraltar). Joyce would have known of it. "Flora Calpensis" was also the pen name of the authoress of *Reminiscences of Gibraltar* (1880) and *The Life of a Rock Scorpion* (1881)'.[75] If Joyce conflated a whole set of historical, literary, and botanical references in the seemingly romantic appellation 'mountain flower' or 'flower of the mountain', Borges succeeded not only in providing a suitable rendition for the two- and four-worded variations of Joyce's epithet, but also went to greater lengths by adding a further significance to the Spanish translation. In his usage of the word *serrana*, Borges brings into the text the fifteenth-century Spanish popular lyric known in Spanish literature as *serrana* or *serranilla*. These pastoral compositions after the Provençal manner typically narrate the amorous encounter between a gentleman [caballero] and a mountain girl [serrana] in the rural setting of the *sierras*, hence its literary denomination.[76] Whilst the development of the *serranilla* produced significant variations in the tone and denouement of the composition, the type of *serranillas* that Borges would have had in mind while translating Molly, are the delicate lyric poems written by the Medieval poet, Íñigo López de Mendoza, famously known as the Marquis of Santillana. In Santillana's *serranillas* the *caballero* tries to obtain the sexual favours of the *serrana* by means of a flattering sensual discourse. In some versions the rural maiden readily submits, while in others she preserves her dignity and condemns the illicit proposals of the 'gentleman'. Borges would have recognized the sexually charged discourse, and closing orgasmic 'Yes' of Molly Bloom, as conforming to the category of erotic *serranilla* in which the *serrana* submits to the proposal of the *caballero*. Indeed, Waisman has convincingly suggested that Borges would have also been aware that: '"yes I will Yes" sounds even more sexually explicit in Borges's Spanish: "sí quiero Sí"' [yes, I want, yes].[77] For instance, Santillana's 'Serranilla IX', concludes with the sexual fulfilment between the gentleman and the rural lady, who seek refuge for their erotic pleasures in the hospitable mountain flowers of Espinama: 'E fueron las flores / de cabe Espinama / los encobridores' [The flowers of Espinama / were our secrecy].[78]

The allusion to the traditional Spanish lyric that Borges laces into the complex cultural fabric of 'Penelope' is not the only Iberian element he reinforces in his Argentine-speaking version of Molly. His choice to preserve most — but by no means all — of Joyce's textual references to places in both Gibraltar and the nearby Andalusia is emphasized through his curious decision to omit other Hibernian topographical and nominal details. It is as if Borges was aware of what Bonnie Kime Scott has referred to as 'the complicated Jewish-Spanish-Gibraltar backgrounds that affect Molly's validity as a mimetic character',[79] and decided to accentuate the composite aspect of Molly's identity. But this crucial decision brought together a fundamental problem: how can an Argentine-speaking Molly Bloom position herself in relation to Joyce's Jewish, Hibernian, and Gibraltarian Molly? Confronted with this further dilemma, Borges opted for exploiting the imperialist ambivalence already implicit in the text, and added a further conflictual element, Argentina, in the already loaded context of Gibraltar. Joyce presented a nostalgic Molly who remembers her Gibraltarian *alter ego* and wonders whether she may still be able to regain her supposed Spanish fluency, this is, to un-translate her Irish self into her former Spanish self. Borges, thus, perceived these various levels at play in Joyce's text and stripped Molly of her Irish guise to disclose her former Spanish layer, only to translate her again into Argentine, achieving a rich version of Molly that, like a palimpsest, is able to reveal its various superimposed scripts at once. This complex act of translation offers a River Plate-speaking Molly Bloom who is able to present, simultaneously, subtle hints of an Irish identity within the colourful, exotic backdrops of Buenos Aires, Gibraltar, and Andalusia. The astute Borges preserved most of the *topoi* related to Gibraltarian and Moorish geography and culture, as well as nearby places in Andalusia. He retained, thus, historical references to 'the old castle thousands of years old' (*U* 18.1592) and translated it into the more compact, fairy tale quality of 'el castillo de miles de años' (*TR1* 202) alluding to the longevity of the Moorish building that as Gifford informs: 'was built by Abu-Abul-Hajez in AD 725'.[80] He also kept topographical information about the mountainous town of 'Ronda' in Andalusian Spain, the port town of Algeciras located in the province of Cadiz, as well as the 'Alameda gardens' and the 'Moorish wall' in Gibraltar. He omitted, however, the reference to Duke Street in Gibraltar as well as the specific allusion to a certain 'Larby Sharons'. Interestingly, Gifford informs us that 'we find no evidence of a Duke Street in Gibraltar' and that Larby Sharons 'does not appear in *Thom's* 1904 or in any of the *Gibraltar Directory and Guidebook(s)*.[81] Borges also takes further liberties with the original by rendering Joyce's idiom 'the devil knows who else' into the standard 'hombres'.

At the other extreme, Borges reiterated the use of the term 'castanets' (castañuelas), a musical instrument that plays a vital role in Andalusian folklore, by employing it as an anaphoric device in the build up of Molly's sexual climax. So, whereas Joyce employs the term only once — 'and the castanets and the night we missed the boat at Algeciras' (*U* 18.1596–97) — Borges utilizes it twice: 'y las castañuelas y aquella noche en Algeciras cuando perdimos el vapor las castañuelas' (*TR1* 202). These translation strategies serve to reinforce the crucial fact that Borges sought to create a polyvalent image of Molly, a hybrid version that fused Irish, Jewish, Spanish, and Argentine identities. Borges was aware of the hybrid aspect of 'Penelope' which, especially in its final pages, offered a version of Gibraltar as the rich confluence of several languages and cultures:

> and the Spanish girls laughing in their shawls and their tall combs and the auctions in the morning the Greeks and the jews and the Arabs and the devil knows who else from all the ends of Europe and Duke street and the fowl market all clucking outside Larby Sharons and the poor donkeys slipping half asleep and the vague fellows in the cloaks asleep in the shade on the steps and the big wheels of the carts of the bulls and the old castle thousands of years old yes and those handsome Moors all in white and turbans like kings asking you to sit down in their little bit of a shop [...] (*U* 18.1586–94)

y las chicas españolas riéndose con sus mantones y peinas y los remates de mañana los griegos y los judíos y los árabes y hombres de todos los rincones de Europa y el Mercado cloqueando y los pobres burritos cayéndose de sueño y los tipos cualquiera dormidos en la sombra de los portales y las ruedas grandotas de las carretas de bueyes y el castillo de miles de años sí y esos moros buenos mozos todos de blanco y con turbantes como reyes haciéndola sentar a uno en su tendencia [...] (*TR1* 202).

Significantly, Andrew Gibson stresses this socio-historical aspect of Gibraltar: 'Above all, however, Joyce emphasizes Gibraltar's racial mix. Historically, it was striking how far, for all the restrictive, colonial legislation, Gibraltar was a melting-pot [...]. Joyce and Molly celebrate the Gibraltarian conflux of peoples'.[82] Just as Joyce immersed Molly in the intricately woven tapestry of Gibraltar that embraced both social mix and a long imperialist history, so Borges extended Joyce's project by incorporating into the text the looming spectre of his native and peripheral Argentina. This allowed him to foster a version of Molly Bloom, or 'Molly Blooms' — as Richard Pearce has recently suggested[83] — whereby several narratives are able to coexist, in a dual consciousness that endows Molly with a renewed, ever-recurring afterlife.

## Notes to Chapter 1

1. Phillip Herring notes: 'The highlight of the symposium may well have been the moving tribute to Joyce by blind Argentine writer Jorge Luis Borges at the Bloomsday Banquet'. See Herring, 'Preface', in *The Centennial Symposium*, ed. by Morris Beja, Phillip Herring, Maurice Harmon, and David Norris (Urbana and Chicago: University of Illinois Press, 1986), p. xii. Unfortunately, no record of this speech has survived.
2. Kearney, *Transitions*, p. 48.
3. Ricardo Güiraldes, *Shadows on the Pampas*, trans. by Harriet de Onís with an intro. by Waldo Frank (London: Constable & Co., 1935).
4. See Lawrence Rainey, *Institutions of Modernism: Literary Elites and Public Culture* (New Haven, CT, and London: Yale University Press, 1998), for an insightful and detailed account of the publishing history of Joyce's *Ulysses*.
5. See Valéry Larbaud, *Lettres à Adrienne Monnier et à Sylvia Beach (1919–1933)*, correspondance établie et annotée par Maurice Saillet (Paris: IMEC, 1991), pp. 85–86. Saillet claims that on 19 June 1922 Güiraldes, his wife and Ocampo collected their three copies of *Ulysses*. Beach's records, however, state that only one copy was purchased. See Glenn Horowitz, *James Joyce: Books and Manuscripts* (New York: Glenn Horowitz Bookseller, 1996), pp. 111–16.
6. See Walter Benjamin, 'The Task of the Translator', in *The Translation Studies Reader*, ed. by Lawrence Venuti, trans. by Harry Zohn (London and New York, Routledge, 2001), pp. 15–23.
7. Karen Lawrence, 'Introduction: Metempsychotic Joyce', in *Transcultural Joyce*, ed. by Karen Lawrence (Cambridge: Cambridge University Press, 1998), pp. 1–8 (p. 1).
8. Larbaud had also a limited knowledge of Portuguese. See John L. Brown, *Valery Larbaud* (Boston; MA: Twayne Publishers, 1981), pp. 163–64.
9. John L. Brown, p. 153.
10. John L. Brown, p. 160, p. 162.
11. See *The Reception of James Joyce in Europe*, ed. by Geert Lernout and Wim Van Mierlo, 2 vols (London: Thoemmes Continuum, 2004).
12. See Fritz Senn, 'The European Diffusion of Joyce', review of *The Reception of James Joyce in Europe*, ed. by Geert Lernout and Wim Van Mierlo (see above) in *James Joyce Broadsheet*, 76 (2007), 1.
13. Larbaud announced Güiraldes's promising literary talents in the July 1920 edition of the N.R.F and also introduced him to the most celebrated writers in Paris. Therefore, Güiraldes's literary reputation changed dramatically after his meeting with Larbaud.

14. See *Barnabooth* and *Fermina Márquez* in Valery Larbaud, *Œuvres*, avec preface de Marcel Arland et notes par G. Jean-Aubry et Robert Mallet (Paris: Gallimard, 1984).
15. Sylvia Beach, *Shakespeare & Company* (London: Faber & Faber, 1959), p. 64.
16. For an example of Borges's *ultraist* poetics see 'Himno del mar' [Hymn to the Sea] which was published in the December 1919 issue of *Grecia* (*TR1* 24–26). Later in his life Borges ironically observed: 'I am still known to literary historians as "the father of Argentine ultraism"'. See *A*, p. 34.
17. This letter belongs to a private collection. It was consulted in Buenos Aires, February 2005.
18. See Blasi, 'Una amistad creadora: las cartas de Valery Larbaud a Ricardo Güiraldes', in *Ricardo Güiraldes: Don Segundo Sombra, edición crítica*, Paul Verdevoye (coordinador) (Madrid: Archivos, 1988), pp. 436, 437, 439, 444, 446.
19. James Joyce, *Ulysse*, traduit de l'anglais par M. Auguste Morel assisté par M. Stuart Gilbert. Traduction entièrement revue par M. Valery Larbaud avec la collaboration de l'auteur. Hollande Van Gelder N 1 (Paris: La Maison des Amis des Livres, 1929).
20. On an Arts and Humanities Research Council-funded trip to Argentina, I visited the 'Museo Güiraldes' in San Antonio de Areco, province of Buenos Aires. The director of the museum, Cecilia Smyth (curiously a descendant of Irish immigrants) showed me this unique copy of the 1929 *Ulysse*.
21. This information was also obtained from Museo Güiraldes.
22. Carlos García (ed.), *Macedonio Fernández/ Jorge Luis Borges: correspondencia 1922–1939*, edición y notas de Carlos García (Buenos Aires: Corregidor, 2000), pp. 93–94. All Spanish translations are mine unless otherwise stated.
23. My description of Xul Solar's painting is based on the painting entitled: 'Los lenguaje del arte moderno' (1925), which belongs to the collection of the Museo Nacional de Bellas Artes, Buenos Aires, Argentina.
24. Robin William Fiddian, 'James Joyce and Spanish-American Fiction: A Study of the Origins and Transmission of Literary Influence', *Bulletin of Hispanic Studies*, 66,1 (1989), 23–39.
25. Valery Larbaud, 'Lettres Argentines et Uruguayennes', *La Revue Européenne*, 34 (1925), 66–70 (p. 70). All translations from Larbaud are mine, unless otherwise stated.
26. Borges's review of *Ulysses* was subsequently included in his first non-fiction collection, *Inquisiciones* [*Inquisitions*] issued in 1925 by Güiraldes's publishing house *Proa*. In the December issue of *La Revue Européenne* Larbaud enthusiastically greeted the volume as, 'le meilleur livre de critique que nous ayons reçu, jusqu'à ce jour, de l'Amérique latine' [the best critical book we have received from Latin America to date]. Larbaud defined the Argentine capital of Buenos Aires as 'plus cosmopolite qu'aucune de nos capitales européennes' [more cosmopolitan than any of our European capitals], and insisted that Borges's creative expression was both 'européenne et américaine' [European and American] and 'très large, très libre, très hardie' [wider, freer, and more audacious] than any perspective that could emerge from Europe. Valery Larbaud, 'Lettres Argentines et Uruguayennes', p. 70.
27. Jorge Luis Borges, 'Invocation to Joyce', trans. by Norman Thomas di Giovanni, in *Poems for James Joyce*, ed. by Bernard Benstock (Kildare: The Malton Press, 1982), pp. 41–42.
28. Derek Walcott, *Omeros* (London: Faber & Faber, 1990), p. 200.
29. Seamus Heaney, *Opened Ground: Poems 1966–1996* (London: Faber & Faber, 1998), pp. 266–67.
30. Heaney, p. 267.
31. See Novillo-Corvalán, 'Literary Migrations: Homer's Journey through Joyce's Ireland and Walcott's Saint Lucia', *Irish Migration Studies in Latin America*, 5.3 (2007), 157–62. Also available online at: http://www.irlandeses.org/0711novillo1.htm.
32. The upper case is Borges's.
33. See Antonio Marichalar, 'James Joyce en su laberinto', *Revista de Occidente*, 17 (1924), 177–202.
34. Jason Wilson, *Jorge Luis Borges* (London: Reaktion Books, 2006), pp. 73–74.
35. Colin MacCabe, *James Joyce and the Revolution of the Word*, 2nd edn (Basingstoke: Macmillan, 2003), pp. 104.
36. Vegh, p. 88.
37. Arthur Power, *Conversations with James Joyce*, foreword by David Norris (London: Lilliput Press, 1999) p. 110.

38. Frank Budgen, *James Joyce and the Making of Ulysses* (London: Grayson & Grayson, 1934), p. 123.
39. Interestingly, Borges's equation of Joyce with Góngora marks the beginning of a negative affiliation between the baroque seventeenth-century Spanish writer — renowned for his obscure linguistic games — and Joyce's Modernist experiments. He reiterated this analogy several times in his literary career. For example, in the prologue of *The Self and the Other* he observed: 'The writer's individual experiments, in fact, have minimal effect except when the innovator resigns himself to the construction of a verbal museum, a game, like *Finnegans Wake* or Góngora's *Soledades*, made up for discussions by literary historians or simple notoriety' (*SP* 147). For a similar comment see the prologue of Borges's translation of Walt Whitman's *Leaves of Grass, Hojas de Hierba* (Barcelona: Lumen, 1991), p. 8, and his 1937 essay 'Kipling and his Autobiography', *OC4* 272. In a 1981 interview with O. Nayarález Borges reinvents Góngora as a 'little Joyce' (*TR3* 366), thus applying his radical theory of literary influence in which Joyce becomes the precursor of Góngora.
40. See Salgado, 'Barroco Joyce', p. 66.
41. Further to this, Anthony Cordingley claims that Borges was the unofficial 'interpreter of Anglophone literary culture to the Argentine and Latin American literary community'. See Cordingley, 'Keeping their Distance: Beckett and Borges Writing after Joyce', in *After Beckett D'après Beckett*, ed. by Anthony Uhlmann, Sjef Houppermans, and Bruno Clément (Amsterdam: Rodopi, 2004), pp. 131–45 (p. 131).
42. The fact that the first complete translation of *Ulysses* into Spanish was undertaken by another Argentine is still a remarkable event. Salas's translation of *Ulysses* was published in Buenos Aires in 1945 and included a prologue by Jacques Mercanton. It remained the only Spanish version for more than thirty years until the appearance of the second Spanish translation by J. M. Valverde in 1976. See *Ulises*, trad. de José María Valverde (Barcelona: Lumen, 1980). A third complete Spanish version of *Ulysses*, translated by Francisco García Tortosa and María Luisa Venegas has been published in Madrid in 1999. See James Joyce, *Ulises*, trad. de Francisco García Tortosa y María Luisa Venegas (Madrid: Cátedra, 1999).
43. Some dubious sources credit Borges with the unlikely role of supervisor of Salas's translation. In an article in the Spanish magazine *Cambio*, Mercedes Monmany argues that Salas's complete version had been 'ordered and revised by Borges'. See Mercedes Monmany, 'El *Ulises* Ilustrado Recuerda la Muerte de James Joyce', *Cambio16*, 1008 (18 March 1991), 90–94 (p. 94). Borges had neither supervised nor corrected Salas's translation, and his only association with this Spanish version is established within the roles of critic and reviewer.
44. Richard Brown, 'Introduction', in *Joyce, 'Penelope' and the Body*, ed. by Richard Brown (Amsterdam: Rodopi, 2006), pp. 11–30 (p. 22).
45. Kathleen McCormick, 'Reproducing Molly Bloom: A Revisionist History of the Reception of "Penelope," 1922–1970', in *Molly Blooms: A Polylogue on 'Penelope' and Cultural Studies*, ed. by Richard Pearce (Madison: University of Wisconsin Press, 1994), pp. 17–40 (p. 17).
46. For example, in opposition to Borges's decision to translate controversial extracts from Molly's soliloquy, Marichalar opted for less contentious passages from 'Ithaca' and 'Penelope' that lacked erotic or sexual references. See Antonio Marichalar, 'James Joyce en su Laberinto'. For further details regarding the larger issue of the reception of Joyce in Spain, see Carlos G. Santa Cecilia, *La recepción de James Joyce en la prensa española (1921–1976)* (Sevilla: Universidad de Sevilla, 1997), pp. 58–60.
47. Edwin Williamson, *Borges: A Life* (New York: Viking, 2004), p. 124.
48. See Alejandro Vaccaro, *Georgie: una vida de Jorge Luis Borges (1899–1930)* (Buenos Aires: Editorial Proa, 1996), p. 189; María Esther Vázquez, *Borges: esplendor y derrota* (Barcelona: Tusquets editores), pp. 79–82; and Rodríguez Monegal, p. 215.
49. Suzanne Jill Levine, 'Notes to Borges's Notes on Joyce: Infinite Affinities' *Comparative Literature*, 49.4 (1997), 344–58 (p. 356).
50. Güiraldes's name was also included in the editorial board of foreign contributors. See Blasi, 'Una amistad creadora', pp. 444–45.
51. Larbaud, '*Ulysse*: Fragments', *Commerce*, 1 (1924), 121–58.
52. Jorge Schwartz, 'Borges y la Primera Hoja de *Ulysses*', p. 721.
53. Sergio Gabriel Waisman, 'Borges Reads Joyce', p. 71.

54. Sarlo, *Jorge Luis Borges: A Writer on the Edge*, p. 136.
55. Kearney, p. 49.
56. Efraín Kristal, *Invisible Work: Borges and Translation* (Nashville, TN: Vanderbilt University Press, 2002), p. 5. However, as we are going to see in Chapter 2, Borges remained much more sceptical about the translation of *Finnegans Wake*.
57. See John Paul Riquelme, 'The Use of Translation and the Use of Criticism', in Fritz Senn, *Joyce's Dislocutions: Essays on Reading as Translation*, ed. by John Paul Riquelme (Baltimore, MD, and London: Johns Hopkins University Press, 1984), p. xxi.
58. Rosa Maria Bollettieri Bosinelli, 'Anna Livia's Italian Sister', in Lawrence, ed., *Transcultural Joyce*, pp. 193–98 (p. 195).
59. See Norman Thomas Di Giovanni, *The Lesson of the Master: On Borges and his Work* (New York and London: Continuum, 2003), p. 69.
60. Borges discusses these two opposite translation approaches in 'Las Dos Maneras de traducir' (See *TR2* 256–59).
61. Don Gifford with Robert J. Seidman, *Ulysses Annotated: Notes for James Joyce's Ulysses* (Berkeley and Los Angeles: University of California Press, 1988), p. 621. It is extremely unlikely that Borges would have known this was a reference to a song.
62. Contrarily to Borges, fellow Argentine Salas Subirat conventionally renders Molly in the customary standard form of 'tú'. See James Joyce, *Ulises*, trad. de J. J. Salas Subirat (Buenos Aires: Santiago Rueda, 2002), pp. 727–28.
63. Vegh, pp. 91–92.
64. For other pertinent examples see Patricia Willson, *La Constelación del Sur: traductores y traducciones en la literatura argentina del siglo XX* (Buenos Aires: Siglo veintiuno, 2004), pp. 117–32. Willson persuasively argues that Borges immersed 'Penelope' in a primarily River Plate background, but neglects to take into account the Gibraltarian and Andalusian elements which are of fundamental importance in Borges's translation. I will argue here that Borges fostered a multifaceted version of Molly Bloom that conflated her Hibernian, Gibraltarian/Andalusian and Jewish identities with a new Argentine signification.
65. For another recent translation of 'Penelope' see Maria Angeles Conde Parilla, 'The Obscene Nature of Molly's Soliloquy and Two Spanish Translations', *JJQ* 33 (1995–96), 211–36 (p. 211).
66. Schwartz, p. 723.
67. Waisman, 'Borges Reads Joyce', p. 65.
68. Levine, p. 356.
69. See Kristal, p. 87.
70. See Patricia Willson, p. 126.
71. Gifford, p. 632.
72. Levine, 'Notes to Borges's Notes on Joyce', 354
73. See Maria Angeles Conde-Parilla, *Los pasajes obscenos de Molly Bloom en español* (Albacete: Ediciones de la Diputacion de Albacete, 1994).
74. See *Ulises*, trad. Salas Subirat (2002), pp. 727–28; *Ulises*, trad. Valverde, pp. 459–60; *Ulises*, trad. García Tortosa y Venegas, pp. 907–08. Conde Parrilla employs Borges's distinctive translation choice of 'flor serrana'. See Conde, *Los pasajes obscenos*, p. 204.
75. Andrew Gibson, *Joyce's Revenge: History, Politics and Aesthetics in Ulysses* (Oxford and New York: Oxford University Press, 2002), p. 271.
76. See Nancy F. Marino, *La serranilla española: notas para su historia e interpretación* (Potomac, MD: Scripta Humanistica, 1987), for a comprehensive and insightful study of the *serranilla*.
77. Waisman, 'Borges Reads Joyce', p. 67.
78. See Guillermo Díaz-Plaja (ed.), *Antología Mayor de la Literatura Española I — Edad Media (Siglos X–XV)* (Madrid: Guadarrama, 1971), p. 859. My translation.
79. Bonnie Kime Scott, *Joyce and Feminism* (Bloomington: Indiana University Press, 1984), p. 61.
80. Gifford, p. 634.
81. Gifford, p. 633.
82. Gibson, *Joyce's Revenge*, p. 261.
83. Richard Pearce, 'Introduction: Molly Blooms: A Polylogue on "Penelope"', in Pearce, ed., *Molly Blooms*, pp. 3–17 (p. 4).

CHAPTER 2

# Borges's Reception of Joyce in the Argentine Press

The trajectory of Borges's reception of Joyce — as we have seen in Chapter 1 — begins in 1925 in a rather turbulent and tempestuous manner, particularly if considered from the standpoint of the rich symbolic meaning conveyed under the title of the avant-garde review *Proa*. The subsequent course of Borges's voyage through Joyce's Hibernian Sea has been characterized by a miscellaneous body of work constituted by notes, book reviews, a condensed biography, and an obituary, which appeared in a number of Buenos Aires periodicals in the late 1930s, as well as a vast number of scattered allusions which conglomerated in his critical work from 1932 onwards.[1] Thus, how did Joyce become throughout the 1930s the repeated focus of attention of Jorge Luis Borges? The first answer to this question has a great deal to do with the emergence of a European critical heritage of a Modernist author of the stature of James Joyce, and the way in which key critical studies, such as Stuart Gilbert's *James Joyce's Ulysses: A Study* (1930), had a considerable impact on the Latin American cultural scene. In his 1925 review of *Ulysses*, Borges anticipated the development of a Joyce industry, predicting that: 'De aquí diez años — ya facilitado su libro por comentadores más tercos y más piadosos que yo — disfrutaremos de él' (*Inq.* 28) ['Ten years from now — his book having been explicated by more pious and persistent reviewers than myself — we will still enjoy it'] (*SNF* 14). Consequently he greeted with enthusiasm the arrival of Gilbert's first book-length study of Joyce's notoriously difficult novel. This attentiveness to the emerging corpus of Joyce criticism is equally implied in Borges's ensuing allusions to yet another pioneering study, Charles Duff's *James Joyce and the Plain Reader* (1932). At the same time, throughout the course of Borges's exploration across Joyce's vast geography we are able to perceive a gradual shift from the youthful tone of the avant-gardist poet and essayist, to the more composed expression of the mature writer, already anticipating his revolutionary compact, classical *ficciones*, and on his way to become, along with Joyce, one of the most revolutionary writers of the twentieth century. The second answer to this question is related to the critical interest and increased speculation that the serialization of *Work in Progress* and the forthcoming publication of *Finnegans Wake* (1939) had been receiving in European and American literary circles. In this manner, the mature Borges who continued and developed his role as unofficial publicist to Joyce was a regular correspondent for a range of Buenos Aires reviews and, therefore, offered a reception of Joyce's work deeply embedded in the historical, cultural, and economic fabrics of Argentina. The aim of this chapter is to offer an informed discussion of Borges's papers on Joyce which appeared in two contrasting Buenos Aires magazines, the strictly literary and cultural journal *Sur* and the mass-marketed ladies' weekly *El Hogar*. The crucial discursive contexts of these two journalistic mediums, I shall argue, are testimony to a decisive period in Argentine culture which becomes particularly apparent in the various ways in which Joyce is read, discussed, interpreted, and translated. Therefore, Borges's papers on Joyce are able to operate both as part of the elitist discourse represented by the group *Sur*, but also as part of the complex socio-economic forces of *El Hogar*. The process through which Borges charts a map of the reception of Joyce in Argentina is also enriched by the wealth of translations, essays, reviews, and testimonies of Joyce's life and works by other national and international writers and critics which were incorporated in the review *Sur*. Equally, it is impossible to discuss the industrious cultural activity of *Sur* during this effervescent period in Argentina without alluding to the personal and literary relationship between the founder of the review, Victoria Ocampo, and the English novelist and critic, Virginia Woolf. Thus, this chapter also details the seminal role that Borges played in the Hispanic reception of Woolf, particularly through his pioneering translations of some of her most celebrated works. On the other hand, Borges's contributions to *El Hogar* may be read as part of a vibrant and multicoloured tapestry that not only interweaved literary, sociological, and economic strands indiscriminately, but also discussed the work of James Joyce in relation to a scintillating repertoire of (super-) concise narratives about other fellow Irish writers such as W. B. Yeats, Oliver St John Gogarty, and Flann O'Brien.

## The Review *Sur*: Cultural Institution, Feminist Front, and Promoter of European Modernism

Founded in 1931 by the Argentine critic, writer, and translator Victoria Ocampo, the literary review *Sur* stands as one of Argentina's most influential 'cultural institution[s]', as John King puts it, which 'helped to shape the course of Argentine letters in the twentieth century'.[2] During its twenty-nine-year existence, *Sur* embodied the revolutionary principles of twentieth-century feminism, principally in Ocampo's defiance to patriarchal discourses through the subject position of a woman whose challenging editorial enterprise led her to overturn the power relations of a predominantly chauvinistic society. With its name famously suggested by the Spanish philosopher Ortega y Gasset over a transatlantic telephone conversation, *Sur* had as its main aspiration the creation of a two-way transmission of culture, a principle that was illustrated in its pictogram of a red arrow pointing downwards, representing the diffusion of Western culture to the southernmost country in the world. Ortega y Gasset's emphasis on the marginality of Argentina contributed towards a conscious repositioning of Argentina as a complex receptacle in which several cultures meet, clash, and intersect. Yet at the same time, in a truly cosmopolitan fashion, the editorial board of *Sur* was integrated by an outstanding cast of writers from Europe, the United States, and Latin America including: Jorge Luis Borges (Argentina), Drieu La Rochelle (France), Ortega y Gasset (Spain),

Alfonso Reyes (Mexico), Jules Supervielle (French-Uruguayan), Waldo Frank (United States), Leo Ferrero (Italian) and Ernest Ansermet (Swiss).

Following the steps of *Revista de Occidente* which founded a publishing house as a means to provide a financial backdrop for the magazine, in 1933 Ocampo inaugurated *Editorial Sur*, an ambitious publishing venture which, as well as bringing out the work of several national writers, also produced translations of a vast number of foreign books.[3] In effect, *Editorial Sur* published the first rendering of Joyce's *Stephen Hero* into Spanish (1960)[4], as well as the first Spanish translation of *Exiles* (1937).[5] 'Spanish has been particularly attracted to Joyce's only play', writes Patrick O' Neill, 'which was to find no fewer than three further Spanish translations'.[6] He also reports that a 'version by Osvaldo López-Noguerol appeared, once again in Buenos Aires, in 1961; a version by Javier Fernández de Castro appeared in Barcelona in 1970; and a fourth translation, by Fernando Toda, appeared in Madrid in 1987 — thus giving Spanish more versions of Joyce's play than exist in any other language'.[7] In line with this increased interest in the dramatic dimension of Joyce's oeuvre, *Sur* published a translation of Marjorie Barkentin's theatrical adaptation *Ulysses in NightTown* (1958) under the title *La noche de Ulises* (1961).[8] In this sense, *Editorial Sur*'s translation of *Stephen Hero*, *Exiles*, and *Ulysses in NightTown* ought to be understood in relation to Victoria Ocampo's larger cultural project to disseminate the works of the most significant writers of the twentieth century in translation. As Lojo Rodríguez points out, 'the works published by the publishing houses *Sur* and *Sudamericana* were distributed throughout the whole of South America and Spain'.[9]

As previously stated, the other modernist writer who merited the attention of Ocampo was Virginia Woolf. In this sense, the most remarkable aspect of the reception of Woolf in the Hispanic world is its immediate association with two towering figures of Argentine letters: Victoria Ocampo and Jorge Luis Borges. Just as Borges encountered Joyce through the intercession of Valery Larbaud, Sylvia Beach, and Ricardo Güiraldes, so Ocampo discovered the works of Virginia Woolf via Beach and Adrienne Monnier. 'When Victoria arrived in Paris that first winter', writes Doris Meyer, 'she went to the rue de l'Odéon to see for herself what Güiraldes had told her was one of the landmarks of Paris, "La Maison des Amis des Livres".'[10] It is not surprising that Victoria Ocampo, an advocate of the rights of women in a patriarchal Argentine society, soon established a close friendship with Beach and Monnier. Indeed, Meyer underlines the important fact that: 'It was Beach who, in 1929, first recommended to Victoria that she read the works of the English novelist and essayist Virginia Woolf, especially a little book published that year entitled *A Room of One's Own*.'[11] Captivated by the diversity and complexity of Woolf's work, Ocampo travelled to London in 1934 and was introduced to Woolf by the English novelist Aldous Huxley, whom she had previously met in Paris. In her fascinating biography, *Virginia Woolf*, Hermione Lee wonderfully captures the immediate fascination between these two different, and yet very similar, female icons of the twentieth century: 'The two women talked avidly, partly in French partly in English, as they stood in the middle of the private view. OCampo [sic] was forty-four. In her youth she had been a famous beauty; she was still, as Virginia said, 'very ripe & rich ... the colour of an apricot under glass.'[12]

## Jorge Luis Borges: Translator of Woolf

If Güiraldes had previously encouraged Borges to translate extracts from Joyce's *Ulysses* for *Proa*, so Ocampo entrusted to Borges the translation of the works of her esteemed acquaintance Virginia Woolf. Thus, on Ocampo's special request, Borges undertook the translation of one of the seminal landmarks of twentieth-century feminism, *A Room of One's Own* (1937), as well as *Orlando* (1937).[13] For the metaphysical and erudite Borges the exercise of translation opened a door to the exploration of female subjectivities, whether Molly Bloom's eroticized and unpunctuated soliloquy — albeit filtered through the perception of Joyce's male authorship — or the clearly defined feminist stance of Woolf's *A Room of One's Own*, and the more complex, ambivalent gender positioning of *Orlando*.[14] Regarding the immediate reception of Borges's translation of *Orlando*, Lojo Rodríguez points out that: '*Orlando* was well received by South American intellectuals: Laura Ayerza (1991, 398) has described how Gabriel García Márquez took Woolf's novel as an inspiration for his *Cien años de soledad*'.[15] To read *One Hundred Years of Solitude* — the watershed of the boom generation and one of the most influential novels of Latin American literature — refracted through Borges's idiosyncratic Spanish translation of *Orlando* is, undoubtedly, a testament to the ambitious cultural project of *Sur*. According to John King, 'Ocampo disseminated Woolf's work in Latin America at a very early date and thus helped to place on the agenda the problems of women in general (Argentine women still did not have the vote) and women writers in particular'.[16] Yet another example of Borges's interest in Woolf is afforded by his concise biography 'Virginia Woolf' that appeared in the October 1936 number of *El Hogar* (see *OC4* 215–16). Woolf embodied for Borges not only a distinctive female voice but also a passageway to Joyce's prominent orchestration of styles in *Ulysses*. Therefore he mentions in his biographical sketch that *Mrs Dalloway* followed Joyce's novelistic tradition of the one-day novel, as well as his exploration of the human psyche with the innovative technique of interior monologue.

## Southerly Winds: Joycean Airs Reach Argentine Shores

The grand cultural project of *Sur* had cast its net wide, sweeping ambitiously between both sides of the Atlantic, creating a multifaceted canvas on which Argentines would be able to observe both their national creativities, as well as the artistic and literary trends currently taking place in the rest of the world. Ocampo was certainly aware that of the most significant European literary influences, James Joyce held pride of place, and therefore she set herself the task to disseminate in Argentina key critical studies of his life and works. In this sense, *Editorial Sur*'s Spanish translations of Joyce did not appear in isolation, but rather emerged in the company of a range of studies by national writers, well-known figures in Joycean scholarship, and French poets and intellectuals. In chronological order, and spanning a period of sixteen years, these papers included:

— Charles Duff's 1932 study *James Joyce and the Plain Reader*, translated as, '*Ulises* y otros trabajos de James Joyce' (translator unknown). See *Sur*, 2 (1932), 86–127.

— Preview of A. Jiménez Fraud's translation of *Exiles*, *Desterrados*. See *Sur*, 35 (1937), 68–86.
— A review of *Finnegans Wake* 'Joyce y los neologismos' [Joyce and the Neologisms] by Jorge Luis Borges. See *Sur*, 63 (1939), 59–61.
— An obituary 'Fragmento sobre Joyce' [A Fragment on Joyce] by Jorge Luis Borges. See *Sur*, 77 (1941), 60–62.
— A study by the avant-garde French writer Armand Petitjean 'El tratamiento del lenguaje en Joyce' [Joyce's Use of Language]. See *Sur*, 78 (1941), 42–59.
— A testimony of Joyce's years in Paris and final days in Zurich by the French poet Louis Guillet. See *Sur*, 87 (1941), 28–42.
— The Argentine poet César Fernández Moreno reviews a translation of C. G. Jung's study of *Ulysses*, ¿*Quién es Ulises?* [Who is Ulysses?] originally published in 1932. See *Sur*, 120 (1944), 79–82.
— An essay by Stuart Gilbert 'El fondo latino en el arte de James Joyce' [The Latin Background in the Art of James Joyce]. See *Sur*, 122 (1944), 11–24.
— A study by the Córdoba (Argentina) poet, critic and translator Enrique Luis Revol, 'Joyce, la literatura y el lenguaje' [Joyce, Literature and Language].[17] See *Sur*, 159 (1948), 75–86.

What this revealing catalogue makes particularly evident is that the diffusion of James Joyce championed by *Sur* was largely conditioned, although by no means exclusively, by three determining and interrelated factors: the early European reception of Joyce's works; Joyce's untimely death in Zurich 1941; and the publication of the complete Spanish translation of *Ulysses* by J. Salas Subirat in Buenos Aires, in 1945. To begin with, Joseph Brooker has persuasively demonstrated that the publication of Stuart Gilbert's *James Joyce's Ulysses* (1930) marked 'the beginning of a gradual process of intensified textual scrutiny [...] [Gilbert] heralds a long-term trend toward completeness and totality in the understanding of Joyce, the belief that his work not only bears but demands exhaustive explication.'[18] In this sense, we can say that Charles Duff's 1932 study follows the hermeneutical trend initiated by Gilbert, but more intently catered for the baffled, non-academic, supposed 'plain reader' of Joyce. In this respect, Jean-Michel Rabaté observes that: 'The book handsomely manages to present the whole scope of Joyce's writings in some fifty pages, while avoiding many traps and keeping the same urbane and balanced tone.'[19] The promise of a James Joyce reference book for dummies made Duff particularly attractive to the inquisitive readers of *Sur* whose limited knowledge of Joyce would have been derived from fragmentary Spanish translations of *Ulysses* (such as Borges's in *Proa* or Marichalar's in *Revista de Occidente*) or the more recent 1929 French *Ulysse*. Indeed, if the 'plain reader' is at the heart of Duff's project — his study was light-heartedly 'DEDICATED WITHOUT MALICE TO THE PLAIN READER'[20] — this is partly because he was deliberately distancing himself from the overall erudite and affected tone of Gilbert's study: 'We may well leave it for learned commentators to amuse themselves with, and assume that the plain reader need not worry too much about it [the *Odyssey*]. If he cannot appreciate the book without it, he will never do so with it.'[21] Moreover, Duff also resorted to Gilbert as 'the best substitute for the original [*Ulysses*]',[22] and, in this way, he advised the 'plain reader who does not happen to possess or have access to a full text of *Ulysses*'[23] to irrevocably and unashamedly turn to Gilbert. The extensive quotations from *Ulysses* interwoven into the texture of

Gilbert's critical analysis certainly offered a valid substitution for a book that had been prohibited in Europe and America. For all its insistence on the substitutional quality of Gilbert's study, Duff's strong assertion largely resonated in Borges's essay 'Narrative Art and Magic' (1932) which was also published in *Sur*, 2 (1932). (Borges would have accessed *James Joyce and the Plain Reader* before its release). Thus, Borges took on board the idea of a 'surrogate *Ulysses*'[24] implicit in Duff's claim, but gave it a twist as he ironically retorted that the reader who did not happen to possess a copy of Gilbert's study should instead turn to Joyce's *Ulysses*: 'Pero la ilustración más cabal de un orbe autónomo de corroboraciones, de presagios, de monumentos, es el predestinado *Ulises* de Joyce. Basta el examen del libro expositivo de Gilbert o, en su defecto, de la vertiginosa novela' (*OC1* 232) ['But the most perfect illustration of an autonomous orb of omens, confirmations, and monuments is Joyce's preordained *Ulysses*. One need only examine Stuart Gilbert's study or, in its absence, the vertiginous novel itself'] (*SNF* 81).[25] This evidence underlines the important fact that Borges's pronouncements on Joyce from 1925 to the 1930s onwards were not produced *ex nihilo* but, instead, the overall pattern that has emerged so far gestures outward and onward, especially in relation to the Joyce critical scenario which gravitated around the figures of Sylvia Beach, Valery Larbaud, Stuart Gilbert and, in this particular case, the British writer and critic, Charles Duff.

The publication of *Finnegans Wake* in 1939 and Joyce's untimely death in Zurich in 1941 constituted two major events in the world of letters that no serious literary publication could have ignored, hence accounting for *Sur*'s editorial decision to incorporate Borges's review and obituary, and notes by the French writers Guillet and Petitjean commemorating Joyce's life and works. What this implies, moreover, is that in the late 1930s Borges would have been keen to demonstrate that he was able to take further his pioneering reception of Joyce's work, and to follow up his 1925 review and translation of *Ulysses* with an ensuing discussion — albeit not so enthusiastic — of *Finnegans Wake* upon its release. It is important to remember, however, that the review of the *Wake* which appeared in *Sur* was an enlarged version of an earlier review previously published in *El Hogar* (both reviews will be jointly discussed in the next section devoted to *El Hogar*).

Upon Joyce's death in Zurich, 13 January 1941, the review *Sur* promptly announced the publication of an obituary article entitled 'James Joyce' by Jorge Luis Borges in its forthcoming February issue.[26] But in a typical Borgesian fashion, the totality (James Joyce) is reduced to a fragment ('A Fragment on Joyce'). This follows in the footsteps of his 1925 shortcut through the labyrinth of *Ulysses* whereby he developed an episodic reading that celebrated the part over the whole, and which unveiled a fragmentary translation of 'Penelope' that strove towards the creation of a decontextualized recreation of the episode. And even his obituary stands midway between 'A Fragment on Joyce' and 'A Fragment on Funes', since a tongue-in-cheek Borges incorporated within the note an early draft of 'Funes the Memorious' and open-handedly awarded it a textual space occupying nearly half of the journalistic column. To some extent the inclusion of Funes at the beginning of 'A Fragment on Joyce' cancels a feature common to all obituaries, namely a biographical summary of the late writer. By eschewing some — but by no means all — of Joyce's biographic details and replacing them with the fictional life and memorizing attributes of his Uruguayan gaucho, Borges disregards the conventions of the obituary and challenges the distinctive eulogizing features of most necrological notes. In spite of this, the Funes digression functions as a textual analogue which is employed as a strategy to allude to Joyce indirectly incorporating, then, a parallel discussion, or alternative fictional angle, from which to subsequently examine the work of James Joyce. In this unconventional obituary, Borges also pays an ironic homage to Gilbert's *James Joyce's Ulysses* and Charles Duff's *James Joyce and the Plain Reader* with the overt declaration:

> Nadie ignora que para los lectores desprevenidos, la vasta novela de Joyce es indescifrablemente caótica. Nadie tampoco ignora que su intérprete oficial, Stuart Gilbert, ha propalado que cada uno de los dieciocho capítulos corresponde a una hora del día, a un órgano corporal, a un arte, a un símbolo, a un color, a una técnica literaria y a una de las aventuras de Ulises hijo de Laertes, de la simiente de Zeus (*Sur* 168).

> Everyone knows that Joyce's book is indecipherably chaotic to the unprepared reader. Everyone knows that Stuart Gilbert, its official interpreter, has revealed that each of the novel's eighteen chapters corresponds to an hour of the day, a bodily organ, an art, a symbol, a color, a literary technique, and one of the adventures of *Ulysses*, son of Laertes, of the seed of Zeus (*SNF* 221).

The immediate implications and overall significance of this declaration, as well as the Funes analogy, will be fully explored in Chapter 3. For the time being, it should suffice to mention that in the wider Latin American context the death of James Joyce did not pass unnoticed and was marked by another influential writer, the Cuban writer, poet and essayist, José Lezama Lima. His essay 'Muerte de Joyce' [Death of Joyce] appeared just one month after Borges's obituary, in the March edition of the Havana review *Grafos*.[27] Just as Borges took to further lengths the Anglophone and Francophone reception of Joyce's works by incorporating critics such as Valery Larbaud, Stuart Gilbert, and Charles Duff, so Salgado claims that Lezama's obituary 'can thus be read as a concentrated, revisionist survey, a catalog of the main critical tendencies that surfaced in response to Joyce's work during Lezama's youth'.[28] He is able to identify in it the numerous voices of 'Wyndham Lewis, Ezra Pound, T. S. Eliot, Valery Larbaud, Herbert Gorman, Stuart Gilbert, E. R. Curtius, and Borges himself among Lezama's sources'.[29] Salgado also reports that: 'On the occasion of Joyce's death, both Marechal and Carpentier published articles praising Joyce's technical innovations in the genre while, at the same time, trying to distance their own creative projects from his influence.'[30]

### Salas Subirat's Magnum Opus: *Ulises*

Yet the event that most resolutely laid claim to the final assimilation of Joyce in the Hispanic world is, undoubtedly, the complete translation of *Ulysses* by J. Salas Subirat. If the extent and scope of Joyce's work had so far been represented by just three complete translations, Dámaso Alonso's *El artista adolescente (retrato)*, Ignacio Abelló's *Gente de Dublín*,[31] and Jiménez Fraud's *Desterrados*, so the translation of *Ulysses*, commissioned by the Buenos Aires publishing house Santiago Rueda, certainly came as a breakthrough in the long-overdue translation of Joyce's influential *Ulysses*. It is then valid to assume that the much-expected Spanish version would have accounted for a renewed interest in Joyce's oeuvre within the intellectual circles of Argentina. Taking advantage of this lively atmosphere of anticipation, Santiago Rueda supplemented the promotion of Salas Subirat's brand new *Ulises* with the publication of a Spanish version of Jung's 1932 study of *Ulysses*, as well as a translation of Herbert Gorman's biography,[32] both of which were marketed as publicity stunts that aimed to attract further attention to their Buenos Aires *Ulises*. It is rather curious, however, that they opted for Jung's psychoanalytical and not-so-congratulatory one-decade-old reading of the novel, rather than for book-length classics such as Gilbert's, or Budgen's *James Joyce and the Making of Ulysses* (1934).[33] Be that as it may, this editorial strategy marked the beginning of a long-standing association between James Joyce and the field of psychoanalysis in Argentina. 'When Joyce reentered Argentina in the 1970s', affirms Francine Masiello, 'it was through an unmistakable linkage to Lacan. Journals such as *Literal* (1973–75) and *Sitio* (1982–83) were devoted to Lacanian Joyce.'[34] She also notes that: 'In 1989, the magazine *Babel* framed Joyce in a single issue, and, in 1991, a seminar on psychoanalysis and literature that recruited some of Argentina's most significant intellectuals was focused on Joyce and language, through the principal lens of Lacan.'[35] The translation of Jung's essay was reviewed by the poet César Fernández Moreno in the October 1944 edition of *Sur*: 'Las solapas del librito que glosamos nos informan que próximamente la editorial Santiago Rueda dará a luz la versión íntegra de *Ulises*, lo cual nos hace pensar que esta publicación viene a manera de avanzada de aquella versión, a explorar el camino, y tantear por anticipado la reacción del público y los poderes públicos'[36] [The dust jacket of this little book under review, informs us that the publishing house Santiago Rueda will soon bring to light the complete Spanish version of *Ulises*, which makes us think that this publication anticipates the translation, paving the way and testing the waters for the ensuing reaction of the general public and of public bodies]. Undeniably, Fernández Moreno is alluding to the scandalous publication history of *Ulysses* and the charges of obscenity, litigation procedures, and censorship in America and various European countries. But the biggest irony here is that at the time of the publication of Salas Subirat's translation the president of the Argentine Republic was Colonel Edelmiro O'Farrell (1887–1980), a descendant of Irish immigrants originally from Co. Longford. Colonel Edelmiro O'Farrell's father, John O'Farrell, embarked on his voyage to Argentina in the mid-nineteenth century and settled down in the district of Lanús located in Greater Buenos Aires, where Edelmiro was born.[37] An army officer and close ally of Juan Domingo Perón, Colonel O'Farrell played a major role in a military coup which landed him the presidency of the country, with Perón standing as vice-president. Would it not seem paradoxical, then, for a president of Irish ancestry to press charges on the grounds of morality against a fellow Irishman? Fortunately enough, the publication of *Ulises* did not raise the alarm of any governmental organization, and the historical launch of the first Spanish translation of Joyce's *Ulysses* was marked by the time in office of the first Argentine president of Irish descent.

In the December 1944 edition of the review, *Sur* deemed it appropriate to salute the ensuing arrival of *Ulises* with a fresh essay by Stuart Gilbert, 'El fondo latino en el arte de James Joyce'. This significant study also appeared in the Paris monthly literary review *Fontaine*, under the title, 'L'ambiance Latine de L'art de James Joyce'.[38] Indeed, Gilbert's new emphasis on the Latin, rather than Hellenic elements of *Ulysses*, was the perfect anticipation for a translation in the Romance languages. The absence of a review of Salas Subirat's translation in *Sur*, however, is explained by the fact that Borges decided to incorporate his 1946 essay, 'Nota sobre el Ulises en español' [A note on the Spanish *Ulysses*], in *Los Anales de Buenos Aires*, the official publication of the Buenos Aires National Library. (Borges's review of Salas Subirat has been fully discussed in Chapter 1, particularly through the light shed by his fragmentary translation of 'Penelope'). It is significant to mention that Salas Subirat published his own apology for the translation in *Contrapunto*, a Buenos Aires review devoted to literature and the arts.[39] The next (and final) appearance of Joyce in *Sur* took place in 1948 as part of a comprehensive study by the Argentine poet and scholar Enrique Luis Revol. Ultimately, *Sur*'s mapping of a Joycean trajectory through its miscellaneous articles and translations laid the foundations for the consolidation of Joyce's work in the crucial decades of the 1930s and 1940s.

### *El Hogar*: Borges, Joyce and Popular Culture

Unlike the avant-garde tendencies of Proa, or the strictly intellectual tone of *Sur*, *El Hogar: ilustración semanal argentina para la mujer, la casa y el niño* [*Home: Argentine illustrated weekly for the lady, home and child*], as the subtitle indicates, had been marketed since its inception in 1904 as a glossy, à la mode periodical publication, targeted at a female audience of Argentina's upper and middle social strata. A distinctive feature of the magazine consisted in its numerous advertising spaces which featured a wide range of female and household commodities, such as upmarket lingerie, beauty products, homeopathic remedies, luxurious confectionery, and the current trends in ladies fashion. *El Hogar*, however, was more than a glossy-popular and had, as Borges's biographer Rodríguez Monegal has observed, 'some literary and cultural aspirations',[40] thus justifying the editorial decision to include the erudite and polyglot Jorge Luis Borges, as one of their regular correspondents.[41] The contextual appearance of Borges's literary notes side-by-side with a variety of publicity spaces destined for mass consumption, as well as in relation to the other not-so-literary columns included in the magazine, cannot be ignored. In effect, it re-inscribes the scholarly Borges within the larger context of popular culture. More importantly the criss-crossing of Borges's literary contributions with columns on fashion and housekeeping resembles the type of publication Joyce's romantic heroine, Gerty MacDowell, pleasurably reads in order to fuel her romantic dreams and gain expert beauty tips. As Don Gifford states, Gerty read 'the *Lady's Pictorial*, "a weekly illustrated journal of fashion, society, art, literature, music and the drama", published in London on Thursday'.[42] Indeed, we learn that Gerty obtains useful fashion tips from the *Lady's Pictorial*: 'A neat blouse of electric blue selftinted by dolly dyes (because it was expected in the *Lady's Pictorial* that electric blue would be worn) [...]' (*U* 13.150–51).

In 'Nausicaa' Gerty's mellifluous and over-sentimentalized discourse is blended with the report of the third-person narrator through Joyce's masterful use of the technique of free-indirect style. Gerty is described as 'slight and graceful, inclining even to fragility' (U 13.53–54) (conventional romantic heroine), but the reader also learns that her beauty has been enhanced by 'Madame Vera Verity, directress of the Woman Beautiful page of the Princess Novelette, who had first advised her to try eyebrowleine which gave that haunting expression to the eyes' (U 13.109–12) (discourse of advertisement). Her facial appearance is also invested with the symbolic attributes of the Virgin Mary: 'The waxen pallor of her face was almost spiritual in its ivorylike purity' (U 13.87–88) and her 'hands of finely veined alabaster' (U 13.89–90) bring to mind the typifying epithet of princess Nausicaa, Gerty's Homeric predecessor, who is referred to in the *Odyssey* as 'she of the white arms'.[43] If we compare the complexly laced set of registers employed in 'Nausicaa' with the beauty pages of *El Hogar*, we soon realize that the Argentine lady reader would have been similarly exposed to the merging of religious, literary, and advertising discourses in the overall printed configuration of the magazine. For example, the Bloomsday June 1939 issue of *El Hogar* in which appeared Borges's review of the *Wake*, featured a publicity space that recalls the type of 'Madame Vera Verity' discourse we tend to associate with Gerty: 'La belleza de los ojos radica en gran parte en su claridad y su brillo'[44] [the beauty of the eyes mainly lies in their sparkle and luminosity]. The beginning of the ad is clearly playing with Christian commonplaces which preached that 'the eyes are the window to the soul', a type of accepted wisdom which is confirmed in the gospel according to Matthew: 'The lamp of the body is the eye. If therefore your eye is good, your whole body will be full of light. / But if your eye is bad, your whole body will be full of darkness'.[45] The biblical metaphor of the eyes as the mirror to the soul may be also identified as belonging to the courtly love Neoplatonic tradition of the beautiful and virtuous lady whose eyes are able to transport the poet-lover to the higher realm of God. The luminous eyes of the angelic lady, whether Dante's Beatrice or Petrarch's Laura, act as a vehicle that connects the poet with the larger love that binds the universe through the eternity of God. Yet the idealized tone of the commercial soon gives way to the more explicit language of the marketplace: 'Se comprende entonces que una sombra obscura colocada sobre los párpados les hace perder en vivacidad [...] Es necesario, sobre todo, una buena higiene de ojos: para esto es preciso lavarlos por la noche y por la mañana con agua de rosas [...]'[46] [It is understood, then, that a dark eye shadow makes the eyelids lose their vivacity [...] It is important to have good eye hygiene: for this reason they should be washed every morning and night with rose water]. Unquestionably, this type of advert is targeting the set of religious and cultural beliefs of a female audience firmly rooted in a patriarchal, Roman Catholic society. Therefore, like Gerty's fusion of Catholicism and fetishism in her devotion to lingerie: 'As for undies they were Gerty's chief care [...] She was wearing the blue set for luck, hoping against hope, her own colour and lucky too for a bride to have a bit of blue somewhere' (U 13.171–81); a range of female targeted advertising spaces in *El Hogar* also amalgamated a Catholic upbringing with the world of consumerism in the dual female roles of virgin and femme fatale.

Equally significant is that this same Bloomsday issue featured a note on the 'Procession of the Corpus Christi', which commemorated the sacrament of the Eucharist in the historical Plaza de Mayo in Buenos Aires.[47] Like the pervasive mystical force of the men's temperance retreat that lingers in the flirtatious and voyeuristic background of 'Nausicaa', so *El Hogar* also dramatizes within its pages a similar type of religious ceremony:

> It was the men's temperance retreat conducted by the missioner, the reverend John Hughes S. J., rosary, sermon and benediction of the Most blessed Sacrament. They were there gathered together without distinction of social class (*U* 13.282–84).

> La tradicional procesión del Corpus Christi, que congregó en la plaza de Mayo a una verdadera multitud. El arzobispo de Buenos Aires, cardinal prima de monseñor Santiago Luis Copello, conduce, bajo el palio, el Santísimo Sacramento'.[48]

> The traditional procession of the Corpus Christi gathered together in a large crowd in the plaza de Mayo. The archbishop of Buenos Aires, cardinal prima do monsignor Santiago Luis Copello, conducts in his pallium, the Most blessed Sacrament.

We can then conclude that just as in 'Nausicaa' Joyce juxtaposes the clichés of romantic literature, the language of advertising, and the influential religious discourse of Roman Catholic Ireland, so Borges's articles in *El Hogar* negotiated a printed configuration that mirrored Joyce's own heterogeneity and polyphonic discourse. Indeed, the manner in which the discourse of advertising is interwoven into Borges's 'high culture' reflects the way in which 'popular culture', namely, newspapers, pulp-fiction, and a wide range of publicities circulate throughout *Ulysses* and indiscriminately merge with Joyce's other literary, philosophical and canonical discourses. As Garry Leonard has observed: 'Advertising — and consumer discourse in general — constitutes a dynamic force every bit as influential on Joyce as, say, the works of Thomas Aquinas, Dante, Shakespeare or Bruno.'[49] If Joyce incorporates into *Ulysses* canonical and popular discourses without imposing any system of hierarchies, so Borges's texts in *El Hogar* dynamically embrace the production of an elite culture in a symbiotic relationship with the popular culture of commercials, pulp fiction, and columns on beauty and practical parenting. Moreover, we also find that the world of advertising infiltrated into some of Borges's columns during this period. In a June 1939 article entitled 'Cuando la ficción vive en la ficción' [When Fiction Lives in Fiction] Borges began with a reference to a commercial commodity, an elaborate biscuit tin displaying a series of Japanese images which revealed to him the notion of infinite regress:

> Debo mi primera noción del problema del infinito a una gran lata de bizcochos que dio misterio y vertigo a mi niñez. En el costado de ese objeto anormal había una escena japonesa; no recuerdo los niños o guerreros que la formaban, pero sí que en un ángulo de esa imagen la misma lata de bizcochos reaparecía con la misma figura y en ella la misma figura, y así (a lo menos, en potencia) infinitamente... (*OC4* 433).

[I owe my first inkling of the problem of infinity to a large biscuit tin that was a source of vertiginous mystery during my childhood. On one side of this exceptional object was a Japanese scene; I do not recall the children or warriors who configured it, but I do remember that in a corner of the image the same biscuit tin reappeared with the same picture, and in it the same picture again, and so on (at least by implication) infinitely ... (SNF 160).]

In the remainder of the note Borges points out that the suggestive iconographic packaging of the confectionery product resembles the metaphysical internal duplications of Josiah Royce, the hall-of-mirrors effect of Velázquez's *Las Meninas*, the tale-within-the-tale devices of *The Arabian Nights* and *Don Quixote*, the inner play in *Hamlet*, and the Chinese-box effects in Meyrink's *The Golem* and Flann O'Brien's *At-Swim-Two-Birds* (SNF 160–61). What remains crucial in this trajectory of infinity represented by the tantalizing Japanese figures is that Borges challenges traditional conceptions of high art by constructing a rich meeting point between the world of culture and the marketplace. In this particular case, Borges is drawing attention to the fact that the discourse of culture may also borrow from the discourse of advertising. If Borges published his papers on Joyce in the mass-marketed *El Hogar* which allowed the polyphonic cohabitation of several discourses, so Joyce published his early stories 'The Sisters', 'After the Race', and 'Eveline' in *The Irish Homestead*, a weekly journal in association with the Irish Agricultural Society. Garry Leonard has persuasively demonstrated that one of the advertisements which featured alongside 'The Sisters' also infiltrated the fictional fabrics of the story:

> Joyce's first short story was printed in an agricultural journal just above an advertisement for mineral water ('Sparkling Montserrat. The Drink for the Gout & Rheumatic') [...] It was only after Joyce saw the story printed that he introduced Eliza's famous verbal slip 'rheumatic wheels' instead of 'pneumatic wheels'. Thus the eminently forgettable soda advertisement ('The Drink for the Gout & Rheumatic') generates the momentary slip of the tongue.[50]

During his four years at *El Hogar* (1936–40) Borges was assigned the fortnightly page of 'Libros y Autores Extranjeros' [Foreign Books and Authors], which consisted of four small sections entitled: 'Essays', 'Concise Biographies', 'Reviews', and a closing (super-) concise section entitled 'Literary Life'. Silvia Barei regards Borges's columns for *El Hogar* as 'una especie de "guía de lecturas", de mapa o de recorrido literario que ciertamente cubría las expectativas de los lectores medios de la época'[51] [as a sort of 'reading guide', a map or literary trajectory that unquestionably fulfilled the expectations of the general reader of the time]. Barei also admits, however, that these journalistic pages were at times over-elaborated, and draws attention to Roberto Alifano's claim that the housewives for whom the magazine was produced would not have been able to fully appreciate the wide cultural background of Borges.[52] Or we may equally claim that what is implied here is that Borges's remarkable level of erudition and fluency in several European languages would have presented a challenge not only to the female readership of *El Hogar* but also to the general reader, male or female. Indeed, Borges's discussion of the experimental and notoriously difficult work of James Joyce would corroborate the view that some columns may have exceeded the cultural expectations of the journal. On the other hand, the conciseness of the notes, the attractiveness of the illustrations and advertisements that accompanied them, and the fact that Borges was aware he was writing for a non-specialized readership lent them an air of accessibility and readability. For instance, Rodríguez Monegal reports that he encountered Borges for the first time in *El Hogar* as a fifteen-year-old boy and read with relish 'a note headed "Literary Life" that was devoted to Joyce and included an anecdote of his meeting with Yeats'.[53] Another childhood testimony of the special gravitation of *El Hogar* in a middle-class home of Argentine society is given by Barei, who warmly evoked the years in which the magazine was purchased by her paternal grandparents.[54] In his introduction of *Textos cautivos*, Enrique Sacerio-Garí seeks to construct a picture of *El Hogar* as 'texto sociológico' [sociological text], which may act as a mirror of 'las imágenes que se proyectaban en la Argentina y el ritmo de vida que esas imágenes perpetuaban semana tras semana en el público lector'[55] [the images that were projected in Argentina, as well as the everyday resonance that those images perpetuated in the weekly audience of the magazine]. Above all, what remains crucial here is the assumption that in the late 1930s Borges discusses Joyce's work not for the select group of scholars, or the limited readership of strictly literary periodicals such as *Sur*, but that he opens up and disseminates his notoriously difficult work to a mass audience. What kind of Joyce emerges, then, from Borges's journalistic notes in *El Hogar*? Or, more precisely, what are the aspects of Joyce that particularly interested Borges? During his four-year employment for *El Hogar* Borges dedicated to Joyce: a capsule biography, 'James Joyce' (1937); a book review of *Finnegans Wake*, 'El Último Libro de Joyce' [Joyce's Latest Novel] (1939); two anecdotes in the section 'Literary Life'; and numerous references in other notes published in the magazine.

### Joyce in a Nutshell

The American critic and translator Suzanne Jill Levine has convincingly demonstrated that 'the Joyce "legend" that Borges fixes on [in his concise biography 'James Joyce'] is one that reflected Borges's own life'.[56] In this way, she argues that at the heart of Borges's biography lies a deliberate interweaving of dates and biographical events that mirrored his own life. Indeed, Levine's claim is corroborated at the beginning of 'James Joyce': 'A los nueve años publicó un folleto elegíaco sobre el caudillo Charles Stewart Parnell' (*OC4* 251); [At the age of nine wrote and published an elegiac pamphlet on the Irish leader Charles Stewart Parnell]. Undoubtedly, Borges stresses the precociousness of Joyce's literary career and the important fact that, like Joyce, he had also translated and published at the tender age of nine the story 'The Happy Prince' by another Irish writer, Oscar Wilde. Almost forty years later, a blind and elderly Borges recalls this decisive event as a watershed in his life: 'When I was nine or so, I translated Oscar Wilde's "The Happy Prince" into Spanish, and it was published in one of the Buenos Aires dailies, *El País*' (*A* 26). It is not surprising, thus, that the multilingual Borges was also fascinated by the account that: '[Joyce] publicó — a los diecisiete años un largo estudio sobre Ibsen en la *Fortnightly Review*. El culto de Ibsen lo movió a aprender el noruego' (*OC4* 251) [Aged seventeen he [Joyce] published a long study on Ibsen in the *Fortnightly Review*. The love of Ibsen led him to the study of Norwegian]. It is clear that at this point Borges was thinking of his teenage years in Geneva, when his fondness for German literature and philosophy led him to the study of the German language. Both Norwegian and German were, of course, self-taught.

Whereas Borges's concise biography of Joyce, as we have been able to see thus far, creates a fascinating overlapping with his own life, it also relied on biographical details drawn from Charles Duff's *James Joyce and the Plain Reader*. For example, Borges perpetrated Duff's inaccuracy in which he claimed that Joyce married Nora at the age of twenty-two.[57] In this sense, an unaware Borges erroneously reports, 'en 1904 se había casado con Miss Norah Healy, de Galway' (*OC4* 251) ['in 1904 he married Miss Norah Healy, of Galway'], and alludes to Nora Barnacle by her maternal surname, 'Healy', as well as spelling her Christian name with an 'h'. Borges's attentiveness to Duff's narrative also compelled him to conclude that Joyce's early works 'no son importantes. Mejor dicho, únicamente lo son como anticipaciones del *Ulises* o en cuanto pueden ayudar a su inteligencia' (*OC4* 251) [are unimportant or, in other words, are only important if viewed as an anticipation of *Ulysses*, or how much they could aid its understanding]. In 1932 Duff had disavowed the value of *Dubliners* and *A Portrait* with the unbending remark that: '*The Portrait* is an interesting work in the history of the technique of the novel, but both it and *Dubliners* pale into insignificance in comparison with the immense conception and wonderful execution of *Ulysses*'.[58]

Yet at the same time Borges was keen to emphasize Joyce's attraction for 'obras vastas, las que abarcan un mundo: Dante, Homero, Tomás de Aquino, Aristóteles, el Zohar' (*OC4* 251) [vast works, those that encompass a universe: Dante, Shakespeare, Homer, Thomas Aquinas, Aristotle, The Zohar]. Undoubtedly, Borges perceived in Joyce's vast cultural heritage the type of encyclopaedic works to which he himself was also attracted. One of the main repercussions of this claim is that it reappeared in Borges's 1941 obituary of Joyce, albeit metamorphosed under the rhetorical guise of one of Borges's most emblematic epigrams: 'Como Shakespeare, como Quevedo, como Goethe, como ningún otro escritor, Joyce es menos un literato que una literatura' (*OC4* 251) [Like Shakespeare, like Quevedo, like Goethe, like no other writer, Joyce is less a man of letters than a literature] (*SNF* 221). Thus, Borges elevates Joyce from individual author to the generic category of 'una literatura', which is represented by the Western tradition of Shakespeare, Quevedo, and Goethe. Borges's dictum may also be read as a premonition of the sheer scale of his own work since, like the mythical Joyce, Borges was on his way to become less a man of letters than a literature.

In the second paragraph of the note Borges reserves his praise for the historical moment in which Joyce composed *Ulysses*. Thus he offers a reading that celebrates Joyce's unfaltering dedication against his own personal vicissitudes and exile, as well as in relation to the larger backdrop of World War I: 'Joyce trabajó el *Ulises* en los terribles años que van de 1914 a 1921 [...] Ocho años consagró a cumplir ese juramento' (*OC4* 251) [Joyce worked on *Ulysses* during the terrible years of 1914 to 1921 [...] he dedicated eight years to fulfil this pledge]. In a grand heroic gesture that mingled the perils of warfare, the tests of exile, and the creation of a work of art, Borges dramatically told his readers of *El Hogar* that: 'En la tierra, en el aire y en el mar, Europa estaba asesinándose, no sin gloria; Joyce, mientras tanto — en los intervalos de corregir deberes de inglés o de improvisar artículos en italiano para *Il Piccollo della Sera* — , componía su vasta recreación de un solo día en Dublín: el 16 de junio de 1904' (*OC4* 251) [On land, air and sea, Europe was assassinating itself, not without glory; Joyce, meanwhile — in the intervals between correcting English coursework and improvising articles in Italian for *Il Piccolo della Sera* — composed his vast recreation of a single day in Dublin: 16 June 1904]. Borges's fondness for elevating Joyce's status from an individual author to a whole literature acquires even greater proportions here: 'Más que la obra de un solo hombre, el *Ulises* parece la labor de muchas generaciones' (*OC4* 251) [More than the work of a single man, *Ulysses* seems the labour of many generations]. Finally, the overall impact of Gilbert's study reappears at the end of the note: 'A primera vista [*Ulysses*] es caótico; el libro expositivo de Gilbert — *James Joyce's Ulysses*, 1930 — declara sus estrictas y ocultas leyes. La delicada música de su prosa es incomparable' (*OC4* 251) [At first sight it [*Ulysses*] seems chaotic; the explanatory book of Gilbert — *James Joyce's Ulysses*, 1930 — reveals its strict and hermetic laws. The delicate music of its prose is incomparable]. Moreover, by repeatedly emphasizing that the composition of *Ulysses* took place within the intense political climate of the 'terrible years' of 1914–21, Borges not only draws attention to the significant contextual background that magnifies Joyce's achievement, but is also commenting, time and time again, on events that correspond with his own personal life. In his autobiographical essay, he recalls: 'We were so ignorant of history, however, that we had no idea that the First World War would break in August. My mother and father were in Germany when it happened, but managed to get back to us in Geneva' (*A* 27). In similar circumstances, Joyce and his family were compelled to leave Trieste and move to Zurich where they stayed until 1919. The fact that Borges and Joyce sought refuge in neutral Switzerland during the war remains a decisive historical intersection, which acquires further significance if we consider that later in their lives both writers, by then blind, returned to Zurich and Geneva respectively, their homes from home and, of course, both died and are buried in Switzerland, the cities of their exile.

Towards the end of the note, Borges summarized the cultural legacy of *Ulysses* and concluded that: 'La fama conquistada por el *Ulises* ha sobrevivido al escándalo' (*OC4* 251) [The fame conquered by *Ulysses* outlasted the scandal]. Scandal, of course, refers to the notorious legal history of *Ulysses* and the gradual lifting of the censorship ban in the United States (1933), Ireland (1934), England (1936) and Australia (1937).[59] The 'fama conquistada' alludes to the fact that for more than a decade *Ulysses* had been the constant focus of critical attention — even in a country as distant as Argentina. Therefore, Borges proclaims the victory of *Ulysses* against legal suits and confiscated copies, and welcomes its recent entry into the literary canon. In this sense, Borges was aware that Gilbert's study sought to legitimize the canonical aspects of the work. As Joseph Brooker has claimed, 'Gilbert insists on the classical stasis of Joyce's work and proved effective in enhancing Joyce's claim for the modern canon.'[60] In the final paragraph, Borges announced Joyce's ensuing enterprise, *Work in Progress*, which he described as 'un tejido de lánguidos retruécanos en un inglés veteado de alemán, de italiano y de latín' (*OC4* 251) [a tapestry of languid puns in an English interwoven with German, Italian and Latin]. As if anticipating his own inexorable fate, he concluded with a short statement that anticlimactically foreshadowed his future Homeric inheritance: 'Está ciego' (*OC4* 152) [He is blind].

## 'After Centuries of Literature': Borges's Reception of *Finnegans Wake*

The most remarkable aspect of Borges's 1939 review of *Finnegans Wake* is that it was opportunely released in Buenos Aires on 16 June, Bloomsday. Only an assiduous admirer and *aficionado* of Joyce's work would give careful consideration to this type of numerological correspondence. Borges's review of Joyce's latest novel, however, sets a marked contrast from the more affirmative tone of his previous 1937 biographical sketch. A baffled Borges begins the note with an allusion to the climate of expectation and speculation that usually arises prior to the publication of a book, particularly of Joyce's untitled, long awaited, and much debated embryonic project, *Finnegans Wake*. Thus Borges announced: 'Ha aparecido, al fin, *Work in Progress*, que ahora se titula *Finnegans Wake*, y que constituye, nos dicen, el madurado y lúcido fruto de dieciséis enérgicos años de labor literaria' (*OC4* 436) ['*Work in Progress* has appeared at last, now titled *Finnegans Wake*, and is, they tell us, the ripened and lucid fruit of sixteen energetic years of literary labor'] (*SNF* 195). This is followed by an apathetic observation, 'lo he examinado con alguna perplejidad, he descifrado sin encanto nueve o diez *calembours*, y he recorrido los atemorizados elogios que le dedican la N.R.F. y el suplemento literario de *Times*' (*OC4* 436) ['I have examined it with some bewilderment, have unenthusiastically deciphered nine or ten *calembours*, and have read the terror-stricken praise in the N.R.F. and the T.L.S.'] (*SNF* 195). This half-hearted introduction is then injected with an acid judgment: 'Los agudos autores de esos aplausos dicen haber descubierto la ley de tan complejo laberinto verbal, pero se abstienen de aplicarla o de formularla, y ni siquiera ensayan el análisis de una línea o de un párrafo...' (*OC4* 436) ['The trenchant authors of those accolades claim that they have discovered the rules of this complex verbal labyrinth, but they abstain from applying or formulating them; nor do they attempt the analysis of a single line or paragraph...'] (*SNF* 195). He then sarcastically continues: 'Sospecho que comparten mi perplejidad esencial y mis vislumbres inservibles, parciales' (*OC4* 436) ['I suspect that they share my essential bewilderment and my useless and partial glances at the text'] (*SNF* 195). An inflexible Borges then demanded the emergence of the type of analytical and systematic guide formerly supplied by Gilbert: 'Sospecho que están clandestinamente a la espera (yo públicamente lo estoy) de un tratado exegético de Stuart Gilbert, intérprete oficial de Joyce' (*OC4* 436) ['I suspect that they secretly hope (as I publicly do) for an exegetical treatise from Stuart Gilbert, the official interpreter of James Joyce'] (*SNF* 195). The reader's guide that Borges so anxiously craved for while composing this review took yet another five years to appear. In 1944 the American critics Joseph Campbell and Henry Morton published the full-length study *Skeleton Key to 'Finnegans Wake'*. In his 1978 *Introduction to*

*English Literature*, co-authored with María Esther Vázquez, Borges commented: 'Al cabo de unos años de labor, dos estudiantes norteamericanos han publicado un libro, desgraciadamente indispensable, que se titula *Ganzúa para Finnegan's Wake*' [*sic*] (*OCC* 854)' [After a few years of work, two North American students published a book, unfortunately necessary, entitled *Skeleton Key to Finnegan's Wake* [*sic*]].[61]

What are we supposed to make of Borges's act of reading? It is unquestionable that he was unconvinced by the *Wake*. If the colossal scope and labyrinthine complexity of *Ulysses* had so far exceeded the possibility of a total reading, then Borges viewed *Finnegans Wake* as the ultimate confirmation of an infinite and unintelligible book which overpowered even the most competent of readers.[62] Secondly, it should not be forgotten that the carefully manipulated pose of the baffled reader that Borges is selling here fits the overall historical pattern of the early reader of the *Wake* described by A. Walton Litz:

> When *Finnegans Wake* first appeared in 1939 most readers familiar with *Ulysses* were confounded by what seemed to be a radical change in Joyce's style and technique. Superficially, the dense language of the *Wake* bore little resemblance to even the most complex sections of *Ulysses*. Only those who had studied the fragments of Joyce's *Work in Progress* published during the 1920's and 1930's were prepared for the new language, realizing that it had developed gradually and inevitably out of the method of *Ulysses*.[63]

Borges's review of the *Wake*, however, suffers a drastic change of tone in the second paragraph in which he brushed aside his previous hostile comments, and expounded a more congratulatory assessment of Joyce's contribution to twentieth-century literature:

> Es indiscutible que Joyce es uno de los primeros escritores de nuestro tiempo. Verbalmente, es quizá el primero. En el *Ulises* hay sentencias, hay párrafos, que no son inferiores a los más ilustres de Shakespeare o de Sir Thomas Browne. En el mismo *Finnegans Wake* hay alguna frase memorable. (Por ejemplo, ésta, que no intentaré traducir: *Beside the rivering waters of, hither and thithering waters of, night*.) En este amplio volumen, sin embargo, la eficacia es una excepción (*OC4* 436).
>
> [It is unquestionable that Joyce is one of the best writers of our time. Verbally, he is perhaps the best. In *Ulysses* there are sentences, there are paragraphs, that are not inferior to Shakespeare or Sir Thomas Browne. In *Finnegans Wake* itself there are some memorable phrases. (This one, for example, which I will not attempt to translate: 'Beside the rivering waters of, hither and thithering waters of, night.') In this enormous book, however, efficacy is an exception (*SNF* 195).]

Borges is full of praise for Joyce's linguistic felicities, but full of scorn for his colossal proportions and his arduous demands on the reader. Consequently, he admires Joyce's verbal artistry, principally the poetic quality of the closing lines of 'Anna Livia Plurabelle', which evoke the night-time, riverside scenery of cyclical renewal and metamorphosis. He admires Joyce's lyrical virtuosity, his ability to conjure up a unique, lofty musicality he deems untranslatable in the Spanish language. Overall, Borges's aesthetic manoeuvre seeks to dismantle the novelistic canvas of *Ulysses* and *Finnegans Wake* in a repeated effort to reinvent Joyce from the standpoint of the fragment, the poem, the aphorism and, occasionally, the *ficción*. The hard-headed Borges repeatedly finds himself hitting the same brick wall in his insistence on demolishing the novelistic edifice of Joyce's work in order to appreciate the disjointed, scattered fragments of the construction. Borges's overall disdain for the novelistic genre is well known, and this pet hate is particularly articulated at the end of his 1954 essay 'A Defense of *Bouvard and Pécuchet*': 'El hombre que con *Madame Bovary* forjó la novela realista fue también el primero en romperla. Chesterton, apenas ayer, escribía: "La novela bien puede morir con nosotros." El instinto de Flaubert presintió esa muerte, que ya está aconteciendo — ¿no es el *Ulises*, con sus planos y horarios y precisiones, la espléndida agonía de un género?' (*OC1* 262) ['The man who, with *Madame Bovary*, forged the realist novel was also the first to shatter it. Chesterton, only yesterday, wrote: "The novel may well die with us." Flaubert instinctively sensed that death, which is indeed taking place (is not *Ulysses*, with its maps and timetables and exactitudes the magnificent death throes of a genre?]' (*SNF* 389). By the same token, in a 1976 colloquium that took place in the University of Michigan, Borges cited the final lines of ALP, which in turn prompted the following observation from Donald Yates: 'I wonder why you said recently "I can't accept a novel because I won't be able to do it and because I'm not interested in it".'[64] Borges's response is slightly biased. The master of the microcosmic and utterly economical *ficción* replies that, undoubtedly, you can get as much from a short story as you can get from a novel: 'I think that the last stories that Kipling wrote are quite as fully packed as any novel. For example, I think that "Children of Antioch" is one of the latest stories he wrote. It is packed as any novel, but it is not more than twenty or thirty pages long.'[65] For the miniaturist, Joyce's Modernist experimentation in the vast field of the novel was a waste of talent. Borges's anti-novelistic stance is lucidly conveyed by Salgado: 'Borges commends not the novelist in Joyce, but rather the polished wordsmith who works and reworks scenes and phrases to improve their cadence and musicality, deftly simulating archaic or contemporary prose styles and capturing their peculiar timbre.'[66] In his 1982 interview with Richard Kearney and Seamus Heaney, Borges summarized this attitude:

> Every time I thought of *Ulysses*, it was not the *characters* — Stephen, Bloom or Molly — that came to my mind, but the *words* which produced these characters. This convinced me that Joyce was first and foremost a poet. He was forging poetry out of prose. My subsequent discovery of *Finnegans Wake* and *Pomes Penyeach* confirmed me in this opinion.[67]

Borges elevates the linguistic virtuosity of *Ulysses* at the expense of the main characters, in spite of the fact that in 1925 he successfully rendered into the variant of River Plate Spanish the lyrically infused sexual reverie of the last two pages of Molly's unpunctuated soliloquy. Borges's disbelief in Joyce's representation of the main characters of *Ulysses* led him to make yet another disparaging comment, 'in the case of *Ulysses* you are told thousands of circumstances about the characters. You know, for example, well, you know that they went twice to the men's room, you know all the books they read, you know the exact positions when they are sitting down or standing up, but you don't really know them. It's as if Joyce had gone over them with a microscope or a magnifying glass.'[68] It may be said that Joyce deems a success what Borges considers a failure, thus, the Joycean victory is the inclusion of an unlimited polyvalency which may produce myriad neologisms, as well as disproportionate amounts of information that prolong the narration excessively. Joyce's aesthetic of expansion both shocked and secretly fascinated Borges. In sum, what concerned him here was to exclusively brand Joyce's art from the viewpoint of his aesthetic of compression and to refract Joyce's epic scale through the brief and measured reading of a *ficción*, poem, or aphorism. This attitude reappeared in *This Craft of Verse*, a volume that collects the Norton lectures Borges delivered in Harvard between the years 1967 to 1968. Here, he invoked the closing lines of 'Anna Livia Plurabelle':

> When I speak of night, I am inevitably — and happily for us, I think — reminded of the last sentence of the first book in *Finnegans Wake*, wherein Joyce speaks of 'the rivering waters of, hitherandthithering waters of. Night!' This is an extreme example of an elaborate style. We feel that such a line could have been written only after centuries of literature. We feel that the line is an invention, a poem — a very complex web, as Stevenson would have had it. And yet I suspect there was a moment when the word 'night' was quite as impressive, was quite as strange, was quite as awe-striking as this beautiful, winding sentence.[69]

For Borges, *Finnegans Wake* comprises universal literature and ought to be cyclically conceived at the wake of a long Western tradition. For Borges, then, the *Wake* is none other than a book made up of an entire tradition, a literary microcosm, and a sort of Aleph enveloping a vast literary universe. Time and time again, Borges likes to praise the infinite qualities of Joyce, such as his ability to sum up the history of the English language. For Borges, thus, Joyce is the ultimate artificer, the successor of Shakespeare. And it is precisely this verbal and stylistic mastery that incorporates 'centuries of literature' which Borges deems both attractive, debatable and, ultimately, untranslatable.

Meanwhile, Borges concluded his *El Hogar* review of *Finnegans Wake* with a negative verdict of Joyce's art of punning: '*Finnegans Wake* es una concatenación de retruécanos cometidos en un inglés onírico y que es difícil no calificar de frustrados e incompetentes' (OC4 436) [*Finnegans Wake* is a concatenation of puns rendered in dreamlike English which it may be hard not to label as frustrated and incompetent]. As Waisman has pertinently suggested, this type of assertion 'marks the beginning of Borges's mostly negative reactions to *Finnegans Wake* [...] Borges concludes by suggesting that Joyce borrows from Jules Laforgue and Lewis Carroll in his verbal experiments, making his barb doubly sharp by asserting that Joyce's precursors obtained better results that he did'.[70]

There is, however, an unmistakable touch of irony, defiance, and playfulness at stake in Borges's remarks on *Finnegans Wake*. How serious is the columnist of *El Hogar*, and how consistent are his views of the *Wake*? This question can only be answered through an examination of the review of the *Wake* which Borges published five months later in *Sur*. For all the hostility and detraction with which Borges imbued these notes, we have to bear in mind that he still decided to have the *Wake* reviewed twice, and for better or worse he undertook the honour, once again, of becoming Joyce's foremost Hispanic critic, which is no small feat when the book under examination is *Finnegans Wake*. A review based on an earlier review, here we get a glimpse of Borges's compositional process as he recycles, expands, and edits his previous material. If in *El Hogar* the review occupied a single page column sandwiched between various adverts, in *Sur* the review is not laced with commercial registers and instead occupies a further two pages. What is then added to this second version? On the one hand, Borges had the opportunity to provide a more detailed account of the *Wake* and to offer a sequel to his Bloomsday review in *El Hogar*. It was as if he closed his first note with the to-be-continued promise, as he comfortably shifted from the mass-market readership of *El Hogar* to the more exclusive readership of *Sur*. On the other, the extra space afforded by *Sur* gave Borges free rein to develop one of his pet themes, the heterogeneous catalogue and the study of a writer's precursors. Like the examination of Kafka's precursors that he would publish more than a decade later, or the catalogue of Funes's precursors he was to incorporate in his 1941 obituary of Joyce, Borges humorously theorized an idiosyncratic genealogy of Joyce's forerunners in *Finnegans Wake*. If in *El Hogar* he suggested that the art of punning had been previously mastered by Lewis Carroll and Jules Laforgue, in *Sur* he extended this list with the wide ranging and disparate names of the English poet and critic Algernon Swinburne; the Buenos Aires minor writer Marcelino del Mazo; the Cuban poet Mariano Brull; the French writer (and Argentine resident) Paul Groussac; the English poet and artist Edward Lear; and the German satirist and translator Johann Fischart. This taxonomy is followed by a systematic exposition of Joyce's coinages, nineteen examples in total, hence the title of the review 'Joyce y los neologismos'. But the most noteworthy aspect of Borges's review is his repeated allusion to Joyce's coinages as 'monstruos' [monsters]. In this manner, the act of deciphering Joyce's 'monstruos verbales' (S 164), he wryly purported, demanded a laborious effort, which was alleviated by the previous exegesis of Stuart Gilbert.[71] According to Borges, the linguistic monstrosities of the *Wake* are grounded in the assumption that they fuse different words in order to create a hybrid linguistic teratology.[72] Their degrees of monstrosity, he contends, vary accordingly, but he identifies some as 'melancólicos' [melancholic], 'incomunicados' [disconnected] and 'desarmados' (this may be read as 'fragmented' or 'unarmed', thus, meaning linguistically vulnerable) (S 165). But similarly to his *El Hogar* review of the *Wake*, the pose of the detractor at times gives way to an encomiastic gesture: '*Secular phoenix*, quizá el más memorable de todos'; ['*Secular phoenix* is perhaps the most memorable of them all'], he wrote, 'alude a cierto verso final de *Samson Agonistes*, en que se llama *secular bird* al fénix de periódicas muertes' (S 166); [it alludes to some final line from *Samson Agonistes*, in which the phoenix of cyclical deaths is called *secular bird*]. Last, but not least, he also interpolated a large footnote in which he positively nodded, and creatively expounded, at what he considered 'la más ilustre frase del libro' [the most celebrated phrase of the book]:

> *The walls are of rubinen and the glittergates of elfinbone.* Marfil, en alemán, se dice *elfenbein*, que debe ser una corrupción de *Elefantenbein*; Joyce traduce literalmente *elfinbone*: hueso de elfo. No de otra suerte los evangelios manuscritos del siglo nueve hacen de *margarita* (perla), *mere-grot*: piedra del mar (S 166).

> [*The walls are of rubinen and the glittergates of elfinbone.* Ivory, in German, is called *elfenbein*, which ought to be a corruption of *Elefantenbein*; Joyce translated *elfinbone* literally: bone of elfo. Inevitably, ninth-century manuscripts of the Gospels turn *margarita* (pearl) into *mere-grot*: stone of the sea.]

Without a doubt, such praise is a far cry from his prior hostile labelling of Joyce's puns as monsters. The promissory aspect of this final stance resurfaces almost three decades later in the Norton lectures he delivered at Harvard. Like an uncanny déjà vu, or as a further example of his prodigious Funes-like memory, a blind Borges recited an almost verbatim version of his 1939 review of lines from Book 2, part 1 of the *Wake*:

> 'Glittergates' is Joyce's gift to us. And then we have 'elfinbone.' Of course, when Joyce wrote this, he was thinking of the German for 'ivory,' *Elfenbein*. *Elfenbein* is a distortion of *Elephantenbein*, 'elephant bone.' But Joyce saw the possibilities of that word, and he translated it into English; and then we have 'elfinbone.' I think 'elfin' is more beautiful than 'elfen.' Besides, as we have heard *Elfenbein* so many times, it does not come to us with the shock of surprise, with the shock of amazement, that we find in that new and elegant word 'elfinbone.'[73]

Borges ended this lecture with a final allusion to Joyce which may be read as a public reconciliation with the Irish writer or, more precisely, with the aesthetic of the baroque: 'I think writers like Góngora, John Donne, William Butler Yeats, and James Joyce are justified. Their words, their stanzas may be far-fetched; we may find strange things in them. But we are made to feel that the emotion behind those words is a true one. This should be sufficient for us to tender them our admiration'.[74] This is precisely the reconciliatory attitude he portrays in his 1982 interview with Heaney and Kearney, whereby he invoked a deeper fraternity with his Irish predecessor: 'Looking back on my own writings sixty years after my first encounter with Joyce, I must admit that I have always shared Joyce's fascination with words, and have always worked at my language within an essentially poetic framework, savouring the multiple meanings of words, their etymological echoes and endless resonances.'[75] If Borges claimed a kinship with Joyce's linguistic artistry, which are then the Joycean echoes, particularly Wakean, that we can find concealed in the complex layers of his fictions?

## Borges's Wakean Twists and Turns

The most compelling example of Borges's Wakean virtuosity may be found in his celebrated story 'Tlön, Uqbar, Orbis Tertius', written one year after his 1939 review of *Finnegans Wake*. What concerns us here, principally, is that Borges devised a sentence in the conjectural, idealist language of Tlön, which brings to mind Joyce's dismantling of grammatical conventions in the composite language of *Finnegans Wake*. It is, we may speculate, as if Borges asked himself the question: what would the language of an imaginary planet devoid of nouns look like? We know that he had recently examined and reviewed *Finnegans Wake* twice. Therefore, Borges was aware that the only real, concrete answer to a wide range of linguistic conjectures was contained in Joyce's inventive polyglot and polysemic novel. For example,

'Borges', first person narrator of the story, observes that our accepted grammatical construction '*surgió la luna sobre el río*' (*OC1* 435) ['the moon rose above the river'] (*CF* 73) is rendered in the imaginary language of Tlön — whose chief characteristic is the lack of nouns — as: '*hlör u fang axaxaxas mlö*' (*OC1* 435), which is in turn translated in Spanish as: 'hacia arriba (*upward*) detrás duradero-fluir luneció' (*OC1* 435). A more succinct Spanish translation (attributed to Borges's friend Xul Solar who was renowned, among other things, as an inventor of languages) is provided: 'upa tras perfluyue lunó' as well as its English equivalent: 'Upward, behind the onstreaming it mooned' (*OC1* 435). If we look more closely at the concise English translation we realize that the phrase bears a thematic and morphological likeness with the passage from 'Anna Livia Plurabelle' that Borges had quoted in his 1939 *El Hogar* review of the *Wake*. Central to Borges's coinage of this grammatically subversive passage is his adherence to specific Joycean verbal arrangements, such as the compounding of nouns with monosyllabic prefixes and suffixes, as well as the incorporation of a gerund at the end of a noun. In this manner, Borges compounds the noun 'stream' with the preposition 'on' and the gerund verb form 'ing' in order to suggest the rhythmic flow of the river: 'onstreaming'. Likewise, Joyce generates an analogous construction by compounding the noun 'river' with the gerund 'ing' in order to evoke the similar image of ever-flowing currents at night-time: 'rivering waters of' (*FW* 216.4). It is important to mention that Robin Fiddian has also emphasized the underlying Joycean 'affinity' in Borges's phrase, but instead reads it in relation to Stephen Dedalus' vision of a ship: 'Moving through the air high spars of a threemaster, her sails trailed up on the crosstress homing, upstream, silently moving, a silent ship'.[76] Here Fiddian makes an equally convincing claim about Borges's borrowing of certain linguistic patterns from Joyce in order to compose a highly experimental phrase. Whereas Borges remained hostile to Joyce's linguistic *monstruos*, he none the less saw Joyce as his literary model for the linguistic speculations of the Berkeleian world of Tlön.

Equally significant is the fact that Borges's biographer Emir Rodríguez Monegal states that in the summer of 1940 Borges composed a valid example of the polyglot writing he had identified in his 1939 reviews of *Finnegans Wake*: 'When Silvina [Ocampo] and Bioy [Adolfo Bioy Casares] married in the summer of 1940 [...] Borges was the best man. To inform Bianco [editor of *Sur*] of the event, which had been decided on rather suddenly, they sent him a telegram written in a language they invented, comprised of English, Italian, and Spanish words.'[77] Adhering to the multilingual and portmanteau principles set forth by Joyce in *Finnegans Wake*,[78] Borges et al. concocted the following message: 'Mucho registro civil, mucha iglesia, don't tell anybodini whateverano'.[79] The point Rodríguez Monegal is making here is that despite Borges's condemnation of Joyce's excessive punning, he nevertheless 'was not immune to that type of verbal wit'.[80] In all the complex ambivalence of Borges's literary relationship with Joyce, a one-time assertion may be readily contradicted by another, and a previous antipathy may become a new sympathy.

## Tales from Ireland: Joyce, Yeats, Gogarty, O'Brien

In his search for a Ulyssean tradition in the twentieth-century novel Borges offered a pertinent commentary of Joyce's Irish successor, namely, the Irish novelist and political commentator Brian O'Nualláin, better known under the pseudonym of Flann O'Brien. Borges was particularly impressed by O'Brien's self-reflexive novel, *At-Swim-Two-Birds* (1939):

> *At Swim-two-Birds* no sólo es un laberinto: es una discusión de las muchas maneras de concebir la novela irlandesa y un repertorio de ejercicios en verso y prosa, que ilustran o parodian todos los estilos de Irlanda. La influencia magistral de Joyce (arquitecto de laberintos, también; Proteo literario, también) es innegable, pero no abrumadora, en este libro múltiple (*OC4* 435).

> [*At Swim-two-Birds* is not only a labyrinth: it is a discussion of the many ways to conceive the Irish novel, and a repertory of exercises in prose and verse which illustrate or parody all the styles of Ireland. Joyce's magisterial influence (also architect of labyrinths; also a literary Proteus) is undeniable, but not disproportionate in this manifold book (*SNF* 162).]

Borges identified in O'Brien a number of fundamental aspects of Joyce's work: the figure of the labyrinth, a twentieth-century parodist, a multilayered work, and the inevitable inscription in an Irish literary tradition. In this way, Joseph Brooker has recently described the work of O'Brien as: 'The most vivid and protracted response to Joyce'.[81] The storyline of *At-Swim-Two-Birds* — which displays a wide range of metafictional devices — would have struck a perfect chord with Borges who at precisely this time started writing the revolutionary *ficciones* that would eventually give him worldwide notoriety. It is also remarkable that O'Brien's book (published in London, March 1939) was already being reviewed by Borges in *El Hogar* as early as 2 June 1939. An essential pioneering impulse lies at the heart of Borges's early reception of O'Brien in Latin America, just as in 1925 he had also deemed himself Joyce's first Hispanic adventurer. Indeed, Borges was tirelessly looking in the vast mirror of Irish art, searching for the manifold figures and reflections that he would later transpose onto his own creative experience. The fraternity between the literatures of Ireland and Argentina — or the way in which the Argentine writer must look to an Irish tradition as an exemplary literary model — remained at the forefront of Borges's seminal lecture 'The Argentine Writer and Tradition'. Across the gulf that separates Borges's utter conciseness and Joyce's (and O'Brien's) novelistic tradition, are hidden a fascinating series of symmetries. For example, Borges's summary of the story line of *At-Swim-Two-Birds* reads, ironically, like a Borgesian fiction:

> Un estudiante de Dublín escribe una novela sobre un tabernero de Dublín que escribe una novela sobre los parroquianos de su taberna (entre quienes está el estudiante), que a su vez escriben novelas donde figuran el tabernero y el estudiante, y otros compositores de novelas sobre otros novelistas. Forman el libro los muy diversos manuscritos de esas personas reales o imaginarias, copiosamente anotados por el estudiante (*OC4* 435).

[A student in Dublin writes a novel about the proprietor of a Dublin public house, who writes a novel about the habitués of his pub (among them, the student), who in their turn write novels in which proprietor and student figure along with other writers of novels about other novelists. The book consists of the extremely diverse manuscripts of these real or imagined persons, copiously annotated by the student (*SNF* 162).]

It reads like the type of infinitely regressive plots Borges would invent and then teasingly credit to imaginary authors such as Herbert Quain in 'A Survey of the Works of Herbert Quain'; or like the endless series of dreams within dreams which dimly occur during the 'unánime noche' (*OC1* 451) [unanimous night] of 'The Circular Ruins'; or the multiple possibilities in the invisible labyrinth of time in 'The Garden of Forking Paths', those dimensions of time which may go on *ad infinitum* and which in turn recall the cyclical nature of *Finnegans Wake*.

Thus Borges's journey through Irish literature gradually progressed from Joyce to Yeats, O'Brien, and Gogarty. In the October 1936 section 'Literary Life' Borges recounts Joyce's often-cited first meeting with Yeats. In Chapter VII of his monumental biography, Richard Ellmann retells Yeats's version of his first exchange with the young Joyce: 'Presently he got up to go, and, as he was going out, he said, "I am twenty. How old are you?" I told him, but I am afraid I said I was a year younger than I am. He said with a sigh, "I thought as much. I have met you too late. You are too old"' (*JJII* 103). What concerns us here is that Borges incorporated his own variation of this anecdote in his bi-weekly column of *El Hogar*. Moreover, he astutely coordinated Joyce's meeting with Yeats with yet another criss-crossing between the two Irish writers, namely Joyce's refusal to sign the petition against Yeats's controversial play *The Countess Cathleen*:

> James Joyce fue el único estudiante que en la Universidad de Dublin se negó a firmar una nota de protesta contra el poeta W. B. Yeats, por su drama 'Countess Cathleen'. Años después, cuando por primera vez se encontraron, Joyce le dijo a Yeats:
> '¡Qué lastima que no nos hayamos conocido antes! Usted es demasiado viejo para ser influenciado por mí.'[82]

> James Joyce was the only student of University College, Dublin who refused to sign a note of protest against W. B. Yeats's drama 'Countess Cathleen'. Several years later, when they met for the first time, Joyce said to Yeats:
> 'We have met too late! You are too old to be influenced by me.'

These anecdotes gave rise to another Irish tale — in this case refracted through Joyce and Yeats — which appeared in the 1938 section of 'Literary Life'. It concerns the famous escape of the poet, novelist, and surgeon Oliver St John Gogarty during the Irish Civil War, coincidentally an anecdote that at the time had highly amused Joyce. As Richard Ellmann reports: 'The only incident that amused him in the Irish Civil War was Gogarty's escape from I.R.A. troops by plunging into the Liffey and swimming to safety' (*JJII* N.535). If in *Ulysses* Joyce turned Gogarty into the infamous and grotesque 'plump Buck Mulligan' (*U* 1.1), Borges similarly saw Gogarty as the subject of literary inspiration; but while a scornful Joyce had mocked him, Borges, fascinated by Gogarty's glorious escape, provided him a more dignified fate by turning the historical incident into a legend of heroism and supernatural intervention. Moreover, this journalistic report on an Irish theme may also be classified as a Borgesian *ficción*, or so called 'fable' in its own right, and due to its conciseness it can be cited in full:

> Durante la última de las guerras civiles de Irlanda, el poeta Oliver Gogarty fue aprisionado por los hombres de Ulster en un caserón a orillas del Barrow, en el condado de Kildare. Comprendió que al amanecer lo fusilarían. Salió con un pretexto al jardín y se arrojó a las aguas glaciales. La noche se agrandó de balazos. Al nadar bajo el agua renegrida, en la que reventaban las balas, le prometió dos cisnes al río si éste lo dejaba en la otra ribera. El dios del río lo escuchó y lo salvó y el hombre cumplió el voto (*OC4* 395).
>
> [Toward the end of the civil war in Ireland, the poet Oliver Gogarty was imprisoned by some Ulster men in a huge house on the banks of the Barrow, in County Kildare. He knew that at dawn he would be shot. Under some pretext, he went into the garden and threw himself into the glacial waters. The night grew large with gunshots. Swimming under the black water exploding with bullets, he promised the river that he would give it two swans if it allowed him to reach the other bank. The god of the river heard him and saved him, and the poet [el hombre] fulfilled his pledge (*SNF* 190).]

Yet it must be mentioned that the main source of Borges's Gogarty *ficción* was *The Oxford Book of Modern Verse*, edited by W. B. Yeats, a book he reviewed for *El Hogar* in May 1937 (see *OC4* 291–92). Significantly, this slim volume had a lengthy introduction in which Yeats justified the somehow disproportionate inclusion of seventeen poems by his friend Oliver Gogarty, whom he deemed 'one of the great lyric poets of our age'.[83] The disproportionateness of the Gogarty entry in the anthology becomes even more apparent if viewed in comparison to the meagre inclusion of only three poems by Joyce. It appears, then, that Borges based his *El Hogar* version of Gogarty's escape on the first-hand account offered by Yeats in his introduction. Yeats's report goes thus:

> Twelve years ago Oliver Gogarty was captured by his enemies, imprisoned in a deserted house on the edge of the Liffey with every prospect of death. Pleading a natural necessity he got into the garden, plunged under a shower of revolver bullets and as he swam the ice-cold December stream promised it, should it land him to safety, two swans. I was present when he fulfilled that vow.[84]

It is unmistakable that Borges offered his readers of *El Hogar* a rewriting of Yeats's résumé of Gogarty's escape, inasmuch as the task of the translator involved, for Borges, an uplifting and re-creative experience. Since Borges's 'tale of Gogarty' is directed to a readership that may not have known the various intricacies of the Irish Civil War, Borges padded his vignette with additional historical details. Therefore, Yeats's indefinite 'twelve years ago' becomes in Borges 'toward the end of the civil war'. Similarly, Yeats's vaguely defined 'enemies' and 'house on the edge of the Liffey' is rendered by Borges as 'some Ulster men' and 'a house on the banks of the Barrow, in County Kildare'. The decorous Borges omits Yeats's 'pleading a natural necessity' and instead substitutes it for the more general 'under some pretext'. In a remarkable fictional twist, Borges poetically infuses Yeats's 'under a shower of revolver bullets' and turns it into 'the night grew large with gunshots'. Finally, Gogarty's salvation plea to the river Liffey is enriched by Borges with a more ritualistic invocation to the pagan powers of the god of the river, who is in turn reported to 'have heard him and saved him'. Borges, of course, was careful to delete Yeats's final intrusion in the narrative, whereby he claimed to have been present 'when he [Gogarty] fulfilled that vow'.

## Notes to Chapter 2

1. See, *OC1*, pp. 232; 262; 266; 363; 418. See also, *S* pp. 27; 140–41; 206; 214. And, *OC4* pp. 217; 235–36; 258; 272; 291; 319; 324; 353; 355; 435.
2. John King, *Sur: A Study of the Argentine Literary Journal and its Role in the Development of a Culture, 1931–1970* (Cambridge: Cambridge University Press, 1986), p. 201.
3. For a list of all the foreign writers translated by *Sur*, see Doris Meyer, *Against the Wind and the Tide: Victoria Ocampo*, with a selection of essays by Victoria Ocampo, trans. by Doris Meyer (Austin: University of Texas Press, 1990), p. 115.
4. James Joyce, *Esteban el héroe*, trans. by Roberto Bixio (Buenos Aires: Sur, 1960).
5. James Joyce, *Desterrados*, trans. by A. Jiménez Fraud (Buenos Aires: Sur, 1937).
6. Patrick O'Neill, *Polyglot Joyce: Fictions of Translation* (Toronto: University of Toronto Press, 2005), p. 72.
7. O'Neill, p. 72.
8. James Joyce, *La noche de Ulises: adaptación dramática por Marjorie Barkentin*, Introducción de Padraic Colum, traducido por Celia Paschero y Juan Carlos Pellegrini (Buenos Aires: Sur, 1958).
9. Laura Mara Lojo Rodríguez ,' "A gaping mouth, but no words": Virginia Woolf Enters the Land of the Butterflies', in *The Reception of Virginia Woolf in Europe*, ed. by Mary Ann Caws and Nicola Luckhurst (London: Continuum: 2002), pp. 218–47 (p. 239).
10. Meyer, p. 101.
11. Meyer, p. 102.
12. Hermione Lee, *Virginia Woolf* (London: Chatto & Windus, 1996), p. 660.
13. Borges later acknowledged, however, that he co-translated *A Room of One's Own* with his mother, Doña Leonor Acevedo de Borges. See Jorge Luis Borges, *En diálogo II*, with Osvaldo Ferrari (Buenos Aires: Sudamericana, 1986), p. 108.
14. For a fascinating study of Borges's translations of Woolf see Patricia Willson, *La constelación del sur*, pp. 132–60.
15. Lojo Rodríguez, p. 235.
16. King, p. 81. King has also persuasively demonstrated the influence that the review *Sur* had on celebrated Latin American writers such as Octavio Paz, Mario Vargas Llosa and, of course, Gabriel García Márquez. See pp. 78–80; pp. 143–44.
17. Revol later published *Teoría del monólogo interior* (Córdoba: Univ. Nacional de Córdoba, 1965) and *La Tradición imaginaria: de Joyce a Borges* (Córdoba: Univ. Nacional de Córdoba, 1971).
18. Joseph Brooker, *Joyce's Critics: Transitions in Reading and Culture* (Madison: University of Wisconsin Press, 2004), pp. 60–61.
19. Jean-Michel Rabaté, 'Modernism and "The Plain Reader's Rights": Duff-Riding-Graves Re-reading Joyce', in *European Joyce Studies: Joyce's Audiences*, ed. by John Nash (Amsterdam: Rodopi, 2000), pp. 29–39 (p. 36). Rabaté also argues that 'Joyce was not only pleased with efforts like Duff's and Ogden's, but also incorporated them into the very substance of *Finnegans Wake*', p. 37.
20. Charles Duff, *James Joyce and the Plain Reader*, with a prefatory letter by Herbert Read, 2nd edn (London: Desmond Harmsworth, 1932), p. 6.
21. Duff, pp. 36–37.
22. Duff, p. 77.
23. Duff, p. 24. This is translated in *Sur* as 'a ese trabajo [Gilbert] habrá de recurrir el lector corriente que no tenga ni pueda procurarse el texto completo de Ulises' (p. 90).

24. See Brooker, p. 61.
25. As I demonstrated in Chapter 1, Borges performed a careful reading of Larbaud's 1921 lecture on Joyce, which was later published in *La Nouvelle Revue Française*. Therefore what ought to be stressed here is that Larbaud's essay stayed in Borges's mind for quite some time, so much so that in his conclusion of 'Narrative Art and Magic', as well as incorporating Duff, he also echoed Larbaud's prior pronouncements: 'We begin to discover and to anticipate symbols, a design, a plan, in what appeared to us at first a brilliant but confused mass of notations [...] and we realise that we are before a much more complicated book than we had supposed, that everything which appeared arbitrary and sometimes extravagant is really deliberate and premeditated', Valery Larbaud, 'The "Ulysses" of James Joyce' *The Criterion*, 1 (1922–1923), 94–103 (p. 97), translator unknown. See also Salgado, 'Barroco Joyce', for an insightful discussion of Borges's references to Gilbert and Larbaud in 'The Garden of Forking Paths'.
26. See the publicity spaces situated at the beginning of *Sur*, 76 (1941).
27. See José Lezama Lima, 'Muerte de Joyce', *Grafos*, 9 (1941), 16. This article was subsequently reprinted in José Lezama Lima, *Obras completas*, 2 vols (México: Aguilar, 1977), pp. 236–38.
28. Salgado, 'Barroco Joyce', p. 79.
29. Salgado, 'Barroco Joyce', p. 79.
30. For a discussion of these essays see Salgado, *From Modernism to Neobaroque: Joyce and Lezama Lima* (Lewisburg, PA: Bucknell University Press, 2001), p. 224, n. 5.
31. See James Joyce, *Gente de Dublín*, trad. Ignacio Abelló (Barcelona: Tartessos, 1942). See also the celebrated 1974 version *Dublineses* by the Cuban writer Guillermo Cabrera Infante (Madrid: Alianza editorial, 1974).
32. See C. G. Jung, *¿Quién es Ulises?*, traducción de Ortega y Gasset (Buenos Aires: Santiago Rueda, 1944). See Herbert Gorman, *James Joyce: El hombre que escribió Ulises*, traducido por Máximo Siminovich (Buenos Aires: Santiago Rueda, 1945).
33. Frank Budgen, *James Joyce and the Making of Ulysses* (London: Grayson & Grayson, 1934).
34. Francine Masiello, 'Joyce in Buenos Aires (Talking Sexuality through Translation)', *Diacritics*, 34.3 (2004), 55–72 (p. 63).
35. Masiello, p. 63.
36. César Fernández Moreno, reseña de C. G. Jung, *¿Quién es Ulises?*, *Sur*, 120 (1944), 79–82 (p. 81), my translation.
37. For a fascinating discussion of the Irish migration to Argentina see Katherine Mullin, 'Don't cry for me, Argentina: "Eveline" and the Seductions of Emigration Propaganda', in *Semicolonial Joyce*, ed. by Derek Attridge and Marjorie Howes (Cambridge: Cambridge University Press, 2000), pp. 172–200 (p. 175).
38. See Stuart Gilbert, 'L'ambiance Latine de L'art de James Joyce', *Fontaine*, 37–40 (1944), 79–88.
39. See *Contrapunto*, 4 (1945), 12. This review also published an essay by Jacques Mercaton, 'James Joyce', translated by José Mora Guarnido, 5 (1945), 2–3.
40. Rodríguez Monegal, p. 286.
41. Rodríguez Monegal also states that 'some of the more established Argentine and Spanish writers contributed regularly to it', p. 286.
42. Gifford, p. 386.
43. Homer, *The Odyssey*, trans. by Robert Fitzgerald (London: The Harvill Press, 1996), p. 116.
44. 'Para ser hermosa: lo que interesa cuidar cuando se hace el arreglo de los ojos', *El Hogar*, 16 de junio, 1939, p. 64.
45. *Holy Bible: The New King James Version* (Nashville: Thomas Nelson, 1982), Matthew 6. 22–23.
46. *El Hogar*, 16 de Junio 1939, p. 64.
47. *El Hogar*, 16 de Junio 1939, p. 46.
48. *El Hogar*, 16 de Junio 1939, p. 46.
49. Gary Leonard, *Advertising and Commodity Culture in Joyce* (Gainesville: University Press of Florida, 1998), p. 12.
50. Leonard, p. 30. See also David Pierce, *James Joyce's Ireland* (New Haven, CT, and London: Yale University Press, 1992) for a reproduction of 'The Sisters' as it first appeared in *The Irish Homestead*, pp. 148–49.
51. Silvia Barei, *Borges y la crítica literaria* (Madrid: Tauro, 1999), p. 42.

52. She is referring here to a claim made by Roberto Alifano. See Barei, p. 42.
53. Monegal, p. 287.
54. See Barei, pp. 11–12.
55. Jorge Luis Borges, *Textos cautivos*, pp. 21–22, my translation.
56. Levine, p. 346.
57. See Duff, p. 31. However, in his 1924 study Gorman also reports that 'In 1904 he married Nora, the daughter of Thomas and Ann Barnacle, of Galway', p. 231.
58. Duff, p. 34.
59. See Vanderham, p. 5.
60. Brooker, p. 76.
61. This typographical mistake is certainly not Borges's. Since by the time he co-authored this book he was totally blind, the error corresponds to the typist.
62. It may be argued that Borges's first acquaintance with *Work in Progress* took place at the end of 1936. This can be deduced from a statement which appeared in a December 1936 note on the Argentine poet Enrique Banchs, whereby he anticipates his hostile reception of the *Finnegans Wake* (see *OC4* 235–37). Borges would have read, however, Duff's brief discussion of ALP in *James Joyce and the Plain Reader*.
63. A. Walton Litz, *The Art of James Joyce: Method and Design in Ulysses and Finnegans Wake* (New York: Oxford University Press, 1964), p. 76.
64. *Jorge Luis Borges: Conversations*, ed. by Richard Burgin (Jackson: University Press of Mississippi, 1998), p. 159.
65. Burgin, p. 159.
66. Salgado, 'Barroco Joyce', p. 69.
67. Kearney, p. 48.
68. Burgin, p. 36.
69. Jorge Luis Borges, *This Craft of Verse*, ed. by Colin-Andrei Mihailescu (Cambridge, MA: Harvard University Press, 2000), pp. 88–89.
70. Sergio Waisman, *Borges and Translation: The Irreverence of the Periphery* (Lewisburg, PA: Bucknell University Press, 2005), pp. 175, 177.
71. Borges is referring here to Stuart Gilbert's article, 'Thesaurus Minusculus: A Short Commentary on a Paragraph of *Work-in-Progress*', originally published in the literary journal *transition*, 16–17 (1928), 15–24.
72. See Waisman, *Borges and Translation*, for an insightful discussion of Borges's analysis of these puns, pp. 178–83.
73. Borges, *This Craft of Verse*, pp. 89–90.
74. Borges, *This Craft of Verse*, p. 85.
75. Kearney, p. 49.
76. Fiddian, pp. 28–29.
77. Rodríguez Monegal, p. 343.
78. Rodríguez Monegal, p. 344.
79. Rodríguez Monegal, p. 344.
80. Rodríguez Monegal, p. 344.
81. Brooker, p. 198.
82. Jorge Luis Borges, *Borges en 'El Hogar': 1935–1958* (Buenos Aires: Emecé, 2000), pp. 18–19.
83. W. B. Yeats (ed.), *The Oxford Book of Modern Verse: 1892–1935* (Oxford: Clarendon Press, 1936), p. xv.
84. Yeats, p. xv.

CHAPTER 3

# James Joyce, Author of 'Funes the Memorious'

## Funes and His Precursors

In 'Kafka and his Precursors' (1951) Borges famously postulated a radical model of reading that dismantled the idea of chronological influence and proposed instead an inverted *modus operandi* in which 'cada escritor crea a sus precursores' (*OC2* 90) ['each writer *creates* his own precursors'] (*SNF* 365). He argued that Kafka's writings allow the construction of a network of shared idiosyncrasies with a series of pre-existent texts, since it is possible to recognize the voice of Kafka in the writings of Zeno, Han Yu, Kierkegaard, Bloy, Browning and Lord Dunsany. Whilst the later writings of Kafka connect all these heterogeneous pieces, without Kafka, the analogy uniting these literatures from different epochs and places would have not been noticed: 'En cada uno de esos textos está la idiosincrasia de Kafka, en grado mayor o menor, pero si Kafka no hubiera escrito, no la percibiríamos; vale decir, no existiría' (*OC2* 89) ['Kafka's idiosyncrasy is present in each of these writings, to a greater or lesser degree, but if Kafka had not written, we would not perceived it; that is to say, it would not exist'] (*SNF* 365). In effect, Borges's suggestion that texts are not isolated entities recalls the similar conclusion he reached in his 1935 essay 'The translators of *The Thousand and One Nights*', in which he stressed that certain works 'sólo se dejan concebir después de una literatura' ['can only be conceived *in the wake of a literature*'] and as a consequence presuppose 'un rico proceso anterior' (*OC1* 411) ['a rich (prior) process'] (*SNF* 108). The richness of this process lies in the conception of a text as the confluence of several pre-existing discourses, a hybrid composite that enters into dialogue with other texts. Borges proposes a retroactive model of reading through which the reading of Kafka will affect the reading of these texts and thus the texts themselves: 'Su labor modifica nuestra concepción del pasado, como ha de modificar el futuro' (*OC2* 90) ['His work modifies our conception of the past, as it will modify the future'] (*SNF* 365). And yet, fundamental to Borges's radical theory on the subject of literary influence is the assumption that 'Kafka and His Precursors' was not created *ex nihilo*, but rather stands as a continuation and development of T. S. Eliot's seminal essay 'Tradition and the Individual Talent' (1919), which is duly quoted as its main intertextual source (see *SNF* 365). The main argument uniting both theses is apparent: Eliot postulates an aesthetic principle, through which writers are not read in isolation, but as part of a living tradition in which the new alters the old, the present modifies the past and, as a result, texts are continually re-valued from the perspective of subsequent texts:

> The existing monuments form an ideal order among themselves, which is modified by the introduction of the new (the really new) work of art among them. The existing order is complete before the new work arrives; for order to persist after the supervention of novelty, the *whole* existing order must be, if ever so slightly, altered; and so the relations, proportions, values of each work of art toward the whole are readjusted; and this is conformity between the old and the new.[1]

If Eliot's theory is applied not just to art but also to criticism, then Borges's 'Kafka and His Precursors' (the really new) posits a modification to the existing order of Eliot's literary system of values. But unlike Eliot's inevitably canonical, Westernized conception of a tradition that strictly comprises 'the mind of Europe',[2] Borges's idea of a tradition is less prescriptive and more wide-ranging, conflating Western, oriental and marginal discourses alike, insofar as it exposes the perspective of a writer located, as Beatriz Sarlo puts it, 'on the limits between cultures, between literary genres, between languages [...] Borges is the writer of the *orillas*, a marginal in the centre, a cosmopolitan on the edge'.[3] Borges, therefore, irreverently articulates what Eliot's innovative yet Eurocentric vision can only insinuate from an inescapably restrictive standpoint. In other words, Borges enlarges, enriches and synthesizes Eliot's theory in the brief, egalitarian and paradoxical phrase: 'cada escritor crea a sus precursores' (*OC2* 90) ['each writer *creates* his precursors'] (*SNF* 365). As a suitable application to his theory he unfolds a concrete case in point, namely a study of Kafka that thoroughly illustrates the idea of a synchronous tradition in which writers may influence both past and future texts. Thus Borges's anatomy of literary influence obeys neither chronological nor coherently or culturally organized systems of thought. If any similarity prevails in his taxonomy of precursors, this is only justified by virtue of the fact that although the heterogeneous pieces do not resemble each other, they nonetheless resemble Kafka.

When studying the central role that Eliot's 'Tradition and the Individual Talent' played in the composition of 'Kafka and his Precursors' it remains a highly instructive methodology to go back to Borges's earlier writings, particularly to a lesser known essay 'Eternity and T. S. Eliot' (1933), originally published in the Buenos Aires review *Poesía*. In this revelatory journalistic piece, which in turn serves as an avant-text of 'Kafka and his Precursors', Borges quotes Eliot extensively, signalling, consequently, a vital interpretative process that foregrounds his subsequent use of the essay (see *TR1* 49–53). The existence of this article highlights the important assumption that the compositional process of 'Kafka and His Precursors' involved a much more complex interweaving of texts. This is signalled at the beginning of the essay, in which Borges warns the reader about the existence of a preceding series of reflections: 'Yo premedité alguna vez un examen de los precursores de Kafka' (*OC2* 88) ['At one time, I considered writing a study of Kafka's precursors'] (*SF* 363).[4] Such a procedure emphasizes, once again, an integral aspect of Borges's practice of writing, which is based on the creation of literary genealogies. Yet Borges's fascination with genealogies is not only concerned with the work of others, but is equally drawn to his own writings, particularly in what Ronald Christ refers as: '[Borges's aim] at creating in us an awareness of his "sources" or "*fuentes*".'[5] Just as Borges sets himself the task of constructing a network of Kafka's precursors via Eliot's seminal essay, so he equally subjects his own rhetoric to analogous exercises that aim to undermine the uniqueness of his writing, and instead privileges the activities of citation, rewriting and plagiarism. He prolixly lists his sources and precursors in the explicatory prefaces and afterwords of his fictions, generously mapping influences of the most varied origins. Central to Borges's activity of appropriation is the assumption that, ultimately, all texts are woven out of pre-existent texts, and no discourse is ever complete since it is always repositioned in relation to preceding or subsequent discourses. This type of intertextual exercise is similarly foregrounded in his 1941 obituary 'A Fragment on Joyce', in which Borges seeks to establish a network of forerunners for his then work-in-progress, 'Funes the Memorious'. In this manner, he anticipates the literary precepts later postulated in 'Kafka and His Precursors' and creates his own precursors by recognizing the voice and mnemonic habits of his character Ireneo Funes in a series of pre-existent texts. With unreserved audacity and customary cheek, he proclaimed Joyce's *Ulysses* and Nietzsche's *Zarathustra* as the 'monstrous' pre-texts of his mnemonic character:

> Del compadrito mágico de mi cuento cabe afirmar que es un precursor de los superhombres, un Zarathustra suburbano y parcial; lo indiscutible es que es un monstruo. Lo he recordado porque la consecutiva y recta lectura de las cuatrocientas mil palabras de *Ulises* exigiría monstruos análogos. (Nada aventuraré sobre los que exigiría *Finnegans Wake*: para mí no menos inconcebibles que la cuarta dimensión de C. H. Hinton o que la Trinidad de Nicea) (*S* 168).
>
> [My story's magical *compadrito* may be called a precursor of the coming race of supermen, a partial Zarathustra of the outskirts of Buenos Aires; indisputably he is a monster. I have evoked him because a consecutive, straightforward reading of the four hundred thousand words of *Ulysses* would require similar monsters. (I will not venture to speak of what *Finnegans Wake* would demand; for me, its readers are no less inconceivable than C. H. Hinton's fourth dimension or the trinity of Nicaea) (*SNF* 220–21).]

For Borges, then, a consecutive, total reading of *Ulysses* demanded the creation of Funes, a fictional character equipped with an infinite memory and, hence, capable of assimilating, in one single reading, the sheer enormity of Joyce's modernist novel. Thus Borges writes his Uruguayan gaucho Ireneo Funes as a Joycean fiction or, more precisely, as the ideal reader of *Ulysses*, and endows him with the all-encompassing memory of his predecessor. If Borges's parenthetical *addendum* is considered part of Funes's precursors, then his network is enlarged by discourses apparently as dissimilar as Joyce's *Finnegans Wake*, C. H. Hinton's fourth dimension and the Christian dogma of the Nicene Creed. Funes, an avid polyglot whose auto-didactical method consists in memorizing entire dictionaries, embodies the type of intellect required for the reading of *Finnegans Wake*, and his persistent state of insomnia, moreover, turns him into Joyce's ideal insomniac, 'as were it sentenced to be nuzzled over a full trillion times for ever and a night till his noddle sink or swim by that ideal reader suffering from an ideal insomnia' (*FW* 120.12–14). As for Borges's eccentric genealogy of Funes it suffices to say that it does not end here. On the contrary, it becomes subsequently expanded in the definitive version of the story that proposes a more extended genealogy, taking on board the names of Pliny the Elder and John Locke.[6] If this is so, Borges's Ireneo Funes acts as the unifying element without whom the network would not have been possible, therefore serving as the central node in an assembly of highly heterogeneous texts. Thus, my proposed sub-heading 'Funes and his precursors' equally aims to unlock Borges's own textual predecessors: James Joyce, Friedrich Nietzsche, John Locke and Pliny the Elder: all of which intersect in the mnemonic eccentricity of his nineteenth-century South American hero.

This chapter explores the pervasive presence of James Joyce in 'Funes the Memorious' both in its embryonic and definitive versions. It will demonstrate that in his 1941 obituary, 'A Fragment on Joyce', Borges uncovered a landscape of memory that charted a genealogy of Funes and his precursors, whereby he declared Joyce's *Ulysses* as the infinite and monstrous precursor of Ireneo Funes, his Fray Bentos gaucho endowed with an infinite memory after a fall from a horse, and who ironically dies in 1889 of pulmonary congestion. It will argue that Borges's 1941 obituary may be read as an anticipation of the literary precepts later postulated in 'Kafka and his precursors', since Borges searches for the voice and mnemonic habits of Funes in Joyce's *Ulysses*. This chapter will show, meanwhile, that the analogies interlinking Funes and *Ulysses*, particularly in the 'Cyclops' and 'Ithaca' episodes, are centred on the subject of memory as an encyclopaedia and literary archive. At the same time, however, it will raise the central question, how do Borges and Joyce negotiate the remembering–forgetting polarity? The chapter will offer a number of answers to this question. Among these, it will underline the crucial fact that Borges and Joyce have incorporated alternative narratives in which they emphasize the conflictual forces inherent in any totalization of knowledge by turning the memories of Funes and the catalogues of the 'Cyclops' and 'Ithaca' episodes respectively into a humorous record of the impossibility and, ultimately, uselessness of a total categorization of knowledge.

## James Joyce and the Making of Funes

In *Borges and His Fiction*, Gene Bell-Villada views 'A Fragment on Joyce' as a 'fascinating documentary record of the artistic transformation of the character Funes in Borges's mind'.[7] Indeed, we have in front of us a multifaceted document that deploys several textual transactions at once: an early draft or pre-text of 'Funes the Memorious', a study in the subject of literary influence, an exercise in comparative literature, an obituary marking the untimely death of James Joyce in Zurich in January 1941, and a journalistic publication in the prestigious Buenos Aires literary review *Sur* for which Borges acted as a regular correspondent. If studied as a work-in-progress of 'Funes the Memorious', then, 'A Fragment on Joyce' constitutes a relevant example of genetic criticism, allowing the reconstruction of the crucial textual processes that took place during Borges's gestation of the character Funes. Such complex exercise validates, moreover, Borges's recurrent thesis that there is no 'texto definitivo' (*OC1* 239) [definitive text] but only a series of 'borradores' [drafts] in an ongoing interpretative process. In effect, the artistic growth of Funes is particularly determined by the several superimposed parchments that emerge as we map out his development from a journalistic column in *Sur* to a fully fledged story in *Ficciones*. This palimpsestual quality is particularly apparent in an extract from 'A Fragment on Joyce' which re-appeared almost verbatim in the 1942 version of the story:

> Nosotros, de un vistazo, percibimos tres copas en una mesa; Funes, todas las hojas y racimos que comprende una parra. Sabía las formas de las nubes australes del amanecer del treinta de abril de mil ochocientos ochenta y dos y podía compararlas en el recuerdo con las vetas de un libro en pasta española que manejó una vez en la infancia (*S* 167).

> [We, at first glance, perceive three glasses on a table; Funes, every leaf and grape on a vine. He knew the shapes of the southernmost clouds in the sunrise of April 30, 1882, and he could compare them in his memory to the veins in the stiff marbled binding of a book he once held in his hands during his childhood (*SNF* 220).]

> Nosotros, de un vistazo, percibimos tres copas en una mesa; Funes, todos los vástagos y racimos y frutos que comprende una parra. Sabía las formas de las nubes australes del amanecer del treinta de abril de mil ochocientos ochenta y dos y podía compararlas en el recuerdo con las vetas de un libro en pasta española que solo había mirado una vez. (*OC1* 488).

> [We, at one glance, can perceive three glasses on a table; Funes, all the leaves and tendrils and fruit that make up a grape vine. He knew by heart the forms of the southern clouds at dawn on 30 April 1882, and could compare them in his memory with the mottled streaks on a book in Spanish binding he had only seen once (*L* 91–92).]

But we should not be fooled here by the similarities between the two extracts. Indeed, as Borges humorously demonstrated in 'Pierre Menard Author of the Quixote', even the ambitious translation undertaken by the French turn-of-the-century writer Pierre Menard failed to guarantee, despite its strict verbatim rendering, exact textual equivalence. What these nearly identical Funes extracts are foregrounding here is the central fact that the procedure of transferring a passage from a text (A) into another text (B) implies the shifting of meaning into a new context. This process produces, consequently, a certain degree of effacement of the textual circumstances of the original text in relation to the new signification it acquires under its new context. By the time Borges completed the 1942 story he made sure that he cleansed it of its previous associations with the 1941 obituary resulting, thus, in the omission of the preliminary comparison between Funes and *Ulysses*, as well as the disappearance of the Joycean frame in which Funes had been initially incorporated. This raises important questions, such as, for instance: what is the trajectory of Funes as a character from his evolutionary growth in 'A Fragment on Joyce' to his ensuing development into his own short story, 'Funes the Memorious'? Does he, as the finished product of the 1942 story eventually published in *Ficciones*, preserve the layers of meaning of the 1941 obituary it has traversed? And, to what extent may the authorial validity of James Joyce, who was subsequently erased from the 1942 version, become, once again, visible through a retroactive reading of the 1941 obituary?

Let us consider, as a preliminary example, a key anecdote from Borges's résumé of the brief life of Funes in 'A Fragment on Joyce', wherein he offers an interesting snapshot of a juvenile Funes engaging in a pictorial reproduction of two chapters from a school manual: 'En la niñez, lo han expulsado de la escuela primaria por calcar servilmente un par de capítulos, con sus ilustraciones, mapas, viñetas, letras de molde y hasta con una errata…' (S 167) ['In childhood, he was expelled from primary school for having slavishly copied out two chapters, along with their illustrations, maps, vignettes, block letters, and even a corrigendum'] (SNF 220).[8] While the ordinary, generalizing memories of school children would only retain selected fragments from a book (or would only be interested in taking a small number of notes to synthesize the main ideas) Ireneo Funes contrarily aspires to a meticulous reconstruction that will allow him the retrieval of even the most infinitesimal and insignificant details. Here, then, Funes is already manifesting his subsequent incapacity for selection and abstraction, an intellectual impediment that Borges thereafter develops as his main mnemonic flaw in 'Funes the Memorious'. Moreover, Borges's reference to a precocious Funes, whose capacity for detail and endeavour for exact representation goes back to his boyhood years, bears a striking likeness to an early anecdote recalled by Joyce's father, John Stanislaus Joyce, when his son James was only seven years of age: 'If that fellow was dropped in the middle of the Sahara, he'd sit, be God, and make a map of it' (JJI 28). This account of the young James charting at the tender age of seven (and in a god-like manner) the vertiginous landscape of the Sahara Desert, reveals Joyce's future delight in cartography, and, as Richard Ellmann remarks, 'his interest in minute detail' (JJII 28). Drawing on John Joyce's anecdote, Eric Bulson views this early account as an anticipation of the geographical realism and totalizing tendencies of *Ulysses*: 'From one of its earliest recorded beginnings, James Joyce's *Ulysses* was a book fated to be written with an encyclopaedic memory and a map'.[9] In his tireless search for parallels between *Ulysses* and his South American gaucho, Borges may well have whispered to himself that if the young Joyce revealed a special knack for mnemonic exercises, so his young Funes should also exhibit early signs of a prodigious memory.[10] Borges's lesson here — if any at all — is that if Funes's school anecdote anticipated his future predilection for taxonomies and absurd catalogues of potentially infinite series, so Joyce's imaginary map of the Sahara foreshadows his fondness for orderly schemes, painstaking detail and naturalistic representation in *Ulysses*.[11]

If Funes stands as the ideal reader of Joyce's epic proportions, namely, as the boundless recipient able to process the whole of *Ulysses*, Borges conversely imposes a principle of compression in his capacity to exemplify a reduced or abridged version of Joyce's book. Just as Fritz Senn argues that 'In some sense *Ulysses* is such a radical translation of the *Odyssey*, from ancient Greek into modern Irish',[12] so in 'Funes the Memorious' Borges provides in turn his own radical translation of *Ulysses*, from Hiberno-English into River Plate Spanish, and above all, from Joyce's grand epic scale to a compressed narrative expression. Yet Borges's miniaturized version of *Ulysses* is constructed as a satirical, compact re-creation of Joyce's gargantuan tendencies. Borges mimics Joyce's endeavour to provide an accurate reconstruction of the Dublin of 16 June 1904, and confers upon Funes the equivalent impulse to provide a round-the-clock reconstruction of an entire day, which in turn demanded another whole day: 'Dos o tres veces había reconstruído un día entero; no había dudado nunca, pero cada reconstrucción había requerido un día entero (*OC1* 488) ['Two or three times he had reconstructed an entire day; he had never once erred or faltered, but each reconstruction had itself taken an entire day'] (*CF* 135). This parodic effect has been noted by César Augusto Salgado: '"Funes the Memorious" can be interpreted as a parody of the baroque modernist novel in its ultimate forms: *Ulysses*, *Finnegans Wake*, and Proust's *Recherche*. Funes's magical, absolute memory recalls *Ulysses*' attempt at the total recollection of Dublin on Bloomsday'.[13] Whereas Joyce dedicated seven years to achieve the enormous scope of *Ulysses*, Borges offers a succinct form of rewriting, a parodic miniature of *Ulysses* that occupies no more than three pages. In the 1941 foreword to *The Garden of Forking Paths* (significantly written the same year as Joyce's obituary) an unashamed Borges pronounces his aesthetics of abridgment: 'Desvarío laborioso y empobrecedor el de componer vastos libros; el de explayar en quinientas páginas una idea cuya perfecta exposición oral cabe en pocos minutos. Mejor procedimiento es simular que esos libros ya existen y ofrecer un resumen, un comentario' (*OC1* 429) ['It is a laborious madness and an impoverishing one, the madness of composing vast books — setting out in five hundred pages an idea that can be perfectly related orally in five minutes. The better way to go about it is to pretend that those books already exist, and offer a summary, a commentary on them'] (*CF* 67).

Only Jorge Luis Borges, the acclaimed master of metaphysical brevity, can blamelessly get away with an irreverent appropriation of *Ulysses*. At this point Borges exhibits one of the most fascinating readings of Joyce to date, that deliberately distances itself from either unconditional eulogy or disapproving critique, in order to propose a dual consciousness that reveals two opposite impulses coexisting within the same discourse. He constructs his dialogue with Joyce as a fruitful dialectic that is both fascinated by Joyce's ability to depict a total reality, and full of scorn for the sheer magnitude of the book. If from this conflictual process is to emerge any possible synthesis, then Borges's resolution is the depiction of a character equipped with an infinite memory (as a cognate to Joyce's total inclusion) in the most thoroughly concise narrative fashion. This fosters the construction of *Ulysses* as precursor of 'Funes the Memorious' or, what is more, if we apply Pierre Menard's technique of 'anacronismo deliberado y de las atribuciones erróneas' (*OC1* 450) ['deliberate anachronism and fallacious attribution'] (*CF* 95) readers would be encouraged to read 'Funes the Memorious' as though it was written by James Joyce. In a further ironic twist, Borges teasingly invites his readers to view Funes as a *multum in parvo* version of *Ulysses*. The critic and translator Sergio Waisman has eloquently summarized this complex meeting point between two of the most revolutionary writers of the twentieth century:

> Joyce asks a question: what would a novel look like that tried to account for every aspect of every single moment of a single day. The answer he gives is *Ulysses* for the daytime, and *Finnegans Wake* for the nighttime. Borges takes

this same question, in response to Joyce, and answers with Funes: a short, clear and concise story that contains a character able to do (because of his perfect memory) what Joyce tried to do.[14]

Just as a total reading of *Ulysses* presupposes the infinite memory of Funes, so the myriad details, lists, catalogues and directory entries in *Ulysses* evoke (and exemplify) the teeming world of Ireneo Funes. Since Funes's memory is infallible, unselective and devoid of abstraction, his reading of *Ulysses* would envisage, of course, less an interpretation than a replication. This totalizing gesture recalls the colossal enterprise of Borges's obsessed cartographers who produced a map of the Empire 'que tenía el tamaño del imperio y coincidía puntualmente con él' (*OC2* 225) ['whose size was that of the Empire, and which coincided point for point with it'] (*CF* 325). Therefore in his transmutation of *Ulysses* into Funes, Borges is still at his most Joycean, carrying to an extreme Joyce's often-cited observation to Frank Budgen (whether taken seriously or not): 'I want, said Joyce [...] to give a picture of Dublin so complete that if the city one day suddenly disappeared from the earth it could be reconstructed out of my book'.[15] If Joyce claims to have reconstructed the myriad aspects that correspond to his conception of Dublin, then Borges engages in a similar procedure by conferring upon Funes not only the mastery of naturalistic representation through his total reconstruction of one entire day of his life, but also an omniscient and omnipresent supremacy: 'Más recuerdos tengo yo solo que los que habrán tenido todos los hombres desde que el mundo es mundo' (*OC1* 488) ['*I, myself, alone, have more memories than all mankind since the world began*'] (*CF* 135).

## Ideal Insomniacs

In a crucial 1976 interview with a group of writers and scholars, later edited by Richard Burgin, Borges revisited the parallels between 'Funes the Memorious' and *Ulysses* that he had publicized in 1941. This testimony emerges by means of another vital link, namely, the persistent insomnia he experienced in the mid-1930s during a scorching summer that he spent in the Hotel *Las Delicias*, located in Adrogué, a city in Greater Buenos Aires:

> When I suffered from insomnia I tried to forget myself, to forget my body, the position of my body, the bed, the furniture, the three gardens of the hotel, the eucalyptus tree, the books on the shelf, all the streets of the village, the station, the farmhouses. And since I couldn't forget, I kept on being conscious and couldn't fall asleep.[16]

Borges then adds that the antidote to his insomniac state lay in his awareness that James Joyce had experienced an analogous situation of acute mnemonic recollection: 'Then I said to myself, let us suppose there was a person who couldn't forget anything he had perceived, and it's well known that this happened to James Joyce, who in the course of a single day could have brought out *Ulysses*, a day in which thousands of things happened'.[17] The significance of this confession lies not only in the fact that Borges seeks refuge in Joyce as a *consolatio memoriae* but also in his conception of *Ulysses* as a *consolatio infinitus*, a type of boundless book that according to him 'contains it all'.[18] Hence Borges argues that the idea of *Ulysses* as an infinite book led to the creation of 'someone who couldn't forget those events and who in the end dies swept away by his infinite memory'.[19] At this point Funes and *Ulysses* amalgamate or, more precisely, Borges confers unto Joyce the authorship of Funes. More importantly, this account forges a mutual reciprocity between Argentine and Irish writers: just as Joyce saves Borges by composing a 'monstrous' book that partakes every detail from reality and rescues him from his lucid nights of insomnia, so Borges complements Joyce by creating an equally 'monstrous' character who not only serves as the ideal reader of *Ulysses*, but also presages the 'ideal insomniac' of *Finnegans Wake*. Significantly, Roland McHugh traces back this *Wake* passage to the French *fin-de-siècle* writer J. K. Huysmans, who proposed in his 1884 novel *A Rebours* [*Against the Grain*] that 'The novel should be a communion between a magic writer & an ideal reader'.[20] Given that Borges endows his hero with a persistent insomnia and an infinite memory, who else but Funes would succeed in transubstantiating this spiritual amalgamation, in other words, author-izing a communion between Borges and Joyce?

Borges's chronic insomnia is projected, then, into his fictional creation Ireneo Funes. In 'Funes the Memorious' the first person narrator remarks: 'le era muy difícil dormir. Dormir es distraerse del mundo' (*OC1* 490) ['It was hard for him to sleep. To sleep is to take one's mind from the world'] (*SNF* 137). In the foreword to *Artificios* Borges declared that the story stands as 'una larga metáfora del insomnio' (*OC1* 483) [a long metaphor for insomnia], thus privileging the insomniac over the mnemonic states, although for Borges total recall and extreme wakefulness are inextricably linked together.[21] Furthermore, the motif of insomnia — together with the implications it produces on the powers of recollection — appears as a significant biographical link between Borges and Joyce. For instance, Frank Budgen's celebrated account of Joyce's prodigious memory highlights not only his ability for committing entire verbal passages to memory, but also the powers of a memory that did not even recede in the hours of the night:

> Joyce's memory for the words of his own compositions and for those of all writers he admired was prodigious. He knew by heart whole pages of Flaubert, Newman, de Quincey, E. Quinet, A. J. Balfour and of many others. Most human memories begin to fail at midnight, and lapse into the vague and à peu près, but not that of Joyce [...] We had been talking about Milton's *Lycidas*, and I wanted to quote some lines of it that pleased me. My memory gave out, but Joyce said the whole poem from beginning to end, and followed it up with *L'Allegro*.[22]

In a 1938 letter to Daniel Brody, Joyce seems to have applied his own precepts of ideal insomnia to himself, declaring that the completion of *Finnegans Wake* was taking 'all day and all night as well' (*SL* 193). (It is also significant that Joyce unfolds Molly's unpunctuated record of past and present memories as an insomniac revelation, albeit with a less lucid power of memory). The theme of insomnia reappears in Borges's work in 1981, in a catechetical piece entitled 'Two Forms of Insomnia', which is strongly reminiscent of what Joyce referred to as the 'mathematico-astronomico-mechanico-geometrico-chemico' discourse of 'Ithaca' (*JJII* 501). Borges poses two questions: 'What is insomnia?' and 'What is longevity' (*SP* 427). In the answer to the first question, he relates, once again, the state of insomnia with acute mnemonic recollection: 'Es pronunciar fragmentos de párrafos leídos hace muchos años, es saberse culpable de velar cuando los otros duermen [...]' (*SP* 426) [It's uttering lines from books read many years ago; it's blaming yourself for staying awake while the others sleep] (*SP* 427). In the same vein, in a 1981 interview Borges described his literary relationship with Joyce as an infinite textual conversation caught up in an endless act of memory: 'Yo sé que en algunas de sus inextricables páginas está Joyce esperándome en pasajes que me han acompañado toda la vida' (*TR3* 367) [I know that Joyce is awaiting me in one of his intricate pages, in passages that have accompanied me all my life].

### Pliny, Author of Funes

In 'Funes the Memorious' a crippled and socially isolated Ireneo Funes greets the narrator with a verbatim recitation, in Latin and Spanish, of the twenty-fourth chapter of the seventh book of Pliny the Elder's *Natural History*:

> Ireneo empezó por enumerar, en latín y español, los casos de memoria prodigiosa registrados por la *Naturalis historia*: Ciro, rey de los persas, que sabía llamar por su nombre a todos los soldados de sus ejércitos; Mitrídates Eupator, que administraba la justicia en los 22 idiomas de su imperio; Simónides, inventor de la mnemotecnia; Metrodoro, que profesaba el arte de repetir con fidelidad lo escuchado una sola vez. Con evidente buena fe se maravilló de que tales casos maravillaran. (*OC1* 488).

> [Ireneo began by enumerating, in both Latin and Spanish, the cases of prodigious memory catalogued in the *Naturalis Historia*: Cyrus, the king of Persia, who would call all the soldiers in his army by name; Mithridates Eupator, who meted out justice in the twenty-two languages of the kingdom over which he ruled; Simonides, the inventor of the art of memory; Metrodorus, who was able faithfully to repeat what he had heard, though it be but once. With obvious sincerity, Ireneo said he was amazed that such cases were thought to be amazing (*CF* 134).]

Not insignificantly, the subject matter of the passage is none other than Memory. Herein, Pliny offers an inventory of outstanding cases of memory which, nonetheless, seem utterly insignificant to the arrogant Funes. Yet this catalogue of mnemonic prodigiousness has been much admired throughout history, as Frances Yates states in *The Art of Memory*, '[Pliny's] little anthology of memory stories in his *Natural History* [was] constantly repeated in the memory treatises of after times'.[23] Regarding Borges's inclusion of Pliny, Bell-Villada asserts that Borges's narrative device proposes 'a typical hall-of-mirrors effect: someone with a perfect memory reciting from memory a passage on memory'.[24] Just as Pliny offers a testimony of exceptional memories from the classical world, so Borges presents his own South-American mnemonic curiosity, insofar as the first-person narrator of the story informs the reader that his account of Funes will contribute to a volume in honour of the Uruguayan prodigy: 'Me parece muy feliz el proyecto de que todos aquellos que lo trataron escriban sobre él; mi testimonio será acaso el más breve y sin duda el más pobre, pero no el menos imparcial del volumen que editarán ustedes'

(*OC1* 485) ['I applaud the idea that all of us who had dealings with the man should write something about him; my testimony will perhaps be the briefest (and certainly the slightest) account in the volume that you are to publish, but it can hardly be the least impartial'] (*CF* 131). But it should be taken into account that whereas Pliny's compact treatise of outstanding memories seeks to provoke admiration, the context of Borges's short-story strips it of its original power to amaze, since by proxy to Funes's absolute memory, the cases that once provoked general amazement become, *mutatis mutandis*, an outdated record of mnemotechnic. And yet it should be noted that Borges omits two relevant details from Pliny's enumeration. First, in *Historia Naturalis* Pliny precedes his list of outstanding memories with a warning about the difficulty of determining which is the most exceptional: 'With regard to memory, a most essential tool in life, it is not easy to say who was the most exceptional since so many men have gained fame for it'.[25] Unlike the more egalitarian Pliny who attributes identical favours to all the men listed in the compilation, Borges confers the entire mastery of mnemotechnic to only one individual, Ireneo Funes, and hence cancels out any other possible exempla that may overshadow the unique powers of his hero. Therefore, Borges deleted the only example from Pliny that might have challenged Funes's mnemonic powers. This is the extraordinary case of Charmadas, who was celebrated in Greece for repeating 'the contents of any volumes in libraries that anyone asked him to recall, just as if he was reading them'.[26] The action of quoting verbatim entire volumes is precisely one of Funes's most coveted attributes, as a shocked narrator becomes the inner audience of Funes's recitation of Pliny. By incorporating Pliny's *Natural History* into 'Funes the Memorious' Borges is, ultimately, writing Funes as a post-scripted *addendum* to Pliny's mnemonic compendium. On the other hand, Borges deviates from Pliny's precepts of memory, since Funes's infallible memory miraculously emerged after his fall off a horse, in an accidental *lapsus* that simultaneously robbed him of his physical mobility and *gifted* him with a prodigious memory. Borges's pattern of fortuitous mnemonic acquisition contrasts, for instance, with Pliny's concluding report about the vulnerability of the faculty of memory: 'No other human function is equally susceptible to upset'.[27] Pliny reports that physical injuries, especially falls, typically inflict upon the victim partial or complete loss of memory. Contrarily to Pliny, Borges overturns previous accounts on the frailty of memory in order to propose the opposite effect, an anomalous case whereby memory is extraordinarily bestowed in a riding accident: 'Me dijo que antes de esa tarde lluviosa en que lo volteó el azulejo, él había sido lo que son todos los cristianos: un ciego, un sordo, un abombado, un desmemoriado' (*OC1* 488) ['He told me that before that rainy afternoon when the blue roan had bucked him off, he had been what every man was — blind, deaf, befuddled, and virtually devoid of memory'] (*CF* 134).

If Borges uses Pliny's treatise as a Chinese box insertion from which to draw further parallels and contrasts with Funes, in a larger scale Pliny's *Historia Naturalis* stands as a metaphor of 'Funes the Memorious'. An ambitiously exhaustive catalogue of facts, or 'history' of *natura* as the universe, Pliny's *Historia Naturalis* stands as a totalizing attempt to integrate a wide range of knowledge and physical phenomena in the confines of a single volume. In a conversation with Roberto Alifano, Borges commented: 'I believe that the first inventor of the encyclopaedia was Pliny, the author of *Historia Naturalis*, in which he compiles in thirty-seven volumes a record of the knowledge of his time and the most diverse materials'.[28] In this sense, 'Funes the Memorious' stands as a parodic commentary of *Historia Naturalis*, turning the principles of cataloguing, classifying and recording every possible aspect of the world into a *reductio ad absurdum*. Just as Funes stands as a successor of Pliny's encyclopaedic impulse, so Joyce's *Ulysses* stands as another avatar of Pliny, another *Book as World*, as Marilyn French puts it: 'Joyce literally set out to create a replica of the world — not a metaphor for it, but a copy of it — reproducing with it all the coincidences, mysteries, and incertitude that pervade actual life'.[29] Similarly, Umberto Eco insists that: 'Joyce thus conceived of a total work, a Work-as-Cosmos [...] The book is also an encyclopedia and a literary summa.'[30] Therefore, Borges and Joyce modelled Funes and *Ulysses* respectively according to totalizing encyclopaedic impulses that aimed to incorporate the whole world in their categorization of knowledge. In a fascinating coincidence, Thomas J. Rice remarks: 'both writers [evinced] an apparent fondness for the '"Eleventh Edition of the *Encyclopedia Britannica*".'[31] Yet, as the leading parodists of the twentieth century, Borges and Joyce transgress the taxonomical logic that prevails in the supposedly all-inclusive, ordered catalogues in an attempt to underline, among other things, their inadequate claim for completion. In *The Fictional Encyclopaedia*, Hilary Clark highlights this dialectic between a desire for totalization and the inevitable limitations of the enterprise:

> Over history, the encyclopaedic enterprise has been characterized by a drive to encircle or include all there is to know. However, this drive has always encountered problems, limitations built into the enterprise itself. No matter how much faith the encyclopaedist(s) may have in the possibility of mastering and communicating the body of knowledge at hand, the totality of this body is an elusive thing. The desire to comprehend knowledge is an erotics recognizing a loss at the very limit of its reach.[32]

As direct descendants of this encyclopaedic tradition, Borges and Joyce are both lured by the magnitude of an enterprise that seeks to embrace all forms of knowledge, and aware that such projects are condemned to fail in their unavoidable incompleteness. Consequently, both emphasize the conflictual forces inherent in any totalization of knowledge by turning the encyclopaedic endeavour for completion into an unavoidable, yet humorous, record of incompletion. For instance, in the 'Cyclops' episode of *Ulysses* the gigantic catalogues that irrupt into the narrative no longer fulfil any principles of systematic relevance, and instead include arbitrary and disconnected series. In this vein, the epic catalogue of 'many Irish heroes and heroines of antiquity' (*U* 12. 176) lists legendary Celtic figures such as Cuchulin and the soldier Owen Roe, side by side a worldwide taxonomy of other historical, literary, and biblical counterparts, ranging from Dante Alighieri, Christopher Columbus, Napoleon Bonaparte, to Tristan and Isolde, and Adam and Eve. As Karen Lawrence argues: 'What begins as a principle of ordering becomes a vehicle of illogic; the category of Irish heroes that commences with Cuchulin suddenly includes the world.'[33] The creation of a catalogue based on absurd and illogical laws of categorization is also one of Borges's pet themes, particularly in

'John Wilkins's Analytical Language'. Just as the catalogue of 'Cyclops' incorporates any random element from the universe, so the disparate numerical system devised by Funes comprises a nonsensical nominal labelling for each number: 'En lugar de siete mil trece, decía (por ejemplo) Máximo Pérez; en lugar de siete mil catorce, el Ferrocarril; otros números eran Luis Melián Lafinur, Olimar, azufre, los bastos, la ballena, el gas, la caldera, Napoleón, Agustín de Vedia' (*OC1* 489) ['Instead of seven thousand thirteen (7013), he would say, for instance, "Máximo Pérez" instead of seven thousand fourteen (7014), the "railroad"; other numbers were "Luis Melián Lafinur", "Olimar", "sulfur", "clubs", "the whale", "gas", "a stewpot", "Napoleon", "Agustín de Vedia"'] (*CF* 136). Funes's babble of disconnected words resembles the arbitrary lists of 'Cyclops', in their all-inclusive accumulation of details any possible element may validly be incorporated into their endless catalogues. What is at stake in Borges's and Joyce's projects, ultimately, is the need to draw attention to the fact that absolute forms of reasoning are condemned to partiality, hence emphasizing the arbitrariness of all systems of thought. As Borges concludes in 'John Wilkins's Analytical Language', 'no hay clasificación del universo que no sea arbitraria y conjectural' (*OC2* 86) ['there is no classification of the universe that is not arbitrary and speculative'] (*SNF* 231).

## Locke, Author of Funes

Towards the end of 'Funes the Memorious', in an attempt to turn Funes's memory into an even more unusual prodigy, the narrator extends the list of 'precursors' of his fictional character. Thus the next mnemonic analogy is linked to the nominalistic language postulated by the British philosopher and empiricist, John Locke. Much like the examples of extraordinary memories provided by Pliny, this new predecessor will be discredited when compared with the unique powers of Funes. The first-person narrator of the story reports thus: 'Locke, en el siglo XVII, postuló (y reprobó) un idioma imposible en el que cada cosa individual, cada piedra, cada pájaro, y cada rama tuviera un nombre propio' (*OC1* 489) ['In the seventeenth century, Locke postulated (and condemned) an impossible language in which each individual thing — every stone, every bird, every branch — would have its own name'] (*CF* 136). It is no wonder that for Funes, even Locke's impossible language in which every particular thing would require a particular name seemed far too general, as he would have devised an even more accurate nomenclature to describe the world: 'Funes proyectó alguna vez un idioma análogo pero lo desechó por parecerle demasiado general, demasiado ambiguo' (*OC1* 489) ['Funes once contemplated a similar language, but discarded the idea as too general, too ambiguous'] (*CF* 136). John Locke's nominalistic idiom ironically proves unsuitably wide-ranging for the supra-empiricist Funes. Indeed, in *Of Memory: Reminiscence, and Writing*, David Farrell Krell suggests that Locke's impossible idiolect anticipated Funes: 'Locke will not have had the advantage of being able to recall Luis Borges' Ireneo Funes — "Funes el memorioso" (1942) — and yet he may have anticipated something of Funes' fate. Which is, one must say, bound to be funereal.'[34] At any rate, Locke participates in the dissemination of a Western mnemonic tradition and, in doing so, proposes an impossible language which, three hundred years later, would be refuted by Ireneo Funes in his nineteenth-century 'arrabal sudamericano' (*OC1* 490) ['South American hinterland'] (*CF* 137). Funes transcends Locke's nominalistic idiom by virtue of his ability to remember '[no sólo] cada hoja de cada árbol de cada monte, sino cada una de las veces que la había percibido o imaginado' (*OC1* 489) ['not only every leaf of every tree in every patch of forest, but every time he had perceived or imagined that leaf'] (*CF* 136). Funes, then, refutes Locke with an even more unfeasible and impractical language which is bound to the flux of time, since any minuscule temporal modification would demand, in turn, a further denomination. These undetected modifications in the perception of average memories, reports 'Borges', highly irritated Funes: 'No sólo le costaba comprender que el símbolo genérico *perro* abarcara tantos individuos dispares de diversos tamaños y diversa forma; le molestaba que el perro de las tres y catorce (visto de perfil) tuviera el mismo nombre que el perro de las tres y cuarto (visto de frente)' (*OC1* 490) ['Not only was it difficult for him to see that the generic symbol "dog" took in all the dissimilar individuals of all shapes and sizes, it irritated him that the "dog" of three-fourteen in the afternoon, seen in profile, should be indicated by the same noun as the dog of three-fifteen, seen frontally'] (*CF* 136). But whereas Borges enlarges Locke with the creation of Funes, Locke nonetheless resorts to God as the supreme example of an infinite memory. In Chapter X of *An Essay*, in the subsection entitled 'On Retention', Locke states that the only memory devoid of forgetfulness or defect is the infinite memory of the Christian God: 'The omniscience of God, who knows all things past, present, and to come, and to whom the thoughts of men's hearts always lie open, may satisfy us of the possibility of this'.[35] We may also add here that in his early essay 'James Clarence Mangan' (1902) Joyce had referred to the unbounded mind of God as, 'that great memory which is greater and more generous than our memory, [for which] no life, no moment of exaltation is ever lost'.[36] Joyce's assertion that God is *infinitus*[37] converges with Borges's similar description in *A History of Eternity* that God's eternity registers the simultaneity of all times, past, present, and future. If Locke and Joyce invoke the memory of God as the ultimate form of perfection since it lacks the defect of ordinary memories, namely, forgetfulness, then Borges views the infallible memory of Funes as a monstrous aberration, an inference that is extended, eventually, to the supreme memory of the Creator and to *Ulysses* and *Finnegans Wake* (see *SNF* 133–34).

## Nietzsche, Author of Funes

In 'On the Uses and Disadvantages of History for Life' (1873) the second essay in a collection entitled *Untimely Meditations*, Nietzsche proposes 'a meditation on the value of history',[38] whereby he condemns Western scientific-historical systems of knowledge for their 'costly superfluity and luxury'[39] and their inability to serve life. As a substitute to this historical overflow, Nietzsche proposes a form of unhistorical living that turns its back on the surplus of historical information that has greatly contributed towards the imprisonment of the individual. Therefore, the excesses of history can only be overcome through the opposite phenomenon of active forgetfulness, a redeeming process that is conceived as the amnesiac antidote to the superabundance of knowledge or excessive remembering. Nietzsche's assault on history, however, should not be understood as a total denial of the importance of history to life. Rather, what is at stake here is that a defunct history, overburdened with useless facts, should give way to a living history infused with the power to serve the individual. In this respect, Edward S. Casey has convincingly argued that Nietzsche, alongside Heidegger, Ebbinghaus and Freud, belongs to a twentieth-century philosophical tradition that approaches 'remembering through the counterphenomenon of *forgetting*.'[40] This tension underlines the significant fact that the act of remembering only exists through its antithetical relationship to oblivion; Mnemosyne (the Greek goddess of remembering) gives way to Lesmosyne (the goddess of forgetfulness). In Greek mythology, the river Lethe purges the souls of the memory of their previous existences. In Book VI of *The Aeneid*, Virgil reports that: 'The god calls in a crowd to Lethe stream / That there unmemoried they may see again / The heavens and wish re-entry into bodies'.[41] In *The Republic* Plato describes the waters of Lethe as the final and inevitable passage towards forgetfulness, hence emphasizing the importance to preserve memories while alive: 'And so, my dear Glaucon, his tale was preserved from perishing, and, if we remember it, may well preserve us in turn, and we shall cross the river of Lethe safely and shall not defile our souls'.[42] These myths act as reminders of the frailty of the faculty of memory, becoming overt exhortations to remember *in vita*, as well as generating the fear of total oblivion, an *horror oblivionalis* which unceasingly validates the process of recollection. In *Memory, History, Forgetting*, Paul Ricoeur offers a compelling examination of the long-lasting dialectic of remembering and forgetting:

> The extraordinary exploits of the *ars memoriae* were designed to ward off the misfortune of forgetting by a kind of exaggerated memorization brought to the assistance of remembering. But artificial memory is the great loser in this unequal battle. In brief, forgetting is lamented in the same way as aging and death: it is one of the figures of the inevitable, the irremediable.[43]

A vindication of forgetfulness overturns the Western binary opposition of memory/forgetting, in order to privilege the second term. In this vein, Nietzsche proposes his own *ars oblivionalis* through active forgetfulness, in what he regards as an indispensable condition for the livelihood of humanity: 'Forgetting is essential to action of any kind, just as not only light but darkness too is essential for the life of everything organic'.[44] In a similar vein, Casey writes: 'To value forgetting instead of vilifying it is to recognize that the forgetting of many details of daily life is not only practically useful — in order to become less distracted and preoccupied — but, in fact, necessary to our well-being, a basis for being-in-the-world.'[45] Thus, Nietzsche offers the chilling parable of a man who was unable to forget:

> Imagine the extremest possible example of a man who did not possess the power of forgetting at all and who was thus condemned to see everywhere a state of becoming: such a man would no longer believe in his own being, would no longer believe in himself, would see everything flowing asunder in moving points and would lose himself in this stream of becoming.[46]

It is thus clear that Nietzsche's vision of a man condemned to a persistent memorious state anticipates the infallible memory of Borges's Funes. In fact, Nietzsche's allegory resembles 'Funes the Memorious' to such an extent that it may even be read as a plot summary of the story. If Nietzsche proposes 'a man who did not possess the power of forgetting', Borges replies that 'His perception and memory were perfect' (*CF* 135). By the same token, Nietzsche's suggestion that his memorious man was incapable of believing in himself, recalls Borges's assertion: 'Su propia cara en el espejo, sus propias manos, lo sorprendían cada vez' (*OC1* 490) [His own face in the mirror, his own hands, surprised him every time he saw them] (*CF* 136). Without a doubt, the similarities between the two texts are striking. But at this point it is relevant to ask how familiar Borges was with Nietzsche's *Untimely Meditations*. Roxana Kreimer has demonstrated that Borges was far more than just familiar with Nietzsche's essay. She has proved that a copy of *Untimely Meditations* was found in his personal library, bearing significant 'subrayado y anotado en los márgenes con su puño y letra' [underlining and annotations on the margins with his own handwriting].[47] Following this decisive evidence it is possible, as a result, to identify a further confluence between Borges and Nietzsche, which is based on the ultimate moral of Nietzsche's parable: 'Thus: it is possible to live almost without memory, and to live happily moreover, as the animal demonstrates; but it is altogether impossible to *live* at all without forgetting'.[48] Unable to exercise any form of *ars oblivionalis* and overwhelmed by his unrelenting powers of recollection, Ireneo Funes seeks refuge in death as the ultimate form of oblivion. As Salgado puts it: 'The story of Borges's disabled genius of memory helps Borges illustrate the empowerment, so crucial to the Nietzschean idea of the Will, that forgetting can bestow.'[49] The family name of Borges's character, Funes, let us not forget, is for this purpose equally emblematic, particularly in relation to Sturrock's insistence that 'his name Funes marks him as *funes(to)*, as someone sad and unfortunate'.[50] Furthermore, Borges confers on Funes the main side effect that Nietzsche assigns to his memorious being: total recall is paid for by the higher price of a constant state of insomnia. Nietzsche says: 'A man who wanted to feel historically through and through would be like one forcibly deprived of sleep.'[51] Consequently this by-product of insomnia becomes an offshoot of the state of total recall. This insomniac feature is, moreover, the point where Borges and Joyce intersect: Funes becomes Joyce's ideal insomniac since a total reading of *Finnegans Wake* would only be achieved with an infinite memory and abstinence from sleep. But if Joyce's last two novels and 'Funes the Memorious' embody the excesses of remembering in their totalizing gestures, how do they in turn negotiate the memory/forgetting polarity? In other words, is it possible to recognize in Borges and Joyce an alternative discourse that is centred neither in total recollection nor in absolute oblivion, but which aims to achieve a higher synthesis out of the interaction of the two conflicting forces? As Paul Ricoeur puts it: 'Could forgetting then no longer be in every respect an enemy of memory, and could memory have to negotiate with forgetting, groping to find the right measure in its balance with forgetting?'[52]

### The Art of Forgetting in 'Funes the Memorious' and 'Ithaca'

In *Remembering: A Phenomenological Study*, Edward S. Casey has persuasively demonstrated that Aristotle's *De Memoria et Reminiscentia* has had a fundamental impact in the Western history of mnemotechnic, contributing to the development of two opposing theoretical approaches to memory, which he labels as 'passivism' and 'activism'.[53] In Aristotle's treatise, this particular distinction emerges from his preliminary differentiation between 'memory' and 'reminiscing' (or 'recollecting'), the first term being associated with a passive form of remembering, while the latter is related to the metaphor of the search as a deliberate attempt to recover the past.[54] On the one hand, Casey points out that for the passivist model, 'remembering is reduced to a passive process of registering and storing incoming impressions. The passivist paradigm is still very much with us, whether it takes the form of a naive empiricism or of a sophisticated model of information processing.'[55] On the other, Casey argues that the 'activist' model 'involves the creative transformation of experience rather than its internalized reduplication in images or traces construed as copies. Echoes of activism are detectable in Plato and Aristotle themselves, especially in the shared conviction that recollection takes place as a search.'[56] If the passivist tradition privileges an operation of memory based on the effortless storage of experience — hence its analogy with the modern computer — the activist paradigm promotes a creative search that involves a retroactive process in which the past is re-collected through language and imagination. However, as John S. Rickard puts it: 'Activist memory is always problematic, for many activist writers on memory doubt the availability of any final truth at the end of their search [...] Thus, the activist tradition sees memory as an intersection between actual experience and interpretation, imagination, and repression.'[57] In this sense, active memory emerges as a deeply personal, subjective and inevitably 'falsified' version of events that overtly declares its impossibility to provide an absolute truth of the past. In the 'Nestor' episode, Stephen Dedalus sums up the core of the activist tradition with his citation from Blake's *A Vision of the Last Judgement*: 'Fabled by the daughters of memory' (*U* 2.7). If remembering is 'fabled' by the muses (who in Greek mythology are the daughters of Zeus and Mnemosyne) then the process of recollection is inevitably filtered through imagination and creativity. By the same token, Borges insists that creative processes are the result of a mixture of 'omisiones y de énfasis, de olvido y de memoria, éste combina alguna de ellas y elabora así la obra de arte' (*OC4* 310) [omissions and emphasis, memory and forgetfulness, which are mixed together to create the work of art]. 'Memory in *Ulysses*', writes Rickard, 'operates in a contested zone constructed by modern philosophical and psychological discourses as well as by older epistemological modes, and thus, predictably, it contains elements of both the passivist and the activists visions of memory.'[58] The same could be applied to Borges, who, as we have seen, analogously deploys a richly intertwined tapestry of discourses of memory and incorporates both activist and passivist undercurrents.

In this final section I will argue that in broad opposition to the surplus of readily available data that prevails in the totalizing archives of Funes and *Ulysses* — particularly in the mathematical catechism of 'Ithaca' — are positioned the non-encyclopaedic memories of the first-person narrator of 'Funes the Memorious', and the strenuous recollection processes of Leopold Bloom and Stephen Dedalus. In this manner, Funes may be said to resemble the meticulous catechist of 'Ithaca', the narrative mind who processes, collects, and classifies large quantities of data throughout the episode. Funes and the catechist intersect in their compulsive creation of taxonomies, endless lists, and in their larger endeavour to overmaster Western knowledge.

What, above all, unites Funes and 'Ithaca' is their industrious self-employment as archivists of an infinitely divisible reality. Funes composes sequences of metonymic associations in an attempt to process the myriad details of his swarming memory and, thus, create potentially vast enumerations linked by an associative system only coherent to his own mnemonic functioning. For Funes, the clouds that adorn the sky remain different throughout each day of his life and cannot be synthesized into a generic whole. This results, of course, in his need to construct further parallels with the countless disparate elements that inhabit his all-absorbing memory. Central to this associative process is the assumption that Funes's correlation of the clouds of the southern sky 'del treinta de abril de mil ochocientos ochenta y dos' (*OC1* 488) ['on the morning of April 30, 1882'] (*CF* 135) — significantly the year of Joyce's birth — with 'las vetas de un libro en pasta española que solo había mirado una vez' (*OC1* 488) ['the veins in the marbled binding of a book he had seen only once'] (*CF* 135), converges with the trajectory of Stephen Dedalus and Leopold Bloom across the city of Dublin. Just as Funes evokes the morning clouds, so the narrative mind of 'Ithaca', captures an example of parallax in the shared perception of a 'matutinal cloud' by Stephen Dedalus and Leopold Bloom from two different points of observation in the morning of 16 June 1904: 'Stephen attributed to the reapparition of a matutinal cloud (perceived by both from two different points of observation, Sandycove and Dublin) at first no bigger than a woman's hand' (*U* 17.27–42). In a 1984 interview with Osvaldo Ferrari, a blind and elderly Borges revealed his familiarity with this Joycean device: '[Joyce] da la hora exacta en que ocurre esa escena, para que uno pueda comparar ese capítulo, que corresponde a la mente de Stephen Dedalus, con el otro, que corresponde a la mente de Leopold Bloom, y entonces hay un momento en el cual los dos se fijan en una nube. Se entiende que ese paralelismo es precioso'[59] ['[Joyce] gives the exact time in which the scene takes place, thus allowing the reader to compare this episode ['Telemachus'], which corresponds to the mind of Stephen Dedalus, with the other, which corresponds to the mind of Leopold Bloom ['Calypso'], hence there is a moment in which both stare at a cloud. It is implied that this parallelism is precious'].

The principle of ordering that characterizes Funes becomes, in turn, the principal narrative mannerism of 'Ithaca'. For instance, the ordinary action of boiling a kettle to make cocoa is turned into a detailed account of successive actions: 'He removed the saucepan to the left hob, rose and carried the iron kettle to the sink in order to tap the current by turning the faucet to let it flow' (*U* 17.160–62). The supposedly inconsequential act of turning on the tap is transformed into a long descriptive report which engages in a regressive series of causalities that trace back the source to the water supply: 'From Roundwood reservoir in county Wicklow of a cubic capacity of 2,400 million gallons, percolating through a subterranean aqueduct of filter mains [...]' (*U* 17.164–66). The associative series that emerge from Funes's mind, derive from his computer-like capacity that fails to limit the amount of information stored and, by the same token, lacks a system able to differentiate between relevant and irrelevant information, hence Funes's response to a shocked narrator: '*Mi memoria, señor, es como vaciadero de basuras*' (*OC1* 488) ['*My memory, sir, is like a garbage heap*'] (*CF* 135). This faulty mechanical functioning that lacks the ability to select, prioritize and filter out unnecessary data, is also one of the main characteristics of Joyce's 'Ithaca'. In a 1921 letter to Frank Budgen, Joyce underlined that the reader of 'Ithaca' '[will] know everything and know it in the baldest coldest way' (*Letters I* 160). As Walton Litz points out: 'This is the technique of much of "Ithaca", an accumulation of details which has no inherent "aesthetic" limits but relies on the epic impact of overmastering fact.'[60] Yet 'Ithaca' also develops an opposing narrative aesthetic through which the information provided in the answers is either disproportionately long or, at times, annoyingly insufficient. In this sense, Karen Lawrence observes: 'This narrative mind amasses facts with no regard for normal conventions of significance and relevance [...] the reader finds himself bombarded with a wealth of data.'[61] Yet this principle of excessive cataloguing produces, on the other hand, an adverse effect of deliberate withdrawal, inasmuch as Funes and the catechist decide, at times, to repress the postulation of an answer or the compilation of a further list. In 'Funes the Memorious', this is evident in the character's refusal to classify the memories of his childhood: 'Lo disuadieron dos consideraciones: la conciencia de que la tarea era interminable, la conciencia de que era inútil. Pensó que a la hora de su muerte no habría acabado aún de clasificar todos los recuerdos de la niñez' (*OC1* 489) ['Two considerations dissuaded him: the realization that the task was interminable, and the realization that it was pointless. He saw that by the time he died he would still not have finished classifying all the memories of his childhood'] (*CF* 136). In 'Ithaca', likewise, the potentially extensive answer to a question is at times undercut by what seems a capricious refusal to answer, and the interrogation is followed by a monosyllabic or single-word response, standing in stark contrast with the elongated, explicative responses previously or subsequently supplied. These one-word rebuttals act as alternative versions that, rather than overstating the course of events, opt for the withholding of information:

> Did either openly allude to their racial differences?
> Neither (*U* 17. 525–26).
>
> Was the clown Bloom's son?
> No (*U* 17. 987–88).

Funes's inability to comprehend the narrator's explanation about the validity of the decimal numerical system: 'Le dije que decir 365 era decir tres centenas, seis decenas, cinco unidades: análisis que no existe en los "números" *El Negro Timoteo* o *manta de carne*' (*OC1* 489) ['I told him that when one said "365" one said "three hundred, six tens, and five ones," a breakdown impossible with the "numbers" *Nigger Timoteo* or a *ponchoful of meat*'] (*SNF* 136), is echoed in the catechist's inability to generate the adequate, commonsensical answers to certain questions. As Fritz Senn puts it: 'It [the catechist] gets everything under control. And misses almost everything. In this sense "Ithaca" is a pedantic triumph and a "protracted failure" (*U* 17.1669) of the occidental preoccupation with taxonomy and intellectual mastery'.[62] In a similar vein, Rickard views the incongruities of 'Ithaca' as '[an illustration] of the defects of voluntary memory, of the assumption that the past is a collection of facts and details that can be easily and simply reassembled'.[63] Whereas most conventional narratives strive towards a foreseeable end, Funes and the catechist ignore the art of closure and would carry on their mnemonic gymnastics *ad infinitum*. Only with an early death of, ironically, pulmonary congestion is Funes's recording engine finally switched off, and only with the sacrificial act of cancelling an answer to the question 'Where?' (*U* 17.2331), which is followed by a bowdlerized orthographical dot, the catechism of 'Ithaca' is finally stopped. ' "Ithaca" is an ending that is not an ending', notes Andrew Gibson, 'in its finality, it fails to finalize things.'[64]

But in opposition to the mnemonic *tour de force* lavishly displayed by Funes and the catechist, we can detect an alternative narrative that struggles to counteract the excesses of memory with the opposite phenomenon of active and selective recollection. Rickard has appropriately referred to the last three episodes of *Ulysses* as 'a quiet explosion of memory [...], which are full of recollecting and reminiscing', stressing that we can detect 'a struggle to remember' which is manifested in Stephen's 'super human effort to try and concentrate and remember' (*U* 16.755) and in Bloom's 'irritation at not finding his key in his pocket "Because he had forgotten and because he remembered that he had reminded himself twice not to forget" (*U* 17.77–79)'.[65] In 'Funes the Memorious' the first-person narrator raises a fundamental problem in a story about a protagonist with an infallible memory:

> Arribo, ahora, al más difícil punto de mi relato. Este (bueno es que ya lo sepa el lector) no tiene otro argumento que ese diálogo de hace ya medio siglo. No trataré de reproducir sus palabras, irrecuperables ahora. Prefiero resumir con veracidad las muchas cosas que me dijo Ireneo. El estilo indirecto es remoto y débil; yo sé que sacrifico la eficacia de mi relato; que mis lectores se imaginen los entrecortados períodos que me abrumaron esa noche (*OC1* 487–88).
>
> [I come now to the most difficult point in my story, a story whose only *raison d'être* (as my readers should know from the outset) is that dialogue of that century ago. I will not attempt to reproduce the words of it, which are now forever irrecoverable. Instead, I will summarize, faithfully, the many things Ireneo told me. Indirect discourse is distant and weak; I know that I am sacrificing the effectiveness of my tale. I only ask that my readers try to hear in their imagination the broken and staccato periods that astounded me that night (*CF* 134).]

In other words, how to recount and rearrange, on the level of discourse, a sequence of events that constitute the story of a man endowed with an infinite memory? This pattern reappears in 'The Aleph' wherein 'Borges' faces the analogous task of describing the infinite aleph, a point in space that contains a universe:

> Arribo, ahora, al inefable centro de mi relato; empieza aquí, mi desesperación de escritor. Todo lenguaje es un alfabeto de símbolos cuyo ejercicio presupone un pasado que los interlocutores comparten; ¿cómo transmitir a los otros el infinito Aleph, que mi temerosa memoria apenas abarca? [...] Lo que vieron mis ojos fue simultáneo: lo que transcribiré, sucesivo, porque el lenguaje lo es. Algo, sin embargo, recogeré (*OC1* 625).

> [I come now to the ineffable center of my tale; it is here that a writer's hopelessness begins. Every language is an alphabet of symbols the employment of which assumes a past shared by its interlocutors. How can one transmit to others the infinite Aleph, which my timorous memory can scarcely contain? [...] What my eyes saw was *simultaneous*; what I shall write is *successive*, because language is successive. Something of it, though, I will capture (SNF 283).]

At this crucial juncture in both stories, Borges foregrounds the limits of language and representation in a form of meta-commentary that brings the narration to a halt in order to examine its own fictional laws and procedures. These remarks also function as a narrator's *apologia* that highlights their mutual ineffability to capture in words, and through imperfect recollection, their infinite revelations. This narrative impasse, however, is reciprocally resolved through the acceptance of the impossibility to attain a total reconstruction of the events. The infinite qualities of Funes, writes Sylvia Molloy, 'only exist in perception itself; *it cannot be told*. While Funes's undistracted attention is busy summoning terms, the narrator wishing to transcribe the series must "clear a space" for narration if he wished to refer the experience — the enumeration of an infinite series — ever so partially.'[66] The counter-narratives of 'Funes the Memorious' and 'Ithaca' are accomplished, thus, through active remembering and a self-confessed quota of forgetfulness. For 'Borges' and for Bloom, the telling of the tale implies, inevitably, an incomplete and imperfect report of the principal facts. Therefore, their deliberately flawed accounts may be re-branded, justifiably, within the sphere of creative recollection.

In 'Ithaca' the catechist stresses that the Hebrew–Celtic cultural exchange between Stephen Dedalus and Leopold Bloom culminated in Bloom's partial intonation of the Zionist hymn: 'Why was the chant arrested at the conclusion of this first distich?' The reply goes thus: 'In consequence of defective mnemotechnic' (U 17.761–66). Here, 'mnemotechnic' should not be read as another word for memory, but as an artificial device for the aid and improvement of natural memory. His 'defective' answer notwithstanding, Bloom gets away by substituting the missing information with 'a periphrastic version of the general text' (U 17.767–68). Whereas the catechist would have presented a full version of the hymn, Bloom seeks refuge, instead, in the paradigmatic axis of language that enables him to substitute one word for another. The act of lapsing into an instance of forgetfulness forges a wide gamut of linguistic and creative possibilities, inasmuch as a lacuna simultaneously takes away meaning but also strives to replace the missing layer with a new script. Moreover, later in the episode, with the imperative command 'catalogue these books' (U 17.1361) the catechist provides a minute inventory of Bloom's shelves. This sequence generates a further series of questions about the polarity of memory and forgetfulness:

> Which volume was the largest in bulk?
> Hozier's *History of the Russo-Turkish War.*
> What among other data did the second volume of the work in question contain?
> The name of a decisive battle (forgotten), frequently remembered by a decisive officer, major Brian Cooper Tweedy (remembered).
> Why, firstly and secondly, did he not consult the work in question?
> Firstly, in order to exercise mnemotechnic: secondly, because after an

interval of amnesia, when, seated at the central table, about to consult the work in question, he remembered by mnemotechnic the name of the military engagement, Plevna (U 17.1414–26).

The redeeming power of amnesia offers, once again, the possibility to fill in a space, to effectuate through the art of memory the recollection of a particular fact. Therefore, Bloom's memory is inevitably affected by 'the access of years' and by 'the action of distraction' (U 17.1916–20). What this makes clear, principally, is the crucial fact that the ordinary memory of Leopold Bloom is condemned (or gifted) with the distortion and partial recollection of facts, like the memory of the first-person narrator of 'Funes the Memorious'. Bloom's memories are dissolved by a combination of lack of attention and the inevitable passing of time. Moreover, Bloom's memory will be gradually swept away by the inexorable current of that mighty usurper of Memory: Death. Borges, in turn, proposes a testament to oblivion at the end of 'The Aleph': 'Nuestra mente es porosa para el olvido; yo mismo estoy falseando y perdiendo, bajo la trágica erosion de los años, los rasgos de Beatriz' (*OC1* 628) ['Our minds are permeable to forgetfulness; I myself am distorting and losing, through the tragic erosion of the years, the features of Beatriz'] (*CF* 288). The only antidote to the mystical revelation of the three-dimensional Aleph is the remedy of forgetfulness, since the potent effects of infinity may only be overcome with an inevitable, yet necessary, void. Death — that other guise of oblivion — is the redeeming force that finally rescues Ireneo Funes from his infallible powers of recollection. Just as Borges clears up the excesses of memory with death and forgetfulness, in 'Ithaca' Joyce proposes a similar redemption by means of a non-heroic formula that merges forgetfulness with forgiveness. If Joyce argued that '[Ithaca] is in reality the end as Penelope has no beginning, middle or end' (*Letters I* 172), then, the longest day in literature, 16 June 1904, culminates with a weary Leopold Bloom breaking free from his Homeric counterpart as he opts for a pacifist acceptance of Molly's infidelity rather than a bloodthirsty revenge on her suitor (Blazes Boylan). This forgiving attitude can only be achieved through forgetfulness, in other words, through the sentiment of 'abnegation' that, as the catechist states, exceeded 'jealousy', just as the sentiment of 'equanimity' surpassed 'envy':

> Why more abnegation than jealousy, less envy than equanimity?
> From outrage (matrimony) to outrage (adultery) there arose nought but outrage (copulation) yet the matrimonial violator of the matrimonially violated had not been outraged by the adulterous violator of the adulterously violated (U 17.2195–99).

After kissing the 'plump mellow yellow smellow melons' (U 17.2241) of Molly's rump, a worn out Bloom loosens himself to the forgetfulness of sleep, while the restless Molly begins her insomniac recollection, so that the book can remember itself infinitely.

## Notes to Chapter 3

1. T. S. Eliot, *Selected Essays* (London: Faber and Faber, 1980), p. 15.
2. Eliot, *Selected Essays*, p. 16.

3. Sarlo, *A Writer on the Edge*, p. 6.
4. For other pre-texts of 'Kafka and His Precursors' see Barei, pp. 155–62.
5. Ronald Christ, *The Narrow Act: Borges' Art of Allusion* (New York: New York University Press, 1969), p. 133.
6. 'Funes el memorioso' was originally published in the Buenos Aires daily *La Nación*, 7 June 1942.
7. Gene H. Bell-Villada, *Borges and his Fiction: A Guide to his Mind and Art* (Chapel Hill: University of North Carolina Press, 1981), p. 99.
8. This biographic detail is not included in 'Funes the Memorious.'
9. Eric Bulson, 'Joyce's Geodesy', *Journal of Modern Literature*, 25.2 (2001–02), 80–96 (p. 81).
10. It is difficult to ascertain whether Borges had knowledge of John Joyce's anecdote. He certainly knew, however, that Joyce had been trained by the Jesuits in Clongowes Wood College, an institution that was renowned for its *memoriter* pedagogy. This detail is mentioned in his 1925 review of *Ulysses* (*Inq.* 24) and in his 1937 capsule biography of Joyce (*OC4* 251). Significantly, Charles Duff, whom Borges had read in 1932, reported in *James Joyce and the Plain Reader* that Joyce was 'gifted with a prodigious, even astounding, memory'. See Duff, p. 31. The same prodigious memory was characteristic, of course, of the Argentine writer.
11. Joyce's portrayal of Dublin as a compendium of street names, parks, public buildings and commercial shops with a statistical, topographical and temporal rigour, has been amply demonstrated in *James Joyce's Dublin: A Topographical Guide to the Dublin of Ulysses*, by Ian Gunn and Clive Hart, with Harald Beck (London: Thames & Hudson, 2004).
12. Fritz Senn, *Joyce's Dislocutions*, p. 16.
13. Salgado, 'Barroco Joyce', p. 71.
14. Waisman, 'Borges Reads Joyce', p. 69.
15. Budgen, p. 69.
16. Burgin, p. 166. Borges gives a similar account in an interview with Roberto Alifano. See 'Funes and Insomnia', in *Twenty-Four Conversations with Borges, including a Selection of Poems: Interviews 1981–1983*, conversations trans. by Nicomedes Suárez Araúz, Willis Barnstone, and Noemí Escandell (New York: Lascaux Publishers, 1984), pp. 27–29 (p. 28).
17. Burgin, p. 166.
18. Burgin, p. 166.
19. Burgin, p. 166.
20. Roland McHugh, *Annotations to Finnegans Wake*, rev. edn (London: Johns Hopkins University Press, 1991), p. 120.
21. A similar theme runs through the 1936 poem 'Insomnia', in which Borges refers to himself as 'un aborrecido centinela [an abhorred watchman] of the city of Buenos Aires (*OC2* 237). In twentieth-century Buenos Aires insomnia becomes the inward, textual recitation of a wakeful mind. Borges's vision finally rolls up in a vivid mnemonic revelation that converges with the larger memory of universal history.
22. Budgen, pp. 180–81.
23. Frances Yates, *The Art of Memory* (London: Routledge and Kegan Paul, 1966), p. 41. In this study Yates offers an unprecedented trajectory of the vast and previously uncharted terrain that constitutes the history of Western mnemotechnics. Yates's survey begins with the legendary Greek poet Simonides of Ceos (the alleged inventor of the art) and is followed by a detailed exposition of the key role that memory played in the Roman sphere of classical rhetoric. She also surveys the art in Greece, paying particular attention to Aristotle's *De Memoria et Reminiscentia* and Plato's *Phaedrus*, which are considered amongst the most influential treatises of memory. Yates then moves to the art of memory that developed in the Middle Ages, mainly through the Christian discourses of Aquinas and Albertus. Her study subsequently concentrates on the more complex memory systems postulated by Giordano Bruno and Raymond Lully. Throughout this magisterial study, Yates emphasizes the enormity of her survey and the crucial fact that Memory conceived as Art and subject matter of a book-length investigation stands neither as an autonomous discipline nor as a complete field of study, but rather emerges as a scattered interdisciplinary project that consequently incorporates a vast array of subjects. The account of the art of memory that I provide in this article is deeply indebted to Yates's

study. For other studies on the subject of memory see Mary Carruthers, *The Book of Memory: A Study of Memory in Medieval Culture* (Cambridge: Cambridge University Press, 1992). For an illuminating commentary of the art of memory in Joyce's *Ulysses*, see Stephen Heath, 'Joyce in Language', in *James Joyce: New Perspectives*, ed. by Colin MacCabe (Brighton: Harvester Press, 1982), pp. 129–48. For an informative and insightful study of Joyce and memory see Jacques Mailhos, 'The Art of Memory: Joyce and Perec', in *Transcultural Joyce*, ed. by Karen R. Lawrence (Cambridge: Cambridge University Press, 1998), pp. 151–73. See also his ' "Begin to Forget it": The Preprovided Memory of *Finnegans Wake*', in *European Joyce Studies 4: Finnegans Wake Teems of Times*, ed. by Andrew Treip (Amsterdam: Rodopi, 1994) pp. 40–67; Klaus Reichert, 'Joyce's Memory', in *Images of Joyce*, ed. by Clive Hart, George Sandulescu, Bonnie K. Scott, Fritz Senn, 2 vols (Buckinghamshire: Colin Smythe, 1998), II, 754–58; and John S. Rickard, *Joyce's Book of Memory: The Mnemotechnic of Ulysses* (Durham, NC, and London: Duke University Press, 1998).
24. Bell-Villada, p. 97.
25. Pliny, the Elder, *Natural History*, trans. with introduction and notes by John F. Healy (London: Penguin, 1991), p. 88.
26. Pliny, p. 88.
27. Pliny, p. 89.
28. Roberto Alifano, *Conversaciones con Borges* (Buenos Aires: Editorial Atlántida, 1984), p. 80, my translation.
29. Marilyn French, *The Book as World: James Joyce's Ulysses* (London: Abacus, 1982), p. 26.
30. Umberto Eco, *The Aesthetics of Chaosmos, the Middle Ages of James Joyce*, trans. by Ellen Esrock (Cambridge, MA: Harvard University Press, 1989), p. 33.
31. Rice, p. 54.
32. Hilary Clark, *The Fictional Encyclopaedia: Joyce, Pound, Sollers* (London: Garland Publishing, 1990), p. 20.
33. Karen Lawrence, *The Odyssey of Style in Ulysses* (Princeton, NJ: Princeton University Press, 1981), p. 109.
34. David Farrell Krell, *Of Memory: Reminiscence and Writing on the Verge* (Bloomington and Indianapolis: Indiana University Press, 1990), p. 79.
35. John Locke, *An Essay concerning Human Understanding*, ed. by Roger Woolhouse (London: Penguin, 1997), p. 151.
36. James Joyce, *Occasional, Critical, and Political Writing*, ed. with an intro. and notes by Kevin Barry, trans. from the Italian by Conor Deane (Oxford: Oxford University Press, 2000), p. 60.
37. This conception of a universal memory brings to mind Jacques Derrida's reading of Joyce, in which he condenses Joyce's legacy as, '[a memory] which is henceforth greater than all your finite memory can, in a single instant or a single vocable, gather up of cultures, languages, mythologies, religions, philosophies, sciences, history of mind and of literatures'. For Derrida, this type of memory surpasses human limitations in order to give way to the workings of a machinist contrivance, hence Derrida's denomination of Joyce's 'hypermnesiac machine', in what he refers to as the 'quasi-infinite speed of the movements on Joyce's cables', as well as in his computerized version of Joyce, compounded in the portmanteau 'joyceware'. See Jacques Derrida, 'Two Words for Joyce', in *Post-Structuralist Joyce: Essays from the French*, ed. by Derek Attridge and Daniel Ferrer (Cambridge: Cambridge University Press, 1984), pp. 145–59 (p. 147).
38. Friedrich Nietzsche, *Untimely Meditations*, ed. by Daniel Breaseale, trans. by R. J. Hollingdale (Cambridge: Cambridge University Press, 1997), p. 59.
39. Nietzsche, p. 59.
40. Edward S. Casey, *Remembering: A Phenomenological Study* (Bloomington and Indianapolis: Indiana University Press, 1987), p. 7.
41. Virgil, *The Aeneid*, trans. by Robert Fitzgerald (London: Harvill Press, 1996), p. 186.
42. Plato, *The Republic*, trans. by Desmond Lee, 2nd rev. edn (London: Penguin, 1987), p. 393.
43. Paul Ricoeur, *Memory, History, Forgetting*, trans. by Kathleen Blamey and David Dellauer (London: University of Chicago Press, 2004), p. 426.
44. Nietzsche, p. 62.

45. Casey, p. 307.
46. Nietzsche, p. 62.
47. Roxana Kreimer, 'Nietzsche, autor de "Funes el Memorioso"', in *Jorge Luis Borges: intervenciones sobre pensamiento y literatura*, ed. by William Rowe, Claudio Canaparo, Annick Louis (Buenos Aires: Paidós, 2000), pp. 189–99 (p. 189). Kreimer claims Nietzsche as the only 'author' of Borges's 'Funes the Memorious', clearly failing to account for the other precursors that similarly contributed to the creation of Funes. However, this is an accomplished and illuminating exposition of Borges's relationship with Nietzsche.
48. Nietzsche, p. 62.
49. Salgado, 'Barroco Joyce', p. 72.
50. John Sturrock, *Paper Tigers: The Ideal Fictions o Jorge Luis Borges* (Oxford: Clarendon Press, 1977), p. 109.
51. Nietzsche, p. 62.
52. Ricoeur, p. 413.
53. Casey, pp. 15–17.
54. See Richard Sorabji, *Aristotle on Memory* (London: Duckworth, 1972), pp. 47–60. This useful study provides a translation of Aristotle's memory treatise *De Memoria et Reminiscentia*.
55. Casey, p. 15.
56. Casey, p. 15.
57. Rickard, p. 10.
58. Rickard, p. 11.
59. Jorge Luis Borges and Osvaldo Ferrari, *Reencuentro: diálogos inéditos* (Buenos Aires: Sudamericana, 1999), p. 37.
60. A. Walton Litz, 'Ithaca', in *James Joyce's Ulysses: Critical Essays*, ed. by Clive Hart and David Hayman (London: University of California Press, 1984), pp. 385–405 (p. 388).
61. Lawrence, *Odyssey of Style in Ulysses*, p. 181, p. 186.
62. Fritz Senn, '"Ithaca": Portrait of the Chapter as a Long List', in *Joyce's 'Ithaca'*, ed. by Andrew Gibson (Amsterdam: Rodopi, 1996), pp. 31–76 (p. 39).
63. Rickard, p. 76.
64. Gibson, *Joyce's 'Ithaca'*, p. 17.
65. Rickard, p. 192.
66. Sylvia Molloy, *Signs of Borges*, trans. by Oscar Montero (Durham, NC, and London: Duke University Press, 1994), p. 118.

CHAPTER 4

# In Praise of Darkness: Homer, Joyce, Borges

In his essay 'On Epic Naiveté' Theodor Adorno offers a view of the function of myth and narrative in Homer's *Odyssey* which may be read as a descriptive note on the Western epic tradition and its unceasing transformative variations throughout history. Adorno argues that the *Odyssey* is:

> none other than an attempt to attend to the endlessly renewed beating of the sea on the rocky coast, and to patiently reproduce the way the water floods over the rocks and then streams back from them with a roar, leaving the solid ground glowing with a deeper color. This roaring is the sound of epic discourse, in which what is solid and unequivocal comes together with what is ambiguous and flowing, only to immediately part from it again. The amorphous flood of myth is the eternally invariant, but the *telos* of narrative is the differentiated, and the unrelentingly strict identity with what is simply identical, with unarticulated sameness, serves to create its differentness.[1]

Adorno's rhythmical and complexly argued account of the epic is worth looking at in more detail. This report invites us to view the *Odyssey* as a metaphorical flight of ever-recurring intersecting currents, an oceanic, mythical undertaking that generations of readers can recognize as part of the same tradition, and yet may be read anew each time. According to Adorno, this process is constituted by a twofold, continuous motion within the epic genre which offers two inter-dependent processes of movement (water) and stasis (rocks). The sound of epic discourse is, thus, oxymoronic, as it is solid and unequivocal (in relation to the rock) but also ambiguous and flowing (in relation to the sea). Much like Penelope's intricate tapestry that involves endless cycles of weaving and un-weaving, the epic follows a similar incessant pattern that simultaneously implies stability and change. Adorno's assertion may also be read, ultimately, as an illustration of the long-standing tradition of the Ulysses myth, from Homer's resourceful wanderer as depicted in the *Odyssey* to Dante's influential account of Ulysses's last voyage in the *Inferno*; from Joyce's transposition of Homer into the scenery of twentieth-century Dublin in *Ulysses* to Borges's cross-cultural reading of the Ulysses myth in his 1948 essay 'The Last Voyage of Ulysses', and his 1949 short story 'The Immortal'.

This chapter examines the Ulysses tradition from the perspective of Borges's revisionary account of the myth. It demonstrates that Borges conflates the Greek, Italian, and Irish avatars of the legendary hero through his use of the metaphor of the ancient explorer and a specific type of nautical imagery. In particular, it argues that Borges's image of the explorer offers a generic category of the Ulysses myth as a journey, a daring quest that may equally stand for the many perils encountered by Homer's Odysseus, Dante's laborious and audacious writing of the *Commedia*, Joyce's stylistic innovations and rewriting of Homer in *Ulysses*, the cutting-edge ethos of his Buenos Aires review *Proa*, his own challenging exploration of Joyce's newly founded geography, and the journey of Joseph Cartaphilus in search of immortality. This chapter also discusses the complex Homeric pattern of seafaring narratives that Joyce develops in 'Eumaeus' and Borges in 'The Improbable Impostor Tom Castro'. In addition, the preliminary section that follows offers an overview of the reception of Homer in English, in an attempt to highlight the crucial fact that Borges's and Joyce's retellings of the Ulysses myth were largely informed by the Homeric tradition they had inherited as twentieth-century writers.[2]

Borges famously opened his seminal essay 'The Homeric Versions' (1932) with a provocative statement on the subject of literary translation:

> Ningún problema tan consustancial con las letras y con su modesto misterio como el que propone una traducción [...] Presuponer que toda recombinación de elementos es obligatoriamente inferior a su original, es presuponer que el borrador 9 es obligatoriamente inferior al borrador H — ya que no puede haber sino borradores. El concepto de *texto definitivo* no corresponde sino a la religión o al cansancio (*OC1* 239).

> [No problem is as consubstantial to literature and its modest mystery as the one posed by translation [...] To assume that every combination of elements is necessarily inferior to its original form is to assume that draft nine is necessarily inferior to draft H — for there can only be drafts. The concept of the 'definitive text' corresponds only to religion or exhaustion (*SNF* 69).]

Borges is challenging fixed notions of authorship and stable conceptions of literary texts. Unlike conventional theorists of translation, he celebrates derivative rather than original creations, inverting the conventional hierarchy, and questioning the notions of originality and the traditional belief in the superiority of the original. This complex process by virtue of which texts are neither situated in a chronological axis nor assessed from strictly canonized standpoints goes hand-in-hand with the type of re-creative translation strategy he practised in his 1925 fragmentary translation of 'Penelope'. If Borges ended his 1946 review of Salas Subirat's complete translation of *Ulysses* into Spanish with a verdict that urged prospective translators of Joyce to adopt a re-creative translation practice, so he concluded 'The Homeric Versions' with a position that similarly illustrated his disbelief in the possibility of attaining a 'faithful' rendition of the original:

> ¿Cuál de esas muchas traducciones es fiel?, querrá saber tal vez mi lector. Repito que ninguna o que todas. Si la fidelidad tiene que ser a las imaginaciones de Homero, a los irrecuperables hombres y días que él se representó, ninguna puede serlo para nosotros; todas, para un griego del siglo diez. Si a los propósitos que tuvo, cualquiera de las muchas que trascribí, salvo las literales, que sacan toda su virtud del contraste con hábitos presentes. No es imposible que la versión calmosa de Butler sea la más fiel (*OC1* 243).

[Which of these many translations is faithful? My reader will want to know. I repeat: none or all of them. If fidelity refers to Homer's imagination and the irrecoverable men and days that he portrayed, none of them are faithful to us, but all of them would be for a tenth-century Greek. If it refers to his intentions, then any of the many I have transcribed would suffice, except for the literal versions, whose virtue lies entirely in their contrast to contemporary practices. It is not impossible that Butler's unruffled version is the most faithful (*SNF* 74).]

Since 'none' or 'all' of these translations is faithful in relation to conveying the 'irrecoverable' cultural and linguistic circumstances of Homer's historical Greece, a tongue-in-cheek Borges then proposes that Butler's Victorian, 'unruffled', prose Homer may be read as the most 'faithful' of them all. Like the cultural abyss that separates the realities of Aristotle and the Islamic philosopher Averroës, in 'Averroës' Search', whose endeavour to translate *The Poetics* is defeated by the fact that he ignores the meaning of the words 'tragedy' and 'comedy', so the translation of Homer participates, to some extent, in a similar process of cultural and linguistic irrecoverability. And yet, this irrecoverable essence — as Borges playfully points out — depends on the eyes of the beholder, as much as the third-person narrator in 'Averroës' Search' seeks to reconstruct the complex circumstances of the historical Averroës about to embark on the translation of *The Poetics*: 'Sentí que la obra se burlaba de mí. Sentí que Averroes, queriendo imaginar lo que es un drama sin haber sospechado lo que es un teatro, no era más absurdo que yo, queriendo imaginar a Averroes, sin otro material que unos adarmes de Renan, de Lane y de Asín Palacios' (*OC1* 588) ['I felt that the work mocked me, foiled me, thwarted me. I felt that Averroës, trying to imagine what a play is without ever having suspected what a theater is, was no more absurd than I, trying to imagine Averroës yet with no more material than a few snatches from Renan, Lane, and Asín Palacios'] (*CF* 241). Ultimately for Borges — and I am also thinking of Walter Benjamin — what becomes paramount here is that a translation is inevitably necessary, despite its questionable inaccuracies, inasmuch as it extends the life of an original, thus inscribing it within a constant need for translatability and, therefore, creative transformation. Where Benjamin, using an identifiably messianic and ghostly terminology, refers to the 'afterlife' of a given work, Borges, in line with his aesthetics of compression and his idiosyncratic practice of writing built on pre-existing texts, unaffectedly utilizes the word *borrador* [draft], to denote the mutability and fluidity inherent in all literary works. The inversion of the original–translation dichotomy is further promulgated by a playful Borges, who praised his own ignorance of Greek as the key factor for his subsequent discovery of a multiplicity of 'Homers':

> El Quijote, debido a mi ejercicio congénito del español, es un monumento uniforme, sin otras variaciones que las deparadas por el editor, el encuadernador y el cajista; la Odisea, gracias a mi oportuno desconocimiento del griego, es una librería internacional de obras en prosa y verso, desde los pareados de Chapman hasta la *Authorized Version* de Andrew Lang o el drama clásico francés de Bérard o la *saga* vigorosa de Morris o la irónica novela burguesa de Samuel Butler (*OC1* 240).

> [The *Quixote*, due to my congenital practice of Spanish, is a uniform

monument, with no other variations except those provided by the publisher, the bookbinder, and the typesetter; the *Odyssey*, thanks to my opportune ignorance of Greek, is an international bookstore of works in prose and verse, from Chapman's couplets to Andrew Lang's 'Authorized Version' or Bérard's classic French drama or Morris' vigorous *saga* or Butler's ironic bourgeois novel (*SNF* 70).]

If the absence of Greek ironically opens up, rather than hinders, an exciting new avenue of knowledge, then Borges and Joyce turned a state of ignorance to a state of enlightenment, and filled their linguistic gap with the overflowing corpus of Homer in languages other than Greek. 'For Borges', writes Levine, 'the great virtue of Homer (Joyce's model) was not his proprietorial originality nor his actuality but the fact that Homer effectively produced a library of English literature, enriching the lives of successive generations of readers.'[3] The richness of the corpus that constitutes the history of Homer in translation is what Hugh Kenner, inscribing Joyce within an identifiable Homeric tradition, refers to under the title 'Mutations of Homer', as well as articulating the crucial and inescapable fact that 'Homer has never been stable'.[4]

This Homeric mutability and/or errancy engenders a series of interrogations throughout *Ulysses* both as part of the underlying assumption that we are in front of a text that is constantly signalling its relation to a larger web of discourses — in this case Homer's *Odyssey* — and to the fact that the work of Homer has been radically shifted across history, language, and culture. The only 'Homer' that Joyce can claim in *Ulysses* is a composite site inhabited by cultural difference and loaded by the several centuries of translation and criticism which have added different layers of meaning to a cultural heritage to which Umberto Eco has referred as 'a case of overinterpretation'.[5] Therefore when, in *Ulysses*, an enthusiastic Buck Mulligan proclaims: 'Ah, Dedalus, the Greeks! I must teach you. You must read them in the original' (*U* 1.79–80), Joyce conveys a mise-en-abyme effect, inasmuch as *Ulysses* is itself a sort of translation of the *Odyssey* and, ironically, Joyce himself was unable to read Homer in the Greek original. Just as in 'Partial Magic in the Quixote', Borges argues that the use of the literary device of Chinese boxes may provoke a reaction of confusion upon readers or spectators: '¿Por qué nos inquieta que el mapa esté incluído en el mapa y las mil y una noches en el libro de *Las Mil y Una Noches*? ¿Por qué nos inquieta que Don Quijote sea lector del *Quijote*, y Hamlet, espectador de *Hamlet*?' (*OC2* 47) ['Why does it disturb us that the map be included in the map and the thousand and one nights in the book of the *Thousand and One Nights*? Why does it disturb us that Don Quixote be a reader of the *Quixote* and Hamlet a spectator of *Hamlet*?'] (*L* 231). We can then transfer this interrogation to Joyce's inclusion of Homer's *Odyssey* within *Ulysses*, thus analogously asking: why does it disturb us that the *Odyssey* be included in *Ulysses*? And, equally, why does it disturb us that Buck Mulligan and Stephen Dedalus be readers of the *Odyssey*? Like the tentative responses to Borges's paradoxes, the answer to these questions would plunge us back again into a conception of literature, language, and translation that defies fixed meanings and proposes playful and irreverent reversals in which Joyce's *Ulysses* may be read as a precursor of Homer's *Odyssey*. Alternatively, Borges proposes the following metaphysical answer: 'tales inversions sugieren que si los caracteres de una ficción pueden ser lectores o espectadores, nosotros, sus lectores o espectadores, podemos ser ficticios' (*OC2* 47) ['these inversions suggest that if the characters of a fictional work can be readers or spectators, we, its readers or spectators, can be fictitious'] (*L* 231).[6]

In this manner, as things stood for Joyce, his relationship with Homer's *Odyssey* was mediated by the long chapter in history that constitutes the reception of Homer in English and other European languages. By this token, the paths that led Borges and Joyce to Homer are informed by a similar tradition of translations, rewritings, and critical assessments. As early as 1930 Stuart Gilbert insisted on Joyce's reliance on Bérard's *Les Phéniciens et l'Odyssée*, particularly highlighting the fact that, like the mercantile Semitic route in which Bérard situated the ancient Greek Homer, so Joyce conflated in Leopold Bloom a syncretic heritage of Hellenic, Semitic (and Hibernian) ancestries.[7] We should also bear in mind, however, that Joseph Brooker has recently undermined Gilbert's highly structured claim, arguing that: 'By the 1950s it was argued that Joyce had pulled Gilbert's leg in directing him to Victor Bérard's study'.[8] Writing on the occasion of Joyce's obituary, an observant Borges also dismissed Gilbert's argument: 'Among these voluntary tics, the most widely praised has been the most meaningless: James Joyce's contacts with Homer, or (simply) with the Senator from the *département de Jura*, M. Victor Bérard' (*SNF* 221). If Borges's contempt for Gilbert's affected parallel demonstrates anything at all, at least it discloses the fact that he was acquainted with Bérard's work and, like Joyce's later critics, did not credit it with any relevance to *Ulysses*. For Borges and Joyce, the Homeric heritage was not only represented by the respected legacy of Chapman and Pope, or the more recent historical/anthropological investigation of Bérard, but also by the scandalously shocking reading of Samuel Butler in *The Authoress of The Odyssey*, where he claimed that the *Odyssey* was written by a woman, more precisely, by a young Sicilian princess who 'had introduced herself into the work under the name of Nausicaa'.[9] In *Borges*, Adolfo Bioy Casares transcribes a 1957 conversation, in which he reports that Borges professed a preference for the *Odyssey* rather than the *Iliad*, as well as the important fact that he was informed by Butler's theory of female authorship.[10] In a similar vein, Brian Arkins dispels any doubt as to which 'Homers' Joyce had read in his lifetime by providing a useful list of the various editions he possessed.[11] Equally useful is the information listed by W. B. Stanford who claims that:

> Professor Stanislaus Joyce has kindly informed me that his brother had studied the following writers on Ulysses: Virgil, Ovid, Dante, Shakespeare, Racine, Fénelon, Tennyson, Phillips, d'Annunzio, and Hauptmann, as well as Samuel Butler's *The Authoress of the Odyssey* and Bérard's *Les Phéniciens et l'Odyssée*, and the translations by Butler and Cowper.[12]

Moreover, Joyce openly and unreservedly confessed that his first acquaintance with the *Odyssey* did not take place via the revered authority of Homer, but through the abridged, highly moralizing Victorian adaptation, *Adventures of Ulysses* by Charles Lamb who, following the success of his *Tales from Shakespeare*, specifically adapted for a child readership.[13] As Bjorn Tysdahl remarks: 'No wonder that when Joyce was given the topic "My Favourite Hero" for an essay, he chose Ulysses (Ellmann 46), and that many years later he recommended Lamb to his aunt Josephine when she found his own *Ulysses* baffling.'[14] By the same token, Hugh Kenner remarks that: 'As the word "adventure" indicates, his first thoughts about the book [*Ulysses*] were rooted in his adolescent reading of Charles Lamb's *The Story of Ulysses* [...] Encountered by Joyce at twelve, this version so impressed itself on his exceptional memory that he seems to have read versions of the Greek text as though they were expansions and rearrangements of Lamb.'[15] Yet at the same time, the heavily mediated version(s) of Homer that Joyce interspersed throughout *Ulysses* reach as far back as the Latin epic model initiated by Virgil in the *Aeneid*. Gérard Genette suggests that: 'The *Aeneid* and *Ulysses* are no doubt, to varying degrees and certainly on different grounds, two hypertexts (amongst others) of the same hypotext: the *Odyssey*, of course.'[16] What Genette is advertising here is an intertextual (or Borgesian) practice of reading that transcends chronological perspectives by situating two historically, linguistically, and culturally distant texts within a synchronic tradition. But, above all, Virgil and Joyce are compounded by a linguistic purpose and an onomastic intersection. In his attempt to bestow a national epic for the *civitas* of Rome, Virgil proudly demonstrated that the grand scale of the epic is as compelling in Latin as in Greek, as well as offering the alternative Latin-based versions of Greek names. Joyce, thus, follows the Latin innovation of Virgil in the *Aeneid* and the vernacular audacity of Dante in the *Commedia*, by composing a modernist version of the epic with a Hibernian inflection of the English language, as well as consciously adhering to a Latinate line that opts for the appellation Ulysses (the Virgilian form) rather than Odysseus (the Homeric form). In a similar sense Fritz Senn observes, 'the book [*Ulysses*] bears in its title the Latin translation of a Greek hero's name'.[17]

In a broader sense, Borges's and Joyce's Homeric heritage has been informed by Chaucer's *Troilus and Criseyde*, which largely relied on Boccaccio's *Filostrato*, and was firmly grounded in French translations/rewritings from Greek or Latin sources. This line is continued by Shakespeare in *Troilus and Cressida*, who in turn adhered to Chaucer's filtered, vernacular, and anachronistic tale of the Trojan lovers, and, even more significantly, by Chapman's celebrated English translation of Homer. We then jump forward to Keats's powerful testament to Chapman's Elizabethan Homer in 'On First Looking into Chapman's Homer', and the fascination of Romantic poets with the cult of the blind rhapsode.[18] The modernist return to Greek mythology exemplified by Eliot's *Waste Land*, and his celebrated 1923 review of *Ulysses*,[19] sought to advertise a model that conjured up both a fragmented, de-canonized, paradoxically 'new' version of the ancient, as well as a retreat to an invented timelessness, a desire to return to a primeval past that will somehow restore meaning to an unstable historical moment. But, as we are going to see throughout this chapter, neither Joyce nor Borges can be pigeonholed in this convenient 'mythical' schema, which is far too restrictive and self-limiting in relation to the complexity of their exercises in translation and rewriting. As Joseph Brooker observes in relation to the appearance of '*Ulysses*, Order and Myth': 'What is striking about [Eliot's] focus is less its novelty than its narrowness, its refusal to take in any other aspects of the text in an article published twenty-one months after Joyce's book appeared.'[20] Thus the inscription of Joyce within the mythical tradition of *Ulysses* should not necessarily signal a unidirectional return to Eliot's 'mythical method'. In this way, as Vanda Zajko proposes, we have to start questioning whether Joyce's relationship with Homer may transcend the limiting, yet highly influential structure imposed by Eliot's mythical reading: 'If we resist the idea that Joyce returns to Homer in order to lend authority to modernity, is it possible to figure the relation of Homer to Joyce in a more dynamic way?'[21] The analysis that follows will testify that it is possible to rethink the relation of Homer and Joyce through Borges by means of a pan-European comparative approach that goes beyond the Eliotic model.

## Greek, Italian, Irish, and Argentine Ulysses

Borges's lifelong interest in the Ulysses theme is condensed in the generic assertion, 'los hombres, a lo largo del tiempo, han repetido siempre dos historias: la de un bajel perdido que busca por los mares mediterráneos una isla querida, y la de un dios que se hace crucificar en el Gólgota' (*OC2* 448) ['throughout history, humankind has told two stories: the story of a lost ship sailing the Mediterranean seas in quest of a beloved isle, and the story of a god who allows himself to be crucified in Golgotha'] (*CF* 400). In 'The Last Voyage of Ulysses' Borges joins the scholarly debate concerning the eternal damnation of the Greek hero Ulysses, who is placed in the eighth circle of Dante's *Inferno*, the section of the Malebolge in which offenders are punished for the sin of fraudulent counselling. At the beginning of the essay, he argues: 'Mi propósito es reconsiderar, a la luz de otros pasajes de la *Comedia*, el enigmático relato que Dante pone en boca de Ulises (*Infierno*, XXVI, 90–142') ['My aim is to reconsider, in the light of other passages of the *Commedia*, the enigmatic tale that Dante places in the mouth of *Ulysses* (*Inferno* XXVI, 90–142)'] (*SNF* 280). Borges is referring, of course, to the compelling tale of the tragic voyage that emerges from the wondrous, elongated flame of the proud Greek hero, who painfully murmurs to Virgil a version of the myth that constitutes Dante's enigmatic addition to the Ulysses legend. He is fascinated by Dante's invention of a new ending, which produces a ramification in the Homeric story and adds further layers of meaning to a rich and complex mythological corpus.[22] The importance of Dante's story in the post-Homeric tradition is emphasized by W. B. Stanford: 'Next to Homer's conception of Ulysses, Dante's, despite its brevity, is the most influential in the whole evolution of the wandering hero.'[23] Borges's fascination with Ulysses calls for further thought and a detailed reading of his critical essay will reveal the several interrelated motives that led to his exploration of the Ulysses myth.

Borges considers an ongoing critical polemic: why is Ulysses punished in the eighth circle of Hell? His exploration of the subject is informed by the two principal camps of scholarly debate surrounding the Dantean episode. One tradition argues that Ulysses is punished for his legendary deceitfulness, chiefly for his plotting of the ruse of the wooden horse that led to the fall of Troy. The other camp, however, states that his punishment results from his more daring, nautical enterprise to embark on a final sacrilegious journey to reach the lands forbidden to man.[24] On discerning Mount Purgatory, Ulysses and his elderly crew incur not the customary wrath of Poseidon — the Greek Pagan deity presiding over the Homeric sea — but the more potent, inexplicable force of a Christian god who mercilessly condemns their human *curiositas* with a crushing death and eternal damnation in the confines of hell:

> Noi ci allegrammo, e tosto tornò in pianto;
> chè della nova terra un turbo nacque,
> e percosse del legno il primo canto.
> Tre volte il fè girar con tutte l'acque:
> Alla quarta levar la poppa in suso
> E la prora ire in giù, com'altrui piacque,
> Infin che 'l mar fu sopra noi richiuso[25] (*Inf* XXVI, 136–42).
>
> [Our celebrations soon turned to grief:
> from the new land there rose a whirling wind
> that beat against the forepart of the ship
> and whirled us round three times in churning waters;
> the fourth blast raised the stern up high, and sent
> the bow down deep, as pleased Another's will.
> And then the sea was closed again, above us.][26]

Borges's interest, undoubtedly, lies in the second tradition, particularly as he is fascinated by the inevitable parallels and contrasts between Ulysses's 'folle volo' and the otherworld voyage undertaken by Dante. 'If Ulysses is in the eighth *bolgia* of the eighth circle because of the "art" of deceit,' writes Boitani, 'God drowned out his earthly life because he was reaching the land where no post-lapsarian mortal, with the exception of Dante Alighieri, is allowed.'[27] If the daring Ulysses embarked on a voyage to a *terra nova* which eventually closed in death and subsequently led him into Hell, then Dante similarly sets out on a journey to explore the kingdom of the dead. Aware of the various critical currents that drew inverted correspondences between Dante and his antitype, Ulysses, Borges, quoting Carlo Steiner's interpretation of Canto XXVI of *Inferno*, claimed: '"Dante, nuevo Ulises, la pisará como un vencedor, ceñido de humildad, y no lo guiará la soberbia sino la razón, iluminada por la gracia"' (*OC3* 355) ['"Dante, a new Ulysses, will set foot there as a victor, girded with humility and guided not by pride but by reason, illuminated by grace"'] (*SNF* 282). In his characteristically erudite way, Borges intermingles his reading of Dante with a quotation from a critical study by the German scholar August Rüegg which adds a further dimension to the Dante/Ulysses parallel:

> Dante es un aventurero que, como Ulises, pisa no pisados caminos, recorre mundos que no ha divisado hombre alguno y pretende las metas más difíciles y remotas. Pero ahí se acaba el parangón. Ulises acomete a su cuenta y riesgo aventuras prohibidas; Dante se deja conducir por fuerzas más altas (*OC3* 355).
>
> [Dante is an adventurer who, like Ulysses, walks along virgin paths, travels across worlds no man has ever glimpsed and aspires to the most difficult and remote goals. But the comparison ends here. Ulysses sets forth on his own account and risks forbidden adventures; Dante allows himself to be guided by higher powers (*SNF* 281).]

For Borges, what is at stake here is that the exploratory missions of Ulysses and Dante — whether sinfully transgressive or divinely approved — implied a burning desire to journey across regions unknown to man in search for uncharted territories. Borges may have also found compelling the implication of forbidden knowledge implicit in this model of literature. The metaphor of the daring explorer becomes paramount in the investigation of Borges's relationship with the Ulysses theme. Equally significant, moreover, is the fact that the pair Dante/Ulysses as filtered through Borges's idiosyncratic prism, travels across literary boundaries and exemplifies the new relationship between Homer, Dante, Joyce, and Borges. Just as Borges labelled Dante the new Ulysses, so in his 1925 review of Joyce's *Ulysses* he similarly branded himself the Hispanic Ulysses of Joyce's Hibernian exploration of the myth: 'Soy EL PRIMER AVENTURERO hispánico que ha arribado al libro de Joyce' (*Inq.* 23) ['I am the first traveler from the Hispanic world to set foot upon the shores of *Ulysses*'] (*SNF* 12). Such reading compounds Borges's interpretation of Dante even further, as it reveals the numerous intricate folds of the Ulysses myth.[28] Thus, the central question to ask here is: can Borges's examination of Dante's Ulysses become a pre-text through which to revisit his previous excursions upon Joyce's newly founded geography? And, equally, can his 1925 review of *Ulysses* and 1948 Dante essay be read as the intertexts of his 1949 short story 'The Immortal'?

First of all, for Borges, a perusal of Canto XXVI of *Inferno* implies, inevitably, an open and fruitful engagement with the other literary afterlives of the Homeric hero. At the end of 'The Last Voyage of Ulysses' he writes:

> Una observación última. Devotas del mar y de Dante, las dos literaturas de idioma inglés han recibido algún influjo del Ulises dantesco. Eliot (y antes Andrew Lang y antes Longfellow) ha insinuado que de ese arquetipo glorioso procede el admirable *Ulysses* de Tennyson. No se ha indicado aún, que yo sepa, una afinidad más profunda: la del Ulises infernal con otro capitán desdichado: Ahab de *Moby Dick* (*OC3* 356).
>
> [A final observation. Devoted to the sea and to Dante, the two literatures written in English have felt the influence of the Dantesque Ulysses. Eliot (and before him Andrew Lang and before him Longfellow) has implied that Tennyson's admirable *Ulysses* proceeds from this glorious archetype. As far as I know, a deeper affinity has not previously been noted: that of the infernal Ulysses with another unfortunate captain: Ahab of *Moby-Dick* (*SNF* 283).]

And yet just as Borges failed to mention Dante's *Commedia* as one of the key sources of his story 'The Aleph',[29] so he equally failed to mention Joyce's *Ulysses* in his examination of the evolution of the Ulysses tradition. But as I will demonstrate here, this failure to acknowledge Joyce is answered, to a certain extent, by the fact that Joyce is tacitly present throughout his exploration of Homer and Dante. For example, the unmistakable Joycean flavour of 'The Last Voyage of Ulysses' led Daniel Balderston to include it amongst the various writings listed in the 'James Joyce' entry of his *Borges: una encyclopedia*.[30]

My argument here is that the theme of the ancient explorer whose ambitious quest is the mapping of new terrains and the difficult endeavour to describe previously unseen geographies, is deeply interconnected with the Buenos Aires avant-garde magazine *Proa*, in which Borges's 1925 review of *Ulysses* and fragmentary translation of 'Penelope' was published. As has been previously discussed in Chapter 1, *Proa* aimed to offer new ways to navigate through the genres of narrative and poetry from a supposedly innovative and groundbreaking point. This is particularly conveyed at the beginning of the review in which Borges proudly describes himself as the first Hispanic adventurer of Joyce's Hibernian Sea. Equally important is the fact that Borges astutely applied to *Ulysses* a recognizable type of nautical imagery, which turned Joyce's experimental novel into a type of enterprise: 'audaz como una proa y universal como la rosa de los vientos' (*Inq.* 28) ['as bold as the prow of the ship, and as universal as a mariner's compass'] (*SNF* 14). Moreover, in 'The Last Voyage of Ulysses' Borges paid a further homage to his former avant-garde forays and did not fail to utilize the crucial noun 'prow' to denote the boldness of Dante's Ulysses journey: 'Cinco meses hendieron el océano, y un día divisaron una montaña, parda, en el horizonte' (*OC3* 354) ['For five months their prow cleaved the ocean, and one day they caught sight of a dark mountain on the horizon'] (*SNF* 280). Indeed — as we have seen in Chapter 1 — Borges was aware of Joyce's deliberate juxtapositions between *Ulysses* and *The Odyssey*. But in spite of this, his 1925 reading of *Ulysses* did not aim to participate in the fashionable critical practice of unravelling parallels between Joyce and his Homeric predecessor but, instead, Borges sought to foster comparisons, or contrasts, with his own linguistic, literary and ideological circumstances in 1920s Buenos Aires.[31] In this sense, it remains fascinating that Borges compared his literary discovery of Joyce's *Ulysses* with a colonizing mission. The young Borges also speaks of *Ulysses*, 'con la vaga intensidad que hubo en los viajadores antiguos, al describir la tierra que era nueva frente a su asombro errante y en cuyos relatos se aunaron lo fabuloso y lo verídico, el decurso del Amazonas y la Ciudad de los Césares' (*Inq.* 23) ['with the license my admiration lends me and with the murky intensity of those ancient explorers who described lands new to their nomadic amazement, and whose stories about the Amazons and the City of the Caesars combined truth and fantasy'] (*SNF* 12). In his interweaving of fact and fiction, Borges's trick to the Buenos Aires readers of *Proa* is to set up a hall-of-mirrors of the prow symbol. Beneath the clear reflection of Joyce's *Ulysses* in the avant-gardist glass of the review, lies a deeper, more complex image that reveals Borges's authorial identification with the legendary Ulysses, in his attempt to offer a portrait of the young artist as an Argentine Ulysses, as he navigates upon the challenging waters of Joyce's Irish variation of the myth. To a further extent — and as I have argued earlier — in the 1920s Joyce's *Ulysses* was also forbidden territory, a prohibited book confiscated by several governmental authorities, as it had become outlawed in the United States, England, Ireland, and most English-speaking countries. At the beginning of *James Joyce and Censorship*, Paul Vanderham rightly quotes Joyce's comment that *Ulysses* 'was one of the world-disturbing sailors'.[32] Hence any reference to Borges's 1925 translation of 'Penelope' ought to take into account the crucial fact that the young avant-garde poet was aware that his voyage through Joyce's *Ulysses* implied an excursion into an unlawful and forbidden geography. The youthful and intrepid Borges embarks on a voyage to Joyce's *terra nova*, a newly discovered territory caught up between the forces of Law and Desire.

In short, Borges traverses the vast ocean of Joyce's literature in order to emerge in the Southern Hemisphere as the Ulysses of Buenos Aires. Hence, as we have seen, his subsequent 1948 speculations about Dante's enigmatic version of the Ulysses story are intricately allied with his prior use of maritime imagery and the metaphor of the ancient explorer in his 1925 review of Joyce. Borges's use of this navigational motif reappears in his poem 'Elegy' in which he proudly invokes his seafaring excursions: 'Oh destino el de Borges, / haber navegado por los diversos mares del mundo' (SP 230) ['Oh destiny of Borges — / to have traversed the various seas of the world'] (SP 231). In another poem he also refers to the alluring call of the sea: 'El mar. El joven mar. El mar de Ulises y de aquel otro Ulises que la gente del Islam apodó famosamente Es-Sindibad del Mar' (OC2 496) ['The sea. The young sea. Ulysses' sea, whom the people of Islam famously called Es-Sindibad the Sailor']. Moreover, in the poem 'The Fourth Element', he asserts: 'Agua, te lo suplico. Por este soñoliento / Enlace de numéricas palabras que te digo. / Acuérdate de Borges, tu nadador, tu amigo. / No faltes a mis labios en el postrer momento' (SP 164) ['Water, I ask a favor. Through this indolent / arrangement of measured words I speak to you. / Remember Borges, your friend, who swam in you. / Be present to my lips in my last moment'] (CP 165).

Yet for all his youthful navigational fervour, it should not be forgotten that the mature Borges identified more closely with Homer and Joyce than with the mythical Ulysses, since he shared with them the destiny of blind bard and weaver of many 'songs for men to come'.[33] The illustrious genealogy of the blind bard from Homer to Joyce and Borges becomes an identifiable narrative thread in their works. In Book VIII of *The Odyssey* the blinded minstrel Demodocus, who has exchanged eyesight for the gift of storytelling, sings the deeds of Odysseus at the court of the Phaeacians. It has been suggested, moreover, that the blind Demodocus singing about Ulysses is a reflection of the blind Homer singing his larger *Odyssey* of the Greek hero. In the 'Lestrygonians' episode of *Ulysses* a compassionate Leopold Bloom helps a blind man make his way through the streets of Dublin (U 8.1078–1108). In a wider epic dimension, the pathetic image of the blinded man 'tapping the curbstone with his slender cane' (U 8.1075) becomes Joyce's tributary acknowledgment to Homer, as he shifts his ancient predecessor across language, literature, and history and finds a suitable analogy in the urban labyrinth of twentieth-century Dublin. 'The figure of the blind man tapping his way around the city streets', suggests Eric Bulson, 'had a personal relevance for James Joyce. His exile and eye troubles made the darkness of the blind stripling immediate enough, and in this specific moment in *Ulysses*, he alludes to the paradox of physical absence and imaginative, geographical proximity.'[34] Similarly Edna O'Brien notes that '[Joyce's] principal model would be Homer — blind Homer, precursor to blind Joyce, who, after labouring the seven years it took to complete "Ulysses", was to suffer from glaucoma, cataracts, and dissolution of the retina.'[35] Like his Irish predecessor Borges also suffered from numerous eye ailments, undergoing his first cataract operation when he was only in his late twenties. It is feasible to conclude that Borges's and Joyce's perceptions of the world would have been deeply affected by their looming blindness. Furthermore, literary and physical blindness pervades the work of the mature Borges, particularly his 1960 collection *The Maker*, and his 1969 poetry book *In Praise of Darkness*. Significantly, Homer and Joyce — along with Shakespeare — are the central literary monuments of these collections. It is no wonder, then, that during the centennial celebrations of Joyce's birth that took place in Dublin on Bloomsday, a blind octogenarian Borges travelled as a guest of honour and relished the irony that, like the blind man of *Ulysses*, he was also wandering across the Dublin of his blind predecessor 'tiptapping his way through its streets with his probing stick'.[36] This frail Borges leaned on a walking stick he had proudly bought in Dublin and reported with glee that a similar one is mentioned 'at the beginning of one of the stories in *Dubliners*'.[37] Another equally fascinating figure of the blind man is conjured up by the St Lucian poet Derek Walcott in *Omeros*, who envisages a chameleon-like Homer who, on his transatlantic journey from ancient Greece to the warm seas of the Caribbean and then back again to Europe, incorporates the afterlives of Homer, Dante and Joyce (and we may say Borges) and successfully blends them in the composite figure of:[38]

> the blind man [who] sat on his crate after the pirogues
> set out, muttering the dark language of the blind,
> gnarled hands on his stick, his ears as sharp as the dog's.
> Sometimes he would sing and the scraps blew on the wind
> when her beads rubbed their rosary. Old St. Omere.
> He claimed he'd sailed round the world. 'Monsieur Seven Seas'
> they christened him, from a cod-liver-oil label
> with its wriggling swordfish. But his words were not clear
> They were Greek to her. Or old African babble.
> Across wires of hot asphalt the blind singer
> seemed to be numbering things. Who knows if his eyes
> saw through the shades, tapping his cane with one finger?[39]

### The Quest for Immortality

The *topos* of the audacious explorer also sets up the larger theme of the story 'The Immortal' in which Borges depicts the journey of a man in search for immortality: a man whose composite identity is gradually disclosed as Homer's: 'También me refirió su vejez y el postrer viaje que emprendió, movido, como Ulises, por el propósito de llegar a los hombres que no saben lo que es el mar ni comen carne sazonada con sal ni sospechan lo que es un remo' (*OC1* 540) ['He also told me of his own old age and of that late journey he had made — driven, like Ulysses, by the intention to arrive at the nation of men that know not what the sea is, that eat not salted meat, that know not what an oar might be'] (*CF* 191). According to Borges, the subject of 'The Immortal', 'es el efecto que la inmortalidad causaría en los hombres' (*OC1* 629) ['is the effect that immortality would have on humankind'] (*CF* 287). The story is constructed as a complex tapestry in which are intricately woven strands from Homer's *Iliad* and *Odyssey*, Dante's account of Ulysses's last journey, Pope's translation of the *Iliad*, the mythical figure of Homer himself, as well as allusions to the legendary figure of the Wandering Jew (chiefly under the name of Joseph Cartaphilus, one of the various onomastic variations of the legend) and the *Arabian Nights* story of Sinbad. Thus Borges depicts the long journey of Joseph Cartaphilus in search of immortality on the one hand, and his retrospective search for mortality, on the other, within a cyclical wandering[40] in which his composite hero becomes an everlasting Homer who — like Dante's Ulysses — embarked on a final voyage and, throughout his immortal trail has written (and forgotten) his *Iliad* and *Odyssey*, has fought in several wars, '[ha copiado] en el siglo trece, las aventuras de Simbad, de otro Ulises' (*OC1* 543) ['has copied down the adventures of Sindbad — another Ulysses'] (*CF* 194), and purchased the six volumes of Pope's translation of the *Iliad*. In his customary way, Borges adds at the end of 'The Immortal' a dubious postscript which functions as a counter-narrative to the prior testimony narrated by Joseph Cartaphilus. A literary critic identified under the pseudonym Dr Nahum Cordovero launches an acid attack that undermines the authenticity of Cartaphilus's narrative, and deems the document 'apocryphal', arguing that it had been plagiarized from the works of Pliny, Thomas de Quincey, Descartes, and Bernard Shaw (*CF* 195). Not arbitrarily, Cordovero's review is entitled *A Coat of Many Colours*. Thus Borges uses the review device as a teasing, humorous ending which, if anything at all, may be read as a lesson in literary theory which foregrounds the important fact that in the sphere of textual interrelations literary discourses are not read or conceived in isolation, but are always positioned in relation to a wider network of pre-existent texts. 'Ironically, then, Cordovero's attack in the Post-script on the integrity of Homer's text is our assurance of its universal validity', writes Ronald Christ, 'the more it is nothing in itself, the more the story is everything.'[41]

Borges's revisionary narrative of the Ulysses theme cannot but bring to mind Joyce's similar creative endeavour in *Ulysses*. 'Both *Ulysses* and "El Inmortal" are a repetition of the *Odyssey* and a voyage through literature', remarks Dominique Jullien, 'thus the story of the Immortal can be read as Borges's response to Joyce's odyssey of a Dublin Jew.'[42] Indeed, Leopold Bloom embodies an Irish Jew who similarly becomes an avatar of Homer's Ulysses, the legendary Wandering Jew, as well as several other nautical aliases, including Sinbad the Sailor.[43] In relation to the Wandering Jew, Timothy P. Martin states that 'In the Wagnerian canon he [Joyce] encountered a rich variety of characters who represent the problem of exile in its full complexity [...] None of Wagner's exiles, however, made as powerful an impression on Joyce as did his "Wandering Jew of the Ocean," the Flying Dutchman.'[44] In relation to Sinbad, Robert Hampson writes: 'Joyce's knowledge of the *Nights* is well documented. Joyce owned an Italian translation in Trieste. When he moved to Paris, he replaced it with the Burton Club Edition. The *Nights*, like the *Odyssey*, was one of the works which was permanently part of Joyce's library.'[45] Borges's lifelong fascination with the *Nights* is well known, particularly his fondness for a wide range of English, German, and Spanish renditions.[46] Joyce's foremost tribute to the *Nights* is conveyed at the end of 'Ithaca' as a weary Bloom invokes the journey of his Oriental predecessor in a rhythmical, alliterative, dreamlike sequence:

> Womb? Weary?
> He rests. He has travelled.
> With?
> Sinbad the Sailor and Tinbad the Tailor and Jinbad the Jailer and Whinbad the Whaler and Ninbad the Nailer and Finbad the Failer [...] (*U* 17.2319–23)

So far, I have demonstrated that in 1925 the young Borges portrayed himself as an Argentine Ulysses navigating through the uncharted waters of Joyce's new epic territory. I argued that Borges extended this metaphor of the explorer to Dante and labelled him the new Ulysses. I showed how this pattern of a journey to a *terra incognita* converges in his story 'The Immortal', in which he fuses the various Greek, Italian, Irish, Jewish and Oriental strands of the Ulysses theme in a man's quest for immortality. To a further extent, this highlights the crucial fact that what attracted the exiled Dante, Joyce, and Borges to the Ulysses archetype was his legendary depiction as outcast or émigré, whether this state is voluntary or involuntary, permanent or transitory, or whether the traveller longs to return to Ithaca, Florence, Dublin, or Buenos Aires. In his poem 'Ars Poetica' Borges invokes the artistic and universal significance of the Ulysses legend: 'Cuentan que Ulises, harto de prodigios, / Lloró de amor al divisar su Itaca / Verde y humilde. El arte es esa Itaca / De verde eternidad, no de prodigios' (*SP* 136) ['They say that Ulysses, sated with marvels, / Wept tears of love at the sight of his Ithaca, / Green and humble. Art is that Ithaca / Of green eternity, not of marvels'] (*SP* 137). The eternity of Ulysses to which Borges is alluding here recapitulates, above all, Joyce's ambitious enterprise in his writing of *Ulysses*. The eternity of Ulysses is nowhere better portrayed than in the mathematical catechism of 'Ithaca', as the reader is afforded a view of the full arch of the Ulysses tradition in Leopold Bloom's grand scale trajectory of the legendary hero:

> Would the departed never nowhere nohow reappear?
> Ever he would wander, self-compelled, to the extreme limit of his cometary orbit, beyond the fixed stars and variable suns and telescopic planets, astronomical waifs and strays, to the extreme boundary of space, passing from land to land, among peoples, amid events. [...] Whence, disappearing from the constellation of the Northern Crown he would somehow reappear reborn above delta in the constellation of Cassiopeia (*U* 17.2012–20).

Joyce's extract has been enriched by W. B. Stanford, who has eloquently referred to this passage as:

> A vast interstellar odyssey and a spectacularly heroic return [...] This is the supreme adventure of Bloom's adventurous mind. It is a conception beyond anything in the previous Ulysses tradition, carrying with it much of that potent scientific romanticism which modern astrophysicists have inherited from ancient astrologers, and much, too, of the spirit of Dante's doomed hero.[47]

For the blind and elderly Borges, a return to Joyce signals a return to Ithaca, a return that goes full circle in relation to his longstanding acquaintance with *Ulysses* and, similarly, from the perspective of the transformative variations of the myth. In his 1968 tributary poem 'James Joyce', a mature Borges, once again the explorer of Joyce's epic geography, voyages through the vastness of his eternal day:

> Entre el alba y la noche está la historia
> universal. Desde la noche veo
> a mis pies los caminos del hebreo,
> Cartago aniquilada, Infierno y Gloria.
> Dame, Señor, coraje y alegría
> para escalar la cumbre de este día. (*OC2* 361)

>     [From the depths of night I've seen
>     at my feet the wanderings of the Jews,
>     Carthage destroyed, Hell, and Heaven's bliss.
>     Grant me, Lord, the courage and joy
>     I need to scale the summit of this day (SP 273).]

Like Dante's Ulysses, who undertakes his last voyage at old age, a frail Borges poetically aspires to reach the summit of Joyce's *Ulysses*. However, this is not a sacrilegious journey since, like Dante the Pilgrim, Borges beseeches God's grace to grant him the *coraje* and *alegría* which are the indispensable qualities in any journey of exploration. As a lifelong traveller of Joyce's topography, Borges knows beforehand that he will never reach the summit of Joyce's monument, insofar as a journey through *Ulysses* involves not a one-way-trip, but infinite excursions into an inexhaustible and wide-ranging geography. Ultimately, in Borges's and Joyce's revisionary treatment of the Ulysses theme is encapsulated a whole epic tradition which, like Adorno's interpretation of *The Odyssey*, preserves the myth through stasis and yet makes it new by 'the endlessly renewed beating of the sea on the rocky coast'. In this sense, 'The Immortal' and *Ulysses* may also be read as an allegory of the ubiquitous presence of Homer in the Western tradition and as the inescapable, overpowering cultural heritage that has haunted Borges and Joyce throughout their lives. In 'The Immortal' Borges follows the grand epic curve of Homer, Dante, and Joyce in a conscious attempt to participate in the retelling of the Ulysses theme. But unlike his epic predecessors Borges reduces their encyclopaedic scale to a miniaturized, compacted form of the epic as short story, vignette, or *ficción* that aims to reduce several centuries of tradition to an economical five-page prose exercise. Even if Dante's retelling is condensed in a single Canto, it still belongs to the larger scope of the *Inferno* and, even more, Ulysses becomes a recurring presence throughout the three Cantiche of the *Commedia*. In 'The Immortal', above all, lies Borges's foremost tribute to Homer's literary immortality, and an unreserved affiliation to a fascinating, yet multifarious tradition he had inherited in the wake of Dante and Joyce.

## The Wine-dark Sea

If for Adorno, the roaring of the sea stands as the sound of epic discourse, this ever-flowing resonance travels from ancient Greece to twentieth-century Ireland in order to converge in the gigantic aquatic catalogue meticulously described in 'Ithaca' (*U* 17.163–228). These oceanic proportions are generated by two questions. First, by the modest, three-worded, preterite interrogation: Did it flow? (*U* 18.163), and then by the more descriptive: 'What in water did Bloom, waterlover, drawer of water, watercarrier, returning to the range, admire?' (*U* 17.183–84). What Joyce listed in a far-reaching, epically inspired catalogue, the more economical Borges encapsulated in the name of a Greek deity of the sea: 'Porque el agua es Proteo' (*SP* 162) ['For water is Proteus'] (*SP* 163), and synthesized its course throughout the globe with two of its ancient rivers: 'Y tu fuga se llama el Éufrates o el Ganges' (*SP* 162) ['Your flights are called the Euphrates or the Ganges'] (*SP* 163). If 'Ithaca' reverberates with an exhaustive record of the various properties and uses of water, then 'Eumaeus' becomes the episode that most strongly suggests the Odyssean seafaring topos, elevating 'Navigation' as its Art and 'Sailors' as its Symbol. In fact, Mary T. Reynolds has pointed out an interesting parallel between the episode and Dante's last voyage of Ulysses: 'A showpiece is Bloom's and Stephen's encounter with the redbearded sailor, whose tale of shipwreck in the southern hemisphere is unmistakably parallel to Dante's account of Ulysses's last voyage in *Inferno 26*'.[48] Reynolds seems to be referring to the gruesome story of Antonio, the Greek sailor and tattooist, who perished at sea eaten by sharks. However, if we consider the vast number of sea stories, both in the northern and southern hemispheres that are woven into the episode, a further series of parallels with Ulysses's tale of shipwreck begin to emerge. Central to this topic are, equally, the many alleged expeditions undertaken by the sailor Murphy, as listed in his dubious record of the world, which he claims to have circumnavigated:

> I was in the Red Sea. I was in China and North America and South America. We was chased by pirates one voyage. I seen icebergs plenty, growlers. I was in Stockholm and the Black Sea, the Dardanelles under Captain Dalton, the best bloody man that ever scuttled a ship. I seen Russia. *Gospodi pomilyou*. That's how the Russians prays (*U* 16.459–63).

Fundamental to the Ulysses theme in this episode is also the exotic postcard from South America, according to Derrida an open text, a public piece of writing,[49] which Murphy suspiciously produces as matter-of-fact evidence to persuade his audience of the numerous perils and out-of-the-ordinary sights he encountered in his many adventures. The episode also displays a cross-current of maritime stories that adorn the (old) narrative of the episode, particularly at the point when 'the others got on to talking about accidents at sea, ships lost in fog, collisions with icebergs, all that sort of thing' (*U* 16.900–01). From the *Flying Dutchman* — the mysterious phantom ship that never returned home — to the tragic case of the Scandinavian ship *Palme* that sank in the Irish sea with its entire crew; from the English ship *Lady Cairns* which in 1904 fatally collided with the German bark *The Mona* with the loss of all crew, to the high-profile nineteenth-century 'Tichborne' (*U* 16.1343) legal case, in which, according to Gifford:

> Arthur Orton (1834–98), a coarse, ignorant butcher [claims to be] Roger Charles Tichborne (1829–54), the heir presumptive of Sir James Francis Tichborne (1784–1862), [who] was lost at sea on the *Bella* in 1854, but his mother refused to believe him dead and advertised for information about his whereabouts.[50]

The other underlying narrative uniting this complex pattern of seafaring tales is put forward by Stephen Dedalus at the beginning of 'Eumaeus', wherein he alerts the reader about the ambiguous, slippery nature of identity throughout the episode: 'Sounds are impostures, Stephen said after a pause of some little time, like names. Cicero, Podmore. Napoleon, Mr Goodbody. Jesus, Mr Doyle. Shakespeares were as common as Murphies. What's in a name?' (*U* 16.362–64). The underlying void that lies behind the façade of the impostor, or the signifier devoid of signified, becomes also the central theme of Borges's *A Universal History of Infamy* (1935): 'Patíbulos y piratas lo pueblan y la palabra infamia *aturde* en el título, pero bajo los tumultos no hay nada. No es otra cosa que apariencia, que una superficie de imágenes; por eso mismo puede acaso agradar' (*OC1* 291) ['Gallows and pirates fill its pages, and that word *iniquity* strikes awe in its title, but under all the storm and lightning, there is nothing. It is all just appearance, a surface of images — which is why readers may, perhaps, enjoy it'] (*CF* 5). To illustrate Stephen's claim, the untrustworthy and hackneyed narrator of 'Eumaeus' refers to Murphy with a wide-ranging onomastic record. Claire A. Culleton has compiled these various appellations: 'Murphy becomes "the communicative tarpaulin" (16.479), "the Skibbereen father" (16.666), "the impervious navigator" (16.1010–11), "Shipahoy" (16.901), and "Jack Tar" (16.1456), almost as if he were given a newer, more animated, moniker with every mention.'[51] Culleton omits, however, the further names of Ulysses Pseudangelos — as Joyce put it in the *schemata* — his Oriental counterpart 'Sinbad' (*U* 16.858) and 'the ancient mariner' (*U* 16.844), an allusion, of course, to Coleridge's *The Rime of the Ancient Mariner*, a poem heavily influenced by Dante's Ulysses.

Joyce's use of the motif of the impostor in 'Eumaeus' runs in juxtaposition to Homer's *Odyssey*, where Odysseus, 'that man skilled in all ways of contending, the wanderer, harried for years on end' (*Odyssey* 13) uses the arts of deception, cunning, and disguise as his main heroic attributes. In Book XIV of the *Odyssey*, Odysseus is physically disguised through the intervention and protection of his Olympic guardian, Athena, in order to conceal his return from the treacherous suitors. On her divine advice, he seeks hospitality in the hut of the swineherd Eumaeus for whom he promptly fabricates a maritime tale of pirates, dangers, and adventures — not unlike his own Odyssey, or the various stories that appear in 'Eumaeus' — in order to conceal his real identity. The histrionic acts of role-play and disguise and the art of storytelling become the means by which imposture is achieved and a counterfeit façade is revealed, a device that Joyce takes to greater lengths in 'Eumaeus'. As Gerald L. Bruns explains in his persuasive analysis of the episode:

> It is good to dwell upon this notion of imposture, because, as it happens, this is the central theme of 'Eumaeus' — a theme around which a tale of masks and roles are woven [...]. The idea that 'Sounds are impostures' adumbrates a basic nominalist formula, according to which a discontinuity is said to prevail between words and things. In the context here the discontinuity is between names and persons, and as the situation develops we are led to wonder, first, whether the keeper of the shelter is really the historical Fitzharris, and, second, whether Murphy is really the romantic figure he purports to be.[52]

In his poem 'Odyssey, Book Twenty-three' (1964) Borges also explores the discrepancy between name and person in Odysseus, and elevates a rhetorical question that brings into the equation the nature of Ulysses as Everyman and Noman that Joyce had explored in 'Ithaca': '¿Dónde está aquel hombre / Que en los días y noches del destierro / Erraba por el mundo como un perro / Y decía que Nadie era su nombre?' (*SP* 204) ['Where is the man now / Who in his exile wandered night and day / Over the world like a wild dog, and would say / His name was No One, No One, anyhow?'] (*SP* 205). Just as Joyce developed the theme of imposture in 'Eumaeus', so in *A Universal History of Infamy* Borges offers the journalistic vignette 'The Improbable Impostor Tom Castro', namely a fictionalized account of the Tichborne legal case that Joyce had already introduced in 'Eumaeus'.[53]

For comparative purposes, I have transcribed their versions of the same story:

*The Tichborne case according to Joyce*

And then, number one, you came up against the man in possession and had to produce your credentials like the claimant in the Tichborne case, Roger Charles Tichborne, *Bella* was the boat's name to the best of his recollection he, the heir, went down in as the evidence went to show and there was a tattoo mark too in Indian ink, lord Bellew was it, as he might very easily have picked up the details from some pal on board ship and then, when got up to tally with the description given, introduce himself with: *Excuse me, my name is So and So* or some such commonplace remark (*U* 16.1341–49).

*The Tichborne case according to Borges*

In the waning days of April, 1854 [...] there had sunk in the waters of the Atlantic a steamship christened the *Mermaid*, bound from Rio de Janeiro to Liverpool. Among the drowned had been one Roger Charles Tichborne, an English military officer brought up in France, and the firstborn son of one of England's leading Catholic families. [...] Bogle decided that it was Orton's duty to take the first steamer for Europe and realize Lady Tichborne's hope that her son had not perished — by declaring himself to be that son (*CF* 15).

The main question to ask here is this: was Joyce's 'Eumaeus' the source for Borges's story? The first tentative answer is no. As is norm with Borges, he provides an 'Index of Sources' and lists Philip Gosse's *The History of Piracy* (1911) as its main source. However I agree with Luis Chitarroni that the most likely reason for this overlap is due to the fact that Borges and Joyce habitually consulted the Eleventh Edition of the *Encyclopaedia Britannica* as an unlimited resource for their writings and, unsurprisingly, the Tichborne case was given a considerable entry.[54] Yet at the same time Borges, who practised a fragmentary, yet paradoxically thorough reading of *Ulysses*, surprised the reader on several occasions with precise and detailed references from 'Scylla and Charybdis', 'Circe', and 'Ithaca', and may well have equally drawn this anecdotal account from Joyce.

In the investigation of the literary relationship between Borges and Joyce, perusing the different ways in which they appropriated a story constitutes a highly instructive and informative methodology. In this case, both versions of the Tichborne case are incorporated within a larger narrative frame: 'Eumaeus', and *A Universal History of Infamy*, in which the chief purpose is the narration of tales of shipwreck, deception, and falsehood. In their fictional adaptations of the historical account we get a glimpse of the sameness and difference of their creative impulses, thus revealing illuminating aspects of the theory and practice of their writings, the fictional laws governing their epic and compressed tendencies, and their recurrent narrative procedures. The fact that Borges and Joyce became interested in the Tichborne case, the fact that they decided to subject it to their highly idiosyncratic, transformative spinning processes and, most of all, the fact that they plunged the finished product within the larger canvas of a book/episode about infamy/deception are significant factors that cannot be ignored. In this way, Joyce offered an additional seafaring interpolation to 'Eumaeus' and Borges a fully developed exercise in prose. Let us then examine more closely the intersections and divergences of their Tichborne versions.

If Joyce dedicates to the Tichborne case a section of 'Eumaeus' permeated by the infectious, clichéd locutions of the third-person narrator — as well as placing it in a dialogic relationship with the several interconnected reports about shipwrecks and deception that integrate the episode — Borges turns his Tichborne vignette into 'ejercicios de prosa narrativa' ['exercise in narrative prose'] that reduces 'la vida entera de un hombre a dos o tres escenas' (*OC1* 289) ['a person's entire life to two or three scenes'] (*CF* 3). Whilst this synthetic technique appears as the fundamental trademark of Borges's writing, we should not forget that in *Stephen Hero* Joyce proposed his theory of the epiphany, which is defined by Stephen as, 'a sudden spiritual manifestation, whether in the vulgarity of speech or of gesture or in a memorable phrase of the mind itself' (*SH* 216). Rather than proposing a clear-cut analogy between Joyce's epiphanies and Borges's journalistic vignettes developed in *A Universal History of Infamy*, I shall argue here that it is possible to recognize some parallels between both forms. For example, Robert Adams Day identifies in the Joycean epiphany an 'extended meditation on the performance of Dante and Ibsen'.[55] Day's endeavour to take the epiphany back to Dante interests us here, as Borges similarly located his concise method within Dante's literary tradition. In his 1980 lecture 'The Divine Comedy' Borges argued that it is possible to recognize in Dante's epic model a poetic artistry whereby the life of a character is captured and condensed in a few lines (*OC3* 213). In this case, Borges states that he has been wrongly praised for introducing this device to fiction, and in his usual self-effacing pose retorted that we owe instead this discovery to Dante's Middle Ages. In retrospect (particularly through his relationship with Joyce) we can recognize that, time and again, Borges approaches a writer from the standpoint of his aesthetics of brevity — in this case Dante — and searches for the fragmentary in the epic, thus turning an encyclopaedic work into a multiplicity of small segments. The invention with which Borges credited Dante is particularly apparent in the story 'Biography of Tadeo Isidoro Cruz', which bears the following epigraph from Yeats's 'The Winding Stair': 'I'm looking for the face I had / Before the world was made' (*OC1* 561). The story closes with the arresting line: 'Cualquier destino, por largo y complicado que sea, consta en realidad de *un solo momento*: el momento en que el hombre sabe para siempre quién es' (*OC1* 562) ['Any life, however long and complicated it may be, actually consists of a *single moment* — the moment when a man knows forever who he is'] (*CF* 213). The far-reaching literary implication we can deduce from this example is that Borges was informed by Dante, but at the same time we can hear some unmistakable echoes of Stephen Dedalus's similar attempt to capture a 'sudden spiritual manifestation'. 'In philosophical and religious terms', writes Vicki Mahaffey, 'epiphany represents an idealistic, even platonic belief in the superiority of the spirit, its ability to transcend materiality.'[56] Borges undoubtedly conveys this idealistic, Platonic search for the spiritual essence of a man's life in the final lines of 'Biography of Tadeo Isidoro Cruz'. But unlike Joyce, who rapidly eschewed the underlying method of his aphoristic epiphanies for the ensuing novelistic scale of *Ulysses* and *Finnegans Wake*, Borges developed this aesthetic of compression and transmuted its essential creative ingredients into the ultimate gold of his Art, the quintessential Borgesian *ficción*. Yet it needs saying that, as Mahaffey points out, the epiphanies reappeared 'in the richer contexts of Joyce's subsequent works'.[57]

If in his account of the Tichborne case Joyce remains closer to the historical facts, Borges blends fact and fiction in his deliberate incorporation of apocryphal elements. Hence, Joyce refers to the ship in which the legitimate Roger Charles Tichborne drowned by its real name, 'Bella' (significantly in Italian and hence highly appropriate in relation to the various references to the Italian language interspersed throughout the episode). Borges, on the contrary, opts for the Homeric name 'Mermaid', as a means to add a Hellenic ingredient to a sea story, as well as to insinuate that the ship was under the spell of the legendary creatures of doom, particularly as he states in *The Book of Imaginary Beings*: 'La *Odisea* refiere que las Sirenas atraían y perdían a los navegantes' (*OCC* 696) ['The *Odyssey* tells us that Sirens attract and shipwreck men'].[58] Borges also succeeds in providing a more detailed profile of the real Tichborne, which highlights his social and economical upper-class milieu. If in 'Eumaeus' Joyce alludes to the tattoo mark in Indian ink (*U* 16.1345) that the legitimate Tichborne had carved on his shoulder during his schooldays (thus setting up a correspondence with the other noteworthy tattoo that Murphy proudly displays to his nocturnal audience in the Cabman's Shelter), Borges omits the reference altogether. On the other hand, as Bell-Villada points out: 'In the Castro story, Borges takes on Bogle (briefly mentioned in the *Britannica* as a Negro servant who gave the real Orton a bit of coaching) and transforms him from the vague supernumerary which he originally was into Orton's coprotagonist and mastermind.'[59] Joyce, we learn, omitted the reference to Bogle. The decisive point at stake here is that Borges and Joyce are modelling their own fictional versions of the same historical material in an attempt to produce an anecdotal account that will fit the overall pattern of their creative projects. Both interlace it in a wider tapestry of stories about deception and/or shipwrecks.[60] Therefore, Borges and Joyce also had the freedom to incorporate into their theme of imposture strands from other sources which added to the multiplicity of meaning they were seeking to convey. And yet, the moulds with which they give shape to their fictional accounts of the Tichborne case participate, moreover, in the larger syncretic tradition of the Ulyssean wanderer. At the beginning of the story Borges alludes to the call of the open sea:

> Sabemos que era hijo de un carnicero, que su infancia conoció la miseria insípida de los barrios bajos de Londres y que sintió el llamado del mar. El hecho no es insólito. *Run away to sea*, huir al mar, es la rotura inglesa tradicional de la autoridad de los padres, la iniciación heroica. La geografía la recomienda y aún la escritura (Psalmos, CVII): *Los que bajan en barcas a la mar, los que comercian en las grandes aguas; ésos ven las obras de Dios y sus maravillas en el abismo* (*OC1* 301).

> [We know that he was the son of a butcher, that his childhood was spent in the gray meanness of the London slums, and that he harkened to the call of the sea. *That* story is not an uncommon one; 'running away to sea' was the traditional English way to break with parental authority — the heroic ritual of initiation. Geography recommended such a course, as did the Scriptures themselves: *'They that go down to the sea in ships, that do business in great waters; these see the works of the Lord, and his wonders in the deep'* (Psalms 107. 23–24) (*CF* 13).]

In 'Eumaeus' Joyce also refers to 'the call of the sea', but, in what is a highly ironic twist for a twentieth-century Ulysses, the uneventful life of Bloom has been starved of maritime adventures. In fact, his limited sea journey involved a boat trip from Dublin to Holyhead: 'nevertheless it reminded him in a way of a longcherished plan he meant to one day realise some Wednesday or Saturday of travelling to London *via* long sea not to say that he had ever travelled extensively to any great extent but he was at heart a born adventurer though by a trick of fate he had consistently remained a landlubber except you call going to Holyhead which was his longest' (*U* 16.499–504). Or, later in the episode the allegedly well-travelled Murphy gradually strips himself of his disguise of voyager, and angrily retorts: '— I'm tired of all them rocks in the sea, and boats and ships. Salt junk all the time' (*U* 16.622–23). Like Borges's 1954 preface to *A Universal History of Infamy* and like Stephen Dedalus's warning at the beginning of 'Eumaeus', we are largely dealing with identities which are 'impostures' or 'just appearance, a surface of images'. The palimpsestic quality of these Ulyssean identities whereby the outer parchment simultaneously reveals and at times contradicts the internal layer(s) of the narrative, become, thus, paramount in a book entitled *Ulysses*, or *A Universal History of Infamy*.

Central to Borges's and Joyce's retelling tales of the Ulysses myth is the assumption that their revisionary, composite fabrics are stitched together with remnants from several cultures, religions, and traditions. Borges and Joyce composed a series of narratives that participate in the Ulysses theme and, therefore, borrow the *topos* of the navigator, the metaphor of the ancient explorer, and the art of deceitfulness. In the difference and sameness of their exercises in appropriation and rewriting, in their complex dialectical relationship we find, once again, the vast novelistic scale of Joyce contra the tight confines of Borges's *ficción*, but equally important, we can also discern the epiphanic mode of Joyce's early writings in synthesis with Borges's economical prose by virtue of Dante's medieval model. Finally, the figure of Homer that looms large in Borges and Joyce may be illustrated with the ending of Borges's moving parable 'The Maker'. In this narrative, a nameless individual, later identified as Homer, experiences a sudden revelation before turning blind:

> En esta noche de sus ojos mortales, a la hora que descendía, lo aguardaban también el amor y el riesgo. Ares y Afrodita, porque ya adivinaba (porque ya lo cercaba) un rumor de gloria y de hexámetros, un rumor de hombres que defienden un templo que los dioses no salvarán y dos bajeles negros que buscan por el mar una isla querida, el rumor de las Odiseas y las Ilíadas que era su destino cantar y dejar resonando cóncavamente en la memoria humana. Sabemos estas cosas, pero no las que sintió al descender a la última sombra (*OC2* 160).

> [In this night of his mortal eyes into which he was descending, love and adventure were also awaiting him. Ares and Aphrodite — because now he began to sense (because now he began to be surrounded by) a rumor of glory and hexameters, a rumor of men who defend a temple that the gods will not save, a rumor of black ships that set sail in search of a beloved isle, the rumor of the *Odysseys* and *Iliads* that it was his fate to sing and to leave echoing in the cupped hands of human memory. These things we know, but not those that he felt as he descended into his last darkness (*CF* 293).]

In this parable of shifting mirrors the blind Borges imagines the precise moment in which Homer conceived his epic oeuvre and yet descended into darkness. Therefore, we can similarly ask, what did Borges and Joyce feel as they created their work and descended into blindness? Like Borges, the blind Joyce looks back to Homer as a means to imagine a further rumour of *Odysseys*, listening to the incomparable music of dactylic hexameters, closing his eyes in order to gain a clear picture of what the eyes of the imagination can only see 'shut your eyes and see' (*U* 3.9) says Stephen Dedalus as he walks into eternity along Sandymount strand. 'I am getting on nicely in the dark' (*U* 3.15) may well have been Joyce's — and also Homer's, Milton's, and Borges's — poignant response at the end of his life. 'Open your eyes now' (*U* 3.25) and the light of the imagination — or the luminocity of the epic tradition — brightens the path of Joyce's and Borges's writings, so that in the eternal sea of literature generations of readers can listen to the 'endless renewed beating of the sea on the rocky coast'.

## Notes to Chapter 4

1. Theodor Adorno, 'On Epic Naiveté', in *Notes to Literature*, trans. by Shierry Weber Nicholsen, 2 vols (New York: Columbia University Press, 1991), pp. 24–30 (p. 24).
2. For an ample treatment of this large subject see *Homer in English*, ed. by George Steiner, with the assistance of A. Dykman (London: Penguin, 1996). See also *The Cambridge Companion to Homer*, ed. by Robert Fowler, 2nd edn (Cambridge: Cambridge University Press, 2006). Simeon Underwood's *English Translators of Homer: From George Chapman to Christopher Logue* (London: Northcote House, 1998) is also a very useful study.
3. Levine, 'Notes', p. 354.
4. Hugh Kenner, 'Mutations of Homer', in *Classic Joyce: Joyce Studies in Italy 6*, ed. by Franca Ruggieri (Rome: Bulzoni Editore, 1999), pp. 25–32 (p. 25).
5. Umberto Eco with Richard Rorty, Jonathan Culler and Christine Brooke-Rose, *Interpretation and Overinterpretation*, ed. by Stefan Collini (Cambridge: Cambridge University Press, 1998), p. 52.
6. Regarding this issue of *Ulysses* and the Homeric original vs. translation, see Keri Elizabeth Ames, 'Joyce's Aesthetic of the Double Negative and his Encounters with Homer's *Odyssey*', in *Beckett, Joyce and the Art of the Negative*, ed. by Colleen Jaurretche (Amsterdam: Rodopi, 2005), pp. 15–48 (p. 15). Her essay 'The Oxymoron of Fidelity in Homer's *Odyssey* and Joyce's *Ulysses*', *James Joyce Studies Annual*, 14 (2003), 132–74 is also a useful discussion of Joyce's affiliation with Homer.
7. Stuart Gilbert, *James Joyce's 'Ulysses': A Study*, 2nd edn (New York: Vintage, 1952), p. 82.
8. Brooker, p. 65.
9. Samuel Butler, *The Authoress of the Odyssey: where and when she wrote, who she was, the use she made of the Iliad, & how the poem grew under her hands*, 2nd edn (London: Jonathan Cape, 1922), p. 8.
10. Adolfo Bioy Casares, *Borges*, edición al cuidado de Daniel Martino (Barcelona: Destino, 2006), pp. 290–97; see also p. 375.
11. See Brian Arkins, *Greek and Roman Themes in Joyce* (New York: Edwin Mellen, 1999), p. 22.
12. W. B. Stanford, *The Ulysses Theme: A Study in the Adaptability of a Traditional Hero* (Oxford: Basil Blackwell, 1954), p. 276, n. 6.
13. Charles Lamb, *Adventures of Ulysses*, with an intro. by Andrew Lang (London: Edward Arnold, 1890).
14. Bjorn Tysdahl 'On First Looking into Homer: Lamb's *Ulysses* — and Joyce's', in *Classic Joyce: Joyce Studies in Italy 6*, ed. by Franca Ruggieri (Rome: Bulzoni Editore, 1999), pp. 279–89 (p. 280).
15. Hugh Kenner, *Ulysses*, rev. edn (Baltimore, MD, and London: Johns Hopkins University Press, 1993), pp. 23–24.
16. Gérard Genette, *Palimpsests*, p. 5.
17. Fritz Senn, *Joyce's Dislocutions: Essays on Reading as Translation*, ed. by John Paul Riquelme (Baltimore, MD, and London: Johns Hopkins University Press, 1984), p. 140.

18. See especially Timothy Webb's up-to-date, informative synopsis in, 'Homer and the Romantics', in Fowler, ed., *The Cambridge Companion to Homer*, pp. 287–310.
19. See T. S. Eliot, *Selected Prose*, ed. by Frank Kermode (London: Faber & Faber, 1975).
20. See Brooker, p. 43.
21. See Vanda Zajko 'Homer and *Ulysses*', in 'Homer in English Translation', in Fowler, ed., *The Cambridge Companion to Homer*, pp. 311–24 (p. 316).
22. It should be noted that Borges had similarly endowed the Argentine cult gaucho poem, *Martín Fierro*, with an alternative ending and fictional resolution. See Borges, 'El Fin' (*OC1* 519–21).
23. Stanford, p. 178.
24. For an illuminating analysis of these two traditions of scholarship see Piero Boitani, 'Shipwreck: Interpretation and Alterity', in *Dante*, ed. by Jeremy Tambling (London: Longman, 1999), pp. 68–85. For a discussion of the evolution of the Ulysses hero from Dante to Joyce and Walcott see also Boitani's essay 'Ulysses in Another World', in *Classic Joyce: Joyce Studies in Italy 6*, ed. by Franca Ruggieri (Rome: Bulzoni Editore, 1999), pp. 33–51.
25. All references to Dante's *Commedia* belong to *La Divina Commedia*, testo critico della Società Dantesca Italiana, riveduto col commento scartazziniano rifatto da Giuseppe Vandelli, dodicesima edizione (Milan: Editore Della Real Casa, 1944), (*Inf* XXVI, 136–42). Further references will be cited parenthetically in the text.
26. Dante Alighieri, *The Divine Comedy*, trans. by Mark Musa, 3 vols (New York: Penguin, 1986), (*Inf* XXVI, p. 309). Further references will be cited parenthetically in the text.
27. Boitani, 'Shipwreck', p. 79.
28. Borges's use of the motif of the explorer is ambivalent in relation to the critical tradition that drew parallels between the voyage of discovery Dante attributes to Ulysses and the subsequent discovery of the New World. See, for instance, his 1981 postscript in 'The Last Voyage of Ulysses' (*SNF* 283). It may be then inferred that he is using the *topos* of the explorer in a non-historical, mythical way. However, I agree with Piero Boitani's assertion that: 'At the beginning of the fourteenth century, Ulysses stands on a triple threshold, that on which, in Dante's conscience, the death of the classical world, the end of Christian philosophy, and the advent of a new world finally clash'. See Boitani, 'Shipwreck', p. 83.
29. Borges's omission of Dante is discussed in Chapter 5.
30. See Daniel Balderston, *Borges: una encyclopedia* (Buenos Aires: Grupo editorial Norma, 1999).
31. Also, we have to remember that since the publication of Stuart Gilbert's 1930 study, Borges rejected the systematic, over-elaborated parallels between the *Odyssey* and *Ulysses*: 'The constant but insignificant parallels between Joyce's *Ulysses* and Homer's *Odyssey*, are still hearing — I will never know why — the impetuous praise of the critics' (*OC1* 417–18).
32. Paul Vanderham, *James Joyce and Censorship*, p. 1.
33. Homer, *The Odyssey*, trans. by Robert Fitzgerald (London: Harvill Press, 1996), p. 154. Further references will be cited parenthetically in the text.
34. Bulson, p. 80.
35. Edna O'Brien, 'Joyce's Odyssey: The Labors of "Ulysses"', *The New Yorker*, 7 June 1999, pp. 82–90 (p. 82).
36. See Kearney, p. 47.
37. See *La Nación*, 6 de agosto 1982, p. 9. The story to which Borges is alluding here is 'A Painful Case', in which Mr Duffy is described 'carrying a stout hazel' (*D* 104).
38. See Patricia Novillo-Corvalán, 'Literary Migrations: Homer's Journey through Joyce's Ireland and Walcott's St Lucia', *Irish Migration Studies in Latin America*, 5.3 (2007), 157–62, also available at http://www.irlandeses.org/0711novillo1.htm, for a discussion of the literary kinship found in the works of Joyce and Walcott.
39. Derek Walcott, *Omeros*, pp. 17–18.
40. It is significant that in 'The Immortal' Borges also alludes to Giambattista Vico's cyclical theory of history which becomes, of course, the main structural pattern of Joyce's *Finnegans Wake*: 'In 1729 or thereabouts, I discussed the origin of that poem with a professor of rhetoric whose name, I believe, was Giambattista; his arguments struck me as irrefutable' (*CF* 193).
41. Ronald Christ, p. 199.
42. Dominique Jullien, 'Biography of an Immortal', *Comparative Literature*, 47 (1995), 136–59 (p. 140).

43. This seafaring motif is discussed in the next section.
44. Timothy P. Martin, 'Joyce, Wagner, and the Wandering Jew', *Comparative Literature*, 42 (1990), 49–72 (p. 50).
45. Robert G. Hampson, 'The Genie out of the Bottle: Conrad, Wells and Joyce', in *The Reception of The Thousand and One Nights in British Culture*, ed. by Peter L. Caracciolo (London: Macmillan, 1988), pp. 218–43 (p. 230).
46. See Borges, 'The Translators of *The Thousand and One Nights*' (*SNF* 92–110).
47. Stanford, p. 221.
48. Mary T. Reynolds, *Joyce and Dante: The Shaping Imagination* (Princeton, NJ: Princeton University Press), p. 38.
49. Jacques Derrida, '*Ulysses* Gramophone', in *A Companion to James Joyce's Ulysses*, ed. by Margot Norris (Boston, MA, and New York: Bedford Books, 1998), pp. 69–90 (p. 73).
50. Gifford, p. 554.
51. Claire A. Culleton, *Names And Naming in Joyce* (Madison: The University of Wisconsin Press, 1994), p. 23.
52. Gerald L. Bruns, *James Joyce's Ulysses: Critical Essays* ed. by Clive Hart and David Hayman (London: University of California Press, 1984), pp. 363–85 (p. 369).
53. Tom Castro was the Hispanic alias of Arthur Orton. Since Borges wrote the stories for the popular Buenos Aires daily *Crítica*, it is understandable that he privileged the Hispanic over the Anglophone version of the name.
54. See Luis Chitarroni, 'Borges y Joyce', in *Joyce o la travesía del lenguaje:psicoanálisis y literatura*, Nada Lasic — Elena Szumiraj (compiladoras), (Buenos Aires: Fondo De Cultura Económica, 1993), pp. 17–25 (pp. 20–21).
55. Robert Adams Day, 'Dante, Ibsen, Joyce, Epiphanies, and the Art of Memory', *James Joyce Quarterly*, 25.3 (1998), 357–62 (p. 361).
56. Vicki Mahaffey, 'Joyce's Shorter Works', in *The Cambridge Companion to James Joyce*, ed. by Derek Attridge, 4th edn (Cambridge: Cambridge University Press, 2003), pp. 185–211 (p. 192).
57. Mahaffey, p. 193.
58. Borges, *Book of Imaginary Beings*, p. 132.
59. Bell-Villada, p. 56.
60. In this sense it is significant that in 'The Widow Ching — Pirate', another of the narratives that integrate *A Universal History of Infamy*, Borges included a reference to the female pirate Anne Bonney, whom he describes as 'una irlandesa resplandeciente, de senos altos y de pelo fogoso, que más de una vez arriesgó su cuerpo en el abordaje de naves' (*OC1* 306) ['a magnificent Irishwoman of high breasts and fiery hair who risked her life more than once in boarding ships'] (*CF* 19).

CHAPTER 5

# Architects of Labyrinths: Dante, Joyce, Borges

The act of reading Dante through the prism of Borges and Joyce implies a radical rethinking of a Western tradition whose interpretative potential has been extended, affected, and reinvigorated by a complex process of literary transactions. The Dantean corpus inherited by twentieth-century Irish and Argentine writers already incorporated six crowded centuries of Dantean scholarship that infused and informed their own afterlives of Dante. By means of these decisive and central historical and cultural negotiations, the Dantean episteme which they encountered constituted a composite legacy that incorporated a vast array of discourses: from Chaucer's pioneering translations/adaptations of the *Commedia* in *The Canterbury Tales*, Milton's inheritance of Dante's Christian epic tradition in *Paradise Lost*, Henry Cary's influential late eighteenth-century rendering of the *Commedia*, to the apogee of Dante's reception in the nineteenth century, particularly in the translations, rewritings and critical re-evaluations of the Romantics, with poets such as Shelley, Byron, Keats and Coleridge openly proclaiming their admiration for Dante. If the Romantics chiefly contributed to the popularization of Dante in English, this reverential dissemination was continued and extended by the Victorian imaginations of Robert and Elizabeth Browning, Thomas Carlyle, Alfred Lord Tennyson, and the significant contribution by the Rossetti family.[1] Equally central is William Blake's innovative visionary iconography of the *Commedia* as depicted in his watercolour illustrations.[2] Therefore, it may be argued that the twentieth-century fascination with Dante's Italian tradition — particularly of writers such as Eliot, Pound, Joyce and Borges — was fundamentally owed to the critical investment that had previously taken place during several centuries of Dantean scholarship.[3] For example, in his essay 'Realism and Idealism in English Literature' Joyce energetically documented the significance Italian writers had had on English literature, insisting that 'its masters were Boccaccio, Dante, Tasso, and Messer Lodovico. Chaucer's *Canterbury Tales* are a version of the *Decameron* or the *Novellino*; Milton's *Paradise Lost* is a Puritan transcript of the *Divine Comedy*' (*CW* 164). As we have already seen in Chapter 4, Borges also recognized the pervasive influence of Dante — chiefly through his Ulysses — in English writing on both sides of the Atlantic (*SNF* 283). Borges, who proclaimed in 'The Argentine Writer and Tradition' his right of unlimited access to the Western archive from the marginal perspective of an Argentine, proudly inherited Dante's writings as part of this recognizable English corpus. As he affirmed in a 1961 conference: 'Llegué de un modo laberíntico a la obra maestra, desde la literatura de una isla septentrional que se llama Inglaterra. Llegué a través de Chaucer, del siglo XIV, y de una versión que no he mirado hace muchos años, la de Longfellow' (*TR3* 71) ['I arrived to this masterpiece [the *Commedia*] in a rather labyrinthine way, through the literature of a northerly island called England. I arrived by means of Chaucer in the fourteenth century and a version of Longfellow that I haven't read for several years'].

This chapter examines the ubiquitous presence of Dante in the works of Borges and Joyce. It explores their respective meetings with the Florentine writer from a literary, historical, and biographical viewpoint. Joyce encountered Dante through a Roman Catholic backdrop and a formative Jesuit upbringing, while Borges's rather belated meeting with Dante took place in the 1930s, yet it became a pivotal and lifelong force in his writings. It argues that in spite of the different circumstances that compelled Borges and Joyce to develop an enduring interest in Dante's works, their encounters are marked by several intersections. Both publicly expressed their unconditional admiration for their Italian predecessor with eulogistic declarations, and yet had the audacity to swap reverence for irreverence in their creative productions, daringly proposing versions of their illustrious *maestro* sprinkled with parody and unmistakably satirical impulses. Both professed a predilection for selected linguistic and thematic aspects of the *Commedia*, which they subsequently blended and moulded to fit the transformative process of their respective writings. Both participated in the post-Dantean tradition of the virtuous lady as a means to offer an inverted female model that endorses attributes far removed from Beatrice's piousness and chastity.

This chapter also investigates the crucial juncture at which Dante meets Joyce in Borges's celebrated *ficciones* 'The Zahir' and 'The Aleph',[4] where he interweaves a complex tapestry of references and allusions to Dante and Joyce respectively that become illuminated through a joint analysis of both stories. I argue that the decisive principle of Borges's encounter with Dante and Joyce implies that their epic proportions can be re-imagined, re-fitted and contracted in the tight, yet infinite confines of a magical panel, memory, coin or minute iridescent sphere also known as the Aleph. It must, therefore, be emphasized that Borges's affiliation with Joyce as a model of infinity and his counteractive disaffiliation as the epitome of fictional overload, brings into play the mediating figure of Dante who, so to speak, stands somewhere in the background or, at times, in the forefront of their conversation, just as Homer and Shakespeare equally participate in the pluralistic forum forged by their complex interactions. Equally, this chapter aims to raise several interrelated questions, such as, how do Joyce and Borges foster afterlives of Dante in the twentieth century? How does Borges create his own compressed, parodic version of the *Commedia*? And in what way is this exercise in rewriting and translation illuminated by his previous condensed version of *Ulysses* in 'Funes the Memorious'? And, finally, what happens when Leopold Bloom's florin embarks on a transcultural voyage from Dublin to Buenos Aires, following the similar journey previously undertaken by Molly Bloom in 1925, and also somehow fulfilling the thwarted expedition never undertaken by Eveline?

## Joyce and Borges, Readers of Dante

The relationship between Joyce and Dante benefited from the early publicity undertaken by Samuel Beckett in his seminal essay: 'Dante...Bruno.Vico..Joyce' that constituted the first study of *Our Exagmination Round His Factification For Incamination of Work-in-Progress* (1929). The chief purpose of this eccentrically titled collection of critical essays (which boasted twelve influential contributors, including the French writer and translator Eugene Jolas and the American poet William Carlos Williams) was to defend *Work in Progress* from the unwelcoming reception of the critics. Beckett's four-way comparative methodology placed Joyce's writings historically in relation to the chronological Italian lineage of Dante, Bruno, and Vico. In his exploration of Joyce's affiliation with Dante, Beckett offers an ample discussion from a linguistic and literary vantage point in which he brings together Dante's treatises and *Commedia* in relation to Joyce's embryonic, untitled, and experimental *Work-in-Progress*. He concluded the essay with 'a last word about the Purgatories'[5] in which he forged a suggestive array of juxtapositions between Dante's and Joyce's purgatorial realms. He asserted that if Dante's Purgatory is 'conical and consequently implies culmination', Joyce's 'is spherical and excludes culmination'. If in Dante's 'there is an ascent from real vegetation — Ante-Purgatory, to ideal vegetation — Terrestrial Paradise,' in Joyce's, contrarily, 'there is no ascent and no ideal vegetation'. If in Dante's there is 'absolute progression and a guaranteed consummation', in Joyce's there is, 'flux — progression or retrogression, and an apparent consummation'. If in Dante's the 'movement is unidirectional, and a step forward represents a net advance' in Joyce's, conversely, 'movement is non-directional — or multi-directional, and a step forward is, by definition, a step back'. Beckett's conclusion insisted on the redeeming, upward journey of Dante's *Purgatorio* as a transitional space leading to Divine salvation, in opposition to Joyce's polyvalent, unfinished, and purgatorial current leading to the further fluidity and uncertainty of an endlessly revolving linguistic motion: 'Dante's Terrestrial Paradise is the carriage entrance to a Paradise that is not terrestrial: Mr. Joyce's Terrestrial Paradise is the tradesmen's entrance on to the sea-shore'. To a further extent, Beckett's intricate pattern of the complex relationship between Joyce and Dante can only anticipate and illuminate his own lifelong dialogue with the Florentine poet. Beckett's 'last word about the Purgatories', paradoxically becomes the first word about *his* Purgatories, as his subsequent rewritings of Dante propose a series of unredeemed characters who are entombed alive in the most austere and desolate of purgatorial landscapes. Principally, Beckett participates in the transformation of Dante's Christian epic of salvation as it conjures up a non-paradisiacal, unconsummated, and perpetual purgatorial model that follows up from his 1929 essay. Beckett foregrounds his appropriation of Dante's vision of the afterlife in his poetic, prose, and dramatic works. In 'Beckett's Purgatories' John L. Murphy asserts that: 'The Catholic tradition — dissected in Joyce — for Beckett becomes another intellectual construction to be mined. While both resurrect Christian models, they reshape and refigure them to suit the needs of not a believer but an agnostic, one who, centuries after Dante, propagates a refurbished purgatorial vision.'[6] Just as

Beckett is advancing his own transformative exercise of Dante in the wake of Joyce, he is equally contributing towards the consolidation of a tradition of Irish writers openly engaged with the aftermath of Dante's medieval vision as it voyages across history, language, and culture to twentieth-century Ireland.[7]

After Beckett's 'Dante...Bruno.Vico..Joyce', the most significant scholarly contribution charting Joyce's relationship with Dante from his early epiphanies to *Finnegans Wake* is Mary T. Reynolds's *Joyce and Dante: The Shaping Imagination* (1981). This ambitious study aims to examine the pervasive influence of Dante in Joyce's entire corpus: 'In all Joyce's work Dante is a massive presence, judged, evaluated, and measured in every dimension.'[8] Reynolds also makes the more subtle proposition that Dante stands at the heart of Joyce's creative impulse or, as she puts it in the compound title of her work, Dante becomes 'the shaping imagination' of Joyce's writing. Since this type of claim runs the risk of excluding other equally central discourses in Joyce's complex intertextuality, she clarifies that Joyce's full-scale literary engagement with Dante is only comparable to his affiliation with Homer and Shakespeare.[9] Reynolds also provides a useful appendix with Joyce's allusions to Dante throughout his entire oeuvre. Apart from Reynolds's study, the Joycean scholarship has recently benefited from Lucia Boldrini's *Joyce, Dante, and the Poetics of Literary Relations: Language and Meaning in Finnegans Wake* (2001). This is an exhaustive investigation that surveys the 'literary relations' between Dante's works and the *Wake*, in an attempt to comparatively demonstrate how Joyce's linguistic plurality, polysemy, and experimentalism are closely intertwined with Dante's treatises, *Commedia* and his epistle to Can Grande della Scala. Boldrini's comparative study adheres to a methodology that aims to unearth what she refers to as '"a Dantean poetics of *Finnegans Wake*", [...] (a conception of the relationship between language and literature, and between theme, structure and style, as well as of the scope of the literary work, and of how a text signifies) which is comparable to the poetics of Dante's works.'[10] Jennifer Fraser's *Rite of Passage in the Narratives of Dante and Joyce* (2002), is likewise another insightful recent study which has enhanced and taken to further lengths Joyce's fascinating relationship with Dante. Her study is carefully constructed around the symbolism of the 'diptych' which 'in late antiquity', she explains, 'were made of wood or ivory, and they were hinged together to close like a book. The inner surfaces of the two panels had recessed surfaces of wax on which one could inscribe a message'.[11] It is therefore suggested throughout the book that the literary works of Joyce and Dante conform to the rich image of the diptych.

On the other hand, a significant corpus of scholarship has demonstrated the noteworthy presence of Dante in Borges's work. The most valuable contribution to date is Humberto Nuñez-Faraco's *Borges and Dante: Echoes of a Literary Friendship* (2006). His study examines three aspects of Borges's relationship with Dante: poetic language, ethics and love. Nuñez-Faraco states that the purpose of his study is 'to reveal the way in which Borges's interests in these issues manifested themselves in his appropriation of Dante and gained prominence within his work as a whole, paying particular attention to the years *c.* 1920–*c.* 1960'.[12] In addition to Nuñez-Faraco's book, there is a wealth of essays that investigate the influence of Dante

— particularly the *Commedia* — in Borges's fiction,[13] a recognizable presence that may be identified in his short stories ('The Aleph', 'The Intruder', 'Death and the Compass', 'The Other Death', 'The Wait'), poems ('Of Heaven and Hell', '*Inferno* V, 129', 'Hunger', 'Conjectural Poem') narrative vignettes ('*Paradiso, XXX, 108*', '*Inferno, I, 32*') and various references to Dante's pagan animal mythology in *The Book of Imaginary Beings* ('Cerberus', The Minotaur', 'Acheron'). Furthermore, Borges, unlike Joyce, engaged in the critical reception of Dante, producing relevant essays in the 1940s which were later compiled in *Nine Dantesque Essays* (1982). He also gave several interviews and conferences on Dante in the last thirty years of his life,[14] and composed the preliminary study of a Spanish prose edition of the *Commedia* translated by Cayetano Rosell with notes by Narciso Bruzzi Costas (1949). As a result of this, his fictional engagement with Dante has to be considered in conjunction to his critical output, particularly as there exists a substantial overlapping and inter-feeding between both productions.

While Borges and Joyce shared a lifelong relationship with Dante, their respective meetings with the Italian poet differ considerably. Joyce's encounter with Dante goes back to his childhood years as part of the religious inheritance of a strict Catholic upbringing which was in turn reinforced by the pedagogical training imparted by the Jesuits. It is also significant that during his studies at University College, Joyce learned Italian and read Dante's *Commedia* in the original. For example, Eco and Santoro-Brienza observe that 'From his early student years, Joyce studied Dante and valued him more than any other poet. Only Homer and Shakespeare are as ubiquitously present in all his writings as Dante is. And Joyce had no hesitation in calling him "the first of the Europeans"'.[15] Joyce's admiration and emulation for Dante led Oliver Gogarty — as Ellmann reports — 'to dub him a little later the Dante of Dublin' (*JJII* 75). Joyce's cultural entrenching in a Dantean universe is also emphasized by David Wallace:

> Joyce grew up knowing Dante as part of the Catholic culture of Ireland: he had a dour governess called 'Dante' Conway; he lived in a house in Blackrock with stained-glass panels in the hall door depicting Dante and Beatrice. His Jesuit educators (like their counterparts in Italy) employed the *Commedia* to enforce Catholic orthodoxy, 'the spiritual refrigerating apparatus invented and patented in all countries by Dante Alighieri'.[16]

In late nineteenth-century Ireland, more than six hundred years after the publication of Dante's *Commedia* and another three hundred since the Basque Christian mystic and founder of the Jesuit brotherhood, St Ignatius of Loyola, composed his influential *Spiritual Exercises*,[17] the Jesuit congregation of Roman Catholic Ireland still adhered to the educational technique based on scholastic conceptions of hell and Loyola's religious and mnemonic technique of 'composition of place'. In Book III of *A Portrait*, Father Arnall's compelling rhetoric effectively borrows from Loyola's *Spiritual Exercises* in order to deliver his dogmatic oration on the eternal punishments reserved for the damned souls in Hell:

> This morning we endeavoured, in our reflection upon hell, to make what our holy founder calls in his book of spiritual exercises, the composition of place. We endeavoured, that is, to imagine with the senses of the mind, in

our imagination, the material character of that awful place and of the physical torments which all who are in hell endure (P 107).

The efficacy of this pedagogical method is based in the intense visualization of the places of Hell and the lasting impression they make on an audience of adolescent boys, particularly under the extreme isolation of a spiritual retreat. Frances Yates argues that Dante's *Inferno* stands amongst the most representative medieval memory systems, and refers to the *Commedia* as a 'mystical art' or 'Dantesque art of memory' which 'could be regarded as a kind of memory system for memorizing Hell and its punishments, with striking images on orders of places.'[18] In this vein, Dante's systematically organized architecture of hell, with its striking iconography of concentric circles, mountains, rivers, woods, icy landscapes, mythological figures, and law of divine retribution based on *contrapasso* (whereby the punishment is commensurate to the nature of the sin committed in life) becomes the exemplary monument of a whole Christian tradition that promotes the accurate and systematic remembrance of hell. Thus, Father Arnall also required that the memories of his 'dear little brothers in Christ' become a *tabula rasa* so that they more easily absorb his hyperbolic eschatological sermon: 'Banish from your minds all worldly thoughts and think only of the last things, death, judgment, hell and heaven', as 'he who remembers these things, says Ecclesiastes, shall not sin forever' (P 93). He also sprinkles his discourse with a further scatological horror, as the dark confines of hell are infused with 'an awful stench. All the filth of the world, all the offal and scum of the world, we are told, shall run there as to a vast reeking sewer' (P 101). This is the type of foul smell that in Canto XI of *Inferno* temporarily halts Virgil and Dante's descent into the Sixth Circle of hell: 'Lo nostro scender conviene esser tardo/ sì che s'ausi un poco in prima il senso/ al tristo fiato'[19] ['Our descent will have to be delayed somewhat/ so that our sense of smell may grow accustomed to these vile fumes'].[20] The effectiveness of Father Arnall's visual, olfactory, and auditory detour of hell leads to Stephen's rapid shift from corporeal pleasures to a spiritual reawakening that culminates in his Act of Contrition and subsequent confession: 'Confess, he had to confess every sin [...] Confess! O he would indeed to be free and sinless again!' (P 118). In Dante's scheme of damnation Stephen would be guilty of lust, an offence that belongs to the sins of Incontinence and is allocated to Circle II of his *terra infernalis*. Once Stephen is purged of his impurity through the sacrament of confession, his previous sinful existence is transformed into 'a life of grace and virtue and happiness' (P 123). But this new spiritual life that closes Chapter III is rapidly overtaken by Stephen's ensuing literary, political and linguistic concerns, insofar as he leaves behind his religious potential as the 'Reverend Stephen Dedalus, S.J.' (P 136) in order to fully embrace the legacy of his mythological predecessor, the pagan Greek artificer Daedalus. In this sense, as Umberto Eco has pointed out, 'Joyce loses his faith but remains faithful to the orthodox system',[21] thus resigning his church but not the medieval model inculcated into him by the Jesuit order in Clongowes and Belvedere. In 'Wandering Rocks' Buck Mulligan sarcastically blames Stephen's existential anxieties and incapacity to fully incarnate his role as an artist to the theological system of thought imparted by the Jesuit order, particularly to the deeply distressing images of hell to which he was exposed as a child:

'— They drove his wits astray, he said, by visions of hell' (*U* 10.1072). As he humorously puts it in 'Telemachus': 'you [Stephen] have the cursed Jesuit strain in you, only it's injected the wrong way' (*U* 1.208–09).

In addition to the highly disturbing visions of hell in *A Portrait*, Joyce conceived the Dantist ideology in terms of both linguistic innovation and political subversion, as Dante openly confronted the structural principles of Italian society, chiefly by advocating the literary use of the vernacular instead of Latin in *De Vulgari Eloquentia*, and in his denunciation of the corruption of church and state, as he unmercifully condemned popes and statesmen to the deepest confines of his *Inferno*. This ideological turn goes hand-in-hand with the Romantic re-evaluation and re-invention of Dante as the revolutionary medieval thinker capable of inspiring radical political changes in societies struggling for emancipation. According to Reynolds, 'Joyce's critical interest in the *Divine Comedy* is his perception of Dante as a critic of society. Joyce took seriously Shelley's dictum that poets are "the unacknowledged legislators of mankind", and architects of social change.'[22] Furthermore, Reynolds highlights a relevant parallel between the situation of the Irish church in Joyce's time and Dante's medieval church: 'In Joyce's Ireland, the issue of anticlericalism, long since dead in England and France, was still as alive as in Dante's time. There was a special attraction for Joyce in Dante's indictment of clerical corruption and his images of simony.'[23]

Unlike Joyce, Borges neither initiated his conversations with Dante via Roman Catholicism, nor engaged in a systematic study of the Italian language.[24] Instead, he only aspired to read Italian in order to gain direct access to Dante and other Italian classics: 'I learned a lot of Italian with Dante. And then I was also taught by Ariosto when I read his *Orlando el Furioso*. They were two magnificent teachers.'[25] This strictly literary pursuit resembles T. S. Eliot's similar confession: 'I am not a Dante scholar; my Italian is chiefly self-taught, and learnt primarily to read Dante; I need still to make constant reference to translations'.[26] Rather surprisingly, perhaps, for a voracious reader of the classics, Borges encountered Dante for the first time in his mid-thirties in an English translation by Dr John Carlyle (Thomas Carlyle's younger brother), which contained a prose rendering in English side-by-side with Dante's Italian (see *A* 44).[27] From a biographical perspective, this literary meeting took place in 1937 while he was unhappily employed as a cataloguer for the Buenos Aires municipal library Miguel Cané. His daily attendance at this government institution involved long tram journeys across the city, which presented him with the opportunity to read an ample catalogue of books, including the *Commedia* (*OC3* 208). Just as Eliot argued that his 'public school knowledge of Italian, a traveller's smattering of Italian, and a literal translation beside the text'[28] aided him during his reading of Dante, so Borges similarly claimed that the fraternity between the Romance languages and a solid Latin education in the prestigious Collège Calvin of Geneva — founded in 1559 by John Calvin[29] — allowed him to read *Inferno* through a constant shifting from translation to original. This type of interpretative process enabled Borges and Eliot to perform a dual reading which offered the added advantage to constantly juxtapose two different linguistic and cultural systems, namely Dante's fourteenth-century vernacular alongside the particular linguistic, historical and cross-cultural idiosyncrasies of the English rendering. This simultaneous reading across two languages goes hand-in-hand with Borges's customary practice of accessing a foreign text in several translations. In his preliminary study of a Spanish edition of the *Commedia*, he ironically advises prospective readers not to perform a monolingual Hispanic reading of the text, but the type of bilingual exercise he had practised with Carlyle.[30] In addition to his polyglot version of Dante, Borges developed a particular fondness for different critical editions of the *Commedia*. This led him to declare in a lecture at the University of Buenos Aires that he possessed in his personal library 'unas once o doce ediciones comerciales comentadas de la *Comedia*, desde las más antiguas hasta las más modernas' [about eleven or twelve annotated editions of the *Commedia*, from the oldest to the modern] and expressed his regret at not having 'la edición de la *Divina Comedia* hecha por el padre de Rosetti' [the Italian edition of the *Commedia* prepared by Rossetti's father].[31]

Contrarily, Joyce's nomadic lifestyle combined with periods of severe impoverishment disallowed him from cultivating the type of bibliophily that was a characteristic feature of the 'librarian author', as John Updike liked to refer to Borges.[32] As regards to Joyce's editions of the *Commedia*, Mary Reynolds argues that he possessed a 'little paperback copy of the *Divine Comedy*, an edition with full notes and commentary by Eugenio Camerini, published by E. Sonzogno (Milan) as a title in the Camerini series of inexpensive editions of the classics'.[33] This, however, does not imply that Joyce had not consulted other critical editions and benefited from further exegetical analysis in his appreciation of Dante. As a matter of fact, Reynolds also informs us that Joyce 'bought a copy of the *Vita Nuova* in Trieste, a book with some intrinsic value. It is an attractive boxed edition of 1911, with the illustrations of Dante Gabriel Rossetti [...]. It seems to have been bought for aesthetic reasons in addition to the obvious connection with Joyce's interest in the pre-Raphaelites.'[34] Borges, who according to Richard Burgin displayed his copy of *Ulysses* on a glass coffee table in his austere Buenos Aires apartment on the Avenida Belgrano,[35] would have certainly treasured this type of edition in his library.

In spite of the different religious and biographical circumstances that drew Borges and Joyce to a lifelong interest in Dante's works, their literary relationship with the Italian poet is marked by several intersections. Both writers cultivated a highly honoured view of Dante and enjoyed expressing their admiration with superlative remarks. In a 1922 lecture Joyce stated that: 'Italian literature begins with Dante and finishes with Dante. That's more than a little. In Dante dwells the whole spirit of the Renaissance' (*JJI* 226). Similarly, in a 1943 essay Borges made an equally definitive statement about Dante, but in a wider gesture to encompass universal literature: 'La *Divina Comedia* es el libro más justificable y más firme de todas las literaturas' (*OC2* 109) ['The *Divine Comedy* is the most justifiable and solid book in all literature'] (*SNF* 238). And in a 1980 lecture he declared: 'Si he elegido la *Comedia* para esta primera conferencia es porque soy un hombre de letras y creo que el ápice de las literaturas es la *Comedia*' (*OC3* 217) [If I have chosen the *Commedia* for this first conference it is because I am a man of letters and I believe that the highest work of literature is the *Commedia*]. Both writers also agree in their predilection for certain linguistic and thematic aspects of the *Commedia*. Reynolds states that Oliver St John Gogarty reported Joyce's fascination with the highly celebrated episode of Paolo and Francesca, in particular with the linguistic virtuosity and rhetorical effects of the passage, which culminates with the alliterative line 'e caddi come corpo morto cade'[36] that Joyce enjoyed reciting from memory. Borges also shared the long-standing interest for Canto V, and admired the same rhythmical consonance of the final line, which he also recited during his 1981 lecture (see *OC3* 211). In his poem '*Inferno* V, 129', he offered a lyrical exercise modelled in Romantic readings of the *Commedia* that offered sympathetic views of the story of Paolo and Francesca. He celebrates an idealistic conception of love which is elevated into an ode that sings about 'todos los amantes que han sido / desde aquel Adán y su Eva / en el pasto del Paraíso' (*SP* 444) ['all the lovers that ever were / since Adam lived with Eve / on the lawns of Paradise'] (*SP* 445).

The adulterous love of Dante's damned lovers also reappears in Joyce's and Borges's works, as they translate the amorous triangle of the two brothers, Paolo and Gianciotto Malatesta, and Francesca di Rimini into the Irish and Argentine fabrics of their works. In this vein, Joyce proposes the new conflictual formula of Bloom–Molly–Boylan in *Ulysses* — albeit with a pacifist resolution that shifts vengeance for equanimity — and the two sets of triads in *Exiles* (1918), a play in three acts that, amongst other things, draws attention to both Joyce's and Dante's condition as outcasts from Ireland and Florence respectively, and their Roman Catholic inheritance. In his 'Notes' to the play, Joyce pondered:

> Why the title *Exiles*? A nation exacts a penance from those who dared to leave her payable on their return. The elder brother in the fable of the Prodigal Son is Robert Hand. The father took the side of the prodigal. This is probably not the way of the world — certainly not in Ireland: but Jesus' Kingdom was not of this world nor was or is His wisdom (*E* 102).

One of the heroines of the play is a twentieth-century avatar of Dante's Beatrice, the twenty-seven-year-old Beatrice Justice, who has become the muse of Richard Rowan's artistic endeavours, and is mysteriously described as 'a slender dark young woman' (*E* 3), hence bringing to mind not only Dante's Beatrice Portinari but also Shakespeare's dark lady. The play focuses on the complex range of love-triangles between Richard–Bertha–Beatrice, and Richard–Bertha–Robert, as it explores the character's mixed feelings of love, jealousy and betrayal. Joyce returned to the jealousy motif in 'Eumaeus', as Stephen Dedalus identified the tension of the triangle integrated by Dante, Beatrice and her real husband: 'the impetuosity of Dante and the isosceles triangle miss Portinari he fell in love with' (*U* 16.886–87), partly to foreshadow the disadvantageous position of Dante (his side being smaller than the other two) and also as an anticipation of the new triad Bloom–Stephen–Molly that emerges in 'Ithaca'.

Just as Joyce transposes Dante's triangular conflict in *Ulysses* and *Exiles*, Borges reallocates the amorous triangle of Canto V in the outskirts of turn-of-the-century Buenos Aires. 'The Intruder'[37] is a study of love, jealousy, and betrayal that stages the filial conflict between two brothers and a woman, Juliana de Burgos, whom they mutually love and, ultimately, decide to sacrifice in order to strengthen their brotherly love. If in Dante's *Inferno* the dishonoured brother enacts his revenge upon Paolo and Francesca who are eventually condemned to Dante's circle of the lustful, in Borges's story of chauvinistic pride and female subjugation the death sentence falls upon Juliana de Burgos, who accepts her sexual and psychological ordeal with total submission. The story ends not with an infernal law of retribution, but with the triumph of the two brothers who reinforce their fraternal ties by means of a shared, secret murder: 'Se abrazaron, casi llorando. Ahora los ataba otro vínculo: la mujer tristemente sacrificada y la obligación de olvidarla' (*OC2* 406) ['Almost weeping, they embraced. Now they were linked by yet another bond: the woman grievously sacrificed, and the obligation to forget her'] (*CF* 351). Nuñez-Faraco suggests that in the story Borges 'makes use of the narrative technique Dante employed in the episode of Francesca da Rimini (*Inferno* V, 73–142), having one of his characters speak for himself as well as for the other — in this case two rival brothers in love with the same woman.'[38] Borges's story about the victimization of Juliana de Burgos by her two male aggressors follows the medieval narrative tradition of the tale of 'patient Griselda' — the literary symbol of the virtuous and long-suffering lady — with existing versions by Boccaccio in Day 10 of the *Decameron*, Petrarch's Latin translation of Boccaccio's story, and Chaucer's reworking of the vernacular Italian and Latin versions in 'The Clerk's Tale'.[39] Kirkpatrick suggests that the ongoing fascination with the tale of Griselda derives from a post-Dantean cult of the image of the lady: 'The Griselda-figure herself offered the post-Dantean writer a number of opportunities to develop the significance of the Lady-image, and to modify according to his own lights the cultural implications of that image.'[40] Interestingly, Joyce refers to the tradition of the tale of patient Griselda in 'Scylla and Charybdis', where an absorbed Eglinton commands Stephen to expand his unorthodox views of Anne Hathaway: ' — We want to hear more, John Eglinton decided with Mr Best's approval. We begin to be interested in Mrs S. Till now we had thought of her, if at all, as a patient Griselda, a Penelope stay-at-home' (*U* 9.618–20). Eglinton adds to the generic categorization of the virtuous-lady-as-Griselda, the female narratives of Penelope and Shakespeare's Anne Hathaway, especially as the 'virtue' of the latter is in the process of being destabilized by Stephen's idiosyncratic theory of Shakespeare's art and life and, ultimately, by *Ulysses* as a whole with the inverted correspondence of Molly Bloom as the unfaithful antitype of Homer's chaste Penelope. Thus the idealization of the lady figure in Dante becomes a literary motif that enables a succession of writers from Petrarch to Joyce and Borges to follow not only a tradition but also to adapt it to their own cultural systems and literary conventions. What Borges performs, in the end, in 'The Intruder' is the masculine translation of a female body (Griselda/Juliana) whom he places in a narrative infused with a predominant patriarchal discourse that focuses on the victimization of a helpless heroine.

## 'A panel whose edges enclose the universe' (*SNF* 267)

In his celebrated story 'The Library of Babel' Borges postulated the existence of an infinite library composed of hexagonal galleries, a secret universe known to contain all possible books on all subjects and languages. In 'The Book of Sand' he toyed with a variation of the same idea and conceived a magical book whose number of pages is infinite. Likewise, in 'The Disk' infinity is contained in Odin's irreversible circle, an unfathomable object that defies the laws of physics and possesses only one side. In 'The Zahir' he fantasized with a twenty-cent coin that convoked a tapestry of infinitely intertwining figures and had the uncanny power to be unforgettable. The reverse of 'The Zahir' — as Borges once declared[41] — is 'The Aleph', which shifts from Islam to Jewish mysticism, and is another microcosm, a minute iridescent sphere that congregated all places in the universe. At the same time, Borges was extremely fond of constructing his own catalogues of infinity and enjoyed unlocking the infinite potential of certain works. In his essay 'Avatars of the Tortoise' (1932) he confessed to having once attempted to compile '[la] móvil historia' ['the mobile history'] of infinity (*OC1* 254), paradoxically poking fun at the fact that an infinite series presupposes no history, since it cancels the sequential notions of beginning and end. While his *Biografía Infinita* never materialized, he nonetheless postulated his own tradition of infinity and included Joyce's *Ulysses* and Dante's *Commedia* as exemplary works. In Chapter 3, I demonstrated how Borges created Joyce's *Ulysses* as a precursor of 'Funes the Memorious' and fused them in a double gesture that comprised both an absolute memory and the sheer monstrosity involved in the act of total recollection. Borges elaborated a critical rhetoric of Joyce that conceived *Ulysses* and *Finnegans Wake* as infinite works, or more precisely, as dense, impenetrable labyrinths. He also enjoyed inventing a larger-than-life version of Joyce that conceived him as the enigmatic, resourceful Irish artificer eternally occupied in the creation of infinite enterprises. This mythical projection featured in his work as: '[el] intrincado y casi infinito irlandés que tejió el *Ulises*' ['the intricate and near-infinite Irishman who weaved *Ulysses*'] (*SNF* 393), and 'arquitecto de laberintos, también; Proteo literario, también' (*OC4* 435) ['also an architect of labyrinths; also a literary Proteus'] (*SNF* 162). Borges's making of a legendary, almost fictional version of Joyce converges with the memorial statement pronounced by an elderly Samuel Beckett on the occasion of Joyce's centennial celebrations: 'I welcome this occasion to bow once again, before I go, deep down, before his heroic work, heroic being'.[42]

In the remainder of this chapter, I shall reveal that Borges wove a pattern of Joycean motifs in the stories 'The Garden of Forking Paths', 'The Zahir', and 'The Disk'. The extent of Borges's complex refraction of Joyce into the tight confines of his *ficciones* has been discussed by Beatriz Vegh, who sees Borges's position as 'a deviation from *Ulysses*'s expanded novelistic format and dreamlike account (especially in "Circe") of a minute totality, towards the condensed fictional format and the hallucinatory accounts of the same minute totality that Borges's own short stories shaped from the mid-1930's.'[43] Thus the question to ask here is, how does Borges translate *Ulysses* and *Finnegans Wake* into his compressed short stories? Or, more precisely, how does he transmute the epic into the aphoristic in his endeavour to offer, like his epigraph from *Hamlet* in 'The Aleph', infinity bounded in a nutshell? (*CF* 274). To begin with, the detectivesque, labyrinthine pattern of 'Death and the Compass' (1944) features a mysterious character named Black Finnegan, who owns a tavern in which the 'Third crime' took place and is described as 'un antiguo criminal irlandés, abrumado y casi anulado por la decencia' (*OC1* 502) ['a former Irish criminal now overwhelmed, almost crushed, by honesty'] (*CF* 150). Borges presents an avatar of a converted H.C.E. who has expiated his previous crimes and is ironically slotted in the dream-like murder scenario of his mathematically engineered story. A further reference to *Finnegans Wake* appears in another labyrinthine tale of espionage, 'The Garden of Forking Paths' (1941), published in a collection of homologous title. In this story, the long misunderstood, complex work of Ts'ui Pen, 'que fue gobernador de Yunnan y que renunció al poder temporal para escribir una novela que fuera todavía más populosa que el *Hung Lu Meng* y para edificar un laberinto en el que se perdieran todos los hombres' (*OC1* 475) ['who was governor of Yunan province and who renounced all temporal power in order to write a novel containing more characters than the *Hun Lu Meng* and construct a labyrinth in which all men would lose their way'] (*CF* 122), stands as a veiled analogue of Joyce's *Wake*. Stephen Albert, the eminent English sinologist unlocks the enigma of Ts'ui Pen's novel by revealing the main secret of his infinite masterpiece about the simultaneity of all times, past, present, and future. Albert's speculations about the possible nature of an infinite work are clearly grounded in the cyclical pattern of *Finnegans Wake*: 'Yo me había preguntado de qué manera un libro puede ser infinito. No conjeturé otro procedimiento que el de un volumen cíclico, circular. Un volumen cuya última página fuera idéntica a la primera, con posibilidad de continuar indefinidamente' (*OC1* 477) ['I had wondered how a book could be infinite. The only way I could surmise was that it be a cyclical, or circular, volume, a volume whose last page would be identical to the first, so that one might go on infinitely'] (*CF* 125). 'Borges had a striking example of such circular work fresh at hand in Joyce's *Finnegans Wake*', writes John T. Irwin; 'the book had appeared in 1939, and Borges had discussed its linguistic innovations in a brief essay published in *Sur* in November of that same year.'[44] The curvilinear pattern of the *Wake* — theoretically grounded on Giambattista Vico's recurring conception of history — revolves around the continuous regeneration of the four cycles of man's history which in turn converge with the circular movement of the reader whose own 'recirculation' is potentially endless in a book that possesses neither beginning nor end. Hence its last inconclusive sentence 'A way a lone a last a loved a long the' (*FW* 628.16–17) that demands a return to the opening paragraph of the book, 'riverrun, past Eve and Adam's, from swerve of shore to bend of bay' (*FW* 3.1–2).[45] If in 'The Garden of Forking Paths' Borges models Ts'ui Pen's *magnum opus* on the manifold pattern of *Finnegans Wake*, so in 'The Zahir' he incorporates Leopold Bloom's distinctive florin as part of an eclectic catalogue of numismatic symbols.

In the prologue to his *Nine Dantesque Essays* (1982)[46] Borges fantasizes about an Oriental library that contains an infinite panel of uncertain origin in which are depicted countless legends, thousands of characters, and myriad shapes and colours. In a typical Borgesian manner, the ambitious panel grows boundless in its enclosure, yet minute in its dimensions in order to encompass the whole universe:

Imaginemos, en una biblioteca oriental, una lámina pintada hace muchos siglos. Acaso es árabe y nos dicen que en ella están figuradas todas las fábulas de las *Mil y una noches*; acaso es china y sabemos que ilustra una novela con centenares o millares de personajes. En el tumulto de sus formas, alguna — un árbol que semeja un cono invertido, unas mezquitas de color bermejo sobre un muro de hierro — nos llama la atención y de ésa pasamos a otras. Declina el día, se fatiga la luz y a medida que nos internamos en el grabado, comprendemos que no hay cosa en la tierra que no esté ahí. Lo que fue, lo que es y lo que será, la historia del pasado y del futuro, las cosas que he tenido y las que tendré, todo ello nos espera en algún lugar de ese laberinto tranquilo... (*OC3* 343).

[Imagine, in an Oriental library, a panel painted many centuries ago. It may be Arabic, and we are told that all the legends of *The Thousand and One Nights* are represented on its surface; it may be Chinese, and we learn that it illustrates a novel that has hundreds or thousands of characters. In the tumult of its forms, one shape — a tree like an inverted cone; a group of mosques, vermilion in color, against an iron wall — catches our attention, and from there we move on to others. The day declines, the light is wearing thin, and as we go deeper into the carved surface we understand that there is nothing on earth that is not there. What was, is, and shall be, the history of past and future, the things I had had and those I will have, all of it awaits us somewhere in this serene labyrinth ... (*SNF* 267).]

Borges then discloses that the infinite engraving he has imagined stands for Dante's *Commedia*: 'He fantaseado una obra mágica, una lámina que también fuera un microcosmo; el poema de Dante es esa lámina de ámbito universal' (*OC3* 343) ['I have fantasized a magical work, a panel that is also a microcosm: Dante's poem is that panel whose edges enclose the universe'] (*SNF* 267). An infinite book, a labyrinth, a microcosm that encompasses a universe, the encapsulation of eternity in a single work, this is, unquestionably, the type of rhetoric that Borges employs when referring to Joyce. Borges's conception of Dante's *Commedia* as an infinite work reappears again in his literary conversations with Osvaldo Ferrari, in a section appropriately entitled 'Dante, una lectura infinita' [Dante, an Infinite Reading], whereby he refers to the *Commedia* as 'ese libro total [en el que] ya está todo' [a total book [in which] is contained everything].[47] Just as in 1925 Borges unashamedly expressed his inability to read *Ulysses* in its entirety, and yet paradoxically claimed to know the inexhaustible book 'con esa aventurera y legítima certidumbre que hay en nosotros, al afirmar nuestro conocimiento de la ciudad, sin adjudicarnos por ello la intimidad de cuantas calles incluye' (*Inq.* 23) ['with that bold and legitimate certainty with which we assert our knowledge of a city, without ever having been rewarded with the intimacy of all the many streets it includes'] (*SNF* 12), so in 1961 he similarly employed the metaphor of the manifold and ever-changing city in order to convey the vastness and unlimited quality of Dante's triple architecture of the otherworld: 'La *Divina Comedia* es una ciudad que nunca habremos explorado del todo' (*TR3* 74) [The *Commedia* is a city that we shall never explore in its entirety].

Borges also relates his infinite conception of the *Commedia* through the numerous interpretations the book has elicited across the centuries. For example, in 'The Pitying Torturer' he examines the self-contradictory nature of Dante's conception of Divine judgement which condemns Paolo and Francesca to the inclement winds of the second circle of the Lustful, in relation to the Pilgrim's compassionate response to the eternal torments of the doomed lovers (see *SNF* 284). This incongruity, he explains, has contributed to the richness and ongoing fascination of the episode. Alberto Manguel also notes that Borges seldom equates his view of the *Commedia* as an infinite book with the infinite readings of the Scriptures via Scotus Erigena's comparison with the iridescent plumage of a peacock:

> Once, after noting that we read now Dante in ways that he couldn't have imagined, far beyond the 'four levels' of reading outlined in Dante's letter to Can Grande della Scala, Borges recalled an observation by the ninth-century mystic Scotus Erigena. According to the author of *On the Divisions of Nature*, there are as many readings of a text as there are readers; this multiplicity of readings Erigena compared to the hues on the tail of a peacock.[48]

In a larger way, Borges's infinite conception of the *Commedia* is interrelated to Dante's epistle to Can Grande della Scala, in which he famously discussed the *Commedia* according to the four-fold model of reading attributed to the Scriptures by Biblical exegetes: the literal, allegorical, moral and anagogical. The key term in Dante's analysis of the interpretative significance of the *Commedia* is 'polysemous, that is, having many meanings'.[49] In this sense, Borges and Joyce aligned their works to Dante's hermeneutical tradition in an attempt to construct their texts as complexly woven fabrics that challenge linear readings and envisage a practice of reading and writing founded on multilayered systems of interpretation. Lucia Boldrini draws attention to a scholarly practice that applies Dante's theological model to the reading of Joyce's oeuvre: 'One of the received notions of Joycean criticism is that Dante's theory of the four levels of meaning is important for all of Joyce's works, and especially for *Finnegans Wake*, the "polysemous" [...] text *par excellence*'.[50] M. Keith Booker has also remarked that 'One of the most obvious parallels between Joyce and Dante is that both writers produce extremely complex texts that generate richly multiple meanings'.[51] Correspondingly, in the Borges scholarship, Matei Calinescu has persuasively argued that Borges's works should be approached not through a linear, single reading, but through a 'Kabbalist [reading that] will try other methods of (re)reading, vertical or circular, intratextual or intertextual'.[52] Despite the fact that Borges's works do not pose the level of linguistic experimentalism in terms of lexical polysemy, neologisms, alterations in syntax and morphology characteristic of Joyce's last two texts, his super-concise *ficciones* are, nonetheless, meticulously carved textual miniatures which compactly stage a wealth of intertextual readings, organized narrative structures, an orchestration of citations in several languages.

### Writing Dante in the Twentieth Century

In most critical studies of Borges's works, 'The Aleph' and 'The Zahir' are discussed in tandem, offering a compact case study of symmetrical narrative patterns, a play of interesting juxtapositions, and a pair of magical objects that possess the exceptional properties to simultaneously mesmerize and disconcert 'Borges', first-person narrator of both fictions.[53] However, in spite of these various intersecting patterns, the magical objects depicted in the two stories do not share the same identical properties, insofar as they denote two religious credos (Hebraism/Islamism), two opposite letters (Alpha/Omega), and two antithetical, yet complementary types of infinity (synchronic/diachronic).[54] According to 'Borges', the Aleph stands for the first letter of the Hebrew alphabet, which in Hebrew lore: 'significa el En Soph, la ilimitada y pura divinidad; también se dijo que tiene la forma de un hombre que señala el cielo y la tierra, para indicar que el mundo inferior es el espejo y es el mapa del superior' (*OC3* 627) ['signifies the En Soph, the pure and unlimited godhead; it has also been said that its shape is that of a man pointing to the sky and the earth, to indicate that the lower world is the map and mirror of the higher'] (*CF* 285). He also compounds the Judaic lore of the Aleph with the groundbreaking theory of set numbers proposed by the Russian born mathematician Georg Cantor (1845–1918) whose theorem about infinity adopts the letter Aleph as the symbol for his transfinite numbers, 'para la *Mengenlehre*, es el símbolo de los números transfinitos, en los que el todo no es mayor que alguna de las partes' (*OC1* 627) ['for the *Mengenlehre*, the aleph is the symbol of the transfinite numbers, in which the whole is not greater than any of its parts'] (*CF* 285). 'Cantor's unique contribution was to consider all the elements of an infinite set to be present (as he said) "at once",' writes Katherine Hayles, 'and thus to posit the number system as a pre-existing, interrelated totality.'[55] This simultaneity is, of course, carefully exploited in 'The Aleph', a point in space which, like Cantor's infinity, contains all points. Borges became acquainted with Cantor's theory in Bertrand Russell's *Introduction to Mathematical Philosophy* (1919) and later in *Mathematics and the Imagination* by Edward Kasner and James Newman, which he reviewed in 1940 (see *OC1* 276–77). But it is essential to note, however, that Borges's idiosyncratic fusion of algebra and Jewish mysticism is informed by the relevant intersection between mathematics and Christianity that takes place in Canto XXXIII of *Paradiso*. In 'The Aleph' the first-person narrator refers to his inability to describe the infinite Aleph on account of the restrictions entailed in a successive and limited linguistic system bound to culture, time, and history. This constitutes, above all, Borges's continued exploration of the ineffability topos, which he also developed, as I have shown in Chapter 3, in 'Funes the Memorious', where the first-person narrator attempts to compose an inevitably partial narrative of a man endowed with an infinite memory. Borges is modelling the motif of the writer's despair about capturing an infinite revelation with an inadequate language system on Dante's similar linguistic *apologia* at his incapacity to lay down for future generations his final vision of the Godhead:

> Da quinci innanzi il mio veder fu maggio
> che 'l parlar nostro, ch'a tal vista cede,
> e cede la memoria a tanto oltraggio
> [...]
> Oh quanto è corto il dire e come fioco
> al mio concetto ! e questo, a quel ch' i' vidi,
> è tanto, che non basta a dicer 'poco' (*Par* XXXIII, 55–57; 121–23).
>
> [And from then on my vision rose to heights
> higher than words, which fail before such sight,
> and memory fails, too, at such extremes.
> [...]

> How my weak words fall short of my conception,
> which is itself so far from what I saw
> that 'weak' is much too weak a word to use (*Par* 392–93).]

Arribo, ahora, al inefable centro de mi relato; empieza, aquí, mi desesperación de escritor. Todo lenguaje es un alfabeto de símbolos cuyo ejercicio presupone un pasado que los interlocutores comparten; ¿cómo trasmitir a los otros el infinito Aleph, que mi temerosa memoria apenas abarca? [...] Lo que vieron mis ojos fue simultáneo: lo que transcribiré, sucesivo, porque el lenguaje lo es. Algo, sin embargo, recogeré (*OC1* 625).

[I come now to the ineffable center of my tale; it is here that a writer's hopelessness begins. Every language is an alphabet of symbols the employment of which assumes a past shared by its interlocutors. How can one transmit to others the infinite Aleph, which my timorous memory can scarcely contain? [...] What my eyes saw was *simultaneous*; what I shall write is *successive*, because language is successive. Something of it, though, I will capture (*SNF* 283).]

If Borges follows Dante's tradition of the human inability to fully grasp and/or describe a vision that transcends our limited intellectual understanding and our inadequate linguistic system (notwithstanding the fact that Borges finds a successful solution with the device of chaotic enumeration), so Joyce equally revisits this problem in 'Ithaca' from the vantage point of geometrical quandaries, as the catechist refers to Bloom's failed attempt to square the circle in 1886:

> Qual è 'l geomètra che tutto s'affige
> per misurar lo cerchio, e non ritrova,
> pensando, quel principio ond'elli indige,
> tal era io a quella vista nova (*Par* XXXIII, 133–36).
>
> [As the geometer who tries so hard
> to square the circle, but cannot discover,
> think as he may, the principle involved,
> so did I strive with this new mystery (*Par* 394).]

> Why did he not elaborate these calculations to a more precise result?
> Because some years previously in 1886 when occupied with the problem of the quadrature of the circle (*U* 17.1070–72).

Dante correlates his inability to describe the mystery of the trinity with the geometer's ongoing and unsuccessful attempts to square the circle. Dasenbrock and Mines argue that Dante introduces this simile in an attempt to emphasize the discrepancy between human and divine understanding: 'The analogy is a close one for Dante: for him, the "new sight" is not capturable by the methods of mathematics because the methods of mathematics are the methods of human beings, and the Divine or the infinite escapes our human comprehension.'[56] Like Dante, Borges exemplifies his difficult task to transmit to future generations his vision of the Aleph with a catalogue of theological and mathematical perplexing notions:

> Los místicos, en análogo trance, prodigan los emblemas: para significar la divinidad, un persa habla de un pájaro que de algún modo es todos los pájaros; Alanus de Insulis, de una esfera cuyo centro está en todas partes y la circunferencia en ninguna; Ezequiel, de un ángel de cuatro caras que a un

tiempo se dirige al Oriente y al Occidente, al Norte y al Sur. (No en vano rememoro esas inconcebibles analogías; alguna relación tienen con el Aleph.) Quizá los dioses no me negarían el hallazgo de una imagen equivalente, pero este informe quedaría contaminado de falsedad. Por lo demás, el problema central es irresoluble: la enumeración, siquiera parcial, de un conjunto infinito (*OC1* 625).

[In a similar situation, mystics have employed a wealth of emblems: to signify the deity, a Persian mystic speaks of a bird that somehow is all birds: Alain de Lille speaks of a sphere whose center is everywhere and circumference nowhere; Ezekiel, of an angel with four faces, facing east and west, north and south at once. (It is not for nothing that I call to mind these inconceivable analogies; they bear a relation to the Aleph.) Perhaps the gods would not deny me the discovery of an equivalent image, but then this report would be polluted with literature, with falseness. And besides, the central problem — even partial enumeration, of infinity — is irresolvable (*CF* 282).]

Joyce's adventurous foray into the field of mathematics owes much, like Borges's, to his acquaintance with Bertrand Russell's *Introduction to Mathematical Philosophy*, in which they not only learned about ancient geometrical pursuits but also became acquainted with theories of infinity. What these examples demonstrate here is that a whole scientific and theosophical tradition becomes the *common locus* in the infinite conversation between Dante, Joyce, and Borges. Whilst Borges and Joyce reveal a clear pattern of Dantean allusions in the complex texture of their narratives, they equally draw attention to the inevitable disparity between Dante's medieval world and their twentieth-century circumstances. In this sense, I concur with Dasenbrock and Mines's assertion that:

> Rather than taking over Dante's material, he [Joyce] is taking over Dante's attitude *towards* his material. Instead of an Aquinas-map, or a Euclid-map, he has what we might call a Russell-map. Like Dante, he is structuring his work with an eye to the best contemporary mathematics and science; the difference is that mathematics and science have changed, and so must the organization of his work.[57]

The shift from an Aquinas-map to a Russell-map is also applicable to Borges, whose Aleph incorporates Dante's medieval model through a transformative process informed by other conceptions of the world and the latest developments in the field of science. Nonetheless, it should be made clear that Joyce and Borges adopt a Russell-map neither as an authoritative discourse nor a definitive orientation, as their emphasis is centred on the fact that there are no absolute or fixed truths in any form of reasoning. Unlike Dante's strict adherence to Ptolemaic and Christian conceptions of the world, Joyce and Borges privilege the arbitrariness of all systems of thoughts. Most of all, this is exemplified in 'Ithaca' (coincidentally in the passage that Borges praised in Salas Subirat's 1945 translation) whereby the catechist exposes Bloom's disbelief in an afterlife and his refusal to adhere to rigid principles with an inventive string of neologisms. This sceptical impulse, which playfully undermines the foundations of Western beliefs, is also employed by Borges in 'El Aleph', as he presents an anti-climatic effect in the 1943 addendum to the story, which further demystifies and discredits the vision of the Aleph in the cellar of Daneri's house as fake:

> That it was not a heaventree, not a heavengrot, not a heavenbeast, not a heavenman. That it was a Utopia, there being no known method from the known to the unknown (*U* 17.1137–41).

> Por increíble que parezca, yo creo que hay (o que hubo) otro Aleph, yo creo que el Aleph de la calle Garay era un falso Aleph (*OC1* 627).

> [Incredible as it may seem, I believe there is (or was) another Aleph; I believe that the Aleph of Calle Garay was a *false* Aleph (*CF* 285).]

This complex interweaving suggests, amongst other things, that Borges and Joyce had the ending of Dante's *Purgatory* very much in their minds while they wrote 'Ithaca' and 'The Aleph' respectively. Another clear example is that they adhered to Dante's image of a constellation of scintillating stars with which he closes each Cantiche:

> e quindi uscimmo a riveder le stelle (*Inf* XXXIV, 139).
> puro e disposto a salire alla stelle (*Purg* XXXIII, 145).
> l'amor che move il sole e l'altre stelle (*Par* XXXIII, 145).

> [And we came out to see once more the stars (*Inf* 383).
> Eager to rise, now ready for the stars (*Purg* 362).
> By the love that moves the sun and the other stars (*Par* 394).]

If the Pilgrim is rewarded with a final stellar vision as he emerges from the realms of Hell, Purgatory, and Paradise, so Bloom and Stephen emerge, 'silently, doubly dark, from obscurity by a passage from the rere of the house into the penumbra of the garden' (*U* 17.1036–38), in order to witness the interstellar spectacle of 'the heaventree of stars hung with humid nightblue fruit' (*U* 17.1036–39).[58] Similarly, 'Borges' is transported from the dark cellar of Daneri's basement to the cosmological, awe-inspiring revelation of the infinite Aleph. A stellar vision, moreover, is conveyed in the final dedicatory of the story. Like several of his poems, essays, and short-stories, 'The Aleph' is dedicated to a female muse, in this case to the Argentine writer and translator Estela Canto,[59] with whom Borges had been deeply in love at the time of writing the story. As Emir Rodríguez Monegal explained:

> Even the person to whom Borges dedicates the story, a young Argentine writer named Estela Canto, has the right Dantesque name: Estela (Stella) was the word Dante chose to end each of the three Cantiche of the *Divine Comedy*; Canto was the name of each division in each Cantica. But the name 'Estela Canto' also means, in Spanish, 'I sing to Estela.'[60]

### From Beatrice to Beatriz, Teodolina, and Bella Cohen

'The Aleph' and 'The Zahir' follow Dante's tradition of unrequited love. Both stories open with the death of their beautiful, yet disdainful heroines, Beatriz Viterbo and Teodolina Villar with whom 'Borges' had been hopelessly in love for many years. Like Dante's lifelong devotion to Beatrice Portinari, the initial grief caused by the demise of these two ladies of upper-class (Teodolina) and middle-class (Beatriz) Argentine society soon represents for 'Borges' the final consolation of his long unrequited love, opening the unconditional prospect to consecrate *in mortem* an affection that had not been reciprocated *in vita*. Just as Dante declares at the end of *La Vita Nuova*: 'Io spero di dire di lei quello che mai non fue ditto d'alcuna'[61] ['I hope to compose concerning her [Beatrice Portinari] what has never been written in rhyme of any woman] (*VN* 99),[62] so 'Borges' similarly states in 'The Aleph', 'muerta yo podía consagrarme a su memoria, sin esperanza, pero también sin humillación' (*OC1* 617) ['now that she was dead, I could consecrate myself to her memory — without hope, but also without humiliation'] (*CF* 275). Edwin Williamson points out that Borges 'believed that it was the pain of thwarted love that had driven the immense narrative machine of the *Divine Comedy*'.[63] If in *Paradiso* the Pilgrim comes to the realization that the transcendental face of Beatrice irradiates more and more beauty as they ascend through the heavenly spheres towards the blinding brightness of God, in 'The Zahir' Borges witnesses a necrophiliac revelation of Teodolina Villar as she miraculously regains her former youth and frivolousness, and grows in beauty and splendour on her deathbed:

> En los velorios, el progreso de la corrupción hace que el muerto recupere sus caras anteriores. En alguna etapa de la confusa noche del seis, Teodolina Villar fue mágicamente la que fue hace veinte años; sus rasgos recobraron la autoridad que dan la soberbia, el dinero, la juventud, la conciencia de coronar una jerarquía, la falta de imaginación, las limitaciones, la estolidez. Más o menos pensé: ninguna versión de esa cara que tanto me inquietó será tan memorable como ésta; conviene que sea la última, ya que pudo ser la primera. Rígida entre las flores la dejé, perfeccionando su desdén por la muerte (*OC1* 590).

> [At wakes, the progress of corruption allows the dead person's body to recover its former faces. At some point on the confused night of June 6, Teodolina Villar magically became what she had been twenty years before; her features recovered the authority of that arrogance, money, youth, the awareness of being the *crème de la crème*, restrictions, a lack of imagination, and stolidity can give. My thoughts were more or less these: No version of that face that had so disturbed me shall ever be as memorable as this one; really, since it could almost be the first, it ought to be the last. I left her lying stiff among the flowers, her contempt for the world growing every moment perfect in death (*CF* 243).]

Similarly, in 'The Aleph', a deeply affected 'Borges' is transported through an iconographic vision — albeit photographically — into the life of his beloved Beatriz as her former beauty and arrogance is revealed in a wide gamut of interconnected images that crystallize her life in an everlasting stillness:

> Beatriz Viterbo, de perfil, en colores; Beatriz, con antifaz, en los carnavales de 1921; la primera comunión de Beatriz; Beatriz, el día de su boda con Roberto Alessandri; Beatriz, poco después del divorcio, en un almuerzo del Club Hípico; Beatriz, en Quilmes, con Delia San Marco Porcel y Carlos Argentino; Beatriz, con el pekinés que le regaló Villegas Haedo; Beatriz, de frente y de tres cuartos, sonriendo, la mano en el mentón... (*OC1* 617).

> [Beatriz Viterbo, in profile, in color; Beatriz in a mask at the Carnival of 1921; Beatriz' first communion; Beatriz on the day of her wedding to Roberto Alessandri; Beatriz shortly after the divorce, lunching at the Jockey Club; Beatriz in Quilmes with Delia San Marco Porcel and Carlos Argentino; Beatriz

with the Pekinese that had been a gift from Villegas Haedo; Beatriz in full-front and in three-quarters view, smiling, her hand on her chin... (*CF* 275).]

And yet the fundamental difference between Dante's Beatrice and her Argentine counterparts resides in the crucial fact that, while Dante bestows upon his Beatrice a higher degree of grace, beauty, and wisdom as they ascend to the eternal light of God, contrarily Borges's Beatriz and Teodolina only irradiate a type of beauty tied up to the earthly sins of vanity, pride, and covetousness. Thus Beatriz only irradiates beauty in the snapshots that a fetishistic Borges worships at the beginning of the story, but is thereafter disintegrated in the shocking images exposed in the revelation of the Aleph: 'vi en un cajón del escritorio (y la letra me hizo temblar) cartas obscenas, increíbles, precisas, que Beatriz había dirigido a Carlos Argentino' (*OC1* 626) ['[I saw] in a desk drawer (and the handwriting made me tremble) obscene, incredible, detailed letters that Beatriz had sent Carlos Argentino'] (*CF* 283). And also in the 'reliquia atroz de lo que deliciosamente había sido Beatriz Viterbo' (*OC1* 626) ['horrendous remains of what had once, deliciously, been Beatriz Viterbo'] (*CF* 283). Nuñez-Faraco has argued that: 'Both in "El Aleph" and in "El Zahir" the image of the dead woman stands as a reminder of the vanity of this world and of the transience of human life.'[64] Borges's satirical reversal of the angelic Beatrice Viterbo into the corrupt and narcissistic versions of Beatriz and Teodolina coalesces with Joyce's similar degrading of Dante's, 'bella donna ch'al ciel t'avvalora' (*Par.* X 93) ['the lovely lady who strengthens you for Heaven'] (*Par.* 122) into the neither beautiful nor heavenly Bella Cohen, the 'massive whoremistress' (*U* 15.2742) who presides at the gates of Joyce's brothel in the infernal confines of Nighttown. M. Keith Booker has convincingly suggested that 'Bella Cohen is intended largely as a parodic revision of Dante's ethereal Beatrice and that one of the targets of this parody is the sort of idealized view of women fostered by Dante's project.'[65] He argues that Joyce 'manages to conflate the myth of woman-as-angel with the equally invidious myth of woman-as-threat, showing that each in fact implies the other and using each to parody and undermine the other.'[66]

It is clear, then, that Borges and Joyce are consciously inscribing themselves in Dante's tradition of woman-as-angel but only as a means to subvert the beatific idealization of the lady in order to introduce the woman-as-threat or, as Booker also proposes, Joyce's transvestite transgression of gender stereotypes with Bella/o Cohen.[67] However, this female antithesis is also present in Dante in the figure of the Siren, who appears in the Pilgrim's dream in Canto XIX of *Purgatory*. Dante demonstrates that beauty lies in the eyes of the beholder as the Pilgrim's gaze turns a hideous female into a beautiful and alluring Siren with whom he becomes instantly spellbound. By means of the divine intersection of a saintly lady, Virgil strips off the Siren's seemingly beautiful façade in order to reveal her repulsive reality and a foul stench: 'L'altra prendea, e dinanzi l'apría / fendendo i drappi, e mostravami 'l ventre: / quel mi svegliò col puzzo che n'uscìa' (*Purg* XIX.31–33) ['He seized the other, ripped her garment off / exposing her as far down as the paunch! / The stench pouring from her woke me from sleep'] (*Purg* 203). This hideous revelation converges with Borges's final horrifying vision in 'The Aleph' that exposes the macabre remains of the otherwise beautiful Beatriz Viterbo. Correspondingly,

Joyce employs an analogous device in 'Circe' as the inanimate image of the nymph is rendered live in the phantasmagoria of 'Circe'. Like the Pilgrim in *Purgatory*, Bloom is spellbound by the deceptive charms of the nymph: 'Your classic curves, beautiful immortal, I was glad to look on you, to praise you, a thing of beauty, almost to pray' (*U* 15.1366–67). The deceptiveness of the nymph is revealed once Bloom rips her veil off in order to expose her ghastly reality, 'her plaster cast cracking, a cloud of stench escaping from the cracks' (*U* 15.3469–70). In this respect, I concur with Booker's conclusion that 'Dante's own use of the siren as a sort of degraded Beatrice prefigures Joyce's depiction of Beatrice as Bella Cohen and in a sense authorizes the connection I am making here'.[68]

The deaths of Beatriz Viterbo and Teodolina Villar set in motion a fictional progression that leads to the narrator's fortuitous encounter with the sacred Islamic coin and his mystical vision of the Aleph in Daneri's basement. In other words, the unrequited love of both heroines and their sudden deaths, serve as the passageway that leads into a magical and mystical journey. In this sense, Borges's narrative scheme goes hand-in-hand with his conviction that Beatrice's disdainfulness towards Dante and her early death, served as the chief motives for Dante's composition of the *Commedia*:

> Enamorarse es crear una religión cuyo dios es falible. Que Dante profesó por Beatriz una adoración idolátrica es una verdad que no cabe contradecir; que ella una vez se burló de él y otra lo desairó son hechos que registra la *Vita Nuova*. Hay quien mantiene que esos hechos son imágenes de otros; ello, de ser así reforzaría aún más nuestra certidumbre de un amor desdichado y supersticioso. Dante, muerta Beatriz, perdida para siempre Beatriz, jugó con la ficción de encontrarla, para mitigar su tristeza; yo tengo para mí que edificó la triple arquitectura de su poema para intercalar ese encuentro (*OC3* 371).
>
> [To fall in love is to create a religion with a fallible god. That Dante professed an idolatrous adoration for Beatrice is a truth that cannot be contradicted; that she once mocked and on another occasion snubbed him are facts registered in the *Vita Nuova*. Some would maintain that these facts are the images of others; if so, this would further reinforce our certainty of an unhappy and superstitious love. With Beatrice dead, Beatrice lost forever, Dante, to assuage his sorrow, played with the fiction of meeting her again. It is my belief that he constructed the triple architecture of his poem in order to insert this encounter into it (*SNF* 300).]

If Borges projects Dante's pattern of unrequited love to 'The Aleph', he also inserts in the story a complex structure of nominal, symbolic, and numerological parallels. It is well known that Dante begins *La Vita Nova* with the central fact that his first encounter with Beatrice took place at the tender age of nine: 'Nove fiate già apresso lo mio nascimento era tornado lo cielo della luce quasi a uno medesimo puncto quanto alla sua propria giratione, quando alli miei occhi apparve prima la gloriosa donna della mia mente'[69] ['Nine times the heaven of the light had revolved in its own movement since my birth and had almost returned to the same point when the woman whom my mind beholds in glory first appeared before my eyes'].[70] Dante then proceeds to gloss a symmetrical chronology of further encounters and dates set on the same numeral. In a similar vein, Borges adheres to Dante's insistence on the importance of numerology and provides an overly precise countdown of

'Borges's' annual visits to Daneri to commemorate the anniversary of Beatriz's birthday. Not insignificantly, 'Borges' informs us that Beatriz died on 30 April 1929, consequently adhering to Dante's symbolic structure constructed around nonary patterns. Moreover, Matei Calinescu wonders about the meticulousness with which temporal markers are interwoven into the narrative and enquires whether this plethora of dates may conceal further secret meanings: 'Are there other numerological implications hidden in the dates, the names, or elsewhere in the text?'[71] Calinescu explains that there is no single answer to the possible symbolic significance of numerical and onomastic references throughout the story and offers, as a way of explanation, the attempts by several critics to decipher the occult meaning of numbers, as well as a parallel with the importance of dates in *Ulysses*.[72] Furthermore, Borges's discussion of Dante's carefully erected configuration of the *Commedia* in terms of its topographical, theological, hermeneutical, and romantic significance is articulated in his collection *Nine Dantesque Essays: 1945–1951*, with a title that acknowledges, once again, the significance of the numeral nine in *Vita Nova* and the *Commedia*. Borges also paid tribute to Dante in the title of the Argentine detective series *El Séptimo Círculo* [*The Seventh Circle*] — appropriately named after the Circle of Violence in Dante's *Inferno*, for which he acted as chief editor alongside his friend and collaborator Adolfo Bioy Casares.

Like most of Borges's translations and appropriations of existing texts, the process involved in 'The Aleph' is re-creative, radical, and, at times, irreverent. In this particular case, the main purpose of the application is to debunk a particular genre or fictional form, yet the exercise is paradoxically peppered with the unmistakable admiration involved in Borges's inscription of 'The Aleph' in a particular Dantean tradition, even if the end result appears more as a parody than as an act of homage. 'The Aleph' is not only about a narrative effect of mystical illumination, but also about the grotesque and humorous figure of Carlos Argentino Daneri, the first cousin of 'Borges's' beloved Beatriz and the owner of the house in Garay Street that encloses the Aleph. To the clearly identifiable onomastic correspondence between Beatrice Portinari and her Argentine counterpart, Beatriz Viterbo, Borges adds the anagrammatical formula that rearranges the first syllable of *Da*nte and compounds it to the last three letters of Aligh*ieri*, in order to turn them into the hybrid form 'Daneri', the parodic Argentine — hence Carlos Argentino — equivalent of Dante. Unsurprisingly, the narrator informs us that the Viterbo family possesses Italian ancestry and that Carlos Argentino's speech and mannerisms betray the heritage of his ancestors: 'A dos generaciones de distancia, la ese italiana y la copiosa gesticulación italiana sobreviven en él' (*OC1* 618') ['At two generations' remove, the Italian *s* and the liberal Italian gesticulation still survive in him'] (*CF* 275). Drawing on Borges's humorous treatment of Dante, Bell-Villada observes: 'Beatrice serves as Dante's guide in *Paradiso*, leading him ever upwards to a joyous and highly contemplative union with God, the cosmos, and herself; here, by contrast, "Borges's" guiding hand is not Beatriz but a tenth-rate Vergil named Carlos Argentino, who leads the narrator downward into a pitlike cellar.'[73]

Throughout the story, 'Borges' pokes fun at Daneri's pompous composition of an epic poem entitled *The Earth* in which: 'Éste se proponía versificar toda la redondez del planeta [en] largos e informes alejandrinos' (*OC1* 620) ['He proposed to versify the entire planet [...] in long, formless alexandrines'] (*CF* 277). In this respect, Daneri's encyclopaedic project may be read — as Emir Rodríguez Monegal has persuasively argued — '[as] a parodic reduction of the *Divine Comedy*'.[74] This type of exercise recalls Borges's parodic compression of Joyce's *Ulysses* in 'Funes the Memorious' and, as we shall see in the next chapter, his miniature rewriting of Shakespeare's Roman tragedy of *Julius Caesar* in the narrative vignette 'La Trama' ['The Pattern']. Further, the totalizing encyclopaedic impulses of Daneri function as a satirical mirror of Dante's epic construction of the *Commedia*, in which he depicts the allegorical journey of Everyman towards the redeeming brightness of God. Contrariwise, Daneri's attempts to seek neither Divine inspiration nor redemption, but to arouse the approval of his literary coterie and, ultimately, to win the Second National Prize for Literature that the first-person narrator believes should have been awarded to him. Borges, in other words, sets up a parodic interplay between Dante and Daneri in which their all-encompassing projects are constantly juxtaposed in an effort to expose the limitations of Daneri's *The Earth* at the expense of Dante's *Commedia*.[75] In this vein, Borges invites his readers to observe a dialectic in his treatment of Dante that on the one hand proposes an (ir)reverent exploitation of the *Commedia* and, on the other, presents a reverential, eulogistic reading in his imaginative revision of the book as an infinite engraving that contains the whole of universal history. Ultimately, as Thiem has persuasively argued, it is possible to read Borges's 'critique of *The Earth* as a critique of the encyclopaedic epic of total vision [which] serves to throw light on Borges's own predilection for brevity, on his peculiar use of Dante, and on the efficacy of his own poem of total vision, "The Aleph".[76] This predilection for brevity is the fundamental force behind Borges's affiliation and disaffiliation with Dante and Joyce, inasmuch as they become the structural models of his stories about total inclusion, and yet their epic proportions are counterpoised to the reductive principle of his fictions.[77]

## Leopold Bloom's 'Irreversible Florin'

In 'The Zahir' the first-person narrator seeks refuge in a Buenos Aires bar after the wake of Teodolina Villar. He orders a brandy and is fortuitously given as small change a twenty-centavo coin, which he later discovers stands as the sacred Islamic symbol. The obsessed and disturbed narrator realises that the powers of the ancient Zahir have congregated in the ordinary Argentine coin, although he is aware that in previous cases the spirit of the Zahir is known to have lived in a tiger, a blind man, an astrolabe, a compass, and a slab of marble. At the moment of receiving the Zahir, 'Borges' compares it with eleven remarkable coins in literature and history, ranging from the Biblical coins exchanged by Judas in the name of Christ, the notes that a wizard turns into paper in *The Arabian Nights*, to 'el florín irreversible de Leopold Bloom' (*OC1* 591) ['Leopold Bloom's irreversible florin'] (*L* 192). Borges's association of 'The Zahir' with Bloom's florin — and the other pieces of silver, obols, drachmas, and pennies listed in the story — strives to create a generic monetary symbol that stands for the whole of universal history: 'Pensé que no hay moneda que no sea símbolo de las monedas que sin fin resplandecen en la historia y la fábula' (*OC1* 590–91) ['The thought struck me that there is no coin that is not the symbol of all the coins that shine endlessly down throughout history and fable'] (*CF* 244). He also chooses Bloom's florin et al. to meditate about the endless possibilities embodied in the possession of a monetary emblem, a reflection not at all dissimilar to Bloom's frequent thoughts about money — albeit charged with Borges's characteristic erudite remarks:

> El dinero es abstracto, repetí, el dinero es tiempo futuro. Puede ser una tarde en las afueras, puede ser una música de Brahms, puede ser mapas, puede ser ajedrez, puede ser café, puede ser las palabras de Epicteto, que enseñan el desprecio del oro; es un Proteo más versátil que el de la isla de Pharos. Es tiempo imprevisible, tiempo de Bergson, no duro tiempo del Islam o del Pórtico (*OC1* 591).
>
> [Money is abstract, I repeated; money is the future tense. It can be an evening in the suburbs, or music by Brahms; it can be maps, or chess, or coffee; it can be the words of Epictetus teaching us to despise gold; it is a Proteus more versatile than the one on the isle of Pharos. It is unforeseeable [imprevisible] time, Bergsonian time, not the rigid time of Islam or the Porch (*L* 192).]

A detailed search for financial transactions in *Ulysses* reveals that during the long day of Leopold Bloom there are countless instances in which cash has been handled. Bloom's capital day is so imperative that it concludes in the 'Ithaca' episode with a detailed one-page inventory — albeit incomplete — of his budget, setting off with a pork kidney and closing with a loan to Stephen Dedalus. The book also records other significant material transactions, such as Mulligan's miraculous discovery of a florin: 'Buck Mulligan brought up a florin, twisted it round his fingers and cried — A miracle' (*U* 1.453) or Mr Deasy's Shakespearean imperative: '*Put but money in thy purse*' (*U* 2.239) to an incredulous Stephen who is in turn reminded of the treachery of Iago. Finally, if we take into account Borges's notoriety for including apocryphal references and imaginary authors in his fictional and critical works, and his famous confession that he had not read *Ulysses* in its entirety, it comes as a surprise to discover that his reference to Bloom's florin is unequivocally corroborated in the mathematical catechism of 'Ithaca':

> What rendered problematic for Bloom the realization of these mutually selfexcluding propositions?
> The irreparability of the past: once at a performance of Albert Hengler's circus in the Rotunda, Rutland square, Dublin, an intuitive particoloured clown in quest of paternity had penetrated from the ring to a place in the auditorium where Bloom, solitary, was seated and had publicly declared to an exhilarated audience that he (Bloom) was his (the clown's) papa. The imprevidibility of the future: once in the summer of 1898 he (Bloom) had marked a florin (2/-) with three notches on the milled edge and tendered it in payment of an account due to an received by J. and T. Davy, family grocers, 1 Charlemont Mall, Grand Canal, for circulation on the waters of civic finance, for possible, circuitous or direct, return.
> Was the clown Bloom's son?
> No.
> Had Bloom's coin returned?
> Never. (*U* 17.973–88)

This textual corroboration raises several questions in relation to Borges's inclusion of Bloom in his catalogue of numismatic symbols. What happens when *Ulysses* enters the superstitious, enigmatic and magical world of 'The Zahir'? Is *Ulysses* enriched by the distinctive attributes of Borges's symbol? Does the Funes–*Ulysses* parallel as explored in Chapter 3, throw any light on the new Zahir–Bloom correspondence? First of all, it is undeniable that Borges used Bloom's florin as one of the literary models for the Zahir. Just as Joyce's disc is 'marked with three notches on the milled edge', Borges's tells the reader at the beginning of the story that the Zahir 'es una moneda común, de veinte centavos; marcas de navaja o de cortaplumas rayan las letras NT y el número dos' (*OC1* 589) ['is an ordinary coin worth twenty centavos. The letters NT and the number 2 are scratched as if with a razor-blade or penknife'] (*L* 189). Later in the story, after much speculation, 'Borges' decides to get rid of the Zahir and, similarly to Leopold Bloom, plunges the idiosyncratic coin into the waters of civic finance. If Bloom is reported to have tendered his florin in payment to the family grocers whose premises are located in south Dublin, 'Borges' operates an analogous transaction and uses his twenty-cent coin to pay for a drink at a local bar situated in the south of Buenos Aires. If Borges offers a metaphysical meditation about the abstract possibilities of financial ownership, Joyce offers a similar speculation with the introduction of the coinage 'imprevidibility',[78] which aims to draw attention to the unpredictability of material gain and loss. It also stands in converse relation to the 'irreparability of the past', as it brings attention to Bloom's paternal anxieties and to his grief over the loss of his son Rudy, who, like the florin irretrievably submerged in the waters of civic finance, is forever lost in the waters of death, that 'undiscovered country from whose bourn / No traveller returns' (*Hamlet* III. 1. 81–82).

What Borges distinctively renders into Spanish as 'el florín irreversible de Leopold Bloom' opens a further intertextual connection with his story 'The Disc'. The first-person narrator of this parable is a woodcutter who has long been a recluse in his hut on the edge of the woods. This mysteriously isolated character is one day visited by an even more mysterious elderly looking stranger who claims to be the king of the Secgens and to possess the disk of Odin:[79]

> — Soy rey de los Secgens. Muchas veces los llevé a la Victoria en la dura batalla, pero en la hora del destino perdí mi reino. Mi nombre es Isern y soy de la estirpe de Odín.
> — Yo no venero a Odín — le contesté. — Yo venero a Cristo.
> Como si no me oyera continuó:
> — Ando por los caminos del destierro pero aún soy el rey porque tengo el disco. ¿Quiéres verlo? [...] — Es el disco de Odín. Tiene un solo lado. En la tierra no hay otra cosa que tenga un solo lado. Mientras esté en mi mano seré el rey (*OC3* 66–67).

> ['I am the king of the Secgens. Many times did I lead them to victory in hard combat, but at the hour that fate decreed, I lost my kingdom. My name is Isern and I am of the line of Odin.'
> 'I do not worship Odin,' I answered. 'I worship Christ.'
> He went on as though he'd not heard me.
> 'I wander the paths of exile, but still I am a king, for I have the disk. Do you want to see it?' [...]

'It is the disk of Odin,' the old man said in a patient voice, as though he were speaking to a child. 'It has but one side. There is no other thing on earth that has but one side. So long as I hold it in my hand I shall be king' (*CF* 478).]

The covetous woodcutter decides to murder the king in order to gain possession of the magical disk. But, in a typical Borgesian twist, the death of Isern also implied the irretrievable loss of the disk. In this sense, if the mathematical catechist of 'Ithaca' unambiguously states that Bloom's florin 'never returned', Borges articulates a more subtle proposition that validates a dual meaning. He converts Bloom's disc into an 'irreversible florin', which implies both an un-returning florin, as well as a florin that, like Odin's disk, possesses only one face. In this vein, Bloom's florin acquires greater meaning in relation to the posterior work of Jorge Luis Borges, allowing the construction of a network of shared idiosyncrasies between the two writers. If according to Borges 'cada escritor *crea* a sus precursores' (*OC2* 90) ['each writer *creates* his precursors'] (*SNF* 365), then we are able to read Joyce in a manner that would not have been possible without Borges's 'The Zahir'. This intersection creates a literary fraternity between Bloom's florin and its Borgesian avatars, the Zahir and the Disc, as Borges confers onto Joyce's coin the magical, infinite qualities characteristic of his own creations. It is also significant to point out, however, that in his 1925 review of *Ulysses* Borges had also performed a numismatic reading of Joyce: 'En su comercio, junto al erario prodigioso de voces que suman el idioma inglés y le conceden cesaridad en el mundo, corren doblones castellanos y siclos de Judá y denarios latinos y monedas antiguas, donde crece el trébol de Irlanda' (*Inq.* 27) ['Aside from the prodigious funds of voices that constitute the English language, his commerce spreads wherever the Irish clover grows, from Castilian doubloons and Judas' shekels to Roman denarii and other ancient coinage'] (*SNF* 14). What is, then, the ultimate effect of Borges's lacing of *Ulysses* into the fabrics of 'The Zahir'? I propose two interrelated answers.

First, 'The Zahir' continues Borges's complex pattern of a magical, yet monstrous object whose main attribute is the supernatural capacity to envelop a whole universe, and whose acquisition produces a side effect of insomnia. In this vein, the Zahir is — like Funes's memory — a magical entity that augments the powers of recollection and cancels the possessor's capacity to forget it: 'El tiempo, que atenúa los recuerdos, agrava el del Zahir' (*OC1* 594) ['Time, which generally attenuates memories, only aggravates that of the Zahir'] (*CF* 248). Just as in 'A Fragment on Joyce' Borges labels Funes and *Ulysses* as monstrous entities in their attempts to achieve a totalization of experience (*SNF* 220–21) so he refers to the Zahir with the same qualifying adjective when he alludes to its 'monstruosa imagen' (*OC1* 594) ['monstrous image'] (*CF* 247). Hence it becomes clear that Borges associates Joyce's writing with an infinite, disturbing object/memory that produces in the narrator a dual sentiment of attraction and repulsion. As I have stated in Chapter 3, Borges confessed that during the 1930s he suffered from insomnia and as a result sought refuge in the fact that Joyce had also suffered from the same ailment and had forged an infinite book, *Ulysses*, 'in which thousands of things happened'.[80] The decisive moral to be deduced from Borges's insomniac account is, therefore, that while Joyce rescued Borges from his nights of insomnia, so Borges fills a hermeneutical gap in Joyce's work by creating the ideal reader, Ireneo Funes, to undertake the total, consecutive reading of *Ulysses* and *Finnegans Wake*. Just as Funes stands as a metaphor of insomnia, so the magical forces of the Zahir produce an alarming state of wakefulness in the narrator, who consults a psychiatrist and ingests sleeping tablets in order to alleviate his lack of sleep. Ultimately, 'Borges', like Funes, longs to swap his state of mnemonic augmentation for the anaesthetizing state of forgetfulness: 'Para perderse en Dios, los sufíes repiten su propio nombre o los noventa y nueve nombres divinos hasta que éstos ya nada quieren decir' (*OC1* 595) ['In order to lose themselves in God, the Sufis repeat their own name or the ninety-nine names of God until the names mean nothing more'] (*CF* 249). If oblivion may be bestowed through the spoken rehearsal of theosophical onomastics, equally 'Borges' hopes that: 'Quizá yo acabe por gastar el Zahir a fuerza de pensarlo y repensarlo; quizá detrás de la moneda esté Dios' (*OC1* 595) ['Perhaps by thinking about the Zahir unceasingly, I can manage to wear it away, perhaps behind the coin is God'] (*CF* 249). Whether 'Borges' encounters God behind the coin is uncertain, but he certainly encounters Leopold Bloom's florin, which underlies his complex and intricate relationship with *Ulysses*. In addition, as Borges stated in his conversation with Richard Burgin, by invoking the name of James Joyce over and over again during his insomniac nights, he conceived the plot of 'Funes the Memorious', an otherwise miniature version of *Ulysses*. In the most paradoxical of manners, the infinity of *Ulysses* allowed him to regain his sleep: 'Each time I suffer from insomnia, I can free myself from memory because this book contains it all, and I can sleep'.[81]

Finally, through the phenomenon of metempsychosis or transculturation, Borges sets Bloom's nomadic coin on a transatlantic voyage from Dublin to Buenos Aires as the Zahir, the new Islamic/Argentine coin. This numismatic diaspora mimics the similar journey undertaken by a 1922 Shakespeare & Company edition of *Ulysses* from Paris to Buenos Aires, which culminated in Borges's conflation of Molly Bloom's Hibernian and Gibraltarian identities with a newly invented River Plate fluency. These various forms of migration symbolically fulfil the frustrated elopement of Eveline to Buenos Aires, hence fostering an Argentine version of Joyce, as well as mapping the waters for further encounters between Borges and Joyce or, eventually, for the dissemination of Joyce's work in Latin America.

## Borges and Joyce, Authors of the *Commedia*

If in 'Pierre Menard Author of the *Quixote*' Borges proposes a *ficción* of a Frenchman who sets himself the arduous task of rewriting Cervantes's *Quixote*, similarly Reed Way Dasenbrock postulates that a whole generation of Anglophone modernist writers aspired to rewrite Dante's *Commedia*, 'One of the ways we could describe an aspiration of virtually all the major modernist writers in English is that they were all trying to write the *Commedia* of the twentieth century.'[82] By the same token, Allen Thiher asserts that: 'In Dante the encyclopedia of the real is given in one self-enclosed book, which, with appropriate adjustment, is a succinct description of the modernist project from Proust and Joyce through Musil and Mann, not to mention the parodist versions thereof later found in Borges and Queneau.'[83] But unlike Borges's fictional Menard who successfully achieved a verbatim, yet paradoxically different, complex exercise in the art of reading across time, culture, and language, not all these modernist transpositions proved equally successful. In particular, Dasenbrock is putting forward a specific case against Pound's much criticized *Cantos*, describing his modernist attempt to reproduce Dante's epic design as 'a disastrous failure'.[84] On the other hand, Pound's Dantist legacy needs to be examined not only from the vantage point of his thwarted efforts to write a *Commedia* of the twentieth century but, principally, from his influential theories of translation that, very much like Borges's Menard, focused on the practice of reading and interpretation. Not insignificantly, in *After Babel* George Steiner includes the name of Ezra Pound amongst the most influential translation theorists of the twentieth century and views his writings on translation as 'the most telling reports on the activity of the translator, and on relations between languages'.[85] Similarly, in *Translation Studies*, Susan Bassnett praises Pound's pivotal contribution to the field: 'The work of Ezra Pound is of immense importance in the history of translation, and Pound's skill as a translator was matched by his perceptiveness as a critic and theorist.'[86]

In opposition to his negative view of Pound, Dasenbrock's verdict of Eliot's creative transformations of Dante remains highly encouraging: 'If modernism has a true "Dantescan voice", that is the voice of Eliot'.[87] But his final words for Joyce are even more assenting: '[In] terms of creative imitation, this means that he was the best imitator of all.'[88] If what is at stake is 'creative imitation' then Borges and Joyce emerge, above all, triumphant in their appropriations of Dante. Their exercises in rewriting are both idiosyncratic and multifaceted, advocating a playful, radical and transformative poetics that shift Dante's medieval world to their twentieth-century circumstances. In effect, what remains decisive for Dasenbrock is the fact that Joyce realised that in order to write a modern *Commedia*, he had to use the knowledge of his time just as Dante had used the knowledge of his. The end result of Borges's and Joyce's complex afterlives of Dante highlights not only the crucial historical, linguistic, and cultural transfer to which Dasenbrock is referring here, but also the ability to combine as much homage and parody in their composite transactions of Dante. If this is so, like the fictional Menard, Borges and Joyce opt for the more challenging method to arrive at the *Commedia*, not by trying to become Dante in fourteenth-century Italy, but via the experiences of Joyce and Borges in their contemporary Ireland and Argentina, and via the mediation of a whole Western tradition of Dantean criticism. Once again, Borges's method of 'anacronismo deliberado y de las atribuciones erróneas' (*OC1* 450) ['deliberate anachronism and fallacious attribution'] (*CF* 95) may produce, at times, versions infinitely more subtle, or richer, than the original.

## Afterword: James Joyce, Author of 'The Aleph'

Alternatively, as far as Borges unites the discourses of Dante and Joyce in the overlapping patterns of 'The Zahir' and 'The Aleph', it is also possible to read in *Ulysses* a complex tapestry of allusions interwoven around the concept of the Aleph. There are thus four interrelated occasions on which Joyce celebrates the Aleph. First, in 'Proteus' as Stephen walks along Sandymount strand he gazes at two midwives and then muses upon the navel-cords that secretly link together the whole of humanity: 'The cords of all link back, strandentwining cable of all flesh. That is why mystic monks. Will you be as gods? Gaze in your *omphalos*' (*U* 3.37–38). This intersecting umbilicus pattern is subsequently extended into a telephone conversation to Eden: 'Hello! Kinch here. Put me on to Edenville. Aleph, alpha: nought, nought, one' (*U* 3.37–40). Stephen's code to Eden brings together the first letter of the Hebrew alphabet, the first letter of the Greek alphabet, followed by three numerals. If these letter-symbols are translated into cardinal numbers they become 11001, creating a figure that recalls the *Arabian Nights* effect of perpetuity as it adds one more digit to a series that represent a conceptual infinity, 11000.[89] Therefore, Joyce articulates in 'Proteus' a relationship between the Aleph and infinity which not only recalls Borges's similar correlation with transfinite numbers, but by situating his entry on the Aleph in conjunction with Stephen's paradisiacal message from Earth to Eden, Joyce also brings to mind Borges's Kabbalistic assertion that the shape of the letter Aleph 'tiene la forma de un hombre que señala el cielo y la tierra, para indicar que el mundo inferior es el espejo y es el mapa del superior' (*OC3* 627) ['is that of a man pointing to the sky and the earth, to indicate that the lower world is the map and mirror of the higher'] (*CF* 285). As he walks through sand, pebbles and shells, opening and closing his eyes from time to time, looking up and down, Stephen speculates about theosophy, literature and metaphysics, and pronounces the letter Aleph. Thus, who other than Stephen Dedalus, who wonders about time and space with his rhetorical question: 'Am I walking into eternity along Sandymount strand?' (*U* 3.18–19) represents Borges's assertion about a man contemplating infinity and signifying the letter Aleph?

The second reference to the Aleph in *Ulysses* takes place in 'Lotus-Eaters' during Bloom's early peregrination through the city of Dublin: 'He crossed Townsend street, passed the frowning face of Bethel. El, yes: house of: Aleph, Beth' (*U* 5.10–11). Don Gifford informs us that 'Beth' and 'El' signify 'House of God' in Hebrew: 'After the city and holy place twelve miles north of Jerusalem, where the ark of the covenant was kept. This is the name of a Salvation Army hall that Bloom passes in Lombard Street East.'[90] Significantly, Joyce's 'House of God' takes us back to Borges's house of the Aleph as we shift across time and space from the Biblical Jerusalem to Joyce's twentieth-century Dublin, and from Townsend Street to Garay Street in Borges's Buenos Aires. There is a proportionate effect of mutation in both houses of Aleph, particularly since Joyce denotes the transposition of the sacred house of Jerusalem to a Salvation Army hall in Dublin, while Borges signals the inevitable demolition of 'la vieja casa inveterada de la calle Garay' (*OC1* 622) ['the old and deeply rooted house on Calle Garay'] (*CF* 280) that contained the Aleph, in order to allow the new venture planned by the landlords Zunino and Zungri.

The third and fourth references take place in 'Circe' and 'Ithaca' respectively, and are concerned with the significance of the letter Aleph in the Hebrew alphabet. In 'Circe' Bloom proclaims his Zionist adherence by displaying 'The ram's horns' (*U* 15.1619) — which according to Gifford signifies a battle trumpet of the ancient Israelites[91] — and utters the first four letters of the Hebrew alphabet: 'Aleph Beth Ghimel Daleth' (*U* 15.1622) in addition to a wealth of references to other Judaic traditions and celebrations. This exploration is revisited in 'Ithaca', as Bloom and Stephen perform a linguistic exchange in which they compare and contrast the Hebrew and Gaelic alphabets respectively:

> How was the glyphic comparison of the phonic symbols of both languages made in substantiation of the oral comparison?
> By juxtaposition. On the penultimate blank page of a book of inferior literary style, entituled *Sweets of Sin* (produced by Bloom and so manipulated that its front cover came in contact with the surface of the table) with a pencil (supplied by Stephen) Stephen wrote the Irish characters for gee, eh, dee, em, simple and modified, and Bloom in turn wrote the Hebrew characters ghimel, aleph, daleth and (in the absence of mem) a substituted qoph, explaining their arithmetical values as ordinal and cardinal numbers, videlicet 3, 1, 4, and 100 (*U* 17.731–40).

It is significant that Joyce intercalates his reference to the Irish and Hebrew languages with a third discourse — albeit neither ancient nor sacred — the soft-core pulp-fiction of *Sweets of Sin*, a volume previously purchased by Bloom (for Molly) in 'The Wandering Rocks' episode. In a typically Joycean gesture, the two revered languages are desacralized through contact with the third profane language of *Sweets of Sin*. This deliberate mixing and clashing of registers produces an effect of hybridization in the novel, as Bakhtin argued in *The Dialogic Imagination*: 'The novelistic hybrid is *an artistically organized system for bringing different languages in contact with one another, a system having as its goal the illumination of one language by means of another*'.[92] This juxtaposition brings back, once again, Borges's debunking of Dante's tradition of the woman-as-angel by including in the mystical revelation of the Aleph the pornographic epistolary correspondence of Beatriz Viterbo. Hence if Joyce authorizes a criss-crossing of the sacred Hebrew and ancient Celtic languages with the bawdy narrative of *Sweets of Sin*, then Borges intersperses the obscene language of Beatriz Viterbo with the mystical revelation of the Aleph.

Above all, the Aleph as an infinite point of convergence in Dante, Joyce, and Borges is best exemplified in Borges's 1941 obituary of Joyce. He concludes the necrological note with a reflection on Joyce's life and oeuvre that brings to mind Beckett's Purgatorial ending in 'Dante... Bruno. Vico.. Joyce', as it emphasizes the Dantean imprint of the book:

> El *Ulises* (nadie lo ignora) es la historia de un solo día, en el perímetro de una sola ciudad. En esa voluntaria limitación es lícito inferior que para Joyce, todos los días fueron de algún modo secreto el día irreparable del Juicio; todos los sitios, el Infierno o el Purgatorio (*S* 169).

[*Ulysses* (as everyone knows) is the story of a single day, within the perimeter of a single city. In this voluntary limitation, it is legitimate to perceive something more than an Aristotelian elegance: it can legitimately be inferred that for Joyce every day was in some secret way the irreparable Day of Judgment; every place, Hell or Purgatory (*SNF* 221).]

## Notes to Chapter 5

1. For a comprehensive examination of the way in which the Victorians appropriated Dante's literary, political and cultural discourses, see Alison Milbank's *Dante and the Victorians* (Manchester: Manchester University Press, 2001).
2. Joyce acknowledged the fact that Blake aspired to become an English *dantisti* in his attempt to learn Italian in order to access the *Commedia* in the original: 'He set about studying Italian to read the *Divine Comedy* in the original and to illustrate Dante's vision with mystic drawings.' See Joyce, *Critical Writings*, p. 179. Similarly, Borges acknowledged Blake's study of Italian in one his lectures at the National University of Buenos Aires. See *Borges professor*, edición, investigación y notas de Martín Arias y Martín Hadis (Buenos Aires: Emecé, 2001), p. 204.
3. See *Dante in English*, ed. by Eric Griffiths and Matthew Reynolds (London: Penguin, 2005) for an up-to-date, detailed anthology of Dante's reception in English from Chaucer to Seamus Heaney.
4. The presence of Dante in 'The Aleph' has been subject of much speculation. Emir Rodríguez Monegal states that Borges playfully disclaimed the story's indebtedness to Dante's *Commedia*: 'Critics [...] have detected Beatrice Portinari in Beatriz Viterbo, Dante in Daneri, and the descent into hell in the descent into the cellar. I am, of course, duly grateful for these unlooked-for gifts' (see Rodríguez Monegal, p. 416). For a discussion of Borges's failure to recognize the *Commedia* as a source see: Jon Thiem, 'Borges, Dante, and the Poetics of Total Vision', *Comparative Literature*, 40 (1988), 97–121.
5. Beckett, 'Dante...Bruno.Vico..Joyce', in *Our Exagmination Round His Factification For Incamination of Work in Progress* (London: Faber & Faber, 1929), pp. 5–22 (pp. 21–22). Further quotations from this essay are also from pages 21–22.
6. John L. Murphy, 'Beckett's Purgatories', in *Beckett, Joyce and the Art of the Negative*, ed. by Colleen Jaurretche (Amsterdam and New York: Rodopi, 2005), pp. 109–24 (p. 122).
7. David Wallace observes, 'an Irish Dante (Yeats, Joyce, Beckett, Heaney) achieves things that are beyond the grasp of the English and Americans'. See Wallace, 'Dante in English', in *The Cambridge Companion to Dante*, ed. by Rachel Jacoff (Cambridge: Cambridge University Press 1993), pp. 237–58 (p. 237).
8. Reynolds, *The Shaping Imagination*, p. 3.
9. Reynolds, p. 3.
10. Boldrini, *Joyce, Dante, and the Poetics of Literary Relations: Language and Meaning in Finnegans Wake* (Cambridge: Cambridge University Press, 2001), p. 13.
11. Jennifer Margaret Fraser, *Rite of Passage in the Narratives of Dante and Joyce* (Gainesville: University Press of Florida, 2002), p. 1.
12. Humberto Nuñez-Faraco, *Borges and Dante: Echoes of a Literary Friendship* (Berlin: Peter Lang, 2006), p. 15.
13. There are several essays that investigate the presence of the *Commedia* in 'The Aleph'. See Maria Bonati, 'Dante en la Lectura de Borges', *Revista Iberoamericana*, 100–01 (1977), 737–44. See also John Thiem, 'Borges, Dante, and the Poetics of Total Vision', *Comparative Literature*, 40 (1988), 97–120, and Matei Calinescu, *Rereading* (New Haven, CT, and London: Yale University Press, 1993), pp. 3–17. For the influence of Dante on 'The Intruder' and other stories see Sylvie Davidson, 'Borges and Italian Literature', *Italian Quarterly*, 105 (1986), 43–49. See also Julio Chiappini's concise volume *Borges y Dante* (Rosario: Editorial Zeus, 1993) for a comparative synopsis and further references on the subject. See also the fourth chapter, 'Blindness: Alephs and Lovers', of María Rosa Menocal's comparative investigation *Writing in Dante's Cult of Truth: From Borges to Boccaccio* (Durham, NC: Duke University Press, 1991), pp. 131–77.

14. For an interview about Dante, see Roberto Alifano, 'La Divina Comedia', in *Ultimas Conversaciones con Borges* (Buenos Aires: Torres Agüero Editor, 1988) pp. 123–30. See also Borges's conference, 'La Divina Comedia', in *Siete Noches* (1980) (*OC3* 207–20) and 'Mi Primer Encuentro con Dante' (1961) in *TR3* 71–74.
15. Umberto Eco and Liberato Santoro-Brienza, *Talking of Joyce*, ed. by Liberato Santoro-Brienza (Dublin: University College Dublin Press, 1998), pp. 61–62.
16. Wallace, p. 252.
17. The Ignatian model was used as a mnemonic guide for composing and delivering sermons and lectures, hence Stephen Dedalus's invocation to Loyola as a patron saint of memory before presenting his Shakespeare theory in 'Scylla and Charybdis' (*U* 9.163). See *The Spiritual Exercises of Saint Ignatius of Loyola*, trans. by Michael Ivens SJ, with an introduction by Gerard W. Hughes SJ (Leominster: Gracewing, 2004).
18. Yates, p. 95, p. 163. For a comparative discussion of Dante's relationship with the art of memory, see Spender Pearce 'Dante and the Art of Memory', *The Italianist*, 16 (1996), 20–61. See also Jerome Mazzaro's 'The *Divina Commedia* and the Rhetoric of Memory', *Rivista di Studi Italiani*, 17.1 (1999), 112–29. See also the 'Introduction' in Borges's *Nine Dantesque Essays* whereby he discusses the differences between the infernal architectures of Dante and Milton, highlighting the contrast between 'Milton's fog and uncertainty' in relation to the 'strictly accurate topography by which Dante engineered his infernal plane'. He also argues that Dante 'devised his topography of death as an artifice demanded by Scholasticism and by the form of his poem' (*SNF* 267–68).
19. All references to Dante's *Commedia* belong to *La Divina Commedia*, testo critico della Società Dantesca Italiana, riveduto col commento scartazzianiano rifatto da Giuseppe Vandelli, dodicesima edizione (Milan: Editore Della Real Casa, 1944), (*Inf* XI, 10–12). Further references will be cited parenthetically in the text.
20. All English translations of the *Commedia* belong to *The Divine Comedy*, trans. by Mark Musa, 3 vols (London: Penguin, 1986), *Inf* 168. Further references will be cited parenthetically in the text.
21. Eco, *The Aesthetics of Chaosmos*, p. 5.
22. Reynolds, p. 18.
23. Reynolds, p. 18.
24. See Jorge Luis Borges, *Nueve ensayos dantescos*, con una introducción de Marcos Ricardo Barnatán y presentación de Joaquín Arce (Madrid: Espasa-Calpe, 1982), p. 46.
25. Borges, *Nueve ensayos dantescos*, p. 46.
26. Eliot, *Dante*, p. 11.
27. See Alighieri, Dante (1933) *La Divina Commedia: Inferno, Purgatorio, Paradiso*, The Italian edited by H Oelsner, English translations by J. A. Carlyle, Thomas Okey & P. H. Wicksteed.
28. Eliot, *Dante*, p. 11.
29. For more details about Borges's secondary education in the Collège Calvin, see Alejandro Vaccaro, *Borges: vida y literatura* (Barcelona: Edhasa, 2006), pp. 57–60.
30. See Dante Alighieri, *La Divina Comedia*, estudio preliminar por Jorge Luis Borges, traducción de Cayetano Rosell y notas de Narciso Bruzzi Costas (Buenos Aires: Jackson editors, 1949), p. xviii.
31. Borges, *Borges professor*, p. 257.
32. John Updike, 'The Author as Librarian', *The New Yorker*, 30 October 1965, pp. 223–46.
33. Reynolds p. 31.
34. Mary T. Reynolds, 'Joyce's Editions of Dante', *James Joyce Quarterly*, 15 (1978), 380–82 (p. 382). Please note that apart from this single reference, all other citations from Reynolds belong to *Joyce and Dante: The Shaping Imagination*.
35. Burgin, pp. 100–01.
36. See Reynolds, p. 83.
37. Andrew Hurley renders the title of the story as 'The Interloper'. See *CF* 348–51.
38. Nuñez-Faraco, p. 20.
39. For an illuminating discussion of the Griselda figure see Robin Kirkpatrick, *Chaucer and the Italian Trecento* (Cambridge: Cambridge University Press, 1983).
40. Kirkpatrick, p. 231.

41. Antonio Carrizo, *Borges, el memorioso* (México: Fondo de Cultura Económica, 1982), p. 236.
42. Samuel Beckett, in 'Foreword' to *James Joyce: An International Perspective*, ed. by Suheil Bushrui and Bernard Benstock (Gerrards Cross: Colin Smythe, 1982), p. vii.
43. Vegh, p. 95.
44. John T. Irwin, *The Mystery to a Solution: Poe, Borges and the Analytic Detective Story* (Baltimore, MD, and London: Johns Hopkins University Press, 1994), p. 20.
45. See Salgado, 'Barroco Joyce', for an illuminating discussion of the numerous Joycean allusions in 'The Garden of Forking Paths', pp. 63–93.
46. This group of essays, originally written between the years 1945–1951, were published separately in several periodical publications. In 1982 Borges granted permission to his publisher, Emecé, to publish them together in book form.
47. Jorge Luis Borges/Osvaldo Ferrari, *En diálogo I* (Buenos Aires: Sudamericana, 1985), p. 198.
48. Alberto Manguel, *With Borges* (London: Telegram, 2006), p. 66.
49. See 'Dante's Letter to Can Grande', trans. by Nancy Howe in *Essays on Dante*, ed. by Mark Musa (Bloomington: University of Indiana Press, 1965), pp. 32–47 (p. 37).
50. Boldrini, p. 35.
51. M. Keith Booker, *Joyce, Bakhtin and the Literary Tradition: Toward a Comparative Cultural Poetics* (Ann Arbor: University of Michigan Press, 1997), p. 82.
52. Calinescu, p. 12.
53. Sturrock argues that 'The Aleph' 'makes a kind of pair' with 'The Zahir', p. 70. See also Bell-Villada's comprehensive discussion of both stories, pp. 212–27; and Calinescu, pp. 3–16.
54. According to Floyd Merrell: 'The Aleph affords a realist image as opposed to the nominalism of the Zahir. One entails a transcendental revelation, the other a series of significant perceptual grasps, or in a way of speaking, one is synchrony, the other diachrony. One is a superposition of all objects, acts, and events in simultaneity, the other a serial collection of particulars with no determinate links.' *Unthinking Thinking: Jorge Luis Borges, Mathematics, and the New Physics* (West Lafayette, IN: Purdue University Press, 1991), p. 8.
55. Katherine Hayles, *The Cosmic Web: Scientific Field Models and Literary Strategies in the Twentieth-Century* (Ithaca, NY, and London: Cornell University Press, 1984).
56. Dasenbrock and Mines, ' "*Quelle vista nova*": Dante, Mathematics, and the Ending of *Ulysses*', in *Medieval Joyce*, ed. by Lucia Boldrini, European Joyce Studies 13 (Amsterdam: Rodopi, 2002), pp. 79–91 (p. 83).
57. Dasenbrock/Mines, 'Dante, Mathematics, and the Ending of *Ulysses*', p. 88.
58. Reynolds also suggests that Joyce compounded this reference with an allusion to Canto II from *Purgatorio*, whereby the Pilgrim sees a ship with the souls of the Redeemed intoning the psalm *In exitu Israel de Aegypto*. See Reynolds, pp. 121–22, for an insightful analysis of Joyce's use of these Dantean extracts in 'Ithaca'.
59. Estela Canto wrote an account of her relationship with Borges in *Borges a Contraluz* (Madrid: Austral, 1989). She also included in this book the previously unpublished love letters that Borges wrote to her during their relationship.
60. Rodríguez Monegal, p. 414.
61. Dante Alighieri, *Vita Nova*, A cura di Luca Carlo Rossi, Introduzione di Guglielmo Gorni (Milan: Oscar Mondadori, 1999), p. 222.
62. Interestingly, Borges quotes this line in his essay 'Beatrice's Last Smile' (see *SNF* 303). He also states that '[...] Beatrice whose beauty increases with each new circle they reach [...] (*SNF* 302).
63. Edwin Williamson, p. 242.
64. Nuñez-Faraco, p. 163.
65. M. Keith Booker, 'From the Sublime to the Ridiculous: Dante's Beatrice and Joyce's Bella Cohen', in *James Joyce Quarterly*, 29 (1992), 357–68 (p. 366).
66. Booker, 'From the Sublime to the Ridiculous', p. 366.
67. Booker, 'From the Sublime to the Ridiculous', pp. 365–66.
68. Booker, 'From the Sublime to the Ridiculous', p. 365.
69. Dante, *Vita Nova*, p. 6–8.
70. Dante Alighieri, *La Vita Nuova*, trans. with an introd. by Barbara Reynolds (London: Penguin, 1969), p. 29.

71. Calinescu, p. 15.
72. See Calinescu, pp. 14–15; pp. 283–84, n.14, n.15, n.16, n.17.
73. Bell-Villada, p. 223.
74. Rodríguez Monegal, p. 414.
75. It has also been argued that Borges is parodying here the Chilean poet Pablo Neruda, particularly his vast poem '*Canto General*'. Nuñez-Faraco points out that Borges may be also attacking the Nicaraguan writer Ruben Darío, the leading poet of the *fin-de-siècle* movement known as *Modernismo* (not to be confused with Modernism in English). Ultimately, I concur with Nuñez-Faraco's assertion in *Borges and Dante* that: 'Daneri embodies a complex web of literary references', p. 45.
76. Thiem, p. 111.
77. See Thiem, pp. 106–19, for a fascinating discussion of the relationship between Borges's 'miniature encyclopedia of the Aleph' and Dante's *Commedia*.
78. It is noteworthy that in his discussion of the abstract possibilities of monetary possession, Borges employs the Spanish invariable adjective 'imprevisible' [unforeseeable] which semantically and grammatically corresponds with Joyce's coinage 'imprevidibility' [unforeseeability], in his discussion of Bloom's florin. Both terms share the negative prefix 'im', followed by the prefix 'pre', which are compounded with the adjective 'visible' in Borges (etymologically related, via French, to the medieval Latin form 'visibilis'), while Joyce directly employs the Latin past form, from 'vidi' ('I saw').
79. It is important to note that Borges and Joyce became, later in their lives, ardent devotees of Norse legend, particularly of the anonymous *Poetic Edda* and Snorri Sturluson's *Edda*. This crucial fact brings a further layer of relevance to Joyce's presence in 'The Disk'. In *Literaturas Germánicas Medievales* (1966) written in collaboration with Delia Ingenieros, Borges offers an illuminating and informative account on the subject (see *OCC* 861–975).
80. Burgin, p. 166.
81. Burgin, p. 166.
82. Dasenbrock, *Imitating the Italians: Wyatt, Spenser, Synge, Pound, Joyce* (Baltimore, MD, and London: Johns Hopkins University Press, 1991), p. 209.
83. Allen Thiher, *Fiction Refracts Science: Modernist Writers from Proust to Borges* (Columbia and London: University of Missouri Press, 2005), p. 20.
84. Dasenbrock, *Imitating the Italians*, p. 214. See also Novillo-Corvalán, review of Line Henriksen, *Ambition and Anxiety: Ezra Pound's Cantos and Derek Walcott's Omeros as Twentieth-Century Epics*, in *The European English Messenger*, 17.1 (2008), 86–87.
85. George Steiner, *After Babel: Aspects of Language and Translation* (Oxford: Oxford University Press, 1998), p. 249.
86. Susan Bassnett, *Translation Studies*, 3rd edn (London and New York: Routledge, 2003), p. 76.
87. Dasenbrock, *Imitating the Italians*, p. 218.
88. Dasenbrock, *Imitating the Italians*, p. 219.
89. In a 1980 lecture, Borges argued that the notion of infinity is consubstantial with the title *The Thousand and One Nights*: 'I believe that it is related to the fact that for us the word "thousand" is almost a synonym of "infinity". To say a thousand nights is to say infinite nights, several nights, innumerable nights. And to say "thousand and one night" is to add one to infinity' (*OC3* 234).
90. Gifford, p. 84.
91. Gifford, p. 477.
92. M. M. Bakhtin, *The Dialogic Imagination: Four Essays by M. M. Bakhtin*, ed. by Michael Holquist, trans. by Caryl Emerson and Michael Holquist (Austin: University of Texas Press, 1981), p. 361.

CHAPTER 6

# Joyce's and Borges's Afterlives of Shakespeare

Jorge Luis Borges published his *Anthology of Fantastic Literature* (1940)[1] one year after the publication of *Finnegans Wake* (1939) and one year before Joyce's untimely death in Zurich (1941), a conjunction of dates that is acknowledged by the fact that the name of James Joyce appears twice in the table of contents of his eccentric treasury of 'fantastic' literature. Closely resembling Borges's wide-ranging model of reading and writing, the anthology unconventionally conflates Western, Oriental, and marginal discourses alike, placing the Taoist Chinese philosopher Chuang Tzu side-by-side with the English writer G. K. Chesterton; the Argentine writer and humorist Macedonio Fernández next to the English ethnologist James George Frazer; the medieval Castilian prince Don Juan Manuel next to James Joyce; and a story by the emerging Argentine writer Silvina Ocampo alongside a one-act play by the American 1936 Nobel Prize winner Eugene O'Neill. As Emir Rodríguez Monegal has remarked: 'To this day it is one of the most curious and unorthodox compilations on the subject [...] The anthology was highly personal and (in the best sense of the word) arbitrary.'[2] But in spite of its eclectic method of selection, the anthology proved to be a decisive compilation that introduced Hispanic audiences to a wide gamut of literature in translation, as well as legitimizing the lesser-known voices of Argentine and Latin American writers. In an interview with Osvaldo Ferrari, Borges proudly claimed that the anthology proved at the time to be 'un libro benemérito, ya que la literatura de la América del Sur [...] ha sido siempre una literatura más o menos realista'[3] [a praiseworthy book, particularly since South American literature has always been more or less realist]. What Borges is stating here is that in comparison to the fertile mode of fantastic fiction that flourished in the nineteenth century in England and the United States, Argentine literature prior to the Latin American boom was characterized by its realist emphasis, particularly if we consider the development in the nineteenth century of a composition known as 'cuadro de costumbres' [sketch of local customs] that largely dominated the literary production of the time. Daniel Balderston observes that the *Antología* 'was an oblique attack on the social realist tradition in Latin American writing [...] suggesting that the writer's first obligation was to tell interesting and challenging stories'.[4] As a result of this, *The Anthology* fostered rich intercultural encounters, in a conscious attempt to renew Latin American fiction by mapping a heterogeneous terrain that offered an unprecedented journey through the fantastic. In negotiating a miscellaneous group of texts under the heading 'fantastic literature', Borges is performing a cultural transaction through which foreign texts in translation are strategically transferred to a new context and, at the same time, national authors are re-evaluated and integrated not only in relation to Western and Oriental discourses alike, but also within the specific category of 'fantasy' that the editors, Borges, Bioy Casares, and Ocampo, were actively seeking to promote.

In this context, it is important to recognize that in the cultural arena of Argentina in the early 1940's James Joyce's *Ulysses* remained the exclusive property of a minority of cultured Anglophone speakers and a French-speaking intellectual elite, such as Victoria Ocampo and the group *Sur*, who had access to the influential 1929 French translation *Ulysse* by Auguste Morel, Stuart Gilbert, and Valery Larbaud, with the collaboration of Joyce himself. Therefore, Joyce's appearance in the anthology would have been credited either to the cultural eccentricity of its editors or, most likely, to Borges's unique acquaintance with his work from his avant-garde days. As I have argued throughout this study, apart from Borges's 1925 translation of the last two pages of 'Penelope' in the avant-garde review *Proa*, and of other similar fragmentary translations that appeared in a few Spanish periodicals throughout the 1920s,[5] there had been no complete rendering of what was proving to become one of the most revolutionary and controversial books of the twentieth century. Borges's rendering of the last two pages of 'Penelope' as well as his careful reinvention of two fragments of *Ulysses* (from 'Scylla and Charybdis' and 'Circe') as fantastic short stories, represented the only picture available to Hispanic readers without access to either the English original or the French translation. Undoubtedly, this event constituted a decisive landmark in the dissemination of Joyce's work in the Hispanic world and, as it will concern us here, it planted the seeds that would later bear the fruits of Borges's literary conversation with Shakespeare and Joyce.

This chapter discusses the way in which Borges and Joyce blended an impressive corpus of Elizabethan, Romantic, Victorian, and contemporary readings of Shakespeare in order to foster their own versions or 'afterlives' of the Bard. By means of a detailed comparative reading of — on the one hand — 'Scylla and Charybdis', the ninth episode of *Ulysses* devoted to the discussion of Shakepeare's art and life, and — on the other — Borges's concise parable 'Everything and Nothing' (1960) and short story 'Shakespeare's Memory' (1980), both of which are entirely dedicated to the exploration of Shakespeare's enigmatic identity, it argues that their affiliation with Shakespeare centres on their conceptions of the playwright as a ghost. Furthermore, this chapter claims that Borges's and Joyce's intersections with Shakespeare reawaken the phantom of Shakespeare in a new language, culture, and history, inasmuch as each 'afterlife' of Shakespeare — to use Walter Benjamin's central metaphor in his seminal essay 'The Task of the Translator'[6] — is conceived as an act of translation. This triple comparative enquiry also attempts to reveal unseen aspects of the relationship between Borges and Joyce through the angle of Shakespeare, whose discourse strengthens and enhances their literary affiliation. It aims to raise several interrelated questions: is it possible to read Borges's 'Shakespeare's Memory' and 'Everything and Nothing' — which Jonathan Bate has described as 'the greatest of all brief allegories of Shakespeare's life'[7] —

through the prism of Joyce's own exposition of Shakespeare in 'Scylla' and 'Circe'? What does Borges's peculiar translation of two fragments of *Ulysses* tell us about his subsequent dialogue with Shakespeare? And, finally, how do Joyce and Borges negotiate the cultural influence that the omnipresent spectre of Shakespeare has exerted throughout the centuries?

## *Ulysses* as an Argentine Ghost Story

I begin with a transcription of the two fragments included in the anthology which, for the sake of clarity and comparative purposes, are side-by-side with Joyce's English version.

> FRAGMENT 1 *(from 'Scylla and Charybdis')*
> What is a ghost? Stephen said with tingling energy. One who has faded into impalpability through death, through absence, through change of manners (*U* 9.147–49).
> DEFINICIÓN DEL FANTASMA
> ¿Qué es un fantasma? preguntó Stephen. Un hombre que se ha desvanecido hasta ser impalpable, por muerte, por ausencia, por cambio de costumbres.[8]

> FRAGMENT 2 *(from 'Circe')*
> (*Stephen's mother, emaciated, rises stark through the floor, in leper grey with a wreath of faded orangeblossoms and a torn bridal veil, her face worn and noseless, green with gravemould. Her hair is scant and lank. She fixes her bluecircled hollow eyesockets on Stephen and opens her toothless mouth uttering a silent word. A choir of virgins and confessors sing voicelessly.*)
> THE CHOIR Liliata rutilantium te confessorum...
> Iubilantium te virginum...
> (*From the top of a tower Buck Mulligan, in particoloured jester's dress of puce and yellow and clown's cap with curling bell, stands gaping at her, a smoking buttered split scone in his hand.*)
> BUCK MULLIGAN
> She's beastly dead. The pity of it! Mulligan meets the afflicted mother. (he upturns his eyes) Mercurial Malachi!
> THE MOTHER
> (*with the subtle smile of death's madness*) I was once the beautiful May Goulding. I am dead
> (*U* 15.4157–74).
> MAY GOULDING
> La madre de Stephen, extenuada, rígidamente surge del suelo, leprosa y turbia, con una corona de marchitos azahares y un desgarrado velo de novia, la cara gastada y sin nariz, verde de moho sepulcral. El pelo es lacio, ralo. Fija en Stephen las huecas órbitas anilladas de azul y abre la boca desdentada, diciendo una silenciosa palabra.
> LA MADRE
> (*Con la sonrisa sutil de la demencia de la muerte.*)
> Yo fui la hermosa May Goulding. Estoy muerta.[9]

The most noteworthy aspect of Borges's translation of Joyce is his endeavour to turn two fragments from 'Scylla' and 'Circe' respectively into self-contained pieces that acquire a new meaning through their immersion in the entirely new context of the anthology. In order to suit this idiosyncratic project of three Argentine devotees of the short story, the fragments acquire independent status as compressed, fantastic vignettes, and therefore adopt their respective titles: 'Definición del Fantasma' and 'May Goulding'. Further, Borges deliberately erased references to other episodes of *Ulysses* that may act as 'textual distractions'[10] and so interfered with the uncanny tone of the anthology. For example, in 'Definición del Fantasma' he excluded the 'tingling energy' that the third-person narrator attributes to Stephen Dedalus in order to draw attention to his enthusiastic yet anxious state of mind before his Shakespearean presentation in front of a hostile audience at Ireland's National Library. On this occasion, Stephen has carefully prepared his public performance in an attempt to win the esteem of an audience composed of Dublin writers, scholars and librarians, particularly John Eglinton, George Russell (AE), and Richard Best, all of whom were active supporters of the Irish literary revival about which Stephen had serious reservations. Stephen's feelings of alienation and displacement become even more acute when he learns that Eglinton failed to invite him to a literary gathering organized by George Moore.

Borges's predilection for 'Scylla' is well documented throughout his complex relationship with Joyce. One year after the publication of the anthology, he referred to the pleasurable activity of reading and re-reading his favorite episodes from *Ulysses*, particularly stressing his fondness for 'el diálogo sobre Shakespeare' (S 168) [the dialogue on Shakespeare]. This tendency resurfaced in his 1946 review of Salas Subirat's Spanish translation of *Ulysses*, in which the majority of his citations are drawn from 'Scylla' (see, for example, *TR2* 234). In addition, in a comprehensive prologue for a special edition of Shakespeare's works in Spanish, he notes that Anne Hathaway gave Shakespeare 'dos hijos, Hamnet (cuyo profético nombre ha sido comentado por Joyce) y Julia' (*Círculo* 166) [she gave him twins, Hamnet (whose prophetic name has been discussed by Joyce) and Judith]. This textual evidence foregrounds the crucial fact that Borges's subsequent dialogue with Shakespeare is mediated by Stephen's ghostly reading of the Bard. In short, a gothic link becomes the fundamental meeting point in his conversation with Shakespeare and Joyce.

In 'May Goulding', on the other hand, Borges excised the stage directions of Buck Mulligan presented in 'particoloured jester's dress of puce and yellow and clown's cap with curling bell' (*U* 15.4166–67) and his customarily mocking speech that refers to the altercation he had with Stephen in 'Telemachus'. Whilst it may be argued that, because 'Circe' is chiefly characterized by its phantasmagorical and hallucinatory histrionics, Borges's omissions were unnecessary, the episode equally contains, as Matthew Creasy has demonstrated,[11] pantomime elements from Shakespearean burlesque, which offer an additional discourse of parody and comic entertainment that Borges probably deemed incompatible with his new version of Joyce. Also deleted from Borges's anthology is the 'choir of virgins and confessors' which foreshadows Stephen's conflictual relationship with Roman Catholicism and his deeply buried psychological trauma from his unwillingness to pray at his mother's deathbed.

Borges's unapologetic subtractions from the source text invite speculation about how the excisions are negotiated in the Spanish text. To begin with, Borges's translation practice may be examined from the perspective of his 1925 fragmentary rendering of 'Penelope', which similarly aimed to turn the last two pages of the book into an autonomous piece intended for the readership of Hispanic audiences. Whereas the two excerpts selected for the anthology belong to two different episodes, 'Scylla' and 'Circe', they are integrated as interconnected pieces with their own separate titles. In this way, Stephen's nominal definition 'what is a ghost?' is promptly followed, and in some way answered, by the uncanny apparition of May Goulding, his dead mother, who in turn serves as an example of the several 'ghosts by death' that populate the anthology. If in 1925 Borges presented to Argentine audiences a fragmentary translation of the last two pages of 'Penelope', in 1940 he similarly promoted a miniaturized version of Joyce's epic proportions filtered through a specific literary predilection: the fantastic short story. This, in turn, goes hand in hand with the revolutionary compressed *ficciones* he was writing at this crucial historical juncture. His displacement of two fragments from *Ulysses* into the anthology thus exhibits a translation practice that imaginatively reinvents the translated text in order to make it fit the specific requirements of his compilation. The overall result is what in his 1929 essay, 'Guido's Relations', Ezra Pound defined as the type of modernist translation that 'falls in the domain of original writing'[12] in which the translator offers a new poem or, in Borges's case, two super-concise fantastic narratives rendered in a manner representative of his aesthetics of brevity.

Just as in 'Scylla' John Eglinton summarizes Stephen's public disquisition on the interrelationship of Shakespeare's art and life at Ireland's National Library as 'He will have it that *Hamlet* is a ghoststory' (*U* 9.141), so in his *Anthology of Fantastic Literature* Borges offers his own epigrammatic version of *Ulysses* as a supernatural tale that establishes a range of dialogic relationships with the other thirty-five interconnected pieces in an eccentric anthology of fantastic literature.[13] Borges is exercising here what Beatriz Sarlo referred to as his idiosyncratic practice of reading obliquely: 'Borges pone en acción algo que seguirá haciendo toda su vida: leer de manera desviada, buscando sólo lo que le sirve, sin ningún respeto por los sentidos establecidos'[14] [Borges performs a lifelong action: reading with a parted eye, only searching for what he needs, and without any respect for the established conventions].

## Searching for Shakespeare

Joyce's and Borges's afterlives of Shakespeare are based on the central premise that their revisions of the Bard have been largely constructed by means of an impressive blending of Elizabethan, Romantic, Victorian, and contemporary interpretations.[15] William M. Schutte has convincingly argued that Joyce constructed Stephen Dedalus's public disquisition on the interrelationship of Shakespeare's life and art out of a wide variety of creative and critical sources, including the biographical scholarly research by Sidney Lee, Frank Harris, and George Brandes, the influential nineteenth-century interpretations of Coleridge, Keats, and Goethe, and the more recent French perspective afforded by Stephané Mallarmé.[16] To this extensive list of sources, Richard Ellmann adds the French writer Dujardin, and the lesser-known volume *A Day with William Shakespeare*, by Maurice Clare, that Joyce had in his apartment in Trieste.[17] An analysis of the sources used by Borges reveals a similar pattern of scholarship, which analogously includes the principal English and German Romantic creative and critical writings on Shakespeare, the presence of a French writer (albeit Victor Hugo, not Mallarmé), contemporary critical studies such as *Crítica Literaria* (1924) by the French-born Argentine intellectual Paul Groussac, and *Introducing Shakespeare* (1939) by the American scholar G. B. Harrison. Like Joyce, Borges was also indebted to Frank Harris's biographical reading of Shakespeare, particularly as it is presented in his 1931 unauthorized biography of the Irish critic and playwright George Bernard Shaw.[18] Not only did this scholarly investigation offer Borges precise details about recent discussions of Shakespeare's life and art but the letter from Shaw that Harris included at the beginning of the biography furnished him with the principal source and outcome of 'Everything and Nothing'. Indeed, in 'A Note on (towards) Bernard Shaw' (1951)[19] Borges suggested that the title 'Everything and Nothing' (note that the title is conveyed in English in the Spanish original) had been inspired by this letter, in which Shaw declared to his biographer: 'Also, you propose to endow me with a soul. Have you not yet found out that people like me and Shakespeare *et genus omne* have no souls? We understand all the souls and all faiths and can dramatize them because they are to us wholly objective: we hold none of them.'[20]

Joyce and Borges conflated several centuries of Shakespearean criticism in order to produce a literary and cultural transfer that articulated a version of Shakespeare as a spectre who, according to Stephen Dedalus, embodies the condition of ghost by virtue of death, absence, and change of manners. Hence, it is possible to read in their conceptions of Shakespeare as a ghost a larger metaphor for the cultural influence the canonical spirit has exerted throughout the centuries. In this vein, Maria Dibattista asserts that: 'A ghost was Joyce's figure for the phenomenon of transculturalism [...] Metempsychosis, the resubstantiation of ghosts Joyce took as his literary model in *Ulysses*, is always a transcultural act, since the reincarnated spirit inevitably returns to different times, altered ways of living.'[21] Similarly, Marjorie Garber applies the 'ghostly' rhetoric employed by Walter Benjamin in 'The Task of the Translator' to Shakespeare's legacy: 'For translation and mechanical reproduction are, precisely, means by which the original and its primacy are put into question. And thus are ways of making — of calling up — ghosts.'[22] In their afterlives of Shakespeare, then, Borges and Joyce utilize an equally recognizable uncanny discourse in a mutual endeavour to highlight the crucial fact that the haunting force of Shakespeare has become an overpowering cultural heritage that reawakens across different languages and cultures. Their converging views of the bard as 'ghost' and 'shadow' are clearly stated at the beginning of 'Scylla' and 'Everything and Nothing':

> — The play begins. A player comes on under the shadow, made up in the castoff mail of a court buck, a wellset man with a bass voice. It is the ghost, the king, a king and no king, and the player is Shakespeare who has studied *Hamlet* all the years of his life which were not vanity in order to play the part of the spectre (*U* 9.164–68).

> Nadie hubo en él; detrás de su rostro (que aun a través de las malas pinturas de la época no se parece a ningún otro) y de sus palabras, que eran copiosas, fantásticas y agitadas, no había más que un poco de frío, un sueño no soñado por alguien (*OC2* 181).
>
> [There was no one in him; behind his face (which even through the bad paintings of those times resembles no other) and his words, which were copious, fantastic and stormy, there was only a bit of coldness, a dream dreamt by no one (*L* 284).]

Stephen's supposedly groundbreaking theory, which is based on historical evidence that Shakespeare played the part of the ghost in *Hamlet*, postulates that Shakespeare identified with the ghost of King Hamlet, an argument that opposed the prevailing view of most nineteenth-century criticism — namely, that Shakespeare identified with Prince Hamlet. Joyce's decision to base the fundamental premise of Stephen's tale of Shakespeare's reading on an uncanny plot twist is continued and developed by Borges in 'Everything and Nothing', where he extends the presiding gothic principle of his narrative by declaring that Shakespeare himself was nothing, as insubstantial and ethereal as a shadow, 'un sueño no soñado por alguien' [a dream not dreamt by anyone]. Later in the story Shakespeare's phantasmal existence is by and large referred to as 'el odiado sabor de la irrealidad' (*OC2* 181) [the hated flavour of unreality] (*Labyrinths* 284). Likewise in 'Shakespeare's Memory' the omnipresent ghost of Shakespeare is variously referred as 'la memoria del muerto' (*OC3* 397) [the dead man's memory], 'el espectro' (*OC3* 398) [the spectre] and with the more general, albeit no less mysterious allusion to, 'el otro' (*OC3* 399) [the other]. In this story Daniel Thorpe offers the narrator (the Shakespearean scholar Hermann Soergel) the memory of Shakespeare: 'Le ofrezco la memoria de Shakespeare desde los días más pueriles y antiguos hasta los del principio de abril de 1616' (*OC3* 394) ['I offer you [...] Shakespeare's memory, from his youngest boyhood days to early April, 1616'] (*CF* 510). Soergel accepts the wondrous memory without hesitation. Yet, the magic gift, as in many Borgesian fictions, turns from joy into terror, and towards the end of the story the narrator re-allocates the memory of the ghost into somebody else's memory. Like the teeming memory of Ireneo Funes, Shakespeare's memory reveals an endless number of details and facts, but lacks the most important aspect of the playwright, his creative genius: 'La memoria de Shakespeare no podía revelarme otra cosa que las circunstancias de Shakespeare. Es evidente que éstas no constituyen la singularidad del poeta; lo que importa es la obra que ejecutó con ese material deleznable' (*OC3* 397) ['Shakespeare's memory was able to reveal to me only the circumstances of the *man* Shakespeare. Clearly, these circumstances do not constitute the uniqueness of *the poet*; what matters is the literature the poet produced with that frail material'] (*CF* 513). The memory of the ghost is neither capable of reproducing Shakespeare's genius nor offering a coherent narrative of his life; instead, it elicits further gaps, uncertainties, and the eerie force of the supernatural. Ultimately, Borges's metaphor reveals the cultural force of the inescapable ghost of Shakespeare which has haunted him and the crucial fact that the mystery of the bard as *incerti auctoris* remains, in spite of ongoing scholarly attempts, an unsolved case. Correspondingly, in 'Scylla' John Eglinton alludes to the obscure, uncharted areas surrounding Shakespeare's life, 'of all great men he is the most enigmatic [...] A shadow hangs over all the rest' (U 9.359–61).

In 'Everything and Nothing' Borges defers any explicit reference to Shakespeare's name until the end of the parable, when the Divinity finally utters the name 'Shakespeare' from a whirlwind. Yet, paradoxically, the reader is also aware throughout the parable that the unnamed protagonist is William Shakespeare. 'Everything and Nothing', thus, deploys the motif of the search on two levels: the playwright's incessant search for an identity and reality that evades him, and the reader's own search for the haunting and slippery construct known as 'Shakespeare'. In this sense, Joyce's and Borges's view of Shakespeare as a ghost converge with Marjorie Garber's observation that: '"Shakespeare" is present as an absence — which is to say, as a ghost. Shakespeare as an author is the person who, were he more completely known, would not be the Shakespeare we know.'[23] In essence, Shakespeare's persona is contradictorily 'known' by his self-effacing canonical status, establishing his identity through a biographical void, and in what Garber refers to as the long-standing investment in the authorship controversy that aims to find 'the "real" ghost writer'.[24]

In 'Scylla', Joyce offers a travesty that mocks these very inquiries. Upon hearing the subject of Stephen's lecture, Buck Mulligan derisively remarks: 'Shakespeare? He said. I seem to know the name' (U 9.508), and later in the episode Stephen compounds his onomastic verdict of the authorship controversy with a pluralized version of Shakespeare's ghostwriters: 'Rutlandbaconsouthamptonshakespeare or another poet of the same name in the comedy of errors wrote *Hamlet*' (U 9.866). When asked by John Eglinton if he believes in his own theory, Stephen elicits one of the most negative retorts in *Ulysses* (U 9.1065–67), and yet still expects to receive payment for his intellectual labours. For Stephen, the art of the Shakespearean Question is not a search for a definite answer but an aesthetic journey merely justified by its own creative — and financial — endeavour, inasmuch as, ultimately, all theories of Shakespeare are equally partial and subject to further refutation. Yet when George Russell objects that Stephen should refrain from 'prying into the family life of a great man' (U 9.181), Stephen, who initially addresses his interlocutors 'superpolitely', rapidly shifts to less courteous retorts: 'Bosh! Stephen said rudely' (U 9.228), and then disregards Russell entirely in order to deliver what John Eglinton calls a 'ghoststory', adding; 'Like the fat boy in Pickwick he wants to make our flesh creep' (U 9.142–43). Later, moreover, Buck Mulligan's burlesque intrusion provides a sort of comic relief to Stephen's solemn and erudite performance.

Central to Stephen's exposition of Shakespeare's condition as a ghost is the assumption that a mature and attractive Anne Hathaway played a vital role in the seduction of the youthful and inexperienced William:

> He chose badly? He was chosen, it seems to me. If others have their will Ann hath a way. By cock, she was to blame. She put the comether on him, sweet and twentysix. The greyeyed goddess who bends over the boy Adonis, stooping to conquer, as prologue to the swelling act, is a boldfaced Stratford wench who tumbles in a cornfield a lover younger than herself. (U 9.256–60).

According to Stephen, then, the forceful Anne Hathaway was the cause of

Shakespeare's ensuing feelings of sexual insecurity, suggesting that the trauma inflicted by her near rape would therefore haunt him forever. Stephen also contends that, while Shakespeare stayed in London, an unfaithful Anne — like Gertrude in *Hamlet* — cuckolded him with his two brothers, Richard and Edmund. Stephen henceforth concludes that Shakespeare, a ghost by absence, turned his supposedly adulterous brothers into the arch-villains of his tragedies, amalgamating sibling rivalry and betrayal in his tragedies *Richard III* and *King Lear*. On a different level, however, another cuckolded figure that fits Stephen's Shakespearean thesis is Leopold Bloom, who is always in the background of 'Scylla', searching for the files of the *Kilkenny People* in the National Library. Stephen's adulterous motif thus also creates a parallel between the unfaithful Anne Hathaway and Molly Bloom. 'Bloom similarly is a ghost by absence', writes Terence Killeen, 'voluntary absence from 7 Eccles Street, where he has left a clear field for Blazes Boylan [...] Bloom has in fact been usurped by Blazes Boylan, as Shakespeare allegedly was by his brothers and Bloom had a son who died young, as Shakespeare's did.'[25]

Anne Hathaway's sexual initiation of Shakespeare is no less important in 'Everything and Nothing', as her vigorous seduction increases Shakespeare's feelings of unreality and insecurity: 'después consideró que en el ejercicio de un rito elemental de la humanidad, bien podía estar lo que buscaba y se dejó iniciar por Anne Hathaway, durante una larga siesta de junio' (*OC2* 181) ['Later he considered that what he sought might well be found in an elemental rite of humanity, and let himself be initiated by Anne Hathaway one long June afternoon'] (*L* 284). Borges continues the theme of Anne Hathaway's seduction in 'Shakespeare's Memory', although in this case sexual initiation is mediated through the personal experience of Hermann Sörgel: 'Recordaría a Anne Hathaway como recuerdo a aquella mujer, ya madura, que me enseñó el amor en un departamento de Lübeck hace ya tantos años' (*OC3* 396) ['I would remember Anne Hathaway as I remembered that mature woman who taught me the ways of love in an apartment in Lübeck so many years ago'] (*CF* 511). Equally, Shakespeare's 'long June afternoon' finds a suitable correspondence in Bloom's marital proposal to Molly and her climatic 'Yes'. In his 1980 prologue to Shakespeare's works Borges insists: 'Anne Hathaway, con la que se casaría en 1582, parece haberle revelado el amor'[26] [Anne Hathaway, whom he married in 1582, appears to have initiated him into love].

Extremely fond of imaginary authors, apocryphal sources and deliberate misreadings, Borges adopted Stephen's tale about Shakespeare's tortuous relationship with Anne Hathaway and his ambivalent condition of ghost-in-life. In this manner, Borges and Joyce present Anne Hathaway as the key *dramatis persona* in Shakespeare's drama and project her early influence as the determinant force in the subsequent scenes of his life. 'Like Stephen', writes Thomas J. Rice, 'Borges notes that the young Shakespeare "allowed himself to be initiated by Anne Hathaway" and, subsequently, "went off to London" having in some sense lost his identity, his manhood, by this sexual initiation.'[27] Rice has also suggested that Borges's fictional retelling of Shakespeare's life follows Stephen Dedalus in employing 'local colour' (*U* 9.158), a literary method which, according to William H. Quillian, resembles the one employed by his nineteenth-century predecessors in that: '[Stephen] assembles a biography of Shakespeare's life, including details about the social life of Elizabethan England'.[28] Just as Stephen sprinkles his lecture with detailed topographical references to Shakespeare's life, such as 'Shakespeare has left the huguenot's house in Silver street and walks by the swanmews along the riverbank' (*U* 9.159–60), so Borges describes Shakespeare's customary visits to public houses and places of ill repute in London: 'Así, mientras el cuerpo cumplía su destino de cuerpo, en lupanares y tabernas de Londres' (*OC2* 181) ['And so, while his flesh fulfilled its destiny as flesh in the taverns and brothels of London'] (*L* 284).

Both men's accounts of Shakespeare's life are also enriched by allusions to and citations from his plays, in an attempt to sustain their arguments with histrionic speeches that act as coded allusions to his life. In 'Everything and Nothing' Borges draws attention to the meta-theatrical utterances of Iago and Richard III, whose self-reflexive lines confess to an audience their evil machinations and their dual identity of actors/characters in order to further his argument about Shakespeare's existential concerns: 'A veces, dejó en algún recodo de la obra una confesión, seguro de que no la descifrarían; Ricardo afirma que en su sola persona, hace el papel de muchos, y Yago dice con curiosas palabras *no soy lo que soy*' (*OC2* 181) ['At times he would leave a confession hidden away in some corner of his work, certain that it would not be deciphered; Richard affirms that in his person he plays the part of many and Iago claims with curious words "I am not what I am"'] (*L* 87). Like Borges, Joyce embeds Stephen Dedalus's Shakespearean thesis with carefully manipulated quotations. In his attempt to impress his library audience, Stephen indiscriminately draws from an inexhaustible Shakespearean archive and certifies that Shakespeare's life is written 'between the lines' of his works (*U* 9.1010).

But if Borges and Joyce begin their speculations on Shakespeare with the central premise that the playwright is 'airy nothing' — an unsubstantial ghost or shadow — their expositions gradually suggest that the Bard encapsulates *everything*. In 'Scylla' this fundamental shift begins to take place with Richard Best's quotation from Coleridge's *Biographia Literaria*: 'A myriadminded man, Mr Best reminded. Coleridge called him myriadminded' (*U* 9.768–69). According to Quillian, 'No criticism of *Hamlet*, not even A. C. Bradley's, has had the enormous influence on subsequent interpretations as Coleridge's fragmentary remarks. Single-handed, he invented the "myriadminded" Shakespeare, conceived, as he tells us, from a direct study of his "myriad-minded" hero.'[29] (Borges singles out this quotation in his review of Salas Subirat's Spanish version of *Ulysses*.) Yet the decisive turning point in 'Scylla' is John Eglinton's crucial statement that temporarily resolves the dialectic of the episode with a reconciling synthesis: 'The truth is midway, he affirmed. He is the ghost and the prince. He is all in all' (*U* 9.1018–19). Unable to contradict such fundamental objection to his theory, Stephen Dedalus energetically agrees with Eglinton's succinct formula: 'He is, Stephen said. The boy of act one is the mature man of act five. All in all' (*U* 9.1020–21). Eglinton follows with a quotation from Dumas *père* — wrongly attributed to Dumas *fils*: 'After God Shakespeare has created most' (*U* 9.1028–29). Stephen, who in *A Portrait of the Artist as a Young Man* equated artistic creation with 'the God of Creation"' (*P* 181) concurs with Eglinton: 'The playwright who wrote the folio of the world and wrote it badly' (*U* 10.46–47).

Similarly, in 'Everything and Nothing' Shakespeare the creative artist becomes father of his entire race, just as God has created humanity. By means of his metaphysical search for substance and his quest for the personal identity he suspects has been denied to him, Shakespeare is able to transcend 'el odiado sabor de la irrealidad' (*OC2* 181) ['the hated flavor of unreality'] (*L* 284). This allows him to exorcize, if only temporarily, the ghostly quality that has haunted his life so far. Therefore, Borges's Shakespeare also becomes 'all in all', the 'myriadminded' man present in all his creations: 'Nadie fue tantos hombres como aquel hombre, que a semejanza del egipcio Proteo pudo agotar todas las apariencias del ser' (*OC2* 181) ['No one has ever been so many men as this man who like the Egyptian Proteus could exhaust all the guises of reality'] (*L* 285).

If in *A Portrait* Stephen equates the artist with God, in 'Scylla' this comparison is projected onto Shakespeare, the creator par excellence, hence allowing Stephen to blend his paternity theories with the new formula of Shakespeare-God.[30] In the interval between *A Portrait* and *Ulysses* Stephen has reconsidered his aesthetics of creation, particularly since he no longer aims to refine himself out of existence, instead, his theory of Shakespeare is modelled — as Schutte points out — 'in his own image'.[31] Like Coleridge's own theory of *Hamlet* — 'I have a smack of Hamlet myself, if I may say so'[32] — Stephen associates the link between Shakespeare's life and works with his own life and anxieties about paternity. In *Ulysses*, his sombre pose, strict black attire, 'Hamlet hat' (*U* 3.390), and mourning for the death of his mother, render him as a self-conscious avatar of Shakespeare's tragic hero. As Haines tells Stephen, 'this tower [Martello] and these cliffs here remind me somehow of Elsinore' (*U* 1.566–67). Further, in 'Proteus', as Stephen walks along Sandymount strand he reflects upon his estrangement from the tower: 'I pace the path above the rocks, in sable silvered, hearing Elsinore's tempting flood' (*U* 3.280–81). In short, Stephen's Shakespearean enquiry incorporates his own ghost story — namely, the phantasm of his mother — which in the *Anthology of Fantastic Literature* Borges astutely places after his definition of a ghost. Ultimately, Stephen aims to answer Shakespeare's (and his own) existential, theological, and creative dilemmas not only through the realm of the uncanny, but also through Christian doctrines of the Nicene Creed. In this manner, he challenges the orthodox Trinitarian doctrine of Nicaea (the Godhead is constituted by Father, Son and Holy Spirit) and proposes instead the notoriously contentious Arian (neither Son nor Holy Spirit are coeternal with the Father) and Sabellian (the Son and Holy Spirit are not Gods but rather aspects of the Father) heretical Trinitarian creeds. As early as 'Telemachus', for example, we see Stephen ruminating about 'the subtle African heresiarch Sabellius who held that the Father was Himself His own Son' (*U* 1.659–60) and, as Kimble Loux has argued, Stephen's journey as an artist is reflected in his passage from one Trinitarian model to another: 'Joyce depicts Stephen's growing confidence in his abilities as an artist as he moves from the Nicene trinity formed by himself and his consubstantial parents, through the Arian and Sabellian trinities of young men.'[33] Stephen's manipulation of Arianism and Sabellianism, furthermore, privileges the supremacy of the Father as the only God over the Son and the Holy Spirit, henceforth allowing Shakespeare, the Father, to become at once the Ghost (King Hamlet) and his own Son (Hamnet/Hamlet). If Shakespeare is conceived as the 'father of all his race', then Stephen repudiates his begetter (Simon Dedalus) — 'Who is the father of any son that any son should love him or he any son?' (*U* 9.844–45) — in order to paradoxically become, as an artist, the father of his own father.

## I AM WHO I AM (Exodus 3. 14)

In an essay entitled 'From Somebody to Nobody' (1950) Borges offers a narrative that surveys the philosophical doctrine of pantheism (whereby nature as a whole is understood as an emanation of God), and its subsequent applications into a clearly defined Romantic corpus of Shakespearean scholarship (Coleridge, Hazlitt, and Hugo) that shifts the pantheistic notion of God into the figure of Shakespeare himself:

> A principios del siglo XIX, ese dictamen es recreado por Coleridge, para quien Shakespeare ya no es un hombre sino una variación del infinito Dios de Spinoza. 'La persona Shakespeare — escribe — fue una *natura naturata*, un efecto, pero lo universal, que está potencialmente en lo particular, le fue revelado, no como abstraído de la observación de una pluralidad de casos sino como la sustancia capaz de infinitas modificaciones, de las que su existencia personal era sólo una.' Hazlitt corrobora o confirma: 'Shakespeare se parecía a todos los hombres, salvo en lo de parecerse a todos los hombres. Intimamente no era nada, pero era todo lo que son los demás, o lo que pueden ser.' Hugo, después, lo equipara con el océano, que es un almácigo de formas posibles (*OC2* 116).

> [At the beginning of the nineteenth century that opinion is recreated by Coleridge, for whom Shakespeare is no longer a man but a literary variation of the infinite God of Spinoza. Shakespeare as an individual person, he wrote, was a *natura naturata*, an effect, but 'the universal which is potentially in each particular opened out to him... not as an abstraction of observation from a variety of men, but as the substance capable of endless modifications, of which his own personal existence was but one.' Hazlitt corroborated or confirmed this: 'He was just like any other man, but that he was unlike other men. He was nothing in himself, but he was all that others were, or that could become.' Later, Hugo compared him to the ocean, which is the seedbed of all possible forms (*SNF* 342).]

Borges offers an elaborate religious and literary pattern that begins with a survey of the various nominal appellations attributed to God and concludes his onomastics of the Creator with the nineteenth-century reinvention of Shakespeare as a symbol of all humanity, the infinite God-like figure that is both the Creator and every one of his own creations. It is evident that this idiosyncratic study of pantheism constitutes one of the chief sources of 'Everything and Nothing'. This is especially apparent in the last paragraph of his parable, in which Borges demystifies the biblical dialogue in the Book of Exodus between God and Moses, by having his Shakespeare ask God to reveal Shakespeare's own identity, not God's:

> Then Moses said to God, 'Indeed, when I come to the children of Israel and say to them, "The God of your fathers hath sent me unto you"; and they shall say to me, "What *is* His name?" what shall I say to them?' And God said to Moses, '*I AM WHO I AM*'.[34]

> La historia agrega que, antes o después de morir, se supo frente a Dios y le dijo: Yo, que tantos hombres he sido en vano, quiero ser uno y yo. La voz de Dios le contestó desde un torbellino: Yo tampoco soy; yo soñé el mundo como tú soñaste tu obra, mi Shakespeare, y entre las formas de mi sueño estás tú, que como yo eres muchos y nadie (*OC2* 182).
>
> [History adds that before or after dying he found himself in the presence of God and told Him: 'I who have been so many men in vain want to be one and myself.' The voice of the Lord answered from a whirlwind: 'Neither am I anyone; I have dreamt the world as you dreamt your work, my Shakespeare, and among the forms in my dream are you, who like myself are many and no one' (*L* 285).]

Unlike Moses, Borges's Shakespeare is no longer interested in finding out the identity of his creator insofar as the revelation of his own identity discloses that God is also made of 'such stuff as dreams are made on, / and our little life is rounded with a sleep' (*Tempest*, IV. 1. 156–58). Borges extends Shakespeare's search for his own identity to God, who, like the playwright, not only dreams his world but is also someone else's dream, thus creating further levels of illusion. In this sense, I concur with Ion T. Agheana's assertion that 'the encounter with God does not resolve Shakespeare's dilemma'.[35] As with the metaphysical concern raised in 'Partial Magic in the *Quixote*', in which Borges asks: '¿Por qué nos inquieta que el mapa esté incluído en el mapa y las mil y una noches en el libro *Las Mil y Una Noches?*' (*OC2* 47) ['Why does it disturb us that Don Quixote be a reader of the *Quixote* and Hamlet a spectator of *Hamlet?*'], the proposed answer — 'Tales inversiones, sugieren que si los caracteres de una ficción pueden ser lectores o espectadores, nosotros, sus lectores o espectadores, podemos ser ficticios' (*OC2* 47) ['These inversions suggest that if the characters of a fictional work can be readers or spectators, we, its readers or spectators, can be fictitious'] (*L* 231) — only blurs the boundary between reality and illusion and elicits, in turn, further interrogations. Moreover, in 'A History of the Echoes of a Name' (1952) Borges postulates that God's reply to Moses ('I AM WHO I AM') may also be read through the prism of Shakespeare's Paroles, the *miles gloriosus* of *All's Well that Ends Well*, who says to his audience: 'Captain I'll be no more, / But I will eat and drink and sleep as soft / As captain shall. / Simply the thing I am / Shall make me live' (*All's Well*, IV. 4. 308.311). According to Borges, Paroles's speech transforms Paroles from one man into all men.[36] If this is so, Paroles is at once 'the thing he is' and the thing that 'everyone is', just as God equally is 'what he is'.[37] In a cyclical way, Borges returns to Paroles's key speech in his aptly titled poem 'The Thing I Am' included in *The History of the Night* (1977) whereby the poetic voice searches for his elusive identity in a personal and cultural archive that uncovers his paternal and maternal genealogies and the boundless memory of a whole Western tradition which resonates in the works of Plato, Homer, Virgil, Dante, and Angelus Silesius (*OC3* 196–97). In 'Shakespeare's Memory', moreover, the narrator, Herman Soergel, uses Parole's speech in a desperate attempt to regain his own individuality. The ability to be many selves results in the impossibility of being one-self, thus circularly returning to Borges's 'Everything and Nothing' and to Shaw's declaration in Harris's biography.[38] Finally, in 'A New Refutation of Time'

(1952) Borges argued that the 'self-less' readers of Shakespeare become Shakespeare himself: '¿Los fervorosos que se entregan a una línea de Shakespeare no son, literalmente, Shakespeare?' (*OC2* 141) ['Are the enthusiasts who devote themselves to a line of Shakespeare not literally Shakespeare?'] (*SNF* 323).

So far, therefore, it is possible to identify in Joyce's and Borges's reinvention of Shakespeare the use of a mixture of discourses borrowed from literary, historical, and theological sources, particularly in their intermingling of fact (the probable), fiction (the improbable/the supernatural), and religion (the superhuman) in their reconstructions of Shakespeare's life. Above all, their interweaving of sources illustrates the extent to which the ghost of Shakespeare loomed large throughout all stages of their works and the complex ways in which they negotiated his ubiquitous presence. This is also epitomized in Stephen Dedalus's presentation of a 'theolologicophilolological' (*U* 9.762) concoction of Shakespeare. We may conclude, then, that Borges's fondness for rhetorical questions and mystical and metaphysical dilemmas — as highlighted in his appropriation of the Biblical episode — explains his decision to include Stephen's 'Definition of a Ghost' in his *Anthology of Fantastic Literature*. Indeed, as Borges may have been well aware, Stephen's initial interrogation — 'What is a ghost?' (*U* 9.147) — is triggered by additional supernatural lines of enquiry based on Shakespeare's own ghost story in *Hamlet*: 'Who is the ghost from *limbo patrum*, returning to the world who has forgotten him? Who is King Hamlet?' (*U* 9.150–51). Just as in 'Everything and Nothing' Borges's Shakespeare asks God who he is, so in 'Scylla' Stephen Dedalus raises a similar biographical and existential concern, as he metaphorically seeks to explain the elusive identity of Shakespeare through the unreality of a ghost, a shadow of a shadow, like Borges's dream of a dream. As Shari Benstock has suggested, Stephen's question also echoes 'the opening of Shakespeare's *Hamlet* ("Who's there?" asks Bernardo, and the five-act drama which follows is an attempt to answer the question).' Benstock argues that 'Stephen's analysis provides answers to both these questions, but the answers are woven into the fictional fabric which is "Scylla and Charybdis": the ghoststories we know as Shakespeare's *Hamlet* and Joyce's *Ulysses* unfold anew as Stephen tells the tale.'[39] For Borges, then, the questions raised in *Hamlet*, the encounter between Moses and God, the various Romantic speculations about Shakespeare's life, Shaw's letter to Frank Harris, and Stephen's definition of a ghost are intertwined precisely because there is no definitive answer to the mystery of the Bard, but rather a series of shifting contexts of reading and interpretation, a version of Shakespeare constantly in motion, travelling across linguistic, geographical, and historical boundaries.

## Transcultural Shakespeare

In 'La Trama' ['The Pattern'], a concise narrative vignette included in *The Maker* (1960), Borges equates the death of the historical Julius Caesar (particularly as it is recorded in Shakespeare's and Quevedo's literary versions of his celebrated final words) with a knife-fight amongst a group of gauchos. In Shakespeare and Quevedo the betrayed Caesar realises that he is about to be murdered by his beloved Brutus and pathetically exclaims: '*Et tu, Brute?*' (*Julius Caesar*, III. I. 79); '¿Y tú entre éstos? ¿Y tú, hijo?'[40] [And you among these? And you, son?].

Borges proposes instead a parallel scenario in which a godson kills his godfather who exclaims, albeit in Argentine slang: '[¡]Pero, che!' [hey, you!] (*OC2* 171). In order to emphasize the importance of the vernacular, Borges then adds that these words should be heard, rather than simply read on the printed page. In this way, the locution 'che' (an idiomatic expression characteristic of the variant of Spanish spoken in Argentina and Uruguay) offered Borges the appropriate idiom with which to translate the historical tragedy of *Julius Caesar* into the tradition of the gaucho, albeit by ironically — and anachronistically — linking the historical scene in the Roman capitol with an isolated terrain in the south of the province of Buenos Aires. Interestingly, at the tender age of nine James Joyce had also creatively engaged with Caesar's last words, when in response to Tim Healy's role in the public humiliation and downfall of Charles Stewart Parnell, he 'wrote a poem denouncing Healy under the title "Et tu, Healy"' (*JJII* 33).

There is yet another aspect to Borges's and Joyce's afterlives of Shakespeare's *Julius Caesar*. In Shakespeare's tragedy, after Caesar has been assassinated, Cassius, who is one of the assassins and also the main conspirator, dramatically drenches his hands with Caesar's blood and then exclaims: 'How many ages hence / shall this our lofty scene be acted over, / in states unborn and accents yet unknown' (*Julius Caesar*, III. 1. 112–14). Cassius's complex speech may be read in several ways. On the one hand, it disrupts the illusion of the theatrical performance as it draws attention to the play as play, and to his condition as an actor impersonating the role of Cassius in one of the many productions of *Julius Caesar*. On the other hand, Cassius's statement may also be read as an anticipation, and validation, of Borges's subsequent staging of the 'lofty scene' of *Julius Caesar* in a remote location of Argentina (the state unborn), and a regional variation of River Plate Spanish (the accent yet unknown). Borges, an attentive reader of Shakespeare had paid careful attention to Cassius's speech. At the end of 'The Pattern' he even offers a translation of Cassius's lines: 'Lo matan y no sabe que muere para que se repita una escena' (*OC2* 171) [They kill him and he does not realise he dies so that a scene may be repeated].

What Borges deploys as a modern Argentine rewriting of Shakespeare's *Julius Caesar*, Joyce transposes into the new historical and geographical context of twentieth-century Dublin. *Ulysses* constitutes not only a radical transposition of Homer's *Odyssey* into the modern Irish scenery of Stephen Dedalus, Leopold and Molly Bloom, but also Shakespeare's *Hamlet* has in turn been superimposed upon the already adapted Homeric frame. If Homer's *Odyssey*, Shakespeare's *Hamlet* and — as we have seen in the previous chapter — Dante's *Commedia*, constitute the principal intertextual sources in *Ulysses*, the history of Julius Caesar — both in its Roman and Elizabethan variations — appears as a significant narrative that is woven into several of the novel's episodes. In 'Nestor', for example, Joyce's version of the historical account focuses (like Borges's) on the instant of the stabbing, but adds a further philosophical argument from Aristotle's *Metaphysics*: 'Had Pyrrhus not fallen by a beldam's hand in Argos or Julius Caesar not been knifed to death. They are not to be thought away. Time has branded them and fettered they are lodged in the room of the infinite possibilities they have ousted' (*U* 2.48–51). In other words, Stephen's concern is primarily with the potential ramifications or 'infinite possibilities' of the other events that could also have been, and which have been 'ousted' by the actual historical event that took place: in this case Brutus's stabbing of Caesar.[41] The Roman tragedy reappears in 'Eumaeus'. When Bloom urges Stephen to eat more solid food, the latter reacts with the dramatic imperative: 'But O, oblige me by taking away that knife. I can't look at the point of it. It reminds me of Roman history' (*U* 16.815–16) — in response to which an incredulous Bloom glances at 'a blunt hornhandled ordinary knife with nothing particularly Roman or antique about it to the lay eye [...]' (*U* 16.818–19) and gently moves it out of Stephen's sight. Amongst the many irreconcilable intellectual differences between Stephen and Bloom is the crucial fact that Stephen conceives the knife that killed Caesar as a generic instrument able to embody, at once, its previous murderous deeds, while Bloom is able to see only a specific, ordinary object devoid of any abstract or historical signification. In this sense, Borges's 'The Pattern' offers a genealogy of the knife that converges with Stephen's generic view of the object, and hence the same filial tragedy is symmetrically translated into the customs of the Argentine gaucho, rendering the homicidal *Knife* as the enduring perpetrator of the deed. This theme is fully developed in Borges's later story 'The Encounter' (1970) about the epic reunion of two knives, in which the duel between the gauchos Uriarte and Duncan (a name that clearly alludes to *Macbeth*) is justified not by their brawly, murderous impulses, but by the ever recurring violence inherent in the daggers:

> Maneco Uriarte no mató a Duncan; las armas, no los hombres, pelearon. Habían dormido, lado a lado, en una vitrina, hasta que las manos las despertaron. Acaso se agitaron al despertar; por eso tembló el puño de Uriarte, por eso tembló el puño de Duncan. Las dos sabían pelear — no sus instrumentos, los hombres — y pelearon bien esa noche. Se habían buscado largamente, por los largos caminos de la provincia, y por fin se encontraron, cuando sus gauchos ya eran polvo. En su hierro dormía y acechaba un rencor humano (*OC2* 421).
>
> [Maneco Uriarte did not kill Duncan; it was the weapons, not the men, that fought. They had lain sleeping, side by side, in a cabinet, until hands awoke them. Perhaps they stirred when they awoke; perhaps that was why Uriarte's hand shook, and Duncan's as well. The two knew how to fight — the knives, I mean, not the men, who were merely their instruments — and they fought well that night [...] In the blades of those knives there slept, and lurked, a human grudge (*CF* 369).][42]

*Julius Caesar* also appears in the episode 'Hades', into which Joyce inserts several lines from the play. Significantly, he appropriates lines that refer to death, interlacing them within a schema of Homeric correspondences that links the burial of Paddy Dignam in Glasnevin, north Dublin, to Odysseus's descent into hell. Bloom's interior monologue translates the words that Mark Anthony delivers to a shocked Roman audience: 'I come to bury Caesar, not to praise him' (*Julius Caesar*, II. 3. 71) into his own discourse, as they are presented without quotation marks (*U* 6. 803). (This is an example of what Claudette Sartiliot refers to as 'the eclipse of quotation'.)[43] Moreover, much of the Shakespearean wisdom that has been injected into Bloom's discourse, as Schutte points out, 'consists largely of literary clichés, some of which he may well use without even knowing that he is quoting'.[44] Bloom's allusion to *Julius Caesar* is furthered in the next line by a reference that ironically links the soothsayer's death-warning to Caesar, 'Beware the ides of March' (*Julius Caesar*, 1. 2. 25), with Paddy Dignam's less heroic and unpredicted death from apoplexy on 13 June 1904: 'His ides of March or June' (*U* 6.803). Bloom's equation of Paddy Dignam with *Julius Caesar* is not the only time the ordinary Dubliner is associated with a Shakespearean hero of noble status. In 'Circe' a funereal Dignam, like the Ghost in *Hamlet*, haunts a tormented Bloom and echoes the Shakespearean lines already quoted by Stephen in 'Scylla': 'Bloom, I am Paddy Dignam's spirit. List, list, O list!' (*U* 15.1219).

Joyce's and Borges's Shakespearean negotiations exhibit a conflicting dynamic that admirably incorporates and adjusts the Shakespearean discourse to suit the requirements of their own narrative purposes of expansion (Joyce) and compression (Borges), and at the same time demystifies its canonical status by fusing it with other non-canonical or vernacular voices that are given equal treatment in their texts. Their mutual endeavour to chart a multidirectional map whereby Shakespeare voyages across language, culture, and history suggests that their revisions of the Bard strive to provoke as much as to reinvigorate a long-standing tradition. Their idiosyncratic guides infuse Shakespeare with a contemporary inflection, inasmuch as the forging of new afterlives of Shakespeare involves not the strict parochial limitation to nationalist tendencies, but, rather, unlimited access to the Western archive from a marginal point of view. In this sense, when Eglinton patriotically postulates the creative instruction that: 'Our young Irish bards [...] have yet to create a figure which the world will set beside Saxon Shakespeare's Hamlet [...]' (*U* 9.43–44), Stephen is aware of the impossibility of returning to a Celtic past as he seeks to create a form of art that transcends the nets of nationality, language, and religion.

It is thus especially significant that in his seminal lecture 'The Argentine Writer and Tradition' (1951) Borges declares Ireland a sister nation in view of its peripheral position in relation to mainstream Europe and famously postulates that the Argentine nation should follow the example of Irish writers who had subversively turned Western discourses to their own advantage: 'Creo que los argentinos, los sudamericanos en general, estamos en una situación análoga; podemos manejar todos los temas europeos, manejarlos sin supersticiones, con una irreverencia que puede tener, y ya tiene, consecuencias afortunadas' (*OC1* 273) ['I believe that Argentines, and South Americans in general, are in an analogous situation; we can take on all the European subjects, take them on without superstition and with an irreverence that can have, and already has had, fortunate consequences'] (*SNF* 426). He also offers, as a further argument against parochialism, Shakespeare's wide-ranging use of a vast number of traditions: 'Creo que Shakespeare se habría asombrado si hubieran pretendido limitarlo a temas ingleses, y si le hubiesen dicho que, como inglés, no tenía derecho a escribir *Hamlet*, de tema escandinavo, o *Macbeth*, de tema escocés' (*OC1* 270) ['I think Shakespeare would have been surprised if anyone had tried to limit him to English subjects, and if anyone had told him that, as an Englishman, he had no right to write *Hamlet*, with its Scandinavian subject matter, or *Macbeth*, on a Scottish theme'] (*SNF* 423). We should note, in this respect, that in 1944 Borges offered yet another afterlife of *Julius Caesar* in his intricate story 'Theme of the Traitor and the Hero'. Here Borges transposes Shakespeare's *Julius*

*Caesar* not to a deserted terrain of the Argentine pampas, but to an Irish scenario in the first half of the nineteenth century: 'La acción transcurre en un país oprimido y tenaz: Polonia, Irlanda, la república de Venecia, algún estado sudamericano o balcánico... [...] Digamos (para comodidad narrativa) Irlanda; digamos 1824' (*OC1* 496) ['The action takes place in an oppressed and tenacious country: Poland, Ireland, the Venetian Republic, some South American or Balkan state ... [...] Let us say (for narrative convenience) Ireland; let us say in 1824'] (*L* 102). Because Borges is aware that the notion of place is not a casual, arbitrary construct, but is deeply embedded in a complex set of historical circumstances, he scans various possibilities for a suitable 'oppressed' country that would fit the rebellious backdrop of the narrative and finally chooses ('for narrative convenience') Ireland. In this respect, Sergio Waisman claims that:

> Here South America is figuratively paralleled with a handful of peripheral European countries. The fact that it is in the periphery where this story could have, and has, occurred is poignant: it is here that history and literature are displaced, mistranslated, rewritten with irreverence; where oppression meets tenacity. It is here that mistranslation functions as a site of innovation, seen as the potential for literary and historical renovation.[45]

In his doubly controversial *ficción* about an oppressed Ireland told from the marginal standpoint of an Argentine who was, in addition, a renowned Anglophone, Borges declares that the Irish rebellion against the English was strategically based on an act of plagiarism, in which the discourse of Shakespeare became the structural master plan for the uprising: 'Nolan, urgido por el tiempo, no supo íntegramente inventar las circumstancias de la multiple ejecución; tuvo que plagiar a otro dramaturgo, al enemigo inglés William Shakespeare. Repitió escenas de *Macbeth*, de *Julio César*' (*OC1* 498) ['Nolan had no time to invent the circumstances of the multiple execution from scratch, and so he plagiarized the scene from another playwright, the English enemy Will Shakespeare, reprising scenes from *Macbeth* and *Julius Caesar*'] (*CF* 145). Borges thus practices and commends the art of stealing from Shakespeare, a talent which in 1945 he credited to two Irish writers: 'George Moore y James Joyce han incorporado en sus obras, páginas y sentencias ajenas' (*OC2* 19) ['George Moore and James Joyce incorporated in their works the pages and sentences of others'] (*SNF* 242).

### Afterword: Joyce and Borges, Translators of Shakespeare

The ghosts of Shakespeare summoned by Joyce and Borges highlight the crucial fact that in the sphere of textual negotiations no literary or historical narrative is ever complete, but is subject to continuous revisions and reincarnations. Thus, Joyce's and Borges's afterlives of Shakespeare draw attention to the fact that the act of reading Shakespeare involves taking part in a pluralistic forum that negotiates a multidimensional textual space in which the Bard embodies a variety of meanings: from unconditional homage to parodic counterpoint, from critical reflection to intertextual framework, from biographical debate to an ambivalent, yet recognizable *Shakespeare* character in their narratives. In this sense, I agree with

Richard Brown's assertion that in 'Scylla' Joyce offers 'a kind of Shakespearean translation, in the sense that it draws on a variety of continental European traditions for reading Shakespeare and in the sense that, for all its universality, it selected and performed various aspects of the life and work for a particular audience in a particular and highly charged historical situation.[46] This is the European tradition to which Borges refers in his 1975 lecture at Belgrano University: '*Hamlet* no es exactamente el *Hamlet* que Shakespeare concibió a principios del siglo XVII, *Hamlet* es el *Hamlet* de Coleridge, de Goethe y de Bradley. *Hamlet* ha sido renacido. Lo mismo pasa con el *Quijote* [...] Los lectores han ido enriqueciendo el libro' (*OC4* 171) [*Hamlet* is not exactly the play *Hamlet* that Shakespeare conceived at the beginning of the seventeenth-century; *Hamlet* is also the *Hamlet* of Coleridge, Goethe and Bradley. Hamlet has been reborn. The same has occurred with *Don Quixote* [...] Their readers have enhanced them] (*OC4* 171).

Ultimately, Borges offers a version of Shakespeare filtered not only through a vast scholarly tradition, but also through his own creative concerns, as he negotiates the legacy of Shakespeare within his own historical and personal situation. In 'Shakespeare's Memory', the blind scholar Herman Soergel projects a mirror of Borges himself who, in 1980, was totally blind.[47] This connection is extended by further autobiographical symmetries such as the parallel of Anne Hathaway's sexual initiation of Shakespeare and the narrator's similar experience with a mature woman, an incident allegedly based on Borges's own life.[48] In this manner, Borges proposes a version of Shakespeare in the form of a composite triad, or hall of mirrors: Herman Soergel, the memory of the ghost and, finally, himself. Similarly, when in 'Circe' Joyce famously positions Stephen and Bloom in front of a mirror: 'The face of William Shakespeare, beardless, appears there, rigid in facial paralysis, crowned by the reflection of the reindeer antlered hatrack in the hall' (*U* 15.3821–24). The recognizable, yet unprecedented reflection of a cuckolded Shakespeare that gazes back at Bloom and Stephen emerges as a hybrid, Trinitarian fusion of the new formula Stephen/Bloom/Shakespeare. Joyce conjures up an ambivalent image, which, like the paradoxical statement pronounced by Shakespeare's Troilus (another cuckold) in *Troilus and Cressida*, 'This is and is not Cressida' (v. 2. 146), offers us a complex Circean hallucination that reads *this is and is not Shakespeare*. Joyce destabilizes our canonical conception of Shakespeare by breaking his venerated image into an ambiguous composite that has been enhanced by Stephen's and Bloom's twentieth-century Irish signification. The Shakespeare that emerges is a richer, multifaceted construct that has been enlarged, like Menard's *Quixote*, by centuries of reading and interpretation and by the new context in which its meaning has been redeployed. Shakespeare still incarnates the figure of the 'myriadminded man' proposed by Coleridge and quoted by Best, but among the myriad faces that constitute his multifarious reflection we can now count Bloom's and Stephen's. Like Borges's Shakespeare in 'Everything and Nothing', the ghostly silhouette that gazes back at Joyce is at once 'everything', all in all, but also 'nothing', 'a ghost, the king and no king' (*U* 9.167). Above all, it is a linguistic, historical, and cultural heritage to be endlessly cited, adapted, and reinvented in their creative works.

## Notes to Chapter 6

1. *Antología de la literatura fantástica*, ed. by Jorge Luis Borges, Adolfo Bioy Casares, Silvina Ocampo (Buenos Aires: Emecé, 2003). The anthology has been translated into English, see *The Book of Fantasy*, ed. and intro. by Ursula K. Le Guin (London: Xanadu, 1988).
2. Rodríguez Monegal, p. 350.
3. Jorge Luis Borges/Osvaldo Ferrari, *Reencuentro: diálogos inéditos* (Buenos Aires: Sudamericana, 1999), p. 148, my translation.
4. See *The Encyclopedia of Contemporary Latin American and Caribbean Cultures*, ed. by Daniel Balderston, Mike Gonzalez and Ana M. López, 3 vols (London & New York: Routledge, 2000), p. 208.
5. See Santa Cecilia, *La recepción de James Joyce en la prensa española* (Sevilla: Universidad de Sevilla, 1997), pp. 16–98.
6. See Walter Benjamin, pp. 15–25.
7. Jonathan Bate, *The Genius of Shakespeare* (Basingstoke and Oxford: Picador, 1997) p. 32. He also offers a compelling analysis of the parable, see pp. 32–33.
8. Borges et al., *Antología*, p. 206.
9. Borges et al., *Antología*, pp. 206–07.
10. See Kristal, p. 87.
11. Matthew Creasy, 'Shakespeare Burlesque in *Ulysses*', *Essays in Criticism*, 55 (2005), 141–42.
12. Ezra Pound, 'Guido's Relations', in *The Translation Studies Reader*, ed. by Lawrence Venuti (London and New York: Routledge, 2000), pp. 26–33 (p. 33).
13. Borges thus stands as a forerunner in stressing the importance of *Ulysses* as a ghost story, particularly if we view his position in relation to such key texts of Joycean scholarship as Shari Benstock's '*Ulysses* as a Ghoststory', *James Joyce Quarterly*, 12 (1975), 396–413, which surveys 'Joyce's exploitation of the "ghostly" nature of Shakespeare's play, and the process by which he makes it a vehicle in the ninth chapter' and Maud Ellmann's 'The Ghosts of *Ulysses*', in *James Joyce's Ulysses: A Casebook*, ed. by Derek Attridge (New York: Oxford University Press, 2004), pp. 83–103 (p. 86), which argues that '*Ulysses* is a book about mourning: about the death of love and its return as fury; about the ghosts who vampirize the ego like the famished spectres of the underworld'.
14. Beatriz Sarlo, *Borges: Un escritor de las orillas* (Buenos Aires: Ariel, 1995), p. 59. My translation.
15. The importance of Shakespeare in Joyce's work has been long acknowledged by critics. See, for example, Morse, 'Mr. Joyce and Shakespeare', *Englische Studien*, 65 (1930–31), 367–81; William Schutte, *Joyce and Shakespeare: A Study in the Meaning of Ulysses* (Hamden, CT: Archon Books, 1971); Ellmann, *The Consciousness of Joyce* (London: Faber & Faber, 1977); and Cheng, *Shakespeare and Joyce: A Study of Finnegans Wake* (Gerrards Cross: Colin Smythe, 1984). In contrast, the relationship between Borges and Shakespeare remains largely uncharted, still lacking full-length studies, comparable to Schutte's and Cheng's, to map a rich area of study in its full complexity and in-depth totality. As things stand, only a few critical essays have been partially devoted to the study of the relationship, for example, Ion Agheana, 'Shakespeare', in *The Meaning of Experience in the Prose of Jorge Luis Borges* (New York: Peter Lang, 1988), pp. 115–25; Vázquez 'La memoria de Shakespeare', *Revista Iberoamericana*, 151 (1990), 479–87; and Costa Picazo, *Borges, una forma de felicidad* (Buenos Aires: Fundación Internacional Jorge Luis Borges, 2001). Tiffany's 'Borges and Shakespeare, Shakespeare and Borges', in *Latin American Shakespeares*, ed. by Bernice W. Kliman and Rick J. Santos (Madison & Teaneck, NJ: Fairleigh Dickinson University Press, 2005), pp. 145–66 is an important exception.
16. Schutte, pp. 153–57.
17. Ellmann, *The Consciousness of Joyce*, p. 59, p. 62.
18. Frank Harris, *Bernard Shaw: An Unauthorized Biography Based on First Hand Information with a Postscript by Mr. Shaw* (London: Victor Gollancz, 1931). In particular, read the chapter 'Greater than Shakespeare?', pp. 247–61.
19. See Borges *OC2* 125–27 or *L* 248–52.
20. Harris, p. xiii.

21. Dibattista, Maria, 'Joyce's Ghost: The Bogey of Realism in John McGahern's *Amongst Women*', in *Transcultural Joyce*, ed. by Karen Lawrence (Cambridge: Cambridge University Press, 1998), p. 21.
22. Marjorie Garber, *Shakespeare's Ghost Writers: Literature as Uncanny Causality* (New York and London: Methuen 1987), p. 16.
23. Garber, p. 11.
24. Garber, p. 3.
25. Terence Killeen, *Ulysses Unbound: A Reader's Companion to James Joyce's Ulysses* (Dublin: Wordwell, 2004), pp. 95–96.
26. Borges, *El círculo secreto*, p. 166.
27. Thomas Rice, 'Subtle Reflections of/Upon Joyce in/by Borges', *Journal of Modern Literature*, 24 (2000), 47–62 (2000) p. 61, n. 63.
28. William H. Quillian, *Hamlet and the New Poetic: James Joyce and T. S. Eliot* (Epping: Bowker Publishing Company, 1983), p. 34.
29. Quillian, *Hamlet and the New Poetic*, p. 5.
30. Rice observes that Borges's fiction 'The Circular Ruins' closely resembles Stephen's paternity theory: 'In Borges' account of the dreamer's origins and conception of the consubstantial, dreamt father and son of "The Circular Ruins," readers of *Ulysses* will likely notice subtle reflections of Stephen Dedalus' account of the "greyedauburn" and "beautiful ineffectual dreamer" Shakespeare's journey downstream from his village of Stratford on Avon, to London — an urban jungle perhaps', p. 61, n. 63.
31. Schutte, p. 89.
32. Coleridge, 'Table Talk', in *The Romantics on Shakespeare*, ed. by Jonathan Bate (London: Penguin, 1992), p. 161.
33. Kimble Loux, '"Am I father? If I were?": A Trinitarian Analysis of the Growth of Stephen Dedalus in *Ulysses*', *James Joyce Quarterly*, 22 (1985), 281–96 (p. 281).
34. New King James Version, Exodus 3. 13–14.
35. Agheana, p. 124.
36. See Tiffany, pp. 145–66, for an insightful discussion of Borges's appropriation of Paroles's lines.
37. In 'The Memory of Shakespeare' the narrator Herman Soergel uses Parole's speech in a desperate attempt to regain his own individuality.
38. It is also possible to detect Keats's theory of 'Negative Capability' in Borges's protean conception of Shakespeare. Keats explained, in a letter of 21 December 1817 to George and Tom Keats: '[...] what quality went to form a Man of Achievement especially in Literature & which Shakespeare possessed so enormously — I mean *Negative Capability*, that is when man is capable of being in uncertainties, Mysteries, doubts, without any irritable reaching after fact & reason.' See John Keats, *Selected Letters*, ed. by Robert Gittings (New York: Oxford University Press, 2002), pp. 41–42.
39. Shari Benstock, '*Ulysses* as Ghoststory', *James Joyce Quarterly*, 12 (1975), 396–413 (p. 402).
40. Francisco de Quevedo, *Marco Bruto*, en *Obras en prosa*, edición clasificada y anotada por Luis Astrana Marín (Madrid: Aguilar, 1932), p. 616.
41. The branching possibilities of Stephen's model of history also recall the labyrinthine pattern of 'The Garden of Forking Paths'. Towards the end of the story Stephen Albert argues that 'Time forks perpetually towards innumerable futures. In one of them I am your enemy' (Borges *L* 53).
42. The homicidal knife also appears in 'El puñal' [The Dagger]. See *OC1* 156.
43. Claudette Sartiliot, *Citation and Modernity: Derrida, Joyce, and Brecht* (Norman and London: University of Oklahoma Press, 1993), p. 20.
44. Schutte, p. 124.
45. Waisman, *Borges and Translation*, p. 139.
46. Richard Brown, 'Translation and Self-translation through the Shakespearean Looking-glasses in Joyce's *Ulysses*', in *Translating Life: Studies in Transpositional Aesthetics*, ed. by Shirley Chew and Alistair Stead (Liverpool: Liverpool University Press, 1999), pp. 339–59 (p. 357).
47. Vázquez, 'La memoria de Shakespeare', p. 483.
48. See Rodríguez Monegal, p. 113.

# CONCLUSION

# The Afterlives of James Joyce in Argentina

James Joyce's legacy in the twenty-first century emerges as a global, multilingual, and pluralistic cultural paradigm which is constantly pointing towards new directions. His revolutionary aesthetic, exploration of the human body, painstaking depiction of the city of Dublin, unprecedented linguistic experimentation, rewriting of Western discourses, and his iconic image as a self-imposed exile have exerted a powerful influence in a great variety of cultural spheres worldwide. He incorporated into the wide and versatile canvas of his art his autochthonous Irish legacy, on the one hand, as well as a cosmopolitan consciousness, on the other. By virtue of this his work is upheld as a symbol which may stand for Irish politics, modernist innovation, or the more multinational light shed by the various European countries in which he resided. Yet Joyce's oeuvre has resonated throughout a wider range of contexts which bear no strict correlation to his life. Most importantly, his work has made powerful waves on the other side of the Atlantic: Latin American countries which had broken free from the shackles of colonial domination in the nineteenth century recognized in Joyce's early works and revolutionary novels their linguistic, literary, and cultural preoccupations. For Latin American writers, thus, inheriting the Spanish language from their European colonizer resembled Joyce's conflictual — yet highly creative — relationship with the English language. Borges's invention of Ireland as sister nation in 'The Argentine Writer and Tradition' — as we have seen in the previous chapter — cast a powerful spell over the imagination of Argentine readers, critics, and writers who have expanded upon the relationship between Ireland and Argentina on a range of artistic levels. While acknowledging the far-reaching impact of Joyce in the Hispanic world in general, I have explored his decisive presence in the work of Borges in particular from his pioneering 1925 review of *Ulysses* and fragmentary translation of 'Penelope' to his 1982 visit to Dublin to commemorate the centenary of Joyce's birth in Dublin (Bloomsday). For this reason, a study of the relationship between Borges and Joyce allows the creation of a broader dialogue between the literatures of Ireland and Argentina, between the point of view of two writers who considered themselves European outsiders, but at the same time embraced a whole Western tradition.

The study of Borges's reception of *Ulysses* and *Finnegans Wake* in the 1930s has involved charting the journey of Joyce through Argentina, which guided the reader through the literary itinerary of *Sur*, the mass-marketed, *à la mode* pages of *El Hogar*, and on to the cultural scene of Buenos Aires at the historical time that marked the publication of the first translation of *Ulysses* into Spanish. Yet at the same time, this orientation underlined the important fact that a larger map of the trajectory of Joyce in Argentina needed to be drawn, and that the specificity of this book in relation to Borges and Joyce could not fully address the ample and rich repertoire of the critical and creative responses to Joyce from 1945 onwards. The conclusion to draw here, therefore, is that the study of the literary interface in Borges and Joyce has taken us all this way, but is able to take us much further. A book-length investigation documenting and analysing the complex interactions between Ireland and Argentina, including the cultural effects of the Irish Diaspora, the construction and dissemination of Ireland in the Argentine imagination, and the ongoing dialogue between Irish and Argentine writers, would indeed offer the appropriate sequel to a study of Borges and Joyce.[1] On the whole, the legacy of Borges's reception of Joyce has been crystallized in the development of a particular line of Argentine literature. The reception of Joyce in Argentina in the wake of Borges uncovers the larger project of an influential generation of writers who extended the trajectory of Joyce's works to the linguistic, historical, and literary circumstances of twentieth-century Buenos Aires in an attempt to renew, transform, and develop the literary production of Argentina. One of the most remarkable events is undoubtedly constituted by the first complete translation of *Ulysses* into Spanish, in 1945, by J. Salas Subirat.[2] We then move onto the experimental city novel *Adán Buenosayres* (1948) by Leopoldo Marechal, widely considered to be the first novel in the Spanish language deeply indebted to *Ulysses*. Equally significant is Julio Cortázar's innovative *Rayuela* (1963) [*Hopscotch* (1966)] which emulates Joyce's Ulyssean tradition by his experimental use of the Spanish language; invention of an infinite work; transgression and parody of previous novelistic traditions; disintegration of linear models of reading; creation of a polyglot, multilayered textual labyrinth; use of the variant spoken in the River Plate area; and his artistic condition as émigré from his native Argentina.[3] As one of the most prominent representatives of the boom generation Cortázar offered an experimental work that would change forever the landscape of Spanish American fiction. In this respect, Cortázar's *Hopscotch* did for the Hispanic world in the 1960s what *Ulysses* had done in the 1920s to Europe and the Anglophone world.[4] Another important successor of Joyce is the post-Latin American boom writer Manuel Puig. In his novels *Boquitas Pintadas* (1969) [*Heartbreak Tango* (1973)] and *The Buenos Aires Affair* (1973) [*The Buenos Aires Affair* (1976)] he employs a particular stylistic feature of *Ulysses*, namely the sentimental, rose-tinted world-view and clichéd linguistic register of the 'Nausicaa' episode. Puig continued and developed the peculiarities of Joyce's thirteenth episode, and in doing so stretched its creative possibilities to book-length proportions, blending it with other significant devices, such as the epistolary genre and a potent mixture of politics, psychoanalysis, and romantic Hollywood movies of the 1930s and 1940s. (This aspect, of course, takes us back to the contextual appearance of Borges's notes in the ladies' journal *El Hogar*.) Finally, it is also imperative to examine the pervasive presence of Joyce in a contemporary writer such as Luis Gusmán, especially his complex novel *En el corazón de junio* (1983) [*In the Heart of June*]. This intricate novel tells the story of Señor Flores, a Hispanic namesake of Leopold Bloom, who has recently undergone a heart transplant and begins a journey of physical and metaphorical self-discovery in search for his donor. The motif of the search sets the stage for a series of parallels with Joyce's work. The most important of these is centred on the political events that took place in Buenos Aires, 16 June 1955, in which thousands of people congregated in the Plaza de Mayo in an attempt to overthrow the Argentine Head of State, Juan Domingo Perón. Therefore Gusmán suggests that the longest day in literature, 16 June 1904 (Bloomsday), acquires a wider historical signification in relation to one of the longest days in Argentine history, 16 June 1955 (Bombsday) that witnessed an unsuccessful *coup d'état* against president Perón in which hundreds of innocent people died. Gusmán's novel may also be read through the light shed by Ricardo Piglia's *Respiración artificial* [*Artificial Respiration* (1994)], an experimental novel that aims to give voice, or breathe air into, the thousands of people who disappeared during a military dictatorship that lasted almost a decade (1976–83). In mapping the afterlives of James Joyce in Argentina it is also crucial to consider the translation history of 'Penelope' particularly since two leading Argentine critics and translators, Enrique Pezzoni and Ramón Alcalde, followed in Borges's footsteps and undertook the translation of the two final pages of Molly Bloom's unpunctuated soliloquy.[5] We may conclude, for the time being, that the fascination of Argentine writers with James Joyce found fertile soil in the hospitable climate of Buenos Aires, literally in its 'good air', and nurtured the seeds that would continue to grow throughout a timely episode of the twentieth and twenty-first centuries.

## Notes to the Conclusion

1. For a full exploration of the literary and cultural relationship between Ireland and Latin America see Laura Izarra and Patricia Novillo-Corvalán (eds), *Irish Migration Studies in Latin America*, 7.2 (2009).
2. See Carlos Gamerro, *El nacimiento de la literatura argentina y otros ensayos* (Buenos Aires: Norma, 2006), for a panoramic overview of the reception of Joyce in Argentina.
3. See Novillo-Corvalán, 'Rereading Cortázar's *Hopscotch* through Joyce's *Ulysses*', *Moveable Type*, special issue: 'The Idea of the New: Discovery, Expression, Reception', 4 (2008), 56–84 (56–57).
4. Novillo-Corvalán, 'Rereading Cortázar's *Hopscotch* through Joyce's *Ulysses*, 74.
5. See Enrique Pezzoni and Ramón Alcalde, 'Molly por Joyce, Borges, Pezzoni y Alcalde', *Voces*, 9 (1995), 18–27.

# BIBLIOGRAPHY

ADORNO, THEODOR, *Notes to Literature*, trans. by Shierry Weber Nicholsen, 2 vols (New York: Columbia University Press, 1991)

AGHEANA, ION T., *The Meaning of Experience in the Prose of Jorge Luis Borges* (New York: Peter Lang, 1988)

ALAZRAKI, JAIME, *Borges and the Kabbalah: And Other Essays on his Fiction and Poetry* (Cambridge: Cambridge University Press, 1988)

ALIFANO, ROBERTO, 'La Divina Comedia', in *Ultimas Conversaciones con Borges* (Buenos Aires: Torres Agüero Editor, 1988), pp. 123–30

—— *Twenty-Four Conversations with Borges, including a Selection of Poems: interviews 1981–1983*, trans. by Nicomedes Suárez Araúz, Willis Barnstone and Noemí Escandell (New York: Lascaux Publishers, 1984)

—— *Conversaciones con Borges* (Buenos Aires: Atlántida, 1984)

ALIGHIERI, DANTE, *La Divina Commedia*, col commento scartazziniano rifatto da Giuseppe Vandelli (Milan: Editore-Libraio Della Real Casa, 1944)

—— *La Divina Commedia: Inferno, Purgatorio, Paradiso*, the Italian edited by H. Oelsner, English translations by J. A. Carlyle, Thomas Okey and P. H. Wicksteed (London: Dent: 1933)

—— 'Dante's Letter to Can Grande', in *Essays on Dante*, ed. by Mark Musa, trans. by Nancy Howe (Bloomington: University of Indiana Press, 1965), pp. 32–47

—— *La Vita Nuova*, trans. with an intro. by Barbara Reynolds (London: Penguin, 1969)

—— *Literature in the Vernacular: De Vulgari Eloquentia*, trans. with an intro. by Sally Purcell (Manchester: Carcanet New Press, 1981)

—— *The Divine Comedy*, trans. by Mark Musa, 3 vols (London: Penguin, 1986)

—— *Vita Nova*, a cura di Luca Carlo Rossi, introduzione di Guglielmo Gorni (Milano: Oscar Mondadori, 1999)

AMES, KERI ELIZABETH, 'Joyce's Aesthetic of the Double Negative and his Encounters with Homer's *Odyssey*', in *Beckett, Joyce and the Art of the Negative*, ed. by Colleen Jaurretche (Amsterdam: Rodopi, 2005), pp. 15–48

—— 'The Oxymoron of Fidelity in Homer's *Odyssey* and Joyce's *Ulysses*', *James Joyce Studies Annual*, 14 (2003), 132–74

ARKINS, BRIAN, *Greek and Roman Themes in Joyce* (New York: Edwin Mellen, 1999)

ATTRIDGE, DEREK, *Joyce Effects: On Language, Theory, and History* (Cambridge: Cambridge University Press, 2000)

AYRES, LEWIS, *Nicaea and its Legacy: An Approach to Fourth-Century Trinitarian Theology* (Oxford: Oxford University Press, 2004)

BALDERSTON, DANIEL, ed., *The Literary Universe of Jorge Luis Borges: An Index to References and Allusions to Persons, Titles, and Places in his Writings* (Westport, CT: Greenwood Press, 1986)

—— *Borges: una encyclopedia* (Buenos Aires: Grupo editorial Norma, 1999)

—— *The Encyclopedia of Contemporary Latin American and Caribbean Cultures*, ed. by Daniel Balderston, Mike Gonzalez and Ana M. López, 3 vols (London and New York: Routledge, 2000)

BAKHTIN, M. M., *The Dialogic Imagination: Four Essays by M. M. Bakhtin*, ed. by Michael Holquist, trans. by Caryl Emerson and Michael Holquist (Austin: University of Texas Press, 1981)
BAREI, SILVIA, *Borges y la crítica literaria* (Madrid: Tauro, 1999)
BARRENECHEA, ANA M., *La expresión de la irrealidad en la obra de Jorge Luis Borges y otros ensayos* (Buenos Aires: Ediciones del Cifrado, 2000)
—— *Borges: The Labyrinth Maker*, ed. and trans. by Robert Lima (New York: New York University Press, 1965)
BASSNETT, SUSAN, *Comparative Literature: A Critical Introduction* (Oxford: Blackwell 1993)
—— *Translation Studies*, 3rd edn (London and New York: Routledge, 2003)
—— 'Comparative Literature in the Twenty-First Century', *Comparative Critical Studies*, 3.1–2 (2006), 3–11
BASTOS, MARÍA LUISA, *Borges ante la crítica Argentina* (Buenos Aires: Hispamericana, 1974)
BATE, JONATHAN, *The Genius of Shakespeare* (Basingstoke and Oxford: Picador, 1997)
BATTISTESSA, ANGEL J., *Ricardo Güiraldes: en la huella espiritual y expresiva de un argentino (1886–1986)* (Buenos Aires: Corregidor, 1987)
BEACH, SYLVIA, *Shakespeare & Company* (London: Faber & Faber, 1959)
BECKETT, SAMUEL, 'Dante...Bruno.Vico..Joyce', in *Our Exagmination Round His Factification for Incamination of Work in Progress* (London: Faber & Faber, 1929), pp. 5–22
—— 'Foreword', in *James Joyce: An International Perspective*, ed. by Suheil Bushrui and Bernard Benstock (Gerrards Cross: Colin Smythe, 1982), p. vii
BELL-VILLADA, GENE H., *Borges and His Fiction: A Guide to his Mind and Art* (Chapel Hill: University of North Carolina Press, 1981)
BENJAMIN, WALTER, 'The Task of the Translator', in *The Translation Studies Reader*, ed. by Lawrence Venutti, trans. by Harry Zohn (London: Routledge, 2001), pp. 15–23
BENSTOCK, BERNARD, ed., *Poems for James Joyce* (Kildare: The Malton Press, 1982)
BENSTOCK, SHARI, 'Ulysses as Ghoststory', *James Joyce Quarterly*, 12 (1975), 396–413
BERNHEIMER, CHARLES, ed., *Comparative Literature in the Age of Multiculturalism* (Baltimore, MD: Johns Hopkins University Press, 1995)
BIOY CASARES, ADOLFO, *Borges*, edición al cuidado de Daniel Martino (Barcelona: Destino, 2006)
BLAMIRES, HARRY, *The New Bloomsday Book*, 3rd edn (London: Routledge, 1996)
BLASI, ALBERTO OSCAR, *Güiraldes y Larbaud: una amistad creadora* (Buenos Aires: Nova, 1969)
—— 'Una amistad creadora: las cartas de Valery Larbaud a Ricardo Güiraldes', in *Ricardo Güiraldes: Don Segundo Sombra, edición crítica*, Paul Verdevoye (coordinador) (Madrid: Archivos, 1988)
BOITANI, PIERO, 'Shipwreck: Interpretation and Alterity', in *Dante*, ed. by Jeremy Tambling (London and New York: Longman, 1999), pp. 68–85
—— 'Ulysses in Another World', in *Classic Joyce: Joyce Studies in Italy 6*, ed. by Franca Ruggieri (Rome: Bulzoni Editore, 1999), pp. 33–51
BOLDRINI, LUCIA, ed., 'Introduction', in *Medieval Joyce* (Amsterdam: Rodopi, 2002)
—— *Joyce, Dante, and the Poetics of Literary Relations: Language and Meaning in Finnegans Wake* (Cambridge: Cambridge University Press, 2001)
—— 'Comparative Literature in the Twenty-First Century', *Comparative Critical Studies*, 3.1–2 (2006), 13–23
BOLLETTIERI BOSINELLI, ROSA MARIA, 'Anna Livia's Italian Sister', in LAWRENCE, ed., *Transcultural Joyce*, pp. 193–98
BONATI, MARIA, 'Dante en la Lectura de Borges', *Revista Iberoamericana*, 100–01 (1977), 737–44
BOOKER, M. KEITH, 'From the Sublime to the Ridiculous: Dante's Beatrice and Joyce's Bella Cohen', *James Joyce Quarterly*, 29 (1992), 357–68

——*Joyce, Bakhtin, and the Literary Tradition: Toward a Comparative Cultural Poetics* (Ann Arbor: University of Michigan Press, 1997)
BORDELOIS, IVONNE, *Un triángulo crucial: Borges, Güiraldes y Lugones* (Buenos Aires: Eudeba, 1999)
——*Genio y figura de Ricardo Güiraldes* (Buenos Aires: Eudeba, 1998)
BORGES, JORGE LUIS, *The Spanish Language in South America: A Literary Problem* (London: Grant & Cutler, 1964)
——*Páginas de Jorge Luis Borges seleccionadas por el autor*, estudio preliminar de Alicia Jurado (Buenos Aires: Editorial Celia, 1982)
——*Textos cautivos: ensayos y reseñas en 'El Hogar' (1936–1939)*, edición de Sacerio-Garí y Emir Rodríguez Monegal (Buenos Aires: Tusquets Editores, 1986)
——*The Book of Fantasy*, ed. by Ursula Le Guin (London: Xanadu, 1988)
——*Obras completas*, 3 vols (Buenos Aires: Emecé, 1990); 4 vols (Barcelona: Emecé, 1996)
——*Obras completas en colaboración* (Buenos Aires: Emecé, 1991)
——*El tamaño de mi esperanza* (Buenos Aires: Seix Barral, 1993)
——*Inquisiciones* (Buenos Aires: Seix Barral, 1994)
——*Borges en revista multicolor: obras, reseñas y traducciones inéditas*, investigación y recopilación de Irma Zangara (Buenos Aires: Editorial Atlántida, 1995)
——*El idioma de los argentinos* (Buenos Aires: Seix Barral, 1996)
——*Textos recobrados*, 3 vols (vol. 1, Barcelona: Emecé, 1997); (vol. 2, Bogotá: Emecé 1997); (vol. 3, Buenos Aires: Emecé, 2003)
——*En Diálogo I*, with Osvaldo Ferrari (Buenos Aires: Sudamericana, 1985)
——*En Diálogo II*, with Osvaldo Ferrari (Buenos Aires: Sudamericana, 1998)
——*Reencuentro: diálogos inéditos*, with Osvaldo Ferrari (Buenos Aires: Sudamericana, 1999)
——*Jorge Luis Borges en Sur: 1931–1980* (Buenos Aires: Emecé, 1999)
——*Collected Fictions*, trans. by Andrew Hurley (New York: Penguin, 1999)
——*Selected Poems*, ed. by Alexander Coleman, trans. by Willis Barnstone, Coleman and others (London: Penguin Press, 1999)
——*Selected Non-Fictions*, ed. by Eliot Weinberger, trans. by Esther Allen, Suzanne Jill Levine, and Eliot Weinberger (New York: Viking, 1999)
——*Labyrinths: Selected Stories and Other Writings*, ed. by Donald A. Yates and James E. Irby, preface by André Maurois (London: Penguin, 2000)
——*This Craft of Verse*, ed. by Colin-Andrei Mihailescu (Cambridge, MA: Harvard University Press, 2000)
——*Borges en El Hogar: 1935–1958* (Buenos Aires: Emecé, 2000)
——*Borges profesor*, edición, investigación y notas de Martín Arias y Martín Hadis (Buenos Aires: Emecé, 2001)
——*The Book of Imaginary Beings*, with Margarita Guerrero, rev. edn, enlarged and trans. by Norman Thomas di Giovanni in collaboration with the author (London: Vintage, 2002)
——*Antología de la literatura fantástica*, ed. by Jorge Luis Borges, Adolfo Bioy Casares and Silvina Ocampo (Buenos Aires: Sudamericana, 2003)
——*El círculo secreto* (Buenos Aires: Emecé, 2003)
BOYLE, FR. ROBERT, SJ, 'Penelope', in *James Joyce's Ulysses: Critical Essays*, ed. by Clive Hart and David Hayman, 2nd edn (London: University of California Press, 1984), pp. 407–33
BROOK, THOMAS, *James Joyce's Ulysses: A Book of Many Happy Returns* (London: Louisiana State University Press, 1982)
BROOKER, JOSEPH, *Joyce's Critics: Transitions in Reading and Culture* (Madison: University of Wisconsin Press, 2004)

BROWN, JOHN L., *Valery Larbaud* (Boston, MA: Twayne Publishers, 1981)
BROWN, RICHARD, 'Translation and Self-translation through the Shakespearean Looking-glasses in Joyce's *Ulysses*', in *Translating Life: Studies in Transpositional Aesthetics*, ed. by Shirley Chew and Alistair Stead (Liverpool: Liverpool University Press, 1999), pp. 339–59
—— *James Joyce and Sexuality* (Cambridge: Cambridge University Press, 1985)
—— 'Introduction', in *Joyce, 'Penelope' and the Body*, ed. by Richard Brown (Amsterdam: Rodopi, 2006), pp. 11–30
BRUNS, GERALD L., *James Joyce's Ulysses: Critical Essays*, ed. by Clive Hart and David Hayman (London: University of California Press, 1984), pp. 363–85
BUDGEN, FRANK, *James Joyce and the Making of Ulysses* (London: Grayson & Grayson, 1934)
BULSON, ERIC, 'Joyce's Geodesy', *Journal of Modern Literature*, 25.2 (2001–02), 80–96
BURGIN, RICHARD, ed., *Jorge Luis Borges: Conversations* (Jackson: University Press of Mississippi, 1998)
BUTLER, SAMUEL, *The Authoress of the Odyssey: where and when she wrote, who she was, the use she made of the Iliad, & how the poem grew under her hands*, 2nd edn (London: Jonathan Cape, 1922)
CALINESCU, MATEI, *Rereading* (New Haven, CT, and London: Yale University Press, 1993)
CANTO, ESTELA, *Borges a contraluz* (Madrid: Austral, 1989)
CARRIZO, ANTONIO, *Borges, el memorioso* (México: Fondo de Cultura Económica, 1982)
CARROLL, ROBERT, 'Borges and Bruno: The Geometry of Infinity in *La Muerte y la Brújula*', *Modern Language Notes*, 94 (1979), 321–42
CARRUTHERS, MARY J., *The Book of Memory: A Study of Memory in Medieval Culture* (Cambridge: Cambridge University Press, 1992)
CASELLI, DANIELA, *Beckett's Dantes: Intertextuality in the Fiction and Criticism* (Manchester and New York: Manchester University Press, 2005)
CASEY, EDWARD S. *Remembering: A Phenomenological Study* (Bloomington and Indianapolis: Indiana University Press, 1987)
CHENG, VINCENT, *Shakespeare and Joyce: A Study of Finnegans Wake* (Gerrards Cross: Colin Smythe, 1984)
CHESELKA, PAUL, *The Poetry and Poetics of Jorge Luis Borges* (New York: Peter Lang, 1987)
CHIAPPINI, JULIO, *Borges y Dante* (Rosario: Editorial Zeus, 1993)
CHITARRONI, LUIS, 'Borges y Joyce', in *Joyce o la travesía del lenguaje: psicoanálisis y literatura*, Nada Lasic, Elena Szumiraj (compiladoras) (Buenos Aires: Fondo De Cultura Económica, 1993), pp. 17–25
CHRIST, RONALD J., *The Narrow Act: Borges' Art of Allusion* (New York: New York University Press, 1969)
CICERO, *On the Ideal Orator (De Oratore)*, trans. by M. May and Jacob Wisse (New York and Oxford: Oxford University Press, 2001)
CLARK, HILARY, *The Fictional Encyclopaedia: Joyce, Pound, Sollers* (London: Garland Publishing, 1990)
COLERIDGE, SAMUEL TAYLOR, *Biographia Literaria*, ed. by George Sampson (London: Cambridge University Press, 1920)
—— 'Table Talk', in *The Romantics on Shakespeare*, ed. by Jonathan Bate (London: Penguin, 1992)
CONDE PARILLA, MARÍA ANGELES, *Los pasajes obscenos de Molly Bloom en español* (Albacete: Ediciones de la Diputación de Albacete, 1994)
—— 'The Obscene Nature of Molly's Soliloquy and Two Spanish Translations', *James Joyce Quarterly*, 33 (1995–96), 211–36
CONLEY, TIM, *Joyce's Mistakes: Problems of Intention, Irony and Interpretation* (Toronto: University of Toronto Press, 2003)

CONNOR, STEVEN, *James Joyce* (Plymouth: Northcote House, 1996)
CONTE, RAFAEL, '*Ulises* a la Carta', *ABC*, 5 September 1992, p. 3
COPLAND, R. A., and G. W. TURNER, 'The Nature of James Joyce's Parody in "Ithaca"', *The Modern Language Review*, 64 (1969), 759–63
CORDELL, D. K., *The Word According to James Joyce: Reconstructing Representation* (Lewisburg, PA: Bucknell University Press, 1997)
CORDINGLEY, ANTHONY, 'Keeping their Distance: Beckett and Borges Writing after Joyce', in *After Beckett D'après Beckett*, ed. by Anthony Uhlmann, Sjef Houppermans, Bruno Clément (Amsterdam: Rodopi, 2004), pp. 131–45
COSTA PICAZO, ROLANDO, *Borges, Una forma de felicidad* (Buenos Aires: Fundación Internacional Jorge Luis Borges, 2001)
CREASY, MATTHEW, 'Shakespeare Burlesque in *Ulysses*', *Essays in Criticism*, 55 (2005), 136–58
CULLETON, CLAIRE A., *Names and Naming in Joyce* (Madison: University of Wisconsin Press, 1994)
CURTIUS, ROBERT ERNST, *European Literature and the Latin Middle Ages*, trans. by Willar R. Trask (London: Routledge & Kegan Paul, 1979)
DASENBROCK, REED WAY, *Imitating the Italians: Wyatt, Spenser, Synge, Pound, Joyce* (Baltimore, MD, and London: Johns Hopkins University Press, 1991)
——— AND RAY MINES, '"Quella vista nova": Dante, Mathematics and the Ending of *Ulysses*', in *Medieval Joyce*, ed. by Lucia Boldrini (Amsterdam: Rodopi, 2002), pp. 79–93
DAVIDSON, SYLVIE, 'Borges and Italian Literature', *Italian Quarterly*, 105 (1986), 43–49
DAY, ROBERT ADAMS, 'Dante, Ibsen, Joyce, Epiphanies, and The Art Of Memory', *James Joyce Quarterly*, 25.3 (1988), 357–62
DE TORRE, GUILLERMO, *Historia de las literaturas de vanguardia II* (Madrid: Guadarrama, 1971)
DERMOT, KELLY, *Narrative Strategies in Joyce's Ulysses* (London: UMI Research Press, 1988)
DERRIDA, JACQUES, 'Two Words for Joyce', in *Post-Structuralist Joyce: Essays from the French*, ed. by Derek Attridge and Daniel Ferrer (Cambridge: Cambridge University Press, 1984), pp. 145–59
———'*Ulysses* Gramophone', in *A Companion to James Joyce's Ulysses*, ed. by Margot Norris (Boston, MA, and New York: Bedford Books, 1998), pp. 69–90
DI GIOVANNI, NORMAN THOMAS, *The Lesson of the Master: On Borges and his Work* (New York and London: Continuum, 2003)
DÍAZ-PLAJA, GUILLERMO, DIRECCIÓN, PRÓLOGO Y NOTAS, *Antología mayor de la literatura española I — Edad media (siglos X–XV)* (Barcelona: Labor, 1958)
DIBATTISTA, MARIA, 'Joyce's Ghost: The Bogey of Realism in John McGahern's *Amongst Women*', in LAWRENCE, ed., *Transcultural Joyce*, pp. 21–37
DUFF, CHARLES, *James Joyce and the Plain Reader*, with a prefatory letter by Herbert Read, 2nd edn (London: Desmond Harmsworth, 1932)
EAGLETON, TERRY, *Literary Theory: An Introduction*, 2nd edn (Oxford: Blackwell, 1996)
ECO, UMBERTO, *The Aesthetics of Chaosmos, the Middle Ages of James Joyce*, trans. by Ellen Esrock (Cambridge, MA: Harvard University Press, 1989)
———'Between La Mancha and Babel', *Variaciones Borges*, 4 (1997), 51–62
——— WITH LIBERATO SANTORO-BRIENZA, *Talking of Joyce* (Dublin: University College Dublin Press, 1998)
——— WITH RICHARD RORTY, JONATHAN CULLER and CHRISTINE BROOKE-ROSE, *Interpretation and Overinterpretation*, ed. by Stefan Collini (Cambridge: Cambridge University Press, 1998)
———'Funes or Memory', in *Conversations About the End of Time*, ed. by Catherine David, Frédéric Lenoir and Jean-Philippe de Tonnac, trans. by Ian Maclean and Roger Pearson (New York: Fromm International, 1999), pp. 189–97

ELIOT, T. S., *Dante* (London: Faber & Faber, 1930)
—— *Selected Essays* (London: Faber & Faber, 1980)
—— *Selected Prose*, ed. by Frank Kermode (London: Faber & Faber, 1975)
ELLMANN, MAUD, 'The Ghosts of *Ulysses*', in *James Joyce's Ulysses: A Casebook*, ed. by Derek Attridge (New York: Oxford University Press, 2004), pp. 83–103
ELLMANN, RICHARD, *James Joyce* (New York: Oxford University Press, 1959)
—— *The Consciousness of Joyce* (London: Faber & Faber, 1977)
—— *James Joyce*, new and rev. edn (New York: Oxford University Press, 1983)
—— *Four Dubliners* (London: Hamish Hamilton, 1987)
FARRELL KRELL, DAVID, *Of Memory: Reminiscence and Writing on the Verge* (Bloomington and Indianapolis: Indiana University Press, 1990)
FERNÁNDEZ MORENO, CÉSAR, RESEÑA DE C. G. JUNG, ¿*Quién es Ulises?*, in *Sur*, 120 (1944), 79–82
FEUER, LOIS, 'Joyce the Postmodern: Shakespeare as Character in *Ulysses*', in *The Author as Character: Representing Historical Writers in Western Literature*, ed. by Paul Franssen and Ton Hoenselaars (London: Associated University Presses, 1999)
FIDDIAN, ROBIN W., 'James Joyce and Spanish-American Fiction: A Study of the Origins and Transmission of Literary Influence', *Bulletin of Hispanic Studies*, 66,1 (1989), 23–39
FISHBURN, EVELYN, ed., *Borges and Europe Revisited* (London: Institute of Latin American Studies)
FOUCAULT, MICHEL, 'What is an Author', in *Modern Criticism and Theory: A Reader*, ed. by David Lodge (London: Longman, 1995), pp. 197–210
—— *The Order of Things: An Archaeology of the Human Sciences* (London: Routledge, 2002)
FOWLER, ROBERT, ed., *The Cambridge Companion to Homer*, 2nd edn (Cambridge: Cambridge University Press, 2006)
FRASER, JENNIFER MARGARET, *Rite of Passage in the Narratives of Dante and Joyce* (Gainesville: University Press of Florida, 2002)
FRENCH, MARILYN, *The Book as World: James Joyce's Ulysses* (London: Abacus, 1982)
GAMERRO, CARLOS, *El nacimiento de la literatura argentina y otros ensayos* (Buenos Aires: Norma, 2006)
GARBER, MARJORIE, *Shakespeare's Ghost Writers: Literature as Uncanny Causality* (New York and London: Methuen, 1987)
GARCÍA, CARLOS, *El joven Borges, poeta (1919–1930)* (Buenos Aires: Corregidor, 2000)
—— *Macedonio Fernández/Jorge Luis Borges: Correspondencia 1922–1939*, edición y notas de Carlos García (Buenos Aires: Corregidor, 2000)
—— 'Comentario a Ivonne Bordelois: *Un Triángulo Crucial: Borges, Güiraldes y Lugones*', *Variaciones Borges*, 9 (2000), 255–58
GARDNER, EDMUND G., 'Imagination and Memory in the Psychology of Dante', in *A Miscellany of Studies in Romance Languages & Literatures*, ed. by Mary Williams and James A. de Rothschild (Cambridge: W. Heffer & Sons, 1932), pp. 275–82
GARDNER, MARTIN, *Logic Machines and Diagrams*, 2nd edn (Brighton: Harvester Press, 1983)
GARMENDIA DE CAMUSSO, GUILLERMINA, 'Jorge Luis Borges y el tiempo', in *Fuego del aire: homenaje a Borges* (Buenos Aires: Fundación Internacional Jorge Luis Borges, 2001), pp. 53–64
GENETTE, GÉRARD, *Palimpsests: Literature in the Second Degree*, trans. by Channa Newman and Claude Doubinsky (Lincoln and London: University of Nebraska Press, 1997)
GERTEL, ZUNILDA, 'Paradojas de la identidad y la memoria de "El acercamiento a Almotásim" a "La Memoria de Shakespeare"', in *El siglo de Borges*, ed. by Alfonso de Toro and Susanna Regazzoni, 2 vols (Madrid: Iberoamericana, 1999), II, 85–99
GIBSON, ANDREW, *Joyce's Revenge: History, Politics and Aesthetics in Ulysses* (Oxford: Oxford University Press, 2002)

——ed., *Joyce's 'Ithaca'*, European Joyce Studies, 6 (Amsterdam: Rodopi, 1996)
——'Introduction', in *Joyce's 'Ithaca'* (as previous), pp. 3–27
Gifford, Don, with Robert J. Seidman, *Ulysses Annotated: Notes for James Joyce's Ulysses* (Berkeley and Los Angeles: University of California Press, 1988)
Gilbert, Stuart, *James Joyce's Ulysses: A Study*, 2nd edn (New York: Vintage, 1952)
——'Thesaurus Minusculus: A Short Commentary on a Paragraph of *Work-in-Progress*', *transition*, 16–17 (1928), 15–24
——'L'ambiance Latine de L'art de James Joyce', *Fontaine*, 37–40 (1944), 79–88
——'El ambiente latino en el arte de James Joyce', *Sur*, 122 (1944), 11–24
Gorman, Herbert, *James Joyce: His First Forty Years* (London: Geoffrey Bles, 1924)
——*James Joyce: El hombre que escribió Ulises*, traducido por Máximo Siminovich (Buenos Aires: Santiago Rueda, 1945)
Griffiths, Eric, and Matthew Reynolds, eds., *Dante in English* (London: Penguin, 2005)
Groden, Michael, *Ulysses in Progress* (Princeton, NJ: Princeton University Press, 1977)
Gross, John, ed., *After Shakespeare: Writing Inspired by the World's Greatest Author* (New York: Oxford University Press, 2002)
Guillet, Louis, 'Recuerdos de James Joyce', *Sur*, 87 (1941), 28–42
Güiraldes, Ricardo, *Obras completas*, prólogo de Francisco Luis Bernárdez (Buenos Aires: Emecé, 1962)
——*Los cuadernos perdidos (1922–1925)* (Buenos Aires: Página 12, 1999)
——*Don Segundo Sombra: Shadows on the Pampas*, trans. by Harriet de Onís with an intro. by Waldo Frank (London: Constable & Co., 1935)
——*Don Segundo Sombra, edición crítica*, Paul Verdevoye (coordinador) (Madrid: Archivos, 1988)
Gunn, Ian, and Clive Hart, with Harald Beck, *James Joyce's Dublin: A Topographical Guide to the Dublin of Ulysses* (London: Thames & Hudson, 2004)
Hampson, Robert, 'Allowing for Possible Error: Education and Catechism in "Ithaca"', in Gibson, ed., *Joyce's 'Ithaca'*, pp. 229–67
——'The Genie out of the Bottle: Conrad, Wells and Joyce', in *The Reception of The Thousand and One Nights in British Culture*, ed. by Peter L. Caracciolo (London: Macmillan, 1988), pp. 218–43
Harris, Frank, *Bernard Shaw: An Unauthorized Biography, based on first hand information with a postscript by Mr. Shaw* (London: Victor Gollancz, 1931)
Hawkins, Peter S., and Rachel Jacoff, eds., 'Still Here: Dante after Modernism', in *Dante for the New Millennium*, ed. by Teodolinda Barolini and H. Wayne Storey (New York: Fordham University Press, 2003), pp. 450–64
Hayles, Katherine N., *The Cosmic Web: Scientific Field Models and Literary Strategies in the Twentieth Century* (Ithaca, NY, and London: Cornell University Press, 1984)
Heaney, Seamus, *Opened Ground: Poems 1966–1996* (London: Faber & Faber, 1998)
Heath, Stephen, 'Joyce in Language', in *James Joyce: New Perspectives*, ed. by Colin MacCabe (Brighton: Harvester Press, 1982), pp. 129–48
——'Ambiviolences: Notes for Reading Joyce', in *Post-structuralist Joyce: Essays from the French*, ed. by Derek Attridge and Daniel Ferrer (Cambridge: Cambridge University Press, 1984), pp. 31–68
Helft, Nicolás, and Alan Pauls, *El factor Borges: nueve ensayos ilustrados* (Buenos Aires: Fondo de Cultura Económica, 2000)
——*Bibliografía completa* (Buenos Aires: Fondo de Cultura Económica, 1997)
Herring, Phillip, 'Preface', in *The Centennial Symposium*, ed. by Morris Beja, Phillip Herring, Maurice Harmon and David Norris (Urbana and Chicago: University of Illinois Press, 1986)
——ed., *Joyce's Ulysses Notesheets in the British Museum* (Charlottesville: University Press of Virginia, 1972)

——ed., *Joyce's Notes and Early Drafts for Ulysses: Selections from the Buffalo Collection* (Charlottesville: University Press of Virginia, 1977)
*Holy Bible: The New King James Version* (Nashville: Nelson, 1982)
HOMER, *The Odyssey*, trans. by Robert Fitzgerald (London: Harvill Press, 1996)
HOROWITZ, GLENN, *James Joyce: Books and Manuscripts* (New York: Glenn Horowitz Bookseller, 1996)
IRWIN, JOHN T., *The Mystery to a Solution: Poe, Borges and the Analytic Detective Story* (Baltimore, MD, and London: Johns Hopkins University Press, 1994)
JALOUX, EDMOND, 'Valery Larbaud', in *The Most Significant Writings from the Nouvelle Revue Française (1919–1940)*, ed. by Justin O' Brien (London: Eyre & Spottiswoode, 1958)
JOYCE, JAMES, *Ulysse*, traduit de l'anglais par M. Auguste Morel assisté par M. Stuart Gilbert. Traduction entièrement revue par M. Valery Larbaud avec la collaboration de l'auteur. Hollande Van Gelder N 1. Exemplaire imprimé pour Madame Adeline del Carril de Güiraldes (Paris: La Maison des Amis des Livres, 1929)
——*Desterrados*, trad. A. Jiménez Fraud (Buenos Aires: Sur 1937)
——*Gente de Dublín*, trad. Ignacio Abelló (Barcelona: Tartessos, 1942)
——*Ulises*, trad. J. Salas Subirat (Buenos Aires: Santiago Rueda, 1945)
——*Ulises*, trad. J. Salas Subirat, 2da ed. revisada (Buenos Aires: Santiago Rueda, 1952)
——*Esteban el héroe*, trad. Roberto Bixio (Buenos Aires: Sur, 1960)
——*La noche de Ulises*, adaptación dramática por Marjorie Barkentin, introd. de Padraic Colum, versión española de Celia Paschero y Juan Carlos Pellegrini (Buenos Aires: *Sur*, 1961)
——*Letters of James Joyce*, 3 vols, vol. 1 ed. by Stuart Gilbert (New York: Viking Press, 1957; reissued with corrections 1966); vols 2 and 3 ed. by Richard Ellmann (New York: Viking Press, 1966)
——*Dublineses*, trad. Guillermo Cabrera Infante (Madrid: Alianza editorial, 1974)
——*Ulises*, trad. José María Valverde (Barcelona: Lumen, 1980)
——*Ulises*, trad. J. J. Salas Subirat (Barcelona: Círculo de Lectores, 1992)
——*Selected Letters*, ed. by Richard Ellmann, 2nd edn (London: Faber & Faber, 1992)
——*Ulises*, trad. Francisco García Tortosa y María Luisa Venegas (Madrid: Cátedra, 1999)
——*A Portrait of the Artist as a Young Man*, ed. by Jeri Johnson (London and New York: Oxford University Press, 2000)
——*Finnegans Wake*, with an intro. by Seamus Deane (London: Penguin, 2000)
——*Dubliners*, with an intro. and notes by Terence Brown, 2nd edn (London: Penguin, 2000)
——*Occasional, Critical, and Political Writing*, ed. with an intro. and notes by Kevin Barry, trans. from the Italian by Conor Deane (Oxford: Oxford University Press, 2000)
——*Ulysses*, ed. by Hans Walter Gabler, with Wolfhard Steppe and Claus Melchior, afterword by Michael Groden, 4th edn (London: Bodley Head, 2002)
——*Ulises*, trad. J. Salas Subirat (Buenos Aires: Santiago Rueda, 2002)
——*Exiles*, intro. by Conor McPherson (London: Nick Hern Books, 2006)
JULLIEN, DOMINIQUE, 'Biography of an Immortal', *Comparative Literature*, 47 (1995), 136–59
JUNG, C. G., *¿Quién es Ulises?*, trad. Ortega y Gasset (Buenos Aires: Santiago Rueda, 1944)
KASNER, EDWARD, and JAMES NEWMAN, *Mathematics and the Imagination*, with drawings and diagrams by Rufus Isaacs (London: G. Bell and Sons, 1949)
KEARNEY, RICHARD, *Transitions: Narratives in Modern Irish Culture* (Manchester: Manchester University Press, 1988)
KEATS, JOHN, *Selected Letters*, ed. by Robert Gittings (New York: Oxford University Press, 2002)

KELLOGG, ROBERT, 'Scylla and Charybdis', in *James Joyce's Ulysses: Critical Essays*, ed. by Clive Hart and David Hayman (Berkeley and Los Angeles: University of California Press, 1984), pp. 147–81
KENNER, HUGH, *Ulysses*, rev. edn (Baltimore, MD, and London: Johns Hopkins University Press, 1993)
—— *Dublin's Joyce* (London: Chatto & Windus, 1955)
—— 'Mutations of Homer', in *Classic Joyce: Joyce Studies in Italy 6*, ed. by Franca Ruggieri (Rome: Bulzoni Editore, 1999), pp. 25–32
KERSHNER, R. B., *Joyce, Bakhtin, and Popular Literature: Chronicles of Disorder* (Chapel Hill and London: University of North Carolina Press, 1984)
KILLEEN, TERENCE, *Ulysses Unbound: A Reader's Companion to James Joyce's Ulysses* (Dublin: Wordwell, 2004)
KING, JOHN, *Sur: A Study of the Argentine Literary Journal and its Role in the Development of a Culture, 1931–1970* (Cambridge: Cambridge University Press, 1986)
KIRKPATRICK, ROBIN, *Chaucer and the Italian Trecento* (Cambridge: Cambridge University Press, 1983)
KREIMER, ROXANA, 'Nietzsche, autor de "Funes el Memorioso"', in *Jorge Luis Borges: intervenciones sobre pensamiento y literatura*, ed. by William Rowe, Claudio Canaparo and Annick Louis (Buenos Aires: Paidós, 2000), pp. 189–99
KRISTAL, EFRAÍN, *Invisible Work: Borges and Translation* (Nashville, TN: Vanderbilt University Press, 2002)
KUMAR, UDAYA, *The Joycean Labyrinth: Repetition, Time and Tradition in Ulysses* (Oxford: Clarendon Press, 1991)
LAMB, CHARLES, *Adventures of Ulysses*, intro. by Andrew Lang (London: Edward Arnold, 1890)
LANSING, RICHARD, *The Dante Encyclopedia* (New York and London: Garland Publishing, 2000)
LAPIDOT, EMA, *Borges and Artificial Intelligence: An Analysis in the Style of Pierre Menard* (New York: Peter Lang, 1991)
LARBAUD, VALERY, 'Valery Larbaud on Joyce (1922)', in *James Joyce: The Critical Heritage*, ed. by Robert H. Deming, 2nd edn, 2 vols (London: Routledge, 1997), I, 252–62
—— '"Ulysses" of James Joyce', *The Criterion*, 1.2 (1923), 94–103
—— '*Ulysse*: Fragments', *Commerce*, 1 (1924), 121–58
—— *Ce Vice Impuni, la Lecture: Domaine Anglais* (Paris: Albert Messein, 1925)
—— 'Lettres Argentines et Uruguayennes', *La Revue Européenne*, 34 (1925), 66–70
—— *Valery Larbaud: Lettre a deux amis*, traduc. de Adelina del Carril (Buenos Aires: Francisco A. Colombo, 1962)
—— *Œuvres*, avec preface de Marcel Arland et notes par G. Jean-Aubry et Robert Mallet (Paris: Gallimard, 1984)
—— *Lettres à Adrienne Monnier et à Sylvia Beach (1919–1933)*, Correspondance établie et annotée par Maurice Saillet (Paris: IMEC, 1991)
LAWRENCE, KAREN, ed., *Transcultural Joyce* (Cambridge: Cambridge University Press, 1998)
—— 'Introduction: Metempsychotic Joyce', in *Transcultural Joyce* (as previous), pp. 1–8
—— *The Odyssey of Style in Ulysses* (Princeton, NJ: Princeton University Press, 1981)
LÁZARO, ALBERTO, 'A Survey of the Spanish Critical Response to Joyce', in *The Reception of James Joyce in Europe*, ed. by Geert Lernout and Wim Van Mierlo, 2 vols (London: Thoemmes Continuum, 2004), II: *Italy, France and Mediterranean Europe*, pp. 422–33
—— 'James Joyce's Encounters with Spanish Censorship, 1939–1966', *James Joyce Studies Annual* (2001), 38–54
LEE, HERMIONE, *Virginia Woolf* (London: Chatto & Windus, 1996)
LE GUIN, URSULA K. (ed.), *The Book of Fantasy* (London: Xanadu, 1988)
LEONARD, GARY, *Advertising and Commodity Culture in Joyce* (Gainesville: University Press of Florida, 1998)

LERNOUT, GEERT, *The French Joyce* (Ann Arbor: University of Michigan Press, 1990)
LEVIN, HARRY, *James Joyce: A Critical Introduction*, rev. augmented edn (Norfolk, CT: New Directions, 1960)
LEVINE, SUZANNE JILL, 'Notes to Borges's Notes on Joyce: Infinite Affinities', *Comparative Literature*, 49.4 (1997), 344–58
—— *The Subversive Scribe: Translating Latin American Fiction* (Saint Paul, MN: Graywolf Press, 1991)
LEZAMA LIMA, JOSÉ, 'Muerte de Joyce', *Grafos*, 9 (1941), 16
—— *Obras completas*, 2 vols (México: Aguilar, 1977)
LITTMANN, MARK E., and CHARLES A. SCHWEIGHAUSER, 'Astronomical Allusions, their Meaning and Purpose, in *Ulysses*', *James Joyce Quarterly*, 2.1 (1964), 238–46
LITZ, A. WALTON, *The Art of James Joyce: Method and Design in Ulysses and Finnegans Wake* (New York: Oxford University Press, 1964)
—— 'Ithaca', in *James Joyce's Ulysses: Critical Essays*, ed. by Clive Hart and David Hayman (London: University of California Press, 1984), pp. 385–405
LOCKE, JOHN, *An Essay Concerning Human Understanding*, ed. by Roger Woolhouse (London: Penguin, 1997)
LOJO RODRÍGUEZ, LAURA MARA, '"A gaping mouth, but no words": Virginia Woolf Enters the Land of the Butterflies', in *The Reception of Virginia Woolf in Europe*, ed. by Mary Ann Caws and Nicola Luckhurst (London: Continuum: 2002), pp. 218–47
LOUX, ANN KIMBLE, '"Am I father? If I were?": A Trinitarian Analysis of the Growth of Stephen Dedalus in *Ulysses*', *James Joyce Quarterly*, 22 (1985), 281–96
LOYOLA, SAINT IGNATIUS, *The Spiritual Exercises of Saint Ignatius of Loyola*, trans. by Michael Ivens SJ and intro. by Gerard W. Hughes SJ (Leominster: Gracewing Printing, 2004)
MACCABE, COLIN, *James Joyce and the Revolution of the Word*, 2nd edn (Basingstoke: Macmillan, 2003)
MACCOMBE, JOHN P., 'Besteglyster and Bradleyism: Stephen Dedalus's Postcolonial Response to English Criticism', *James Joyce Quarterly*, 39 (1992), 717–33
MADTES, RICHARD E., 'Joyce and the Building of Ithaca', *ELH*, 31 (1964), 443–59
MAHAFFEY, VICKI, 'Joyce's Shorter Works', in *The Cambridge Companion to James Joyce*, ed. by Derek Attridge, 4th edn (Cambridge: Cambridge University Press, 2003), pp. 185–211
MAILHOS, JACQUES, '"Begin to forget it": The Preprovided Memory of *Finnegans Wake*', in *Finnegans Wake: 'Teems of Times'*, ed. by Andrew Treip, European Joyce Studies, 4 (Amsterdam: Rodopi, 1994), pp. 40–67
—— 'The Art of Memory: Joyce and Perec', in LAWRENCE, ed., *Transcultural Joyce*, pp. 151–73
MANGUEL, ALBERTO, *With Borges* (London: Telegram, 2006)
MARICHALAR, ANTONIO. 'James Joyce en su Laberinto', *Revista de Occidente*, 17 (1924), 177–202
MARINO, NANCY F., *La serranilla española: notas para su historia e interpretación* (Potomac, MD: Scripta Humanistica, 1987)
MARTIN, GERALD, *Journeys Through the Labyrinth: Latin American Fiction in the Twentieth Century* (London: Verso, 1989)
MARTIN, TIMOTHY P., 'Joyce, Wagner, and the Wandering Jew', *Comparative Literature*, 42 (1990), 49–72
MASIELLO, FRANCINE, 'Joyce in Buenos Aires (Talking Sexuality through Translation)', *Diacritics*, 34.3 (2004), 55–72
MAURER, KARL, '"Faut-il avoir vu l'enfer pour le decrier?": La Vision de l'enfer selon Dante, Ignace de Loyola et Akutagawa', in *The Force of Vision*, 6 vols (Tokyo: 13th Congress of the International Comparative Literature Association, 1995), I: *Dramas of Desire*, ed. by Ziva Ben-Porat and Hana Wirth-Nesher, pp. 115–23
MAZZARO, JEROME, 'The *Divina Commedia* and the Rhetoric of Memory', *Rivista di Studi Italiani*, 17.1 (1999), 112–28

McCormick, Kathleen, 'Reproducing Molly Bloom: A Revisionist History of the Reception of "Penelope", 1922–1970', in Pearce, ed., *Molly Blooms*, pp. 17–40
McHugh, Roland, *Annotations to Finnegans Wake*, rev. edn (London: Johns Hopkins University Press, 1991)
—— *The Sigla of Finnegans Wake* (London: Arnold, 1976)
McIntyre, J. Lewis, *Giordano Bruno* (London and New York: Macmillan, 1903)
Menocal, María Rosa, *Writing in Dante's Cult of Truth: From Borges to Boccaccio* (Durham, NC: Duke University Press, 1991)
Mercaton, Jacques, 'James Joyce', trans. by José Mora Guarnido, *Contrapunto*, 5 (1945), 2–3
Merrell, Floyd, *Unthinking Thinking: Jorge Luis Borges, Mathematics, and the New Physics* (West Lafayette, IN: Purdue University Press, 1991)
Meyer, Doris, *Against the Wind and the Tide: Victoria Ocampo*, with a selection of essays by Victoria Ocampo, trans. by Doris Meyer (Austin: University of Texas Press, 1990)
Milbank, Alison, *Dante and the Victorians* (Manchester: Manchester University Press, 2001)
Missana, Sergio, *La máquina de pensar de Borges* (Santiago: Lom ediciones, 2003)
Molloy, Sylvia, *Signs of Borges*, trans. by Oscar Montero (Durham, NC, and London: Duke University Press, 1994)
—— 'Lost in Translation: Borges, the Western Tradition and Fictions of Latin America', in Fishburn, ed., *Borges and Europe Revisited*, pp. 8–20
Monmany, Mercedes, 'El *Ulises* ilustrado recuerda la muerte de James Joyce', *Cambio16*, 1008 (18 March 1991), 90–94
Morris, Pam, ed., *The Bakhtin Reader: Selected Writings of Bakhtin, Medvedev, Voloshinov* (London: Arnold, 1994)
Morse, B. J., 'Mr Joyce and Shakespeare', *Englische Studien*, 65 (1930–31), 367–81
Mullin, Katherine, 'Don't Cry for Me, Argentina: "Eveline" and the Seductions of Emigration Propaganda', in *Semicolonial Joyce*, ed. by Derek Attridge and Marjorie Howes (Cambridge: Cambridge University Press, 2000), pp. 172–200
Mulrooney, Jonathan, 'Stephen Dedalus and the Politics of Confession', *Studies in the Novel*, 33.2 (2001) 160–79
Murillo, L. A., *The Cyclical Night: Irony in James Joyce and Jorge Luis Borges* (Cambridge, MA: Harvard University Press, 1968)
Murphy, John L., 'Beckett's Purgatories', in *Beckett, Joyce and the Art of the Negative*, ed. by Colleen Jaurretche (Amsterdam and New York: Rodopi, 2005), pp. 109–24
Murray, Edmundo, *Devenir irlandés: narrativas íntimas de la emigración irlandesa a la Argentina (1844–1912)*, con un prólogo de Hilda Sábato (Buenos Aires: Eudeba, 2004)
Nietzsche, Friedrich, *Untimely Meditations*, ed. by Daniel Breaseale, trans. by R. J. Hollingdale (Cambridge: Cambridge University Press, 1997)
Nolan, Emer, *James Joyce and Nationalism* (London: Routledge, 1995)
Novillo-Corvalán, Patricia, Review of María Angeles Conde Parrilla, *Los pasajes obscenos de Molly Bloom en español*, *James Joyce Broadsheet*, 69 (2004), 2
—— 'Literary Migrations: Homer's Journey through Joyce's Ireland and Walcott's St. Lucia', *Irish Migration Studies in Latin America*, 5.3 (2007), 157–62
—— Review of Line Henriksen, *Ambition and Anxiety: Ezra Pound's Cantos and Derek Walcott's Omeros as Twentieth-Century Epics*, in *The European English Messenger*, 17.1 (2008), 86–87
—— 'Rereading Cortázar's *Hopscotch* through Joyce's *Ulysses*', *Moveable Type*, 4 (2008), 56–84
—— and Laura Izarra, eds., *Irish Migration Studies in Latin America*, 7.2 (2009)
Nuñez-Faraco, Humberto, *Borges and Dante: Echoes of a Literary Friendship* (Berlin: Peter Lang, 2006)

Nuño, Juan, *La filosofía de Borges* (México: Fondo de Cultura Económica, 1986)
O'Brien, Edna, 'Joyce's Odyssey: The Labours of "Ulysses"', *The New Yorker*, 7 June 1999, pp. 82–90
O'Neill, Patrick, *Polyglot Joyce: Fictions of Translation* (Toronto: University of Toronto Press, 2005)
Ortega, Julio, and Elena del Río Parra, eds., *'El Aleph' de Jorge Luis Borges*, edición crítica y facsimilar (México DF: El Colegio de México, 1995)
Ortiz, Eduardo, 'The Transmission of Science from Europe to Argentina and its Impact on Literature: From Lugones to Borges', in Fishburn, ed., *Borges and Europe Revisited*, pp. 108–23
Osteen, Mark, *The Economy of Ulysses: Making Both Ends Meet* (New York: Syracuse University Press, 1995)
Parrinder, Patrick, *James Joyce* (Cambridge: Cambridge University Press, 1984)
Pearce, Richard, ed., *Molly Blooms: A Polylogue on 'Penelope' and Cultural Studies* (Madison: University of Wisconsin Press, 1994)
——'Introduction: Molly Blooms: A Polylogue on "Penelope"', in *Molly Blooms* (as previous), pp. 3–17
Pearce, Spencer, 'Dante and the Art of Memory', *The Italianist*, 16 (1996), 20–61
Petit de Murat, Ulises, '¿Quién sos vos para no discutirme?' *La Maga*, año 1, 22 (10 June 1992), p. 17
Petitjean, Armand, 'El tratamiento del lenguaje en Joyce', *Sur*, 78 (1941), 42–59
Pezzoni, Enrique, and Ramón Alcalde, 'Molly por Joyce, Borges, Pezzoni y Alcalde', *Voces*, 9 (1995), 18–27
Piette, Adam, *Remembering and the Sound of Words: Mallarmé, Proust, Joyce, Beckett* (Oxford: Clarendon Press, 1996)
Pierce, David, *James Joyce's Ireland* (New Haven, CT, and London: Yale University Press, 1992)
Pimentel Pinto, Julio, 'Borges, una poética de la memoria', in *Jorge Luis Borges: intervenciones sobre pensamiento y literatura*, ed. by William Rowe, Claudio Canaparo and Annick Louis (Buenos Aires: Paidós, 2000), pp. 155–65
Plato, *The Republic*, trans. by Desmond Lee, 2nd rev. edn (London: Penguin, 1987)
Platt, L. H., 'The Voice of Esau: Culture and Nationalism in "Scylla and Charybdis"', *James Joyce Quarterly*, 29 (1991–92), 737–50
Pliny the Elder, *Natural History*, trans. with intro. and notes by John F. Healy (London: Penguin, 1991)
Pound, Ezra, 'Guido's Relations', in *The Translation Studies Reader*, ed. by Lawrence Venuti (London and New York: Routledge, 2000), pp. 26–33
Power, Arthur, *Conversations with James Joyce*, foreword by David Norris (London: Lilliput Press, 1999)
Quevedo, Francisco de, *Marco Bruto*, en *Obras en prosa*, edición clasificada y anotada por Luis Astrana Marín (Madrid: Aguilar, 1932)
Quillian, William H., 'Shakespeare in Trieste: Joyce's 1912 Hamlet Lectures', *James Joyce Quarterly*, 12 (1974–75), 7–15
——*Hamlet and the New Poetic: James Joyce and T. S. Eliot* (Epping: Bowker Publishing Company, 1983)
Rabaté, Jean-Michel, 'Joyce the Parisian', in *The Cambridge Companion to James Joyce*, ed. by Derek Attridge (Cambridge: Cambridge University Press, 1990), pp. 83–103
——*Joyce Upon the Void: The Genesis of Doubt* (London: Macmillan, 1991)
——'Modernism and "The Plain Reader's Rights": Duff-Riding-Graves Re-reading Joyce', in *European Joyce Studies: Joyce's Audiences*, ed. by John Nash (Amsterdam: Rodopi, 2000), pp. 29–39
Rainey, Lawrence, *Institutions of Modernism: Literary Elites and Public Culture* (New Haven, CT, and London: Yale University Press, 1998)

READ, FORREST, ed., *Pound/Joyce: The Letters of Ezra Pound to James Joyce, with Pound's Essays on Joyce* (New York: New Directions, 1967)
REICHERT, KLAUS, 'Joyce's Memory', in *Images of Joyce*, ed. by Clive Hart, George Sandulescu, Bonnie K. Scott, Fritz Senn, 2 vols (Gerrards Cross: Colin Smythe, 1998), II, 754–58
REVOL, A., *Teoría del monólogo interior* (Córdoba: Univ. Nacional de Córdoba, 1965)
—— *La tradición imaginaria: de Joyce a Borges* (Córdoba: Univ. Nacional de Córdoba, 1971)
REYNOLDS, MARY T., *Joyce and Dante: The Shaping Imagination* (Princeton, NJ: Princeton University Press, 1981)
—— 'Joyce's Editions of Dante', *James Joyce Quarterly*, 15 (1978), 380–82
RICE, THOMAS J., 'Subtle Reflections of/upon Joyce in/by Borges', *Journal of Modern Literature*, 24 (2000), 47–62
RICKARD, JOHN S., *Joyce's Book of Memory: The Mnemotechnic of Ulysses* (Durham, NC, and London: Duke University Press, 1998)
RICOEUR, PAUL, *Memory, History, Forgetting*, trans. by Kathleen Blamey and David Dellauer (London: University of Chicago Press, 2004)
RIQUELME, JOHN PAUL, *Teller and Tale in Joyce's Fiction: Oscillating Perspectives* (Baltimore, MD, and London: Johns Hopkins University Press, 1983)
—— 'The Use of Translation and the Use of Criticism', in Fritz Senn, *Joyce's Dislocutions: Essays on Reading as Translation*, ed. by John Paul Riquelme (Baltimore, MD, and London: Johns Hopkins University Press, 1984)
RODRÍGUEZ MONEGAL, EMIR, *Jorge Luis Borges: A Literary Biography* (New York: Dutton, 1978)
ROWE, WILLIAM, 'How European is it?', in FISHBURN, ed., *Borges and Europe Revisited*, pp. 21–36
RUCKER, RUDY, *Infinity and the Mind: The Science and Philosophy of the Infinite* (Brighton: Harvester Press, 1982)
RUNNING, THORPE, 'Borges' Ultraist Poetry', in *Jorge Luis Borges*, ed. with an intro. by Harold Bloom (New York: Chelsea House Publishers, 1986), pp. 199–225
SALAS, HORACIO, *Borges: una biografía* (Buenos Aires: Planeta, 1994)
—— 'Martín Fierro y Proa', en *La cultura de un siglo: América Latina en sus revistas*, Saúl Sosnowski editor (Buenos Aires: Alianza Editorial, 1999)
SALAS SUBIRAT J., '*Ulises*', *Contrapunto*, 4 (1945), 12
SALGADO, CÉSAR AUGUSTO, 'Barroco Joyce: Jorge Luis Borges's and José Lezama Lima's Antagonistic Readings', in LAWRENCE, ed., *Transcultural Joyce*, pp. 63–97
—— *From Modernism to Neobaroque: Joyce and Lezama Lima* (Lewisburg, PA: Bucknell University Press, 2001)
SANTA CECILIA, CARLOS G., *La recepción de James Joyce en la prensa española (1921–1976)* (Sevilla: Universidad de Sevilla, 1997)
SARLO, BEATRIZ, *Borges: un escritor en las orillas* (Buenos Aires: Ariel, 1995)
—— *Jorge Luis Borges: A Writer on the Edge*, ed. by John King (London and New York: Verso, 1993)
—— *Una modernidad periférica* (Buenos Aires: Nueva Visión, 1988)
SARTILIOT, CLAUDETTE, *Citation and Modernity: Derrida, Joyce and Brecht* (Norman and London: University of Oklahoma Press, 1993)
SAUSSY, HAUN, ed., *Comparative Literature in an Age of Globalization* (Baltimore, MD: Johns Hopkins University Press, 2006)
SCHUTTE, WILLIAM M., *Joyce and Shakespeare: A Study in the Meaning of Ulysses* (Hamden, CT: Archon Books, 1971)
SCHWARTZ, JORGE, 'Borges y la primera hoja de *Ulysses*', *Revista Norteamericana*, 100–01 (1977), 721–26

SCHWARZ, DANIEL R., *Reading Joyce's Ulysses* (London: Macmillan, 1987)
SCOTT, BONNIE KIME, *Joyce and Feminism* (Bloomington: Indiana University Press, 1984)
SCOTT, JOHN A., *Understanding Dante* (Notre Dame, IN: University of Notre Dame Press, 2005)
SEIDEL, MICHAEL, *Epic Geography: James Joyce's Ulysses* (Princeton, NJ: Princeton University Press, 1976)
SENN, FRITZ, *Joyce's Dislocutions: Essays on Reading as Translation*, ed. by John Paul Riquelme (Baltimore, MD, and London: Johns Hopkins University Press, 1984)
—— 'The European Diffusion of Joyce', *James Joyce Broadsheet*, 76 (2007), 1
—— '"Ithaca": Portrait of the Chapter as a Long List', in GIBSON, ed., *Joyce's 'Ithaca'*, pp. 31–76
SHAKESPEARE, WILLIAM, *The Norton Shakespeare: Based on the Oxford Edition*, Stephen Greenblatt, general ed. (New York and London: Norton, 1997)
SHAPIRO, HENRY L., 'Memory and Meaning: Borges and *Funes el memorioso*', *Revista Canadiense de Estudios Hispánicos*, 9 (1985), 257–65
SILVESTRI, LAURA, 'Borges y Dante o la superstición de la literatura', in *El siglo de Borges*, ed. by Alfonso de Toro and Fernando de Toro, 2 vols (Vervuert: Iberoamericana, 1999), I: *retrospectiva-presente-futuro*, pp. 385–408
SITMAN, ROSALIE, *Victoria Ocampo y Sur: entre Europa y América* (Buenos Aires: Lumiere, 2003)
SORABJI, RICHARD, *Aristotle on Memory* (London: Duckworth, 1972)
SPIVAK, GAYATRI, *Death of a Discipline* (New York: Columbia University Press, 2003)
STALEY, HARRY C., 'Joyce's Catechisms', *James Joyce Quarterly*, 6.1 (1968), 137–53
STANFORD, W. B., *The Ulysses Theme: A Study in the Adaptability of a Traditional Hero* (Oxford: Basil Blackwell, 1954)
STEINER, GEORGE, *The Death of Tragedy* (London: Faber & Faber, 1961)
—— ed., *Homer in English*, with the assistance of A. Dykman (London: Penguin, 1996)
—— *After Babel: Aspects of Language and Translation* (Oxford: Oxford University Press, 1998)
—— *What Is Comparative Literature?* (Oxford: Clarendon Press, 1995)
STEVENS, ADRIAN, 'Hermann Broch as a Reader of James Joyce: Plot in the Modernist Novel', in *Londoner Symposion: Hermann Broch: Modernismus, Kulturkrise und Hitlerzeit* (London: Londoner Symposion, 1991)
STURROCK, JOHN, *Paper Tigers: The Ideal Fictions of Jorge Luis Borges* (Oxford: Clarendon Press, 1977)
SULLIVAN, KEVIN, *Joyce Among the Jesuits* (New York: Columbia University Press, 1957)
THIEM, JOHN, 'Borges, Dante, and the Poetics of Total Vision', *Comparative Literature*, 40 (1988), 97–121
THIHER, ALLEN, *Fiction Refracts Science: Modernist Writers from Proust to Borges* (Columbia and London: University of Missouri Press, 2005)
TIFFANY, GRACE, 'Borges and Shakespeare, Shakespeare and Borges', in *Latin American Shakespeares*, ed. by Bernice W. Kliman and Rick J. Santos (Madison and Teaneck, NJ: Fairleigh Dickinson University Press, 2005), pp. 145–66
TYSDAHL, BJORN, 'On First Looking into Homer: Lamb's *Ulysses* — and Joyce's', in *Classic Joyce: Joyce Studies in Italy 6*, ed. by Franca Ruggieri (Rome: Bulzoni Editore, 1999), pp. 279–89
UNDERWOOD, SIMEON, *English Translators of Homer: From George Chapman to Christopher Logue* (London: Northcote House, 1998)
UPDIKE, JOHN, 'The Author as Librarian', *The New Yorker*, 30 October 1965, pp. 223–46
VACCARO, ALEJANDRO, *Georgie: una vida de Jorge Luis Borges (1989 — 1930)* (Buenos Aires: Editorial Proa, 1996)
—— *Borges: vida y literatura* (Barcelona: Edhasa, 2006)

VAN BOHEEMEN-SAAF, CHRISTINE, 'Joyce's Answer to Philosophy: Writing the Dematerializing Object', in *Joyce, 'Penelope' and the Body*, ed. by Richard Brown (Amsterdam: Rodopi, 2006), pp. 31–46
VANDERHAM, PAUL, *James Joyce and Censorship: The Trials of Ulysses* (London: Macmillan, 1998)
VÁZQUEZ, MARÍA ESTHER, *Borges, sus días y su tiempo* (Buenos Aires: Vergara, 1999)
—— '"La memoria de Shakespeare": el último juego de Borges', *Revista Iberoamericana*, 151 (1990), 479–87
—— *Borges, esplendor y derrota* (Barcelona: Tusquets editores, 1996)
VEGH, BEATRIZ, 'A Meeting in the Western Canon: Borges's Conversation with Joyce', in *English Joyce Studies: Joyce's Audiences*, ed. by John Nash (Amsterdam: Rodopi, 2000), pp. 85–98
VIEIRA, ELSE RIBEIRO PIRES, 'Liberating Calibans: Readings of Antropofagia and Haroldo de Campos' Poetics of Transcreation', in *Post-colonial Translation: Theory and Practice*, ed. by Susan Bassnett and Harish Trivedi (London and New York: Routledge, 1999), pp. 95–113
VIRGIL, *The Aeneid*, trans. by Robert Fitzgerald (London: Harvill Press, 1996)
WAISMAN, SERGIO, *Borges and Translation: The Irreverence of the Periphery* (Lewisburg, PA: Bucknell University Press, 2005)
—— 'Borges Reads Joyce: The Role of Translation in the Creation of Texts', *Variaciones Borges*, 9 (2000) 59–73
WALCOTT, DEREK, *Omeros* (London: Faber & Faber, 1990)
WALLACE, DAVID, 'Dante in English', in *The Cambridge Companion to Dante*, ed. by Rachel Jacoff (Cambridge: Cambridge University Press, 1993), pp. 237–58
WEBB, TIMOTHY, 'Homer and the Romantics', in FOWLER, ed., *The Cambridge Companion to Homer*, pp. 287–310
WENINGER, ROBERT, 'James Joyce in German-speaking Countries: The Early Reception, 1919–1945', in *The Reception of James Joyce in Europe*, ed. by Geert Lernout and Wim Van Mierlo, 2 vols (London and New York: Thoemmes Continuum, 2004), I: *Germany, Northern and East Central Europe*, pp. 14–50
—— 'Comparative Literature at a Crossroads? An Introduction', *Comparative Critical Studies*, 3.1–2 (2006), xi–xix
WHITMAN, WALT, *Leaves of Grass, Hojas de Hierba*, trad. Jorge Luis Borges (Barcelona: Lumen, 1991)
WILLIAMSON, EDWIN, *Borges: A Life* (New York: Viking, 2004)
WILLSON, PATRICIA, *La Constelación del Sur: traductores y traducciones en la literatura argentina del siglo XX* (Buenos Aires: Siglo veintiuno, 2004)
WILSON, JASON, 'The Mutating City: Buenos Aires and the Avant-garde, Borges, Xul Solar, and Marechal', *Hispanic Research Journal*, 4.3 (2003), 251–69
—— *Jorge Luis Borges* (London: Reaktion Books, 2006)
—— 'Jorge Luis Borges and the European Avant-Garde', in FISHBURN, ed., *Borges and Europe Revisited*, pp. 68–80
WOOD, MICHAEL, *Children of Silence: Studies in Contemporary Fiction* (London: Pimlico, 1998)
WOODALL, JAMES, *The Man in the Mirror of the Book: A Life of Jorge Luis Borges* (London: Sceptre, 1996)
YATES, FRANCES, *The Art of Memory* (London: Routledge and Kegan Paul, 1966)
YEATS, WILLIAM BUTLER, ed., *The Oxford Book of Modern Verse: 1892–1935* (Oxford: Clarendon Press, 1936)
ZAJKO, VANDA, 'Homer and *Ulysses*', in FOWLER, ed., *The Cambridge Companion to Homer*, pp. 311–24

# INDEX

Acevedo de Borges, Leonor (Borges's mother)  65 n. 13
Adorno, Theodor  93, 107, 114 n. 1
Agheana, Ion T.  163, 170 n. 15, 171 n. 35
Alifano, Roberto,  51, 67 n. 52, 78, 90 n. 16, 91 n. 28, 148 n. 14
Alighieri, Dante:
   and Borges  3, 9, 20, 21, 53, 94, 99–107, 113, 115 n. 29, 117–50
   and Joyce  3, 9, 50, 53, 79, 97, 98, 106, 108, 109, 111, 113, 116 n. 48, 116 n. 55, 117–50
   *Commedia*:
      *Inferno*  93, 99, 100, 115 n. 24, 115 n. 26, 115 n. 28, 121–23, 125–26, 129–30, 134, 138
      *Purgatorio*  119, 134, 136
      *Paradiso*  119, 121, 131–34, 138
   *De Vulgari Eloquentia*  123
   'Letter to Can Grande della Scala',  120, 130, 149 n. 49
   *Vita Nuova*  124, 135, 137, 149 n. 61
Alonso, Dámaso  15, 46
Anderson, Margaret  17
Appiah, Anthony  1
Aquinas, Thomas  50, 53
Aristotle  53, 84, 23 n. 90, 92 n. 54, 95, 165
Attridge, Derek  66 n. 37, 91 n.37, 116 n. 56, 170 n. 13
Auerbach, Erich  2

Balderston, Daniel  101, 115 n. 30, 151, 170 n. 4
Bakhtin, M. M.  146, 149 n. 51, 150 n. 92
Barei, Silvia  51– 52, 66 n. 51
Barnacle, Nora (Mrs James Joyce)  53
Bassnett, Susan  1–2, 10 n. 1, 10 n. 7, 10 n. 14, 144, 150 n. 86
Bate, Jonathan  152, 170 n. 7, 171 n. 32
Beach, Sylvia  12, 15, 16, 25, 36 n. 5, 37 n. 15, 42, 45
Beckett, Samuel  38 n. 41, 114 n. 6, 119–20, 127, 147 nn. 5, & 7, 149 n. 42
Bell-Villada, Gene H.  71, 77, 90 n. 7, 112, 138, 150 n. 73
Benjamin, Walter  12, 36 n. 6, 95, 156, 170 n. 6
Benstock, Shari  164, 171 n. 39
Bérard, Victor  95, 96, 97
Bianco, José  61
Bioy Casares, Adolfo  61, 97, 114 n. 10, 138, 152, 170 n. 1
Blake, William  16, 84, 117, 147 n. 2
Boitani, Piero  100, 115 n. 24
Boldrini, Lucia  2, 10 n. 12, 130, 147 n. 10, 149 n. 56
Bollettieri Bosinelli, Rosa Maria  30, 39 n. 58

Booker, M. Keith  130, 136, 149 n. 51, 149 n. 65
Borges, Jorge Luis:
   'A Defense of *Bouvard and Pécuchet*'  57
   'A Fragment on Joyce'  44, 45, 70–77
   *A History of Eternity*  81
   *Anthology of Fantastic Literature*  4, 5, 151–55, 161, 164, 170 n. 1
   'A Survey of the Works of Herbert Quain'  63
   'Avatars of the Tortoise'  127
   'Averroës' Search'  95
   'Autobiographical Essay'  17, 54
   'Biography of Tadeo Isidoro Cruz'  111
   'Death and the Compass'  121, 127–28
   *Fervour of Buenos Aires*  22–23
   'Funes the Memorious'  4, 68–89
   'Everything and Nothing'  152, 156–64, 169
   'From Somebody to Nobody'  162
   '*Inferno V*, 129'  121, 125
   'Kafka and His Precursors'  68–71
   'Joyce's *Ulysses*'  6, 17, 21–24, 31, 40, 46, 101–02
   'Invocation to Joyce'  18, 37 n. 27
   'James Joyce' (capsule biography)  52–55
   'James Joyce' (poem)  106–07
   'John Wilkins's Analytical Language'  80
   'Joyce and the Neologisms'  44, 58–60
   'Joyce's Latest Novel'  52, 55–58
   *Nine Dantesque Essays*  99–102, 121, 128–29, 148 n. 24
   'Partial Magic in the Quixote'  96–97
   'Pierre Menard, Author of the Quixote'  5, 25, 72, 74, 143–44
   'Review of Salas Subirat's *Ulises*'  28–30
   'Shakespeare's Memory'  152, 157–64, 169, 171 n. 37
   'The Aleph'  87–89, 121, 127, 130–39, 145–46, 147 n. 4, 150 n. 75
   'The Argentine Writer and Tradition'  9, 167, 172
   *The Book of Imaginary Beings*  112, 116 n. 58, 121
   'The Book of Sand'  127
   'The Circular Ruins'  63, 171 n. 30
   'The Disk'  127, 141–42
   'The Encounter'  166
   'The Immortal'  104–07, 115 n. 40
   'The Infinite Language'  28–29
   'The Garden of Forking Paths'  63, 74, 127–28, 171 n. 41
   'The Homeric Versions'  94–96
   'The Intruder'  121, 125–26
   'The Library of Babel'  126–27

'The Language of the Argentines' 31–32
'The Last Page of *Ulysses*' 7, 13, 15, 17, 25–36, 45
'The Literary Life: Oliver Gogarty' 63–65
'The Pattern' 164–66
'The Translators of the Thousand and One Nights' 68, 116 n. 46
'The Zahir' 127, 130–43, 145, 150 n. 78
'Theme of the Traitor and the Hero' 167–68
'Tlön, Uqbar, Orbis Tertius' 60–61
'Two Forms of Insomnia' 76–77
*Universal History of Infamy* 94, 109–14, 116 n. 60
'When Fiction Lives in Fiction' 50–51, 62
Borges, Norah 17
Botana, Natalio 25
Bradley, A. C. 160, 169
Brooker, Joseph 44, 54, 62, 65 n. 18, 97, 98
Brown, Richard 26, 38 n. 44, 169, 171 n. 46
Bruno, Giordano 50, 90 n. 23, 119, 120, 146, 147 n. 5
Budgen, Frank 24, 26, 38 n. 38, 66 n. 33, 75, 76, 86
Bulson, Eric 73, 90 n. 9, 103
Burgin, Richard 67 n. 64, 75, 124, 143
Butler, Samuel 13, 95, 97, 114 n. 9

Cabrera Infante, Guillermo 66 n. 31
Calinescu, Matei 130, 138, 147 n. 13
Calvin, John 123, 148 n. 29
Campos, Haroldo de 3, 10 n. 14
Canto, Estela 134, 149 n. 59
Cantor, Georg 131
Caraffa, Brandán 16
Carlyle, John 123, 124, 148 n. 27
Carlyle, Thomas 117, 123
Carroll, Lewis 58, 59
Casey, Edward S. 82, 84, 91 n. 40
Cervantes, Miguel de 25, 143
Chapman, George 95, 96, 97, 98, 114 n. 2
Chaucer, Geoffrey 98, 117, 118, 1260, 147 n. 3, 148 n. 39
Chesterton, G. K. 57, 151
Christ, Ronald J. 70, 90 n. 5, 105, 115 n. 41
Coleridge, Samuel Taylor 13, 109, 117, 155, 160, 161, 162, 169, 171 n. 32
Conde Parilla, María Angeles 32, 39 n. 74
Cordingley, Anthony 38 n. 41
Cortázar, Julio 173, 174 n. 3
Creasy, Matthew 154, 170 n. 11
Culler, Jonathan 1, 114 n. 5
Curtius, Robert Ernst 46

Dante, *see* Alighieri, Dante
Dasenbrock, Reed Way 132–33, 143, 144, 149 n. 56, 150 n. 82
Darío, Rubén 150 n. 75
Day, Robert Adams 111, 116 n. 55
De Torre, Guillermo 15, 17, 26
Derrida, Jacques 2, 91 n. 37, 108, 116 n. 49, 171 n. 43
Di Giovanni, Norman Thomas 37 n. 27, 39 n. 59

Dibattista, Maria 156, 171 n. 21
Donne, John 60
Duff, Charles 40, 43–46, 53, 65 n. 19, 66 n. 25, 90 n. 10
Dujardin, Édouard 155

Ebbinghaus, Hermann 82
Eco, Umberto 79, 91 n. 30, 96, 114 n. 5, 122, 148 n. 15
Eliot, T. S. 14, 46, 68–70, 89 n. 1, 98–99, 101, 115 n. 19, 117, 123, 144
Ellmann, Maud 170 n. 13
Ellmann, Richard 13, 63, 73, 97, 121, 155, 170 n. 15

Fernández, Macedonio 37 n. 22, 151
Fernández Moreno, César 44, 47, 66 n. 36
Ferrari, Osvaldo 65 n. 13, 85, 92 n. 59, 129, 149 n. 47, 151, 170 n. 3
Fiddian, Robin W. 17, 37 n. 24, 61
Fischart, Johann 59
Flaubert, Gustave 57, 76
Fraser, Jennifer Margaret 120, 147 n. 11
Frazer, James George 151
French, Marilyn 79, 91 n. 29
Freud, Sigmund 82

Gamerro, Carlos 174 n. 2
Garber, Marjorie 156, 158, 171 n. 22
García Márquez, Gabriel 43, 65 n. 16
García Tortosa, Francisco 33, 38 n. 42, 39 n. 74
Genette, Gérard 5, 10 n. 19, 98, 114 n. 16
Gibson, Andrew 34, 36, 39 n. 75, 87, 92 n. 62
Gifford, Don 35, 39 n. 61, 48, 108, 145, 146
Gilbert, Stuart 21, 37 n. 19, 40, 44–45, 46, 47, 48, 54, 55, 59, 65 n. 23, 66 nn. 25 & 38 & 71, 97, 114 n. 7, 115 n. 31, 152
Goethe, Johann Wolfgang von 53, 155, 169
Gogarty, Oliver St. John 41, 62–65, 121, 125
Góngora, Luis de 8, 24, 38 n. 39, 60
Gorman, Herbert 46, 47, 66 n. 32, 67 n. 57
Groussac, Paul 59, 169
Güiraldes, Adelina de 12, 16
Güiraldes, Ricardo 12–17, 27, 36 n. 3, 36 n. 5, 36 n. 13, 37 nn. 18 & 20 & 26, 38 n. 50, 42, 43
Gusmán, Luis 173–74

Hampson, Robert 105, 116 n. 45
Harris, Frank 155, 156, 164, 170 n. 18
Hathaway, Anne 126, 154, 158, 159, 169
Hazlitt, William 162
Heaney, Seamus 8, 12, 20, 21, 29, 37 n. 29, 57, 60, 147 nn. 3 & 7
Heap, Jane 17
Helft, Nicolás 6, 10 n. 22
Herring, Phillip 36 n. 1
Hinton, C. H. 70

Homer:
   and Borges  3, 8–9, 20–21, 24, 25, 27, 37 n. 31, 53, 55, 93–116, 118, 120, 163
   and Joyce  3, 8–9, 20–21, 24, 25, 27, 49, 55, 89, 93–116, 118, 120, 121, 126, 165, 166
   *The Iliad*  97, 104, 105, 117 n. 9
   *The Odyssey*  21, 25, 44, 49, 66 n. 43, 73, 91 n. 33, 93, 96–98, 102–09, 112–14, 114 n. 6 & 9, 115 nn. 31 & 33 & 35, 165
Hugo, Victor  156, 162
Huxley, Aldous  42
Huysmans, J. K.  76

Ibsen, Henrik  52–53, 111, 116 n. 55
Irwin, John T.  128, 149 n. 44

Jolas, Eugene  119
Joyce, James:
   *A Portrait of the Artist as a Young Man*  16, 53, 116, 121–23, 160–61
   *Dubliners*  22–23, 53, 104
   'After the Race'  51; 'A Painful Case' 115 n. 37; 'Eveline' 13, 51, 66 n. 37, 118, 143; 'The Sisters' 51
   *Exiles*:  42, 44, 125, 182
   *Finnegans Wake*  4, 9, 30, 38 n. 39, 39 n. 56, 40, 44–45, 52, 55–61, 63, 65 n. 19, 67 n. 62, 67 n. 63, 70, 74, 76, 81, 83, 90 n. 20, 91 n. 23, 111, 115 n. 40, 120, 127, 128, 130, 143, 147 n. 10, 151, 170 n. 15, 172
   *Stephen Hero*  42
   *Ulysses*:
      'Telemachus'  85, 123, 154, 161
      'Nestor'  84, 165
      'Proteus'  145, 161
      'Calypso'  85
      'Lotus Eaters'  145
      'Hades'  166
      'Lestrygonians'  103
      'Scylla and Charybdis'  110, 126, 148 n. 17, 152, 153, 154, 155, 156–64, 167, 169
      'Wandering Rocks'  122, 146
      'Cyclops'  71, 79, 80
      'Nausicaa'  18, 49–50, 173
      'Circe'  110, 127, 137, 146, 152, 153–55, 167, 169
      'Eumaeus'  94, 108–13, 125, 166
      'Ithaca'  21, 38 n. 46, 71, 76, 84–89, 92 n. 60, 92 n. 62, 105, 107, 109, 110, 125, 132, 133–34, 140, 142, 146, 149 n. 58
      'Penelope'  6, 7, 8, 13, 15, 17–18, 21, 25–36, 38 n. 44, 38 n. 45, 39 nn. 64 & 65, 45, 48, 94, 101, 102, 152, 155, 172, 174
Joyce, John Stanislaus  73
Jung, C. G.  44, 47, 66 n. 32, 66 n. 36

Kafka, Franz  59, 68, 69, 70, 71, 90 n. 4

Kearney, Richard  8, 11 n. 29, 12, 29, 57, 60
Keats, John  98, 117, 155, 171 n. 38
Kenner, Hugh  96, 98, 114 nn. 4 & 5
Killeen, Terence  159, 171 n. 25
King, John  10 n. 17, 41, 43, 65 n. 2
Kipling, Rudyard  38 n. 39, 57
Kirkpatrick, Robin  126, 148 n. 39
Kreimer, Roxana  83, 92 n. 47
Kristal, Efraín  30, 32, 39 n. 56

Laforgue, Jules  58, 59
La Rochelle, Drieu  41
Lamb, Charles  97–98, 114 n. 13
Lang, Andrew  95–96, 101, 114 n. 13
Lange, Norah  26–27
Larbaud, Valery  12–18, 21–22, 25, 27, 29, 36 nn. 5 & 8 & 13, 37 nn. 14 & 18 & 19 & 25 & 26, 38 n. 57, 42, 45, 46, 66 n. 25, 152
Lawrence, Karen  11 n. 28, 12, 36 n. 7, 79, 86, 91 n. 33
Lee, Hermione  42, 65 n. 12
Leonard, Gary  50, 51, 66 n. 49
Levine, Suzanne Jill  38 n. 49, 52, 96
Lezama Lima, José  11 n. 28, 46, 66 nn. 27 & 30
Linati, Carlo  21
Litz, Walton  56, 67 n. 63, 86, 92 n. 60
Locke, John  71, 80–81, 91 n. 35
Lojo Rodríguez, Laura Mara  42, 43, 65 n. 9
Longfellow, Henry W.  101, 118
López de Mendoza, Íñigo (Marqués de Santillana)  34
Loux, Ann Kimble  161, 171 n. 33
Loyola, Saint Ignatius  121, 148 n. 17

Mahaffey, Vicki  111–12, 116 n. 56
Mallarmé, Stephané  155, 156
Manguel, Alberto  130, 149 n. 48
Manuel, Don Juan (Infante)  151
Marechal, Leopoldo  17, 46, 173
Marichalar, Antonio  21, 37 n. 33, 38 n. 46, 44
McHugh, Roland  76, 90 n. 20
Milton, John  76, 114, 117, 148 n. 18
Molloy, Sylvia  88, 92 n. 66
Monnier, Adrienne  14, 16, 25, 36 n. 5, 42
Morel, Auguste  16, 27, 29, 37 n. 19, 152
Morris, William  95–96
Murat, Ulises Petit de  10 n. 27

Neruda, Pablo  150 n. 75
Nietzsche, Friedrich  70, 71, 81–83, 91 n. 38, 92 n. 47
Nuñez-Faraco, Humberto  120, 126, 136, 147 n. 12, 150 n. 75

O'Brien, Edna  103, 115 n. 35
O'Brien, Flann  41, 51, 62
Ocampo, Silvina  151–52, 170 n. 1
Ocampo, Victoria  12, 36 n. 5, 41–43, 61, 65 n. 3

O'Neill, Eugene 151
Ortega y Gasset, José 41, 66 n. 32

Parnell, Charles Stewart 52, 165
Paz, Octavio 65 n. 16
Perón, Juan Domingo 47, 174
Petrarca, Francesco 49, 126
Piglia, Ricardo 174
Plato 82, 84, 90 n. 23, 91 n. 42, 111, 163
Pliny the Elder 71, 77–80, 91 n. 25, 105
Pope, Alexander 97, 104–05
Portinari, Beatrice 125, 134–35, 138, 147 n. 4
Pound, Ezra 46, 56, 91 n. 32, 117, 120, 144, 150 n. 82, 155, 158, 170 n. 12
Power, Arthur 24, 37 n. 37
Pratt, Mary Louise 1
Proust, Marcel 74, 143, 150 n. 83
Puig, Manuel 173–74

Quevedo, Francisco de 53, 164, 171 n. 40, 180

Rabaté, Jean-Michel 44, 65 n. 19
Reyes, Alfonso 14, 42
Reynolds, Mary T. 108, 116 n. 48, 120, 123, 124–25, 148 n. 34, 149 n. 58
Rickard, John S. 84, 87, 91 n. 23
Ricoeur, Paul 82, 83, 91 n. 43
Riquelme, John Paul 30, 39 n. 57, 114 n. 17
Rojas Paz, Pablo 16
Rodríguez Monegal, Emir 6, 10 nn. 20 & 23, 38 n. 48, 48, 52, 61, 66 n. 41, 134, 139, 147 n. 4, 151
Rosetti, Dante Gabriel 124
Russell, Bertrand 131, 133

Said, Edward 2
Salas Subirat J. 4, 7, 25, 28–29, 33, 39 n. 62, 39 n. 74, 44, 46–48, 94, 133, 154, 160, 173
Salgado, César A. 11 n. 28, 46, 57, 66 n. 25, 66 n. 30, 74, 83, 149 n. 45
Santa Cecilia, Carlos G. 38 n. 46, 170 n. 5
Sarlo, Beatriz 10 n. 17, 28, 69, 155, 170 n. 14
Savitsky, Ludmila 16
Saussy, Haun 1–2, 10 n. 3
Schutte, William M. 155, 161, 166, 170 n. 15
Schwartz, Jorge 11 n. 28, 27, 32, 38 n. 52
Scott, Bonnie Kime 34, 39 n. 79, 91 n. 23
Senn, Fritz 14, 36 n. 12, 39 n. 57, 73, 86, 92 n. 62, 98, 114 n. 17
Shakespeare, William:
and Borges 3, 9, 53, 56, 58, 98, 103, 118, 120, 151–69
and Joyce 3, 9, 50, 53, 56, 58, 97, 98, 103, 108, 118, 120, 121, 125, 151–69

*Hamlet* 51, 96, 127, 141, 155–65, 167, 169, 171
*Julius Caesar* 139, 164–68
*Macbeth* 166–68
*Troilus and Cressida* 98, 169
Shaw, George Bernard 105, 106, 163–64, 170 n. 18
Solar, Xul 16, 37 n. 24, 61
Spivak, Gayatri 2, 3, 10 n. 9
Stanford, W. B. 97, 99, 06, 114 n. 12
Steiner, George 114 n. 2, 144, 150 n. 85
Sturrock, John 83, 92 n. 50, 149 n. 53
Supervielle, Jules 42
Swinburne, Algernon 59

Tennyson, Lord Alfred 97, 101, 117
Thiher, Allen 143, 150 n. 83
Torre, Miguel de 15, 17, 26, 148 n. 14
Tysdahl, Bjorn 97, 114 n. 14
Tzu, Chuang 151

Updike, John 124, 148 n. 32

Vaccaro, Alejandro 38 n. 48, 148 n. 29
Valverde, José María 33, 38 n. 42, 39 n. 74
Vanderham, Paul 7, 10 n. 26, 102
Vargas Llosa, Mario 65 n. 16
Vázquez, María Esther 38 n. 48, 56, 170 n. 15
Vega, Lope de 24
Vegh, Beatriz 11 n. 28, 23, 31, 127
Vico, Giambattista 115 n. 40, 119, 120, 128, 146, 147 n. 5
Virgil 18, 19, 20, 21, 82, 91 n. 41, 97, 98, 99, 122, 136, 163

Waisman, Sergio 11 n. 28, 27, 32, 34, 58, 67 n. 70, 67 n. 72, 74, 168
Walcott, Derek 20–21, 37 nn. 28 & 31, 104, 115 nn. 24 & 38, 150 n. 84
Wallace, David 121, 147 n. 7
Weninger, Robert 3, 10 n. 16
Williams, William C. 119
Williamson, Edwin 26–27, 38 n. 47, 135
Willson, Patricia 11 n. 28, 32, 39 n. 64, 65 n. 14
Wilson, Jason 22, 37 n. 34
Woodall, James 6, 10 n. 21
Woolf, Virginia 41–43, 65 n. 9, 65 n. 12, 65 n. 14

Yates, Donald 57
Yates, Frances 77, 90 n. 23, 122
Yeats, William Butler 41, 52, 60, 62–65, 67 n. 83, 111, 147 n. 7

Zajko, Vanda 99, 115 n. 21